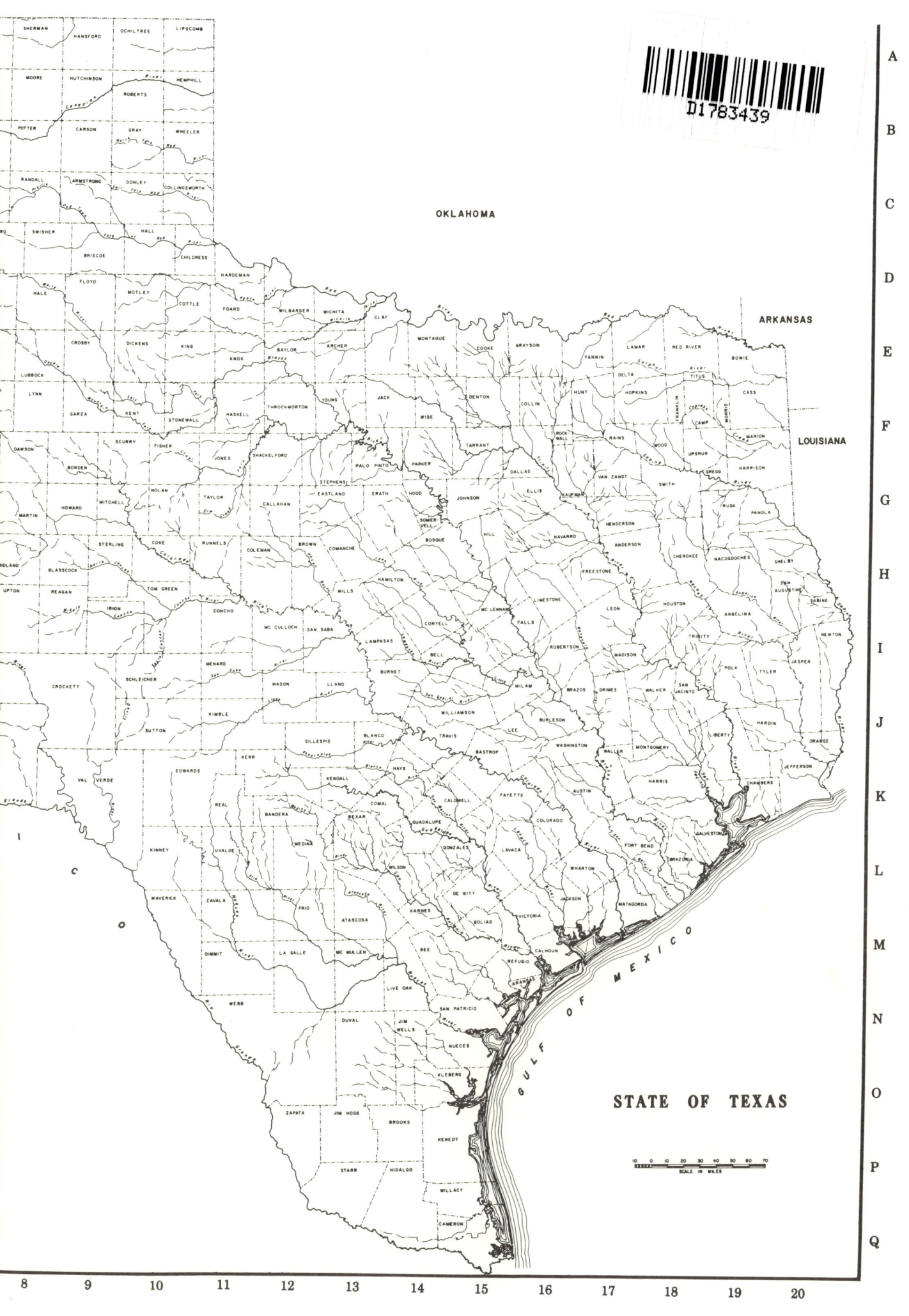

The Explorers' Texas

Donated to the
Centro Cultural Hispano de San Marcos
From the
 Center for the Study of the Southwest
Brazos Hall • Texas State University–San Marcos

The Explorers' Texas

The Animals They Found

Volume 2

Del Weniger

EAKIN PRESS ★ AUSTIN, TEXAS

FIRST EDITION

Copyright © 1997
By Del Weniger

Published in the United States of America
by Eakin Press
An Imprint of Sunbelt Media, Inc.
P.O. Drawer 90159 ★ Austin, TX 78709-0159

ALL RIGHTS RESERVED. No part of this book may be reproduced in any form without written permission from the publisher, except for brief passages included in a review appearing in a newspaper or magazine.

ISBN 1-57168-100-0

2 3 4 5 6 7 8 9

Library of Congress Cataloging-in-Publication Data

Weniger, Del.
    The explorers' Texas : the animals they found / Del Weniger.
      p.   cm.
    Includes bibliographical references and index.
    ISBN 1-57168-100-0
    1. Mammals — Texas — History. I. Title.
QL719.T4W45   1996
599.09764--dc20
                                                       96-2845
                                                            CIP

*To my wife, Nell,
without whose love and support,
often material, this book could not
have been written.*

Acknowledgments

I sincerely acknowledge the help of others in the accomplishment of this work. The huge amount of research necessary was aided by the preliminary reading done many years ago by numerous members of the Sierra Club's San Antonio Group. Further research was made possible by generous grants from the Ewing Halsell Foundation and the Robert J. Kleberg, Jr. and Helen C. Kleberg Foundation. Libraries which made the study possible by preserving and making available the words of explorers include Our Lady of The Lake University Library, Trinity University Library, Daughters of The Republic of Texas Research Library, Center for American History at The University of Texas, Texas State Library, North Carolina State University Library, and Duke University Library.

Contents

Introduction		1
1	The Buffalo in Texas	9
2	The Deer Story in Early Texas	33
3	Antelopes: The Texas Speedsters	39
4	Texas Elk	46
5	The Texas Bighorn Mountain Sheep	52
6	The Bears of the Texas Hills	55
7	Wolves at the Door	63
8	Texas Cats	79
	The Jaguar	79
	The Texas Lion	84
	The "Dainty Ocelot"	94
	The Wild Bobcat	96
	The Rare Rio Grande Cats	97
9	Texas Little Foxes	99
10	Texas Hogs: Native and Naturalized	101
	Mexican Hogs: The Only Native Texas Ones	101
	Feral Hogs: The Dogs of the French	107
11	More Than Critters	110
	The Raccoon	110
	The Ringtail	111
	The Badger: Texas Underground Fighter	113
	The Pole Cats Which Were Skunks	115
	The Aquatic Carnivores in Texas	122
	The Rat of the Trees	124
	Texas Armadillos	127
12	The Rodents as They Were in Texas	132
	Texas Beavers	132
	Prairie Dogs: The Original Urban Texans	134
	Texas Underground Rodents	142
	The Texas Tree Squirrels	142
	Early Texas "Inferior Animals"	145
13	They Rushed Around the Texas Brush	148
	The Jack Rabbits: Texas Hares	149
	The Cottontails: Texas *Sylvilagus*	156

14	Merely Noted in Passing	159
	Bats Moving In	159
	The Porpoise Problem	161
	Texas' Actual Sea Monsters	162
15	Absent Without Leave	164
	The Muskrat Didn't Ramble That Much	164
	Is the Porcupine a Native Texan?	166
	Has the Coati Really Come In?	168
	Seals: Our Immigrant Refugees	169
Notes		173
Bibliography		183
Index		195

Illustrations

Map 1. Where buffalo were found	11
Early Buffaloes	16-17
Maps 2-5. Buffaloes by Season	23
Antelopes (*Harper's Weekly* Illustration)	44
American Elk by Audubon	47
Map 6. Texas counties in which bears were found	60
Wolves attacking buffalo	66
Early artist's conception of wolves	68
Prairie Wolf by Audubon	69
Red Texas Wolf by Audubon	77
The Jaguar by Audubon	80
Cougar by Audubon	86
The Ocelot by Sir William Jardine	94-95
Collared Peccary by Audubon	102
Ring-tailed *Bassaris* by Audubon	112
Texas Skunk by Audubon	115
Otter by William Daniell	122
Opossum (eighteenth-century)	124
Nine-banded Armadillo by Audubon	127
Texas Hare by Audubon	150

Introduction

THE PURPOSES OF THE BOOK

Today's Texas fascinates us. We travel immense distances to experience the many wonders of the state. We even surround ourselves with the most perfect images of its scenes and its creatures that can be produced with brush, camera or pen.

This is entirely commendable as love of either homeland or adopted land — up to a point. But there is a frenzy underlying our rush to get out and experience Texas as well as to decorate everything from the best spaces on our walls to the choice spots on our coffee tables with images of what is out there, which must indicate a deep fear that today's Texas is transitory and threatened.

We know in our hearts that the threat is real, so this is not another book written to make that more obvious. It is instead an attempt to reveal, by researching what the animal populations of this land were like in its pristine, unaffected-by-modern-humans condition, something of what Texas was originally like and what we have already done to it. To show this would seem reason enough for this book's existence, since only by discovering what the natural Texas actually was and comparing that with what it is now, can we intelligently project the futures of either our animals or ourselves.

A second aim of this book is to help make it possible for today's explorer of Texas to know whether what is met with out there now is the same as what was there originally — in any sense the genuine Texas that once was. I hope the book makes it possible to tell whether any creature you meet in Texas is Texas stock in its native situation or whether it must be assumed to be an immigrant or an import of historic times.

There is yet a third purpose for this book. I want to help you who only get to explore in fancy to play out your imaginary expeditions. The aim is to let you know what animals you can realistically imagine coming across while you fancy yourselves La Salle or Bowie or Mrs. Austin venturing into the wilderness in their particular decades — buffaloes, elk, bears and wolves, down to prairie dogs and rabbits.

Also, I intend to show how the presettlement locations of our animals either duplicate or diverge from the maps of their more recent ranges. This is important because it should, once again, show how profound the effects of our modern developments have been upon Texas.

Beyond all this, I construct this book in a special way which I hope will help make up for a particular lack looming large, particularly in today's youths. This deficiency is their inability, due to their being deprived of experiences in unmodified natural communities, to even imagine the wilderness creatures of Texas as they once were. In my more than forty years of teaching about living things I have seen this blindness gradually developing, and it is the most pronounced ever in today's youngsters. It has become frustrating to find my illustrations drawn from both farmyard and wilderness gone ineffective unless I spend extra time and effort explaining them. This is because present-day urbanites who have never been on a farm or off the concrete any farther than the lawn simply cannot imagine a hen guarding her chicks, a litter of ravening piglets mauling a sow, a herd of cattle in flight — let alone a buffalo stampede, a cougar stalking, cactus in a broiling desert or moss-shrouded cypress in a drowned swamp. The tense silence of an alligator gliding in moonlit water or the philharmonic sounds of night-time coyotes are, like most wilderness experience, inconceivable to our deprived young suburbanites. So I go to extra lengths to gather and repeat here the most graphic word pictures of the Texas plants and animals as found and described by our explorers, in order to hopefully stimulate today's imaginations so that they can at least with their minds' eyes see the original Texas creatures in their primeval situations.

This is also an attempt to make up for the lack of serious studies of Texas' natural history during its exploratory and first settlement period in comparison with the many studies of what its flora and fauna were like during both prehistoric and more recent times. This curious gap is due to the early historical period coming too late to be the subject of geological analysis and ending before more than just the first practitioners of organized scientific investigations came upon the Texas scene.

THE PERIOD COVERED

This is an attempt to discover what the fauna of Texas was like as discovered and before settlement and modern practices modified it. The period dealt with here runs from the time of the first explorations in Texas, of which contemporary records are preserved which are complete enough that locations can be plotted with acceptable confidence, down to the date when we have the most reasons to believe that the wilderness of this state was no longer intact. This would be from the late seventeenth century until about 1860, and means that the journals of some of the first explorers into Texas — Coronado, for instance — cannot be used as sources here. While it is apparently true that Coronado passed through some of what was to become Texas, in spite of the best efforts of many scholars it seems to remain doubtful that we can trace his path with such certainty that we can be sure he was in this or that future county when he reported specific things. His accounts, and those of some others, are therefore so general as to be of little use to us, and are surpassed anyway by those of other explorers, the locations of whose reports can be pin-pointed at least down to the chosen level.

The closing date of 1860 is, of course, a more or less arbitrary cut-off date for the historic wilderness period, because no one can say that in this or that particular year the last of Texas' original wilderness was modified or eliminated. Yet I did not choose it capriciously. I chose it because it is easily demonstrated that after that date, in most of Texas, the plant and animal populations were being so altered that the original living communities were no longer all intact or recognizable. This date seems to mark approximately the middle of the gradual process of turning Texas from what it was found to be into something different.

For those who may think that 1860 is too early a date for marking the end of wilderness Texas, I bring in a statement from one of the earliest histories of Texas about the state of natural things here at an even earlier date. I must quote it at length because of its significance concerning the social as well as the natural history of Texas toward the end of what I call the exploratory period.

David B. Edward, in his *History of Texas,* published in 1836, wrote: "It will be well also, for the emigrant to remember, that the animals once so numerous throughout the woods and prairies of Texas, are either pretty much destroyed, or retreating to the upper region of the country, from whence they are fast taking their final leave. . . . The inhabitants [of Texas] in general are (or rather were) composed of a class who had been unfortunate in life . . . who in a great measure were banished from the pleasures of life, and almost from its necessaries. So much so, that many of them had to rely upon the precariousness of the chase alone, for their first year's support. . . . But where [in recent years] were all those flocks of deer, buffalo, and bear, which at that time so plentifully abounded in the country? Either destroyed by so many depredating upon them for a living, or driven by a continual pursuit to the upper parts of the province, where it was as much as a man's life was worth to follow them! Again, while smoke-dried horse flesh has come to be in such repute among the whites, where were the poor blacks, in these [recent] days of privation and suffering? They were ranging and ransacking every creek and pond, for fish, frogs, and even alligators. Yes, Colonel Groce of the Brazos lost many a good negro, who might have been living yet, had they always been successful in their alligator hunts."[1]

So the 1860 cut-off date is a little late in some places. And some would imagine that in other places — particularly in northwest Texas — the primeval wilderness remained intact well beyond this date. Of course there were remote pockets where it must have, but when the buffaloes were hardly more than ten years from being wiped out, *pastores* had founded numerous settlements from which they were herding countless sheep over northwest Texas,[2] the Spanish had been along the Rio Grande for a couple of hundred years, and there was already a lumbering industry in the Franklin Mountains,[3] is it too early to say that even West Texas was losing its virgin character by that date? I believe I have chosen 1860 correctly as at least near the latest date when the deflowering of Texas had not yet proceeded to the point where her elementary character was in doubt.

THE SOURCES OF KNOWLEDGE ABOUT THE PERIOD OF OUR INTEREST

With a desire for knowledge about the flora and fauna of this early historical period aroused, where do we look to gratify it? The answer to this question is very important.

The first and major source of knowledge about the creatures of that time has to be the surviving written reports of Texas' explorers. I believe that the eyewitness accounts of those who were here at that time have a legitimate priority. These are first-hand records of actual observations noted down contemporaneously, and mostly lying for long in various archives or buried in almost forgotten volumes. As such they fairly beg for someone to take them seriously. I try to do this by gathering all of these statements which are available to me — literally thousands of accounts found in 360 different items written by 290 different explorers. I organize them and then present the explorers' picture of each creature built up by putting their various statements together, even as a mosaic is brought to be by assembling the varicolored bits available to the artist. These are our primary sources on this subject.

And there is precedence for this sort of effort. The most outstanding previous example which I have seen of the compilation and use of pioneers' accounts in a modern animal study is Frank Gilbert Roe's *The North American Buffalo, A Critical Study of the Species in Its Wild State*.[4] Where most other recent authors merely quote a handful of early reports to set a tone for whatever theories they wish to champion, Roe genuinely tries to survey the early accounts of eyewitnesses, attempts to summarize the points they make, then considers the theories of more recent scientists and others who couldn't have been there at the times under consideration, and finally attempts to render coherent and valid conclusions about the buffalo's history based upon the totality. Even though he deals with only one animal, the fact that he attempts to accomplish this for the animal over its whole international range and to include its total history down to the present produces a very large and complex tome. Although I am dealing with various animals, my limiting this study to Texas and to only the exploratory era results in a much shorter, though by no means simple, work. The point is that the precedence of the explorers' testimony is recognized, respected, and built upon.

KEEPING THE PRIMARY SOURCES PRIMARY

These explorers of ours are legendary for having been a mixed bag of humanity. They ranged all the way from European aristocrats out on intercontinental larks, through European intelligentsia coming here as refugees, military officers on campaigns or searching out overland routes, promoters, soldiers actual or of fortune, missionaries, surveyors, settlers, a few wives of such men, to several other persons who chose to remain anonymous. Any general statement about their approaches to nature, beyond saying that they just observed what they found and wrote about it, would be unfair to some if not to all of them.

We can't even generalize about why they wrote their observations down. Some had to write official journals and reports, some just reported on their own. Some were writing letters home, some wrote to attract immigrants, while several wrote to forewarn prospective immigrants of the dangers and difficulties they would encounter if they came here. Some seem merely to have written from the inner urge which propels so many pens. It seems safe to say that not over half a dozen of them had any special interest in or knowledge of animals. Few were focusing on the fauna of the wilderness or show any motivation to describe the animals of Texas any more than any of its other features.

This poses a real problem as we go through their statements. We can't take time to get to know all these 290 explorers personally. Besides, of some of them we know only their names, and of several not even that. Including even the barest biography and analysis of those for whom that is possible would add scores of pages to this book.

There is another reason why I prefer not to try to bring these explorers to life before us as individuals. It is because I do not want to evaluate their accounts by the personalities, educations, vocations or characters of those who wrote them. Who would

I make myself if I judged that because Dr. Roemer and Mr. Olmsted were highly educated, Captains Pope and Marcy were military officers, the Abbe Domenech and Father Menzel were churchmen, etc., their accounts were sober, accurate, truthful and to be taken seriously, while because Elijah Hicks and Josiah Pancoast were poorly educated and used poor grammar, McCullough and Holland were mere soldiers, Frederick Marryat also wrote fiction, and Eliza Johnston and Mary Austin Holley were women, their accounts are exaggerated, inaccurate and suspect?

The aforementioned author, Roe, tries to so evaluate his early witnesses. But this causes his work to be full of stated or implied judgments like: such-and-such explorer said so-and-so, and he is a trustworthy witness, so we must credit what he reports, but so-and-so pioneer is apparently a naive or even untrustworthy source, so what he says may not actually have happened like he said at all. This not only compounds the length of Roe's study and casts a tentative pall over everything in it, but sets up the author as a supercilious judge, on the basis of nothing but hearsay and prejudice, of persons dead long before he was born.

I choose to be no such judge, but to let the reports speak for themselves. Since each account is only one among many, if an explorer is bearing false witness or even exaggerating, any significant falsity in his report will make it stand out from the others as an obvious anomaly. When I draw a range map by marking all the locations where various explorers say they found an organism, any significant mistaken identity will be isolated and obvious out there in left field as surely as it would be on the most recent biogeographer's map. It is intended to present such composite pictures and maps here and to draw attention to both positive consistencies and glaring inconsistencies as they appear. Instead of letting any one word-artist, whether explorer or the latest zoologist, paint his subjective picture of the original Texas fauna, we are going to build a picture of those wilderness animals which is a mosaic in which any false report will stand out and be noted like the misplaced red piece among the blue chips of the mosaic's sky.

It is the accounts that are primary here, not the people. I choose to judge the people by their accounts instead of presuming to accept, reject or even rank the reports by my opinion of their authors. So, unless there is some special reason for it, I only introduce each explorer the first time he appears in the text by a sentence or two indicating the barest knowledge of who he was. Anyone who feels he needs to know more can find most known details about these people in any good Texana library.

CONTEMPORARY ACCOUNTS VERSUS REMINISCENCES

It is a given in some circles that the accounts left by such persons as our explorers — genteel travelers, traders, missionaries, soldiers, adventurers, hunters, poor immigrants, some miscreants, and others such as they were — are not very useful and perhaps better off ignored because such people were bound to be at best often mistaken and at worst biased when writing about plants and animals. A secondary aim of this study is to check this assumption. I feel we have a unique opportunity to do that here. But the results we find may be so surprising as to appear unbelievable to some. This surprising outcome results from one discovery made in the process of this study. And this discovery seems to me to be the most important outcome of the whole study, because it seems to explain why writings by explorers and pioneers have had such poor press and to show that their accounts written down contemporary with the observations they made do not deserve such a blanket stigma.

Early in this study, when statements of those who had been in Texas during the exploratory period, whether written down at the time of the observations or years later as recollections, were all included, the pictures resulting from this hodgepodge turned out to be distorted images full of paradoxes and of elements out of line with our knowledge from other sources. There seemed to be no consistent and intelligent explorers' picture of early Texas' natural environment at all, and I almost aborted my study.

Roe obviously faced the same dilemma in his study of the buffalo. He used many early accounts of that animal, but he relied indiscriminately upon eyewitnesses' reports written down and so finalized at or very near the time of observations and upon reminiscences of those who saw the phenomena, but were only writing — or in some cases telling orally — what they remembered after many years had gone by. So Roe had to wade through countless descriptions, some immediate and many recalled as much as fifty years later. And in the mass of these he has had to point out many contradictory statements. So he is reduced to trying to weigh one pioneer against another, to evaluating both those who were writing reports immediately upon observation and those who had become old story-tellers. He is reduced to judging some as "strong sources" and others "doubtful sources." And from all this he has tried to come up with something consistent. Occasionally this proved impossible, and he has had to leave a point in doubt.

But the happenstance recounted in the introduction of the first volume based on this material, *The Explorers' Texas: The Lands and Waters*, caused me to separate the reports of actual eyewitnesses written down on the spot or immediately afterwards, from all reminiscences, and I consider this the single most unique and important feature of this project based upon one of its most important discoveries.

Seen by themselves, the reminiscences were a pile of often contradictory materials yielding many unbelievable or contradictory assertions. This is perhaps because of the time interval between observations and recording, which allows opportunity for memory to distort and for egos to restructure recollections into statements readjusted more to pride and prejudice's desires. By contrast, reports of observations made or events participated in, which were recorded immediately, before there could be time for either conscious or unconscious adjustments, presented so many consistent and believable pictures that they themselves spotlighted the few misguided ones. I therefore eliminated all reminiscences from my sources, and, basing everything on actual on-the-spot reporting, get the remarkably consistent pictures of the early Texas denizens here presented.

This is a matter of actual, immediately reported observations versus folklore. The often artful, fascinating legends and beliefs which make up folklore, having a time interval before the telling giving opportunity for it, come to include tales in the sense of exaggerations and outright yarn-spinnings. These are the kiss of death as far as factual knowledge is concerned and the precursors of pseudoscience. But there is this other category — that of sober, on-the-spot reporting of observed phenomena by eyewitnesses. This is the essentially unembellished testimony of the explorers before time for consciously or unconsciously concocted story lines intervenes. It is unfortunate there is no name for this reportage to set it off from folklore. It has been too seldom taken seriously as factual and its stories, being uncrafted, do not rate a category as literature.

It should be realized that any explorer who was self-conscious enough to stop on a trail, crouch in a tent, squint before a campfire, firebrand or candle in order to write down his observations of wilderness life must have felt himself an eye of civilization scouting the wilds for a host of others. This must have brought him great excitement, but also a great sense of responsibility. These pioneers must have observed under the spell of this excitement and reported — even if only to the folks back home —under the sobering effect of this responsibility. Unless we judge them to have been perverse, the results should be accuracy and completeness. And we are not disappointed. Wayne Franklin, in his book, *Discoverers, Explorers, Settlers, The Diligent Writers of Early America*, expresses what we find very clearly, writing: "When the [early] American traveler stops in his career and surveys the actual surrounding world — trying to break through the descriptions which have been laid over it, and to render in prose exactly what is to be seen beneath them — one is likely to sense, as in the passage quoted here (written in 1713, by Antoine de la Mothe Cadillac to Ponchartrain, Minister of Marine and Colonies, about some gardens on Dauphine Island), a refreshingly critical mind at work."[5] It is this sort of writing which I have searched out, and upon which I have based the conclusions of this book.

IT'S THEIR WORDS OVER OURS

This is almost a book of quotations. I have attempted to portray as nearly as possible every element of the original Texas in the actual words of our pioneers instead of in my own. I make no apology for this because I see good reasons why this is a strength instead of a weakness.

First, the picture we want to see emerge here is theirs — not ours. So neither our up-to-date statistics, graphics or word artistry could likely portray the things they were seeing either so accurately or so directly as the words they themselves wrote on the spot. In fact, our retelling can falsify. There is already too much bandied around about what they are supposed to have said. I choose to quote what they did say.

Second, the way they said things is often significant. Sometimes it is so artful as to stimulate imaginations far beyond anything our modern idioms, likely prosaic because so far removed from the reality, could generate. My words in retelling their experiences could hardly be expected to surpass their originals, so I defer to them.

Third, I have noted that a secondary but important goal of this work is to provide an opportunity to evaluate our explorers as observers and reporters of the animals they encountered. Therefore they deserve to be heard directly. They have already been judged too often *en masse, in absentia* and on generalities. It is high time to examine them individually, to weigh their very own words — which is the only way they can actually be allowed to testify in their own defense — and to listen to what they have to say on testable specifics. This is the only way to not put words in their mouths.

And fourth, many of the quotations used are taken from yellowing tomes or crumbling old periodicals which never made it into or were long ago culled from libraries of general use, which only survive at all buried deep in special collections or archives, and which may never make it onto microfilms or computer lists. The repeating of them verbatim seems like a rescuing of their words from very near oblivion. It is a laying of them out where they may be seen a little longer, and so almost the same sort of worthwhile process as that of digging up fragile masterpieces and setting them out for the public in modern museums.

FINDING OUR WAY IN THEIR WILDERNESS

A few words must be included about our methods of calculating the locations of our explorers when they were making their observations. In most instances where their reports are more specific than writing about Texas in general or a named region of the state, their observations are embedded in itineraries of expeditions, diaries of outings, or recountings of travels. Many of such itineraries and diaries have been carefully studied by historians who have published maps and annotations of the routes taken. I have used these whenever available.

However, I have gone beyond this. Itineraries typically start each telling with a statement such as: "Leaving Mustang Spring . . ." or some such major feature of the scene like a river or creek, canyon or peak, caprock or inlet. From this starting point they then say something like: "we traveled so many miles [or leagues] in such a direction, where we saw this or that animal." My method has been to first locate the stated starting point of the telling. In many cases this is a well-known feature of Texas geography. We have pin-pointed those less known by using detailed geological maps and the statements in the 22,874 early Texas survey field notes read for this study. Having located the identifiable anchor point of the telling, we have measured on our maps to discover in what present county the direction and distance given by the explorer puts the observation. In cases where the unit of distance is known to have had varying lengths, such as the league has, we have plotted with both the shortest known length used and the longest. This rarely puts the results in different counties, but if it or any other ambiguity does, I willingly state the location with an "either/or." It is only in instances where the specific known location of the observation is stated by the explorer himself that I narrow the location below this county level.

NAMES, NAMES, ANYBODY GOT MORE NAMES?

It is obvious that most of this state's explorers did not use recognized scientific names for the living things they wrote about, and this may be a stumbling block for some to whom scientific nomenclature is gospel and any other names suspect. We may as well deal with this problem before going any further.

The first reason why the pioneers seldom used scientific names is that, very simply, many of the creatures they met up with had not yet been described and named legitimately — which is to say named by recognized scientists in the prescribed way. Various of our explorers were out here struggling through the Texas wilderness in order to send specimens of these new creatures back East to the scientists sitting in their comfortable offices so those pundits could coin their scientific names for the new organisms. But even that process was only beginning in Texas this early. Only within the last fifteen years of the period I propose to deal with had Texas become U.S. territory or the Smithsonian been set up as a center for studies of the nation's natural history. And only in 1859 did Baird's *The Mammals of North America* appear. These developments have been said to have "ushered in a modern era of group endeavor (as opposed to personal performance, a la Audubon), exactitude, and a forbidding accumulation of technical weight."[6] Translate that into a statement that only during the last decade of our period of study did organized science start to look at Texas wilderness. There were, as yet, few scientific names to replace terms with which the explorers communicated.

Add to the above that what scientific nomenclature had already been built up by 1860 was still virtually a private language used by only the scientifically initiated. Yet it was necessary for wilderness pioneers to be able to communicate with each other with a minimum of misunderstanding about creatures which could be vital resources to be sought out or mortal dangers to be avoided. That common names functioned adequately in the frontier's crisis situations makes it seem such off-hand devaluations of the vernacular as we sometimes hear are hardly warranted. However, there are other ways to tell which animals the pioneers are writing about. The descriptive talents of those frontiersmen is too often underestimated. The common names the explorers use will be relied upon here to identify only major and distinct animal types. For indicating closely related species or any forms having closely similar relatives in the same region, the explorers' clearly stated descriptions or clear pictures containing the distinguishing characteristics of the form have to be present in his account.

I hope the naming problem, while I admit it makes necessary much wisdom on the part of all of us, does not deter us from digging out and recognizing the kernels of truth about the explorers' Texas, even when they are buried under the piles of names caused by our failure to equal Adam in naming all things well.

NEW VIEWS OF OLD THINGS?

I have already been told, "There is no presently demonstrable scientific basis for many of these old statements or your interpretations of them, so how dare you presume to build upon them!" But this book does not claim to be a new scientific study. It is a history book! It is an attempt at a biological *history* — a history of Texas animals during a certain past historical period. As such it may be rather a new thing, but it exactly parallels numerous histories of human events of the same period which have been widely presented. I realize that this approach presents the same difficulty which any bold statement of history poses for scientific thinkers. But all I ask here is for the reader to approach this book with what any historical work must meet in its readers if it is to be taken seriously — what has elsewhere been called a hermeneutics of sensible faith instead of a hermeneutics of automatic skepticism. This positive attitude might be expressed by something like the following: The explorers were clearly the only eyewitnesses to Texas as it then was. As our forebears, they should be presumed to have been intelligent, observant, and reputable until proved otherwise. So where the logic is sound, the arguments in this study will be granted credence until disproven by actual physical evidence marshalled apart from modern theorizing.

I have put forth much effort to survey the scientific literature bearing on these explorers' reports, so as to interpret their statements as correctly as possible in the light of scientific knowledge. But scientific thought is constantly being added to and changing, so the specialist will always have new theories which I have not seen. Readers, over time, will themselves have to take these new scientific developments into account.

But in answer to criticisms which I already see of my method and of my presuming to play a historian interpreting the past, I can do no better than to quote once again Frank Gilbert Roe, as, in closing his voluminous study, he dealt with the same sort of critics. He wrote. "Where I ventured to criticize biologists or zoologists, it has been for their pronouncements as historians. In dealing with an animal now extinct as a free wild species in its most characteristic native habitat, the first task is to ascertain and classify the historical evidence, and not until this has been done can biological investigation proceed with much profit."[7] I am attempting to do this historical spadework for the animals of Texas.

Some have applauded my gathering and presentation of the pioneers' accounts, but questioned my right to interpret these accounts, particularly where my interpretations fly in the face of some presently and widely held opinions. Once again I will let Roe, whose methods I am following in my own less grand study, answer for me. He expresses his position — and the one I also take — in his concluding summary as follows: "Inevitably at times, in adducing and commenting upon evidence concerning the habits of the buffalo or the Indian, or in discussing the various beliefs or assertions respecting them, the character, the degree of inherent credibility, the contemporaneous authority or some such feature of the evidence under consideration has naturally given rise (in a study professedly critical) to occasional utterances of a 'judicial' character. These have been more commonly negative, tending to illustrate the apparent influence of the testimony under discussion upon the fortunes of some perhaps widely accepted but not soundly authenticated belief.... It will be widely perceived ... that the mere labour involved in the collection and arrangement of the evidence contained in the present work, could scarcely be performed during the space of several years without the author reaching broad conclusions. Some of these are provisional and tentative, in certain respects at least. Others are more fixed and definite. While no student should close his mind to the possibility of further evidence necessitating a recasting of his views on any subject — perhaps very drastically — I must acknowledge that I cannot conceive what the nature of the new evidence could be that would require the abandonment of the latter class of conclusions, which I have been driven to form from my study of the evidence now existing."[8] If my work spurs on the search for such new evidence, even in attempts to discredit my interpretations, this will be a further reason for this study's presentation.

So on with the expeditions! Fan out over the wilderness expanses! Tell us, explorers, what creatures, great or small, you found in the untamed wilds of Texas!

1

The Buffalo in Texas

In any accurate picture of the Texas the explorers found, the American buffalo must loom in the foreground. This animal's prime importance to the Indians was established for all time when Gen. Phil Sheridan convinced the Texas legislature that the more quickly the buffaloes were exterminated the more quickly the Indians would be starved into submission — and when history proved him correct.

The buffalo's importance to the explorers is clear from the diaries of the early Spanish expeditions, where the numbers of wild *vacas* (buffaloes) slaughtered from day to day are religiously given as the best indications of how well the parties subsisted and how easy the journeys were. Without the buffaloes the country would have been not only much more vacant of animal life, but also of Native Americans, and for much longer of explorers, settlers and even of modern developments such as railroads. One recent student of such things puts it thus: "... no other wild animal was so important to the development of the North American continent as the massive, long-haired beast of the plains."[1]

DOES A TEXAN CALL IT BUFFALO OR BISON?

This primal animal was not without relatives in other parts of the world, and so was not spared the usual confusion when it came to naming it. A quite similar cousin existed in Europe. Because this European animal was familiar to the ancients, it had several names coined for it. Perhaps the oldest, traceable to ancient Greek, was the term *bonasus*. This word is still applied to the European animal, it being designated scientifically as *Bison bonasus*. But another Greek name for the European animal was *bison*. This word came down through the Latin to become the *wisand* of the Teutonic and *wisunt* of the Germans, and to remain the bison of modern English use. It was also settled upon by Linnaeus in the first scientific naming of the American animal, and ours therefore remains officially *Bison bison L.*

But there was yet another ancient name, the Greek word *Boúbalus*. This became the Latin *Búfalus*, the French *boeufs*, and our modern buffalo. This name may have been used for the European animal also, but it later became applied especially to the wild cows discovered in Asia and Africa — hence the term, water buffalo, and that animal's scientific name, *Bos bubalus*.

So what was the name they used for the American animal when it was first discovered? The earliest Spanish explorers merely called them *vacas* (cows), *toros* (bulls), or adopted the Indian name, *cibola,* for them. It is as though the Spanish did not know the old European names or else chose to avoid all of them in referring to what they found here. It appears that the latter may have been the case, since Vicente de Zaldivar, when describing the animals in 1589, wrote that their horns "resembled those of the *búfalo.*"[2] This shows that he knew that term, and appears to be the first use of the word in American letters. Espejo, however, named the Pecos River the *Rio de las Vacas* in 1583, because, "travelling along its banks for six days, a distance of about thirty leagues, we found a great number of the *vacas* [cows] of that country."[3] The earliest French explorers called them *boeufs*. An example was La Salle's *La Riviere Aix de Boeufs* for the Texas river on which he built his Fort St. Louis.

The earliest English explorers to meet with these animals called them wild cows also, but by 1729, they were definitely "buffaloes" to Col. William Byrd and his surveying party, who even christened a watercourse in Virginia as Buffalo Creek because of sighting numbers of them there. The general use of the name "buffalo" instead of "bison" by the explorers and settlers from then on is attested to by the dozens of Buffalo Creeks, Buffalo Gaps, etc. on maps of almost the whole continent and the absence of Bison Creeks or other features using this word.

It may have been the consciousness of being on a new continent which they related more to Asia and Africa than to Europe which prompted early Texans to use the word "buffalo" for the animal they found here, but they always did. It is Buffalo Bayou, not Bison Bayou, buffalo grass, not bison grass. Only three of all the pre-1860 writers in English or German I have found used the word "bison" at all. General Wavel, in an 1835 guidebook for immigrants, where he was trying so hard to be understood by the Europeans that he used every name he knew, wrote: "The wild animals to be met with in Texas, are the buffalo, or the bison, known in this country [Europe] as the bonassus..."[4] And Mrs. Holley, writing in 1836, said, "The buffalo — commonly so called, but termed by naturalists the bison — is found in Texas astonishingly gregarious."[5] Even for such a scientist as Dr. Baird, when as late as 1857 he was doing the technical write-up of the animals encountered on the western railroad surveys, the animal was "the buffalo" and its scientific name was *Bos Americanus*.[6] Science's growing insistence on the name "bison" for our American species came because of Linnaeus, and although it may be technically more correct, and it is fashionable now to imply that using the term "buffalo" is being common at best and showing ignorance at worst, to have been "in" with the explorers and settlers one would have to have spoken of buffalo, not bison.

Lt. Col. Richard Irving Dodge summed it up best when he wrote in 1877, "I suppose I ought to call this animal the 'bison'; but, though naturalists may insist that 'bison' is his true name, I, as a plainsman, also insist that his name is buffalo. As buffalo he is known everywhere, not only on the plains but throughout the sporting world; as buffalo 'he lives and moves and has his being'; as buffalo he will die; and when, as must soon happen, his race has vanished from earth, as buffalo he will live in tradition and story."[7] In this account of the explorers' view of things, we therefore choose to use their name for him.

WHERE IN TEXAS WERE THE BUFFALO?

That the buffalo was almost always upon the stage where early Texas history materialized is shown by the fact that I have been able to assemble 276 separate statements written by eyewitnesses before 1860 about experiencing buffaloes in Texas, and these from locations in 130 of the present counties of the state. Map 1 shows the present counties of Texas in which there was at least one sighting of buffaloes between the coming of the first explorers and 1860.

The scattering of the explorers' sightings of buffaloes in northwest Texas is more an indication of which counties explorers happened to leave accounts of passing through than of any local buffalo ranges, because we know from other evidence that they ranged the whole of the Panhandle and high plains and into all adjacent territories. There were droves of them next door in Oklahoma and they still existed in New Mexico at that time.

Because there have been some statements of doubts about buffalo being in New Mexico in historic times, it is perhaps worthwhile to digress to establish this point. Capt. Vicente de Zaldivar described a herd of 100,000 buffaloes somewhere near present Tucumcari, New Mexico, in 1598.[8] Writing in 1834 as an eyewitness, Jean Louis Berlandier said: "Persecuted in the western regions of the United States, bison are driven from their ranges by Anglo-American activity, though they still appear in Texas and New Mexico."[9] Reed states that, "In historic times, the range of the bison in New Mexico... extended into the east slope of the mountains in the headwaters of the Canadian River (high up, into the upper valleys of the Vermejo), to the vicinity of Las Vegas, to the Lincoln region, and to the Salt Basin on the west side of the Guadalupes...."[10]

Map 1 shows how generally buffaloes were reported throughout Central Texas. It is remarkable evidence both of how completely these animals ranged over this part of the state and how thoroughly the explorers covered and reported the area. A few of their accounts from the different centuries involved are quoted here to demonstrate the time of the buffalo's presence in local ranges over the exploratory period.

From east-central Texas in 1691, we have the testimony of Don Domingo de Teran. Reporting his travel, which was apparently from present Colorado or Fayette County across western Austin and then Washington counties, he wrote: "On the

Map 1.
Where Texas Buffalo were found.

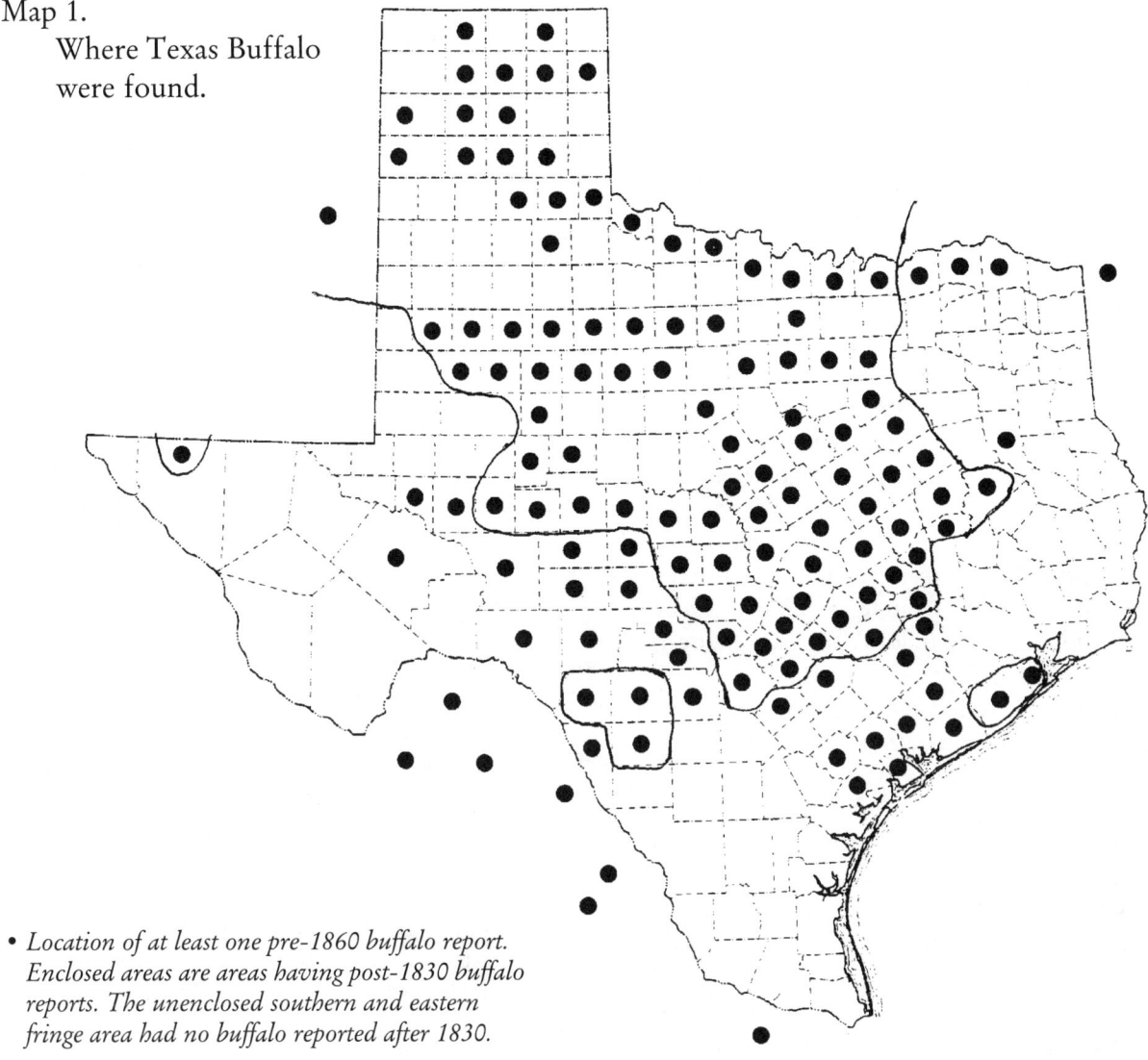

• Location of at least one pre-1860 buffalo report. Enclosed areas are areas having post-1830 buffalo reports. The unenclosed southern and eastern fringe area had no buffalo reported after 1830.

said day, July 22nd of the same year, our royal standard moved forward [from the Colorado River] toward the north, a quarter northeast. After traveling five leagues in the said direction, following a narrow trail with woods on either side, we camped upon an *ARROYO*, where there was water in holes only. The surrounding country was filled with buffaloes. Great numbers of them were in the nearby woods.... On the 23rd of the said month, our royal standard advanced six leagues in the same direction over a level country and we camped on another *arroyo*, the water being almost filled with buffaloes, because of the great number in the vicinity."[11]

In the same year, Fray Damian Manzanet used almost the same words when describing the many buffaloes he found when apparently in present Robertson and Brazos counties.[12]

Juan Dominguez de Mendoza gives the evidence concerning the buffaloes in west central Texas at that time. In 1684, when probably in northwestern Concho County, he wrote, "The country is well supplied with . . . beeves [buffalo], and many other kinds of animals. . . . Eighty beeves [buffalo] have been killed, rather more than less." When apparently in eastern Sutton County, he wrote, "The beeves [buffalo] that were killed by the whole camp were two hundred, rather more than less."[13]

The part that the buffaloes played on that fateful day in 1691, when the Spanish discovered the San Antonio River and named the site for the city to be built on its banks, shows how great the area's buffalo population was at that time. Manzanet wrote: "Wednesday, [June] 13 . . . On this day, there were so many buffaloes that the horses stampeded and forty head ran away. These were collected with the rest of the horses by hard work on the part of the soldiers.... I called this place San Antonio De Padua.... Wednesday, 15. We left San Antonio de Padua and traveled east, a quarter northeast.... After going five leagues, we halted upon an intermittent *arroyo*. There were a great many buffaloes...."[14]

From the eighteenth century we have ample accounts of the buffalo in the central part of the state. From the more northerly parts we have reports like that of Don Athanase de Mezieres, dated about 1788, and describing his movements through today's McLennan and Bosque counties just west of the Brazos River: "In order to reach the pueblo I departed from the western course which I had followed up to that time, travelling through broad and pleasant plains, interspersed with numberless woodlands, but having the defect of a scarcity of water, such as is there being dirty and contaminated because of the great concourse of animals. The number of wild cattle [buffaloes] that we encountered was incredible. After a short distance they increased so that we were passing among innumerable herds...."[15] From out in southern Menard, eastern Kimble and perhaps some of extreme west Gillespie counties, we have Lafora's 1767 statement: "The woods covering all this region consist of live-oak, chaparral, and mesquite, and they shelter many herds of buffaloes and a large number of bears."[16] From down in northeastern Travis and northwestern Bastrop counties we have the 1727 statement of Brigadier Rivera, who reported: "I traveled eight leagues straight to the northeast.... At the end of the third league, I crossed the Rio de San Marcos [the Colorado River], which carries much water.... I saw fewer buffaloes on this day than on the preceding one.... In the day of the 24th, I travelled eight leagues, in the same direction as on the previous day, over a level country without any timber. I saw more than two hundred head of buffaloes. I stopped on the south bank of the *arroyo* which they call the upper Las Animas [probably Brushy or Yegua Creek]."[17]

From the earlier part of the nineteenth century we have ample testimony to the presence of the buffalo in Central Texas. A few samples follow.

Concerning northern McLennan and Hill counties, Dr. Ferdinand Roemer wrote in 1849, "After leaving this wooded bottom [site of present Waco] behind us, we entered a sparse oak forest which led us to an open, undulating prairie extending toward the north and east in an immeasurable distance.... When on the following morning at daybreak we entered the prairie on which mesquite trees grew scatteringly, the first object that met our view was a buffalo herd, quietly grazing near us. I had long cherished the wish to see this largest mammal of the American continent in its wild state.... Now all of a sudden a whole herd stood before us.... During the course of the day, we saw more herds, numbering three to four hundred...."[18]

Those of us who have never imagined the Hill Country full of buffaloes should ponder the statements of Jean Louis Berlandier. While describing his 1828 hunting expedition to the headwaters of the Guadalupe River, he wrote concerning a day's travel from near the site of present Ingram to that of present Hunt, Texas, in Kerr County: "During our march, we encountered vast herds of buffalo."[19] When in what is today northwestern Bandera County he had the following remarkable experience: "At daybreak the fog was so dense that we could hardly identify the direction we should follow. We walked slowly and in silence. The darkness of the fog was so great that at times we almost tripped over buffalos."[20]

Although it is not evidence of the first order, being a reminiscence and not an eyewitness account, I include the following statement for its special interest. It was made by Alex. W. Terrell and is concerning a happening of 1837 or 1838. According to Terrell, "Jacob Harrell was then the only white frontier settler where Austin is located, and no white man lived on the waters of the Colorado above him. His cabin, and a stockade made of split logs to protect his horses from the Indians, were built at the mouth of Shoal Creek, near the river ford. There Lamar and Fontaine ... and their ranger escort camped for the night, and were awakened next morning early by Jake Harrell's little son, who told them that the prairie was full of buffalo. Lamar and his men were soon in the saddle, and after killing all the buffalo they wanted were assembled by a recall sounded by the bugler on the very hill where now stands the State Capitol building. ... Willis Avery, whose posterity still live in Texas, told me that Lamar killed on that hunt with his holster pistol near where the Avenue Hotel now stands the largest buffalo bull he ever saw."[21]

While in southern Bastrop or Caldwell County in 1835, Charles B. Shain reported: "On the 24th [of December], I killed three buffaloes; and two others were killed by some of the rest of the company. We must have seen five or six hundred that day."[22]

That at least some of these buffaloes were still down in the San Antonio area in 1836 is made clear by Jose Enrique de la Pena, whose report of that time says: "On the 30 of March, the day began with abundant rain but our march continued. . . . As commanding officer of the brigade, I advanced [from Bexar] to Cibolo Creek in order to reconnoiter the ground, and during two hours in the afternoon, in the neighborhood of the road, I saw hundreds of buffalo in herds."[23]

Such are the statements from the first half of the nineteenth century — droves of buffaloes all over Central Texas. But after the middle of the century things were apparently different. I have found only one statement concerning buffaloes in this part of the state after 1850, and that is by J. De Cordova, who wrote in 1858: "The great Colorado sulphur spring is situated on the southwestern bank of the Colorado River, about seventy-five miles above the city af Austin, in this [San Saba] county . . . to the sportsman it furnishes a few buffalo. . . ."[24] After that, concerning buffaloes in Central Texas there is only a profound silence.

What happened by this time? Dr. Ferdinand Roemer, quoted before about finding vast herds of buffalo in 1849 much farther north where the wilderness had still hardly been invaded, wrote also in 1849 about the situation down near the settlements: "Of the wild quadrupeds of mammals appearing in the region of New Braunfels, the American deer is the largest, for the buffalo, which at the time when the first settlers came here under Prince Solms, were still seen on the heights north of New Braunfels, had retreated long ago and did not come within many miles of the city."[25]

Lt. A. W. Whipple pictured the situation in his report of 1853 and 1854: "If not in these days, they [the buffalo] formerly ranged south as far as the waters of the Brazos, Colorado, and other Texas rivers, where there are vast hunting grounds for the great Comanche and Kioway tribes of Indians. The noble wild animal upon which these red men of the plains mainly subsist is already becoming greatly diminished in numbers, by the restraints of the settlements, and by the military occupancy of their grounds."[26]

The picture the explorers leave us of Central Texas is complete. According to them the Hill Country, the Blackland Prairies and the Edwards Plateau were, when they found them, one grand pasture teeming with buffalo. They made use of them as they would, dining upon them, shooting them for sport, generally harrassing them. So according to their own admissions, by 1850, their activities and those of the settlers who were already following them up into the area had caused the mighty buffalo — really a timid pushover — to forsake forever the southern parts of these woods and prairies he had apparently enjoyed for millenia and to hang on only tentatively to the northern parts of Central Texas. Interestingly, all this was prime hunting country for the Indians. It should be food for our thoughts that the buffalo could have coexisted here with the Indians for nobody knows how long, but couldn't survive the first generation of explorers and settlers.

North and Central Texas were originally teeming with buffalo. That is clear. But what about the extremities of the state?

Map 1 makes it clear that those who were there at the time found few, if any, buffalo in extreme East Texas. Except for sightings in two counties, Houston and Cherokee, and in several counties on the northern border, the Trinity River marked a distinct limit to their range in northern Texas. It is a gratifying confirmation of our explorers' veracity and of our mapping method to find Fray Solis stating this same thing in 1767, as follows: "In this part of the country, the region immediately east of the Trinity River, there are no bison. . . ."[27] And except for two counties on the Gulf Coast, the Brazos marked the same sort of a limit in the south.

This lack of buffalo in East Texas is hard to understand. It can hardly be because they were there but missed, because explorers had tramped all over the area, a large part of it had already been surveyed, and settlements were already scattered all over it before 1860. Also, buffaloes were known to have originally ranged on east to within sight of the Atlantic Ocean. But they must have shunned East Texas from before the time of the earliest explorations. Two early statements make that clear.

The Talon brothers, survivors of La Salle's expedition and one of whom was for some years a captive of the Cenis Indians in East Texas, stated during their interrogation back in France, "But for these, that is to say the Cenis [a nation whose village] is about one hundred leagues inland [Note: thought to have been in the Caddo area of northeast Texas], they cultivate the soil and grow maize or corn, beans and pumpkins of diverse kinds, with other sorts of vegetables and roots, of which they don't know the name. They grow tobacco, but little, and only for their use. They also raise horses, of which they make use only to transport their meats, being obliged to go very far to hunt the buffalo, which are so savage and flee so much the inhabited regions that they are only found at 15 or 20 leagues around the villages."[28]

Fray Francisco Casanas de Jesus Maria confirmed the Talons' report of no buffalo in extreme East Texas. In a letter to the viceroy of Mexico, dated August 15, 1691, written from the Tejas Indian territory of northeast Texas, he stated: "The Indian men have only one occupation, hunting. Although they are very skilled in shooting arrows, they are not able to kill a sufficient amount of the game mentioned to supply their wants; and, it therefore becomes necessary for them to make use of the buffalo. So, at various times in the year, the Indians come together for the purpose of going out to hunt buffalo. The nearest place they can be found in about four days' travel from this place."[29]

This is strange, since buffaloes were clearly just across in Arkansas and Louisiana as late as the beginning of the nineteenth century. Several statements establish that. Thomas Freeman, in his journal of his 1806 expedition up the Red River, wrote, when near present Fulton, Arkansas, "Buffaloe tracks were first seen by the hunters of the party in the Vicinity of this Hill."[30] Dan L. Flores, editor of Freeman's journal, says in a note to this, "According to Joseph Paxton, as late as the 1790s, Caddo and Bodcau Prairies were the resort of large herds of bison. Paxton de Sevier, Mount Prairie, Ark. Terr., August 1, 1828, HOUSE DOC. 78, 29th Cong. 2d. sess., p. 10."

Henry Kerr, in his jaunt up the Red River, two or three days after leaving Natchitoches, Louisiana, and when just past a main Indian village, reported seeing many buffalo. The year was 1809, and his word picture of the deer and buffaloes and the huge amount of verdure then present in the Red River prairies is so fine that it is worth repeating here. He wrote: "We now passed extensive prairies. . . . These plains afford a rich pasture to the deer and buffalo, which may be seen in droves; still they are very wild. . . . I discovered a beaten path . . . I followed for three or four miles, where it forked; I kept the main path. I soon found the weeds and grass were getting high. . . . The weeds had now become as high as my head, when I found fresh signs of game, and undiscovered I crawled within twenty paces of several deer, feeding like sheep. I singled out one that was nearest, and took deliberate aim, when my gun snapped; they instantly threw up their heads. I again cocked, and just as they were making off, I brought one down. It now seemed as if bedlam had broke loose. Herds of deer and buffalo were running in every direction, leaping to the top of the weeds to discover from whence the alarm proceeded. . . ."[31]

In spite of all this, our explorers maintain that at that date there had not been buffaloes in East Texas for over a hundred years. Somewhere between 1715 and 1721, Espinosa wrote, "the buffalo is distant more than forty leagues [100 miles] from the Texas country [the area of the Tejas Indians of the Trinity and Angelina Rivers], and to secure a supply of dried meat the Indians all go well armed because at this time if they fall in with the Apaches the two murder each other unmercifully."[32] And Father Gaspar Jose Solis wrote in 1767, "Now, in these places (those which are to the east of the Rio de la Trinidad), there are few deer, no buffaloes, some turkeys, and many bears."[33]

The consensus of the explorers is that buffaloes were, from the time of the first explorers, rare if found at all in extreme East Texas, even though they were ranging in herds both east and west of there. When we look for reasons for their absence in this corridor up into their larger range, we find only one explanation ventured by anyone who was there at the time. Dr. Roemer observed that they quickly fled the vicinity of American settlements, and the Talon brothers had long before that credited the fact of their not being in East Texas to their having fled that Indian "inhabited region." The testimony is thus that the numerous Indians of East Texas, with their settled lifestyles, their comparatively large population centers, their agriculture and their organized hunting, had already so affected the environment of East Texas as to render it untenable for the buffalo. If this was true, then it means these Indians were already well on the way to modernity — were already achieving the modern human's ability to fundamentally change his environment. This is in sharp contrast to the small to nonexistent effects of the nomadic Indians of northwest and Central Texas upon their surroundings and contradicts our often-cherished imagination of all Indians as ecologically innocent primitives not involved in the human assault upon nature.

Looking down the Texas coast from the Trinity River with the early explorers, we would have seen plenty of buffaloes. Enriquez Barroto wrote in his diary that when he was sailing down the Gulf Coast in 1687, he spied animals on the beach which were buffaloes. He put a party ashore at a spot best calculated to have been in what is now Brazoria County, between San Luis Pass at the west end of Galveston Island and the mouth of the Brazos River, to hunt them.[34]

The early presence of ample buffaloes on down in what is now Jackson County is attested to by the fact that La Salle named the river which he encountered there *LES VACHES* [the cattle], "on account of the number of buffaloes found there," as Yoakum put it in his great history of Texas published in 1855.[35] It is still the Lavaca River, and Port Lavaca is thus a testimony to buffaloes on the coast.

Victoria and Calhoun counties' seventeenth-century buffaloes were well attested to. Henri Joutel, of La Salle's party, described them as they were in 1685: "We called it [Garcitas Creek] *la Riviere aux Baeufs*, that is the River of Bullocks, by reason of the great number of them there was about it. These Bullocks are very little like ours [the European bonasus], there are Thousands of them, but instead of Hair they have a very long curl'd sort of wool."[36]

Immediately the Spanish came looking for these French intruders, and in 1690, Gen. Alonso De Leon wrote: "... we set out in the same direction [east] over some plains which were covered with buffalo, to cross the arroyo of the French [Garcitas Creek], and having crossed it, we continued to the old settlement."[37] In 1691, Teran got there, and he wrote, "... we suspended our journey remaining on the said bank [of the Guadalupe River] because it was necessary to go down from this location to the Fort [old Fort St. Louis] in search of vessels and people.... On the 7th of the said month, our royal standard and camp continued the march in search of the Old Fort, the vessels, and the people belonging thereto. We traveled toward the north [east], a quarter north about two leagues of this distance being through a wooded region. We then made three additional leagues toward the southwest through a level country. Here there were more than a thousand head of buffaloes...."[38]

That the huge animals persisted on the central part of the Gulf Coast into the first half of the nineteenth century is well attested. Mary Austin Holley, in a letter written in 1838, said: "The county surveyor is here finishing the survey of this place. He told me he was lately surveying near Dickson's [in present Galveston County] & was on my league — adding that it was a very beautiful tract indeed.... He saw there a herd of 30 Buffalo, & numerous mustang horses ... he added it would be a glorious stock farm. Its being a haunt for Buffalo & Mustang — & deer innumerable — shows that."[39]

In 1840, George W. Bonnell wrote: "Between Galveston bay and the Brazos are great quantities of wild game; and on this bayou [Chocolate Bayou], buffaloes are found in considerably abundance."[40] In a book published in 1840, S. S. Colt wrote: "... in the northern parts [of Texas], buffaloes, almost without number.... A few buffaloes are found near the Gulf."[41] And in a book published in 1841, Orceneth Fisher repeated Colt's words exactly,[42] doubling the testimony, but leaving himself open to some suspicions concerning possible plagiarism.

In close parallel to the situation of East Texas, we have a lack of buffaloes in South Texas. From Calhoun County, the southernmost county on the coast where they were seen, the known sightings of them describe an arc retreating back up to Bexar County and then terminating on the west in Maverick County. To establish this southwestern-most anchor of their range, we have statements such as that of Manzanet, who wrote in 1691: "Sunday, [June] 3. Espiritu Santo Day, after mass, we left San Fernando and Rio del Norte [the Rio Grande] because the place was lacking in pasturage for the cattle and horses. We continued toward the north, over broken country, with arroyos, hills and mesquite woods. It was like this for about three leagues. After that the country is good and level.... During all the previous days, we had seen many buffaloes. Today there were more."[43]

Below the line of this arc, there is no report of a single buffalo in South Texas throughout the century and a half during which they were still clinging to the territory just north of it — even when the retiring deer, antelope and elk were still down there. We even have eyewitness testimony that they weren't there, and about where their range ended, since General De Leon wrote in 1689, when in present Goliad County, "we moved forward, east-northeast, in search of a great river which the guide told us we should find and which we reached at two in the afternoon. We travelled six leagues, the first three over some hills, and the rest of the way over some hills that were timbered and marked with ravines. It was necessary in some places to clear

A very early illustration of some of the world's bovines, with some early names used for them. The topmost (called here Bos bubalos: *buffalo) is apparently the water buffalo of India and/or the cape buffalo of Africa. The second down (called* Zebu) *is the zebu, found from China to east Africa.*

away the timber so as to pass through. The country was the most pleasant that we had traversed; the river [the Guadalupe] is not very full and has a good ford; its banks are covered with timber. Six buffaloes — the first we had seen for a hundred leagues [coming from Coahuila] — were killed along the way."[44]

Does this mean that the buffalo never ranged into deep South Texas and the once lush Mustang Desert was always empty of them? Some research into the fauna of adjoining Mexico might help in answering this, and it yields the interesting fact that buffaloes were common at that time deep into Mexico.

We have just read that Manzanet stated in 1691, after crossing the Rio Grande near present Eagle Pass and after traveling through Coahuila, that, "During all the previous days, we had seen many buffaloes." Corroborating this account of them in Coahuila at that time is a statement written in 1690, by General De Leon. When near present Guerrero, Coahuila, he wrote, ". . . we set out towards the north for the Rio Grande. The company camped on its bank, and some buffalo were found."[45] And Teran reported at about the same time that he found Indians hunting the buffalo between the Rio Grande and the Rio Sabinas in Mexico.[46] These statements would scatter them widely in Coahuila.

Early scientists knew well that the buffalo ranged until comparatively recently into Mexico. Spencer F. Baird, in his 1857 write-up of the mammals encountered on the surveys for the western railroads, wrote: "The American Buffalo was formerly found throughout the entire eastern portion

The upper illustration on this page (labeled here simply Bison) *and the lower (called* Bos taurus, urus *or wild bull) probably represent the European bison and the American buffalo, although there are no clues as to which is meant to be which.*

of the U.S. to the Atlantic ocean, and as far south as Florida . . . to the south it extended over the entire Mississippi valley, through Texas and into Mexico."[47] J. A, Allen, in his 1875 "History of the American Bison," placed it in northeastern Mexico down to latitude 25°.[48] Judge Bethel Coopwood, in an article written in 1900, shows evidence from Mexican archives and from the statements of old Mexican settlers that buffaloes were abundant around the locale of present Monterey and Saltillo in 1556 to 1560, that buffalo herds had in early times crossed the Rio Conchas and gone to the foot of the Sierra de San Carlos, that they were south of Matamoros as late as 1808, and that they were below Laredo until about 1840.[49]

Although some more recent students have failed to read these older statements and so speak of it as only a more northern animal, the buffalo was the "Mexican cow" by virtue of being a Mexican resident until very recent times. Erik K. Reed is one more recent scientist who realizes this, writing; "Further south, however, west of the lower Rio Grande in Coahuila and northern Tamaulipas, bison survived to the nineteenth century."[50] Any who have read the explorers' accounts carefully would not be surprised at Mexican buffaloes nor at the idea that they ranged, until comparatively recently, very much farther into Mexico than even these scientists suggest. Ferdinand Lindheimer, for instance, the famed botanist of Texas and certainly a credible observer, when he was living in Mirador in the state of Veracruz, wrote in a letter dated January 17, 1835: "The animal world here is not any less remarkable [than the vegetable]. Lions (without mane) and tigers are not infrequent here (3 tigers were slain here the day before we arrived). Stags, a small type of deer, buffaloes, badgers, rabbits, anteaters, apes, skunks, are the larger mammals of this area."[51]

So why were there no buffalo during these same times in deep South Texas? The situation is quite similar to that of East Texas, each comprising a region without buffaloes surrounded in all landward directions by them. And the only clue given to any reason for their lack in South Texas is the same as that for East Texas. Jean Louis Berlandier stated it in 1828: "Before thousands of them had been killed, they used to cross the Rio Grande. We know through old accounts that they used to visit [the state of] Nuevo León. The residents of Texas, both military and civilian, annually participate in the hunt for buffalo and bear.... In spite of the small population the number of Mexican oxen (as they are called by Spanish authors) diminishes every day. They were completely killed off in Florida, where they were persecuted by the Anglo-Americans. Meanwhile, they continue to resist in Texas. Toward the end of the seventeenth century, they used to travel farther south. In the eighteenth century they came to the vicinity of San Antonio de Bejar from where they have disappeared in our time."[52]

So as explanation of their absence in South Texas we have the suggestion that they were hunted and hounded out of there, even as they were later everywhere. And this looks to be true. Certainly there does not seem to be a lack of anything the buffaloes needed in the natural environment. Since it later provided so handsomely for the horses gone wild that it became known as the Mustang Desert, the country could have supported quantities of them and given them ample room to run. But if they were hunted and frightened away it was not in this time of the explorers, because we have seen that the buffaloes were already absent from the Texas side of the Rio Grande Valley when the earliest explorers first came. We therefore have, as in the East Texas situation, the inference that they were already eliminated from South Texas by the Indians before the explorers came. For this to be true it would have taken many Indians, but this is no problem. Anyone reading the earliest explorers' accounts of the lower Rio Grande Valley for what they tell of the Indians found there will learn that the valley was a center of several Indian cultures before the Spanish came. And a further parallel with East Texas emerges. Here in the lower Rio Grande Valley were the only large, permanent, agricultural settlements of Indians the explorers found since East Texas. Perhaps it was true here, as the Talons stated about East Texas, that the Indians in permanent population centers were "obliged to go very far to hunt the buffalo, which are so savage and flee so much the inhabited regions that they are only found at 15 or 20 leagues [38-50 miles] around the villages." So the inference seems to be that the buffalo's range had already been restricted in these two places by the presence of mankind before the explorers came, and the logical conclusion following this was already there to be seen by any who might have cared, that the buffaloes could survive only nomadic hunters and gatherers and would be eliminated by the spread of civilization even without the war of extermination which was waged upon them to hurry the job.

One other extremity of Texas remains to be evaluated as buffalo country. It is the trans-Pecos West Texas — and the clues to buffalo out there are so few that many have missed them entirely. D B. Hiatt, for instance, listened to the present traditions of the region and wrote, "I have heard that buffalo never crossed the Pecos River."[53] But the old-timers of his day had forgotten the really early explorers such as Juan Dominguez de Mendoza, who wrote in 1684, "... we set out from this place, which was given the name San Juan del Rio. It is in a beautiful plain. In its environs there are four high mesas; from the small one toward the north flows a spring; within three arquebus shots, apparently, there issue five other springs, all beautiful; and within the distance of half a league a most beautiful river is formed.... Three *toros* [buffaloes] were killed in this place, and with them came relief to the great need which all the camp suffered."[54]

Both Bolton and Williams, who often disagree about specific locations of these very early reports, agree that this was at the site of present Fort Stockton and the beautiful river was Tunis Creek. This puts the buffaloes quite a ways west across the Pecos and establishes that they did at that very early time range into the trans-Pecos at least that far. But it is true that all of the explorers, the California-bound travelers and the military expeditions who crossed that country in the next century and a half never mentioned a buffalo out there again. Only the mention of finding *"bois de vacas"* [buffalo chips] in extreme northern Hudspeth County,[55] yields any later trans-Pecos trace of them, and this is only evidence that a few of them must have strayed down from eastern New Mexico, where we know they persisted that late. So we have to say that the evidence is that however far they may have formerly roamed southwest, they had forsaken the trans-Pecos area no later than during the eighteenth century. But we might have anticipated it. Knowing the permanent population centers of Indians which existed and prompted Spanish missions along the adjacent part of the Rio Grande by that time, we can once again imagine the buffalo being pushed back from this part of its range by the encroachment of mankind, even as it looks to have been in East and South Texas. That the process of hounding them away from the area was well along when the very first explorers came is shown by Diego Perez de Luxan's report. The year was 1582, and he was writing about the Indians he encountered in Mexico, a short distance southwest of what is now Presidio, Texas, when he said: "These people . . . cover themselves with well tanned skins of the *cibula*. These hides they tan and soften by beating them with stones until they are soft. They fight with bows and arrows. The bows are Turkish, all reinforced and very strong, and the strings are made from the sinews of the buffalo. For these people ordinarily go after the meat and skins where they [the buffalo] roam, which is about thirty leagues [75 miles] from this province."[56] The distance given here would take these Indians close to no other place where buffaloes have been specifically reported except Mendoza's Fort Stockton area, making it appear that the animals were already under pressure from concerted Indian raids upon them in the trans-Pecos that early.

BUFFALO IN NUMBERS BEYOND COMPREHENSION

In general, the explorers have told us that they found the buffalo over all of Texas except deep East Texas, the extreme south and the very far southwest of the state. We must imagine the preponderance of the state with these animals once roaming over it. But can we imagine the number of them which were here?

Most of us have some idea that there were very many buffaloes out on the high plains, everywhere from Texas into Canada. Many of us have read estimates of their total numbers at their heyday. These run from around thirty million[57] to sixty to seventy-five million,[58] or as high as fifty to one hundred twenty-five million. Roe, after an exhaustive discussion, settles upon around forty million as the most likely number for the total buffalo population at its zenith.[59]

Another way to perhaps visualize the great quantities of these animals which existed is to imagine the incredible sizes of their main herds. Thomas Farnham, when on the Santa Fe Trail in 1839, spent three whole days passing through an uninterrupted herd of buffaloes which he estimated covered 1,350 square miles of country. This made it a mass of buffaloes larger than the state of Rhode Island.[60] Lewis and Clark saw an estimated twelve million in one herd,[61] and an unknown traveler to California in 1849 wrote that while in the Indian territory of Oklahoma he had "no hesitation in saying that from fifty to a hundred thousand were in sight at once."[62]

It even taxed the proverbial Texian braggadocio for our explorers to state the huge numbers of buffalo in this state. When exploring in the Llano and San Saba rivers area of Central Texas in 1684, Mendoza simply wrote, "the number of buffalo is so great that only the divine Majesty, as owner of all, is able to count them."[63] An indication that he was probably right comes from his statement that his party killed 4,030 of them in one place in that area. When in the region of McLennan, Bosque, Falls and Somervell counties, just west of the Brazos River, Don Athanase de Mezieres wrote in about 1788, "The number of wild cattle that we encountered was incredible. After a short distance they increased so that we were passing among innumerable herds — a precious and inexhaustible supply from which these natives secure their food, clothing, shelter, and articles of trade."[64] Perhaps Amangual made the ultimate Texian statement when he wrote, as he was apparently in present Scurry County in 1808, "today an infinite number of buffaloes was seen in the arroyo . . . and as far as one could see, the country was covered with buffaloes."[65] Although their numbers were surely not infinite, there were obviously very many buffaloes in Texas. As late as 1822, and as far southeast as Robertson County, near present Hearne, Texas, W. B. Dewees wrote, "You would scarcely believe me, were I to tell you of the vast herds of buffalo which abound here; I have frequently seen a thousand in a day between this place, and the mouth of Little River."[66] And still later, in 1840, they were still in North Texas in such numbers, for Moore wrote then, "The country overshadowed by the Cross Timbers abounds in game, being frequented by immense herds of buffalo. . . ."[67]

BUFFALO: THE FIRST TEXAS NOMADS

But most of us probably have incorrect ideas about where in Texas those buffalo masses were. We have had so many pictures of buffalo herds spread across the huge open expanses of the Great Plains and so few representations of them among trees that we imagine the plains were constantly covered with buffalo, and we can hardly imagine those huge animals gliding through the shadows of deep forests or crashing through swamps. Yet any careful reading of the explorers' records shows that we have misconception here.

For instance, Lt. A. W. Whipple wrote an official report on the Llano Estacado — the great high plain of extreme northwest Texas — in 1853 and 1854. At that time — no more than twenty years before the buffalo hunters were killing millions of buffalo in the very same place — Whipple wrote: "This is a dry, and generally timberless tract of country, extending over a distance of about one hundred and ninety miles. Over this region, and the western portions of the last [the high prairies of western Oklahoma and northwest Texas], immense herds of buffaloes range at certain seasons of the year, but they evidently make no prolonged stay here; passing from the waters of the Arkansas and Canadian rivers, south to those of Red river and its tributaries, and thence back again. If not in these days, they formerly ranged south as far as the waters of the Brazos, Colorado, and other Texan rivers, where there are vast hunting grounds for the great Comanche and Kioway tribes of Indians."[68]

Thomas Falconer left eyewitness testimony of the plains without buffaloes when he wrote in 1842 about his experience northwest of present Amarillo, on the Canadian River: "On the 23rd [of September] we reached the Rio Escaravadra (*escarbadura*, scraping). The Mexicans stated that, when the stream did not run, water was obtained in the channel by scraping or digging up the ground. It lay in a broad chasm about 100 feet below the level of the prairie.... Our course was kept westerly and near to the line of the river, sometimes camping on it at night, and other times halting at lagunes [playa lakes] on the prairies, where were frequently flocks of wild ducks. Some few antelopes were killed. It was not buffalo season, and we saw none, but there were signs of immense herds having traversed the country."[69]

So it is clear that while the plains could be swarming with buffaloes at some times, at others they could present only a ghostly emptiness, the millions which one knew had to be somewhere wholly absent from those huge pastures. Where could they have gone?

We have seen Whipple's statement that at times the buffaloes were on the Arkansas and Canadian rivers and at other times they were down on the rivers of lower Texas, and that the great Indian hunting grounds were not on the Llano Estacado but down on these rivers. Yoakum, when in his history he is discussing the site of La Salle's murder, gives us a clue which turns us in the right direction, and we find them in most unlikely places for what are so often called "dwellers of the plains." Yoakum wrote, "At that season of the year (March), the buffaloes were down in the timber, and the Indians also in pursuit of them. Hence, La Salle met more Indians on this second tour, and Nika had no difficulty in finding buffalo...."[70]

Note Yoakum's statement carefully. He says that the buffaloes were sometimes "down in the timber." And many explorers verify this. We have seen Teran's report that in July of 1691, when he was in present Colorado, Fayette and Austin counties, "The surrounding country was filled with buffaloes. Great numbers of them were in the nearby woods."[71] And we have had Lafora's statement in 1767, when he was in Kimble and Gillespie counties, that "The woods covering all this region ... shelter many herds of buffaloes...."[72]

The explorers have made it clear. From what they tell, in their original mode the buffaloes were great travelers. Their congregation into their great herds did not mean they were settled. These huge masses were almost always moving. Out on the high plains, at one time one might encounter many square miles of buffaloes — an awesome congregation— but they were all going, they could cover great distances, and the same stretch of plain might be completely empty of them when seen again. This would be because sometimes they were far off along some *Rio de Las Vacas,* "down in the timber" of the Hill Country or the prairies — even down on the Gulf shore — but you couldn't count on finding them there either. The point is that they were always moving, and that originally, before mankind restricted them, they owned the whole of what was to become Texas to the extent that they roamed it all. Moore summed it up in 1840, at the very end of their age of free travel: "Vast droves of buffalo frequent the whole unsettled portion of Texas, and a few months since were found in great numbers in the immediate vicinity of the capitol. The droves of these animals, often cover the whole face of the country for miles in extent near the sources of the Colorado and Brazos. They annually migrate from the northern to the southern sections of the country, and are pursued in these migrations by the Comanches and other Indians, who chiefly depend upon these herds for their food."[73]

But Moore presents us with a new question to be settled. Does their ceaseless wandering mean that they were migratory animals in any large sense?

This question is not a simple one to answer, even though there are plenty of opinions on it. As for our pre-1860 eyewitnesses, we have just seen Moore's flat statement that they migrated annually. Freeman made a similar statement, writing in 1806, of "immense herds of Buffaloes, upon which the Indians almost entirely subsist, moving their camps, as these animals migrate with the season, from North to South and back again."[74] And St. John, in 1844, wrote, "The buffalo is a migratory beast. . . ."[75] Other explorers don't make such definite statements, but imply a migration when they speak of buffaloes going "south in winter and north in summer."[76] Still others, like Bracht, speak of how the buffaloes "range," "drift" and "stray," implying movement here and there, but not calling this a concerted migration.[77] It would seem that the explorers are not conclusive on the question. While all saw buffaloes continually moving, some believed it was migration but some did not commit themselves on it.

It is strange that some, writing more recently, even though the buffaloes were all gone and they have no direct observations of their own to base their opinions upon, become more definite in their statements. Don H. Biggers, for instance, has written: "In habit they [the buffaloes] were migratory, drifting south to the Rio Grande in winter, and north into the Dominion of Canada in summer. . . . It was literally one vast herd ebbing north and south with the seasons."[78] J. I. Hill maintained it thus: "Unlike most other terrestrial animals of America, so long as he roamed at will over the vast plains, the Buffalo had settled migratory habits. . . . This was most noticeable in the great Western pasture region, where the herds were more numerous, and their movements more easily observed. The herds that wintered in Texas and the Indian Territory migrated to Nebraska, Colorado, and Wyoming in the spring. The winter herds of Colorado, Wyoming and Nebraska went to the prairies along the Saskatchewan and the Great Slave Lake."[79] Mari Sandoz believed that there were four great herds, and that each herd migrated annually around a great circle three hundred to four hundred miles across, being in the north of its circle in summer and south in winter. She said her "Texas herd," for instance, wintered down toward the Pecos and Concho and summered north in southeast Colorado and southwest Kansas.[80]

But this idea that the buffalo migrated is not universally accepted. For instance, Tom McHugh, in one of the greatest studies of this animal, states that the annual north-south migration is "still argued," though "discredited," and says that George Catlin, the great artist of the plains, stated that the buffaloes were not migratory.[81] Others could be quoted to this same effect, and we have ourselves a quandary. Did or did not the buffaloes migrate, and why the confusion, from the very first, over the question?

There is total agreement that the buffaloes moved. Everybody who was there saw that. The confusion is over whether this movement was migration or not, and here there is plenty of room for disagreement. To see why, ask by what means simple explorers on the scene, or even accomplished scholars after all the buffaloes were gone, could tell whether the moving was migration or not; or, for that matter, how many bothered to learn specifically what it took to make a going migration.

We are more fortunate than most of the explorers probably were in that we can take down a dictionary and find the answer to what migration is. And when we do, we find that movement becomes migration when it is either a going from one place of abode to another "with a view to residence," or a "passing periodically" from one place to another.

As for the first meaning, no observer whose record we have has spoken of the buffaloes residing anywhere or described any place as their abode. They did not have a winter home, a summer home — any home. They only had ranges. The animal was the paragon of the nomad — the one ceaselessly on the road, the homeless traveler — so his drifting was certainly not a migration from one place of abode to another. It was the opposite of that — a continual straying.

But did he pass "periodically" from here to there? We have seen that some have claimed that, and this becomes the crux of the matter. Did he move regularly, seasonally back and forth to and from anywhere? If he did he migrated. If he didn't, he did not.

It's not surprising that the explorers themselves — only passing through, with no opportunity to stay and observe the presence or absence of buffalo in any given area over any series of seasons, and with no one of them having any overall view of the whole scene — were unclear and even disagreed about whether the buffaloes came and went regularly or not. And it is to be expected that there would be disagreement among scholars trying to decide the issue later, after the animals were already restricted in their movements or eliminated. Too bad that there were no wildlife experts back then to tag buffaloes and see whether any individuals actually trekked from the Pecos or the Brazos all the way to Nebraska or Wyoming and back or not. If only we had something by way of actual data to tell us where the buffaloes were from season to season and whether there were regular, seasonal times when they were here or there.

If we take the explorers' accounts seriously, there is something like this right before us. The 276 pre-1860 sightings of buffaloes in 130 present Texas counties, which form the basis for our Map 1, have another dimension. Many of them are from itineraries of expeditions, diaries of trips, or other material specific enough that they state on what month and day the buffaloes were present at a given site. By adding the factor of the seasons in which the buffaloes were seen in each county, we have solid data — apparently the first ever assembled — about where the animals were in each season, and so evidence of whether or not they migrated. If buffaloes migrated, then I should get a two-tiered map, with summer sightings in only North Texas — or maybe none at all in Texas if they had gone clear to Colorado and Wyoming as some have said — and winter sightings all over Central Texas but with few if any in North Texas. On the other hand, if they did not migrate, but only made erratic and unorganized movements, then my map would be a patternless hodge-podge at all seasons.

Which does the seasonal factor give me? It produces the accompanying almost featureless maps (Maps 2–5). To summarize it verbally, buffaloes were either present or absent in any particular region during any given season randomly, during the 250 years of my explorers' sightings. For instance, buffaloes were in Central Texas in each of the four seasons during some years and absent in others. Specifically, I have all four season records from Milam, Robertson, Burleson, Washington, Austin, Bastrop, Edwards, and Kimble counties — evidence that at least in some years they were not off migrating. They were present in spring and summer — when, if they migrated, they should have been way up north — in many years in many counties of south-central Texas, from Maverick, Zavala, Uvalde, Medina, Bexar, Wilson, and Guadalupe to Colorado, Austin, and Brazoria counties. They were also present in fall or winter of some years not only down in Central Texas, where they should have migrated to, but also up in Stonewall, Throckmorton, Fisher, Jones, and Shackelford counties, as well as way up in Oldham, Sherman, and Ochiltree counties of the northern Panhandle. And there were some peculiar groupings, such as their having been found in some years in Calhoun County in winter, but sometimes also in Victoria and Jackson counties in the spring and Brazoria County in the summer.

In general, all that can be said is that they could appear or disappear in any part of their range in any season — with one exception. They were never reported in the Panhandle during the dead of winter, even though they were sometimes along the Canadian River during all three other seasons.

So what can we say with certainty about the buffaloes' traveling? We can say that before they were restricted by man (1) they were always moving, (2) they could be present or absent at almost any given site in their immense Mexico to Canada range in any season of any year, (3) but the movements of any particular individuals or herds were not migrations, but erratic, unpredictable shiftings from place to place as range and weather conditions dictated.

Larry Barsness sums it up the best in his recent and most beautiful book on the buffaloes: "No man knew what locality might please them any one year. The Musselshell [River], which they loved, might see them several seasons and then see them not at all for several seasons. During summer months they might seek high, breezy places away from insects, and thus seem, to men following rivers, to have deserted the country. One man rode from Manitoba to Rocky Mountain House, good buffalo country, and saw not a buffalo — only chips from other seasons. The Pawnee once came off the plains discouraged by a bad winter hunt only to find buffalo thick near their villages. In the fall buffalo moved toward a place of good winter feeding and protection from storms — usually wooded land, perhaps in a local

Buffaloes by Season

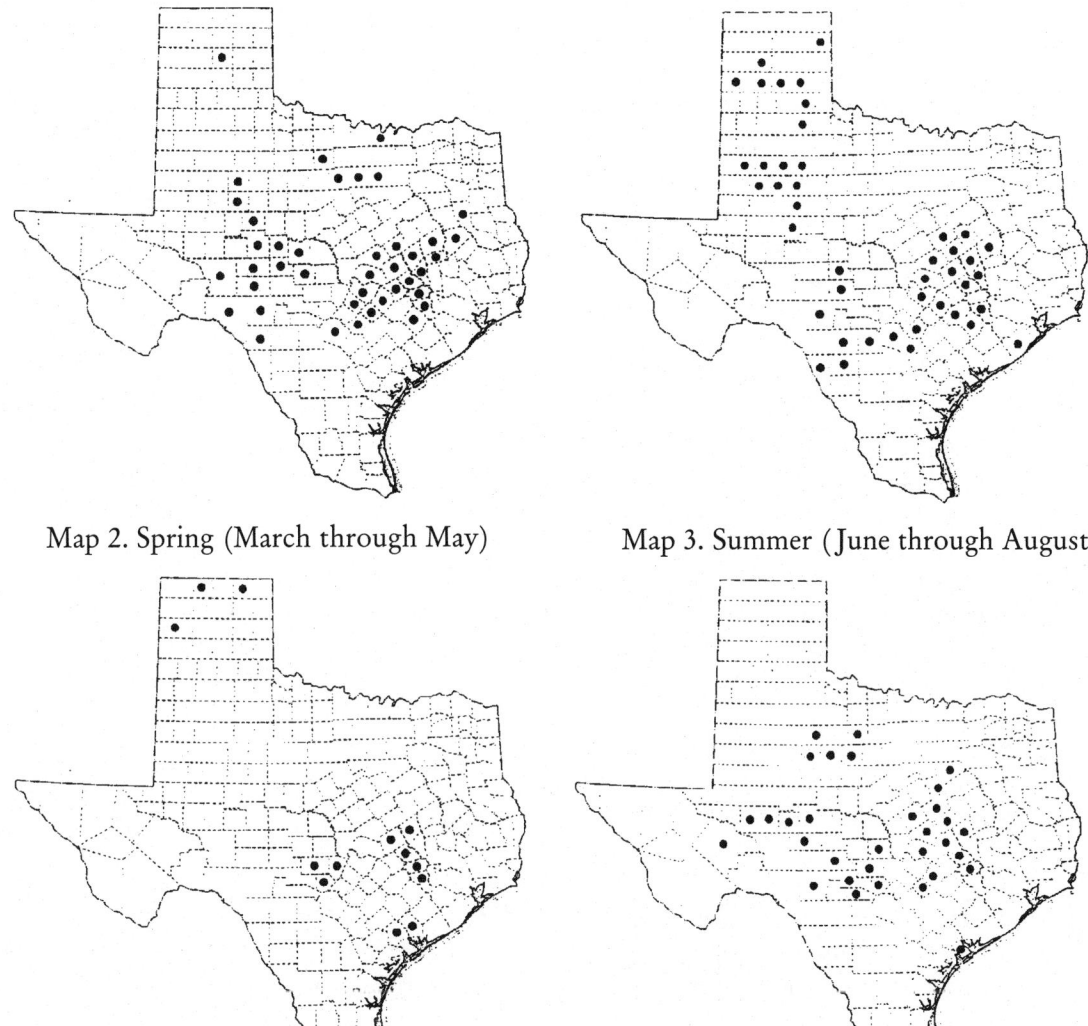

Map 2. Spring (March through May)

Map 3. Summer (June through August)

Map 4. Fall (September and October)

Map 5. Winter (November through February)

Marked counties are those having pre-1860 reports of herds of buffalo present in the seasons indicated. These animals probably were underreported in northwest Texas because of that region having been belatedly explored. However, their reported presences seem to indicate little if any pattern of seasonal migration within this state.

mild climate. They moved haphazardly.... Yet even these cannot be called migration. Instead they are erratic absences, for these herds might not return ... come spring, but wander elsewhere.... If buffalo had moved more predictably, no mountain man need ever have unsqueamishly eaten grasshopper or rattlesnake saying 'Meat's meat.' At any time he could have found a 'migration route' and slaughtered meat.... At times not even the famed Red River hunters filled their meat carts."[82]

We must therefore say that our Texas explorers caught the reality of the buffaloes' constant coming and going, but were so briefly present themselves that they never saw the whole picture and so never understood the wholly erratic nature of their movements. So some of them mislead us with their false assumptions of regular migrations which our tabulation of their own sightings in different seasons of different years prove did not at that time take place.

We can be thankful that we limit our picture to

the time of the explorers. This means we do not have to trace the dismal story of the bisecting of the original international mass of buffaloes by the barriers of the railroads and the swaths of death their hunters and settlers cut through it, into what the later observers called the northern and southern herds and finally into the four herds of Sandoz. Others have traced how each of these penned masses actually did wheel around in what many took for migrations in their desperate attempts to avoid the hunters and to find shelter, food and water in its ever-shrinking and more inadequate range.[83]

A TEXAS BUFFALO WAS JUST A BUFFALO

Pioneers in other parts of the continent maintained that there were different kinds of buffaloes. Explorers north of Texas described "mountain buffaloes" or "blacks" and "buffers" or "Mealys." This distinction persisted. These two kinds became respectively the "woods buffalo" and the "plains buffalo," and finally *Bison bison athabascae* and *Bison bison bison*. Much has been written concerning the reality or lack of reality of this division, and real conflicts were waged over the replacing of the original woods buffaloes of Canadian preserves with plains buffaloes imported from the south.

But we apparently never have had to worry about this distinction in Texas. In the hundreds of passages about buffaloes in this state's early writings, I have found no mention of any such subspecies. In fact, two of the earliest explorers make specific statements about the buffaloes' uniformity. The Talon brothers, reporting on their seventeenth century observations in Texas, testified: "All of them [the buffaloes], male as well as female, are of a reddish black color."[84] And Don Juan de Onate, detailing his 1601 trip through the future Texas Panhandle, wrote, "All these cattle are of one color, namely brown, and it was a great marvel to see a white bull in such a multitude."[85] So apparently we had only *Bison bison bison* in Texas, even though they were often found in our forests as well as on our plains.

However, we see here that Onate noted seeing a white buffalo bull. What an example of beginners luck that in 1601 he happened upon what no later explorer reports being fortunate enough to see in Texas in all of the following 250 years! But we know that Onate was not dreaming. His account is actually a fine example of the completeness of the explorers' picture of their world when it is built up as a collage of all their observations, because we know from explorers and fur traders of more northern latitudes that albino buffaloes existed, even though they were extremely rare.

WHEN IS A BUFFALO HERD A HERD?

Observers of the buffaloes in their heyday tell of "herds" of from a few hundred to hundreds of thousands or perhaps a million strong. They speak of their "covering the countryside," and moving more or less in unison the same direction, or, when surprised, stampeding in awesome masses. Shouldn't we question whether such masses could exist without some sort of internal structure? Did any of our explorers notice any organization in these masses?

Only a very few of those who worked their ways through extensive buffalo populations paid sharp enough attention to notice the animal's social organization — and that should not surprise us — but several did.

J. Wright Mooar was one of the greatest of the buffalo hunters. Having stalked and killed thousands of the animals as a leader in the great buffalo slaughter, he had to have studied their habits. As reported by Don H. Biggers, Mooar said that the true buffalo grouping which should be called a herd was not whatever happened to be in view at a given time, but "a family group . . . of from a few hundred to many thousands." He continued, saying that often there were so many herds in proximity that it appeared as one herd, but that these herds were real, separate units, and that he had "frequently stood on an eminence and counted as many as half a dozen herds within a few hundred yards of each other. Some of these herds were contentedly grazing, others peacefully lying down, and others marching along with military precision, but all headed in the same direction."[86]

Although he was not fortunate enough to have hunted in Texas, Richard Irving Dodge resided on the plains for over thirty years, from 1849 onward, and is recognized as among the greatest possessors of firsthand knowledge of our frontier game animals and perhaps the most eloquent in describing them. He wrote, "The whole country appeared one mass of buffalo moving slowly to the northward, and it was only when actually among them that it could be ascertained that the apparently solid mass was an agglomeration of innumerable small herds, of from fifty to two hundred animals separated from the surrounding herds by greater or less space, but still separated."

This is the same herd structure as Mooar described. It is this which is the real herd unit, not the overall mass covering a valley, a region or an interstate expanse. And Dodge's observation is specific enough that he can go on to describe the dynamics of this buffalo herd. He first denies in no uncertain terms that this herd is organized by or that the members are "retainers of some specially powerful bull who keeps proper order and subjection among them. Nothing is farther from the truth. The association is not only purely instinctive, voluntary, free from the domination of power, of sexual appetite, or individual preferences, but is most undoubtedly entirely accidental as to its individual components."

This is an exact denial of what Mooar apparently meant by a herd being a family group, but Dodge is emphatic and gives the details of what he had observed: "I have, unobserved, carefully watched herds while feeding. I have seen two or more small herds merge into one, or one larger herd separate into two or more. This is done quietly, gradually, and as it were accidentally, in the act of feeding, each buffalo seeming only intent on getting his full share of the best grass. The cows and calves are always in the centre, the bulls on the outside. When two feeding herds approach each other and merge into one, the only perceptible change — and this is so gradual as scarcely to be noticeable — is that the bulls on the sides of contact work themselves out towards a new circumference, which is to enclose the whole; and when a larger herd breaks by the same gradual process into smaller ones, the bulls instinctively place themselves on the outside of each. When pursued the herds rush together in one compact plunging mass. As soon as the pursuit is over, and the buffalo are sufficiently recovered from their fright to begin feeding, those on the outside of the mass gradually detach themselves by breaking into small herds, until the whole large herd is in the normal condition. If each dominant bull had on such occasions to run through the whole great herd to look up his lost wives, children, and dependents, his life would not only be a very unhappy but a very busy one."[87]

THE MOST OVERRATED STAMPEDE

Having related accounts of buffaloes filling the country from horizon to horizon and having noted statements like Dodge's that "when pursued the herds rush together in one compact plunging mass," it seemed I should write next an exciting section about the horrible, death-dealing buffalo stampedes. After all, the stories we were raised on about the hazards of our pioneer forebears' existences often featured fearsome episodes of humans, horses, wagons, tepees, and even trains and cabins having been run over by tides of insane, unstoppable buffaloes. So I returned to my Texas pioneers' writings prepared to pick the most grisly of such stories come down to us and feature them here.

But I was disappointed. The nearest to this which I did find was the comparatively tame account left by Dr. Ferdinand Roemer of his really easy escape from such a stampede in Central Texas in 1849. He described it this way: "On leaving the [Little River] bottom we had an immeasurable prairie, covered with mesquite trees, before us. After a ride of several hours we came to a little brook called Willes Creek where buffaloes in great numbers were grazing. They covered the grassy prairie separated into small groups and far distant on the horizon they were visible as black specks. The number of those clearly seen must have been not less than a thousand. When several hundred of them, disturbed by our presence, bolted, the ground resounded as at a charge of a regiment of cavalry. In their fright the herd came directly toward us and we had to hurry to get out of their reach, as they do not change the course of their flight, but trample under foot any object confronting them."[88]

The rest of the actual eyewitness accounts of buffalo stampedes were even more tame. W. B. Dewees' story of experiencing one in 1830 is typical: "We encamped that night a short distance from the road, half way between Gonzales and Bexar [San Antonio]. A short time after midnight, we were awakened by the trampling of hoofs, which seemed to be coming in the direction of our encampment. We listened! The sounds grew more distinct! Was it a cavyyard of horses, running in the prairie, or was it a party of Indians coming upon us? And how should we escape, were questions which rapidly suggested themselves to our minds. They advanced nearer, and yet more near; what must we do? to attempt to fly is vain. At length we secreted ourselves, as well as we could, behind a Musquit tree; the night was dark, and we knew our enemy could not see us till they were close upon us. They came up, the sight of our fire seemed to frighten them, and separated the company. I now crept cautiously from my place of concealment to see who was our foe. To my great relief I found it to be a vast herd of buffaloes. Our horses had been frightened by their coming, and one of them which was tied had broken his fastenings and gone with the buffaloes, followed by the other, although hobbled."[89]

By now I was thoroughly confused. I had Dr. Roemer's statement that buffaloes would never change their courses and would trample anything before them, but I had Dewees' conflicting testimony that his campfire had split such a stampede and that even a hobbled horse, which could certainly not dodge the charge, had not been run down. I soon found other statements of early Texans who seemed to regard buffalo stampedes as harmless. J. P. Simpson even looked upon one as "agreeable." He wrote: "In the month of May, 1838, being desirous of taking a buffalo hunt, he and five others went in ox wagons to the cross timbers west of where Whitesboro now stands. They killed a few buffaloes that evening and were feasting on them that night when they were suddenly alarmed by a noise as of rushing mighty waters. They flew to their arms and prepared for an attack by the Indians, but to their very agreeable surprise, it was an immense herd of traveling buffaloes."[90]

Beyond these rather off-hand, unconcerned accounts of the things, I had not one firsthand Texas account of buffalo stampedes killing anyone or even destroying anything. Where was the Texas braggadocio on this, anyway?

Research further afield was clearly necessary, so I went into the general literature on buffaloes. This turned up plenty of tales of buffalo stampedes. The earliest recorded is probably that observed by Coronado in 1541, when his men fired at a large herd and they stampeded across a ravine, the first individuals falling into it and, after their bodies had filled the ravine, the rest running over the first. There are numerous accounts from explorers of herds being stampeded by hunters, by thunder and lightning, by prairie fires, or even by the sounds of trains. And some of these stampedes carried many individual buffaloes over banks into rivers where they drowned or into bogs where they mired down. The stampedes were clearly of mortal danger to the buffaloes themselves, but this didn't tell me anything about the danger from these mad masses to others.

There are vivid accounts from explorers of being caught in front of such stampedes, and of the heroic measures which seemed to have saved life, limb and property. Major Dodge's telling of such a narrow escape experienced in the Arkansas River country in 1870 is typical. As the animals bore down upon him he says he stood his ground and fired at them, dropping several of the nearest buffaloes directly in front of him, and he credits this with splitting the herd so that it rushed by the dead animals and himself on either side. Others even claimed to have accomplished this feat of splitting the herd and saving themselves by just standing firm and waving blankets or by shouting in the faces of the oncoming monsters.

In reading of these episodes, I will admit that I didn't question the efficacy of these heroic actions. They sounded so great, I was as gullible as any rube hearing Buffalo Bill boast of his bravery. Still, I became a little bothered because I could find no Texan who boasted of diverting the stream of death with his bravado. Didn't our Texans ever save themselves so heroically, and if, as it appeared, they did not, then were our Texas buffaloes — perish the thought — some way less fearsome?

I have to admit that I did not solve the enigma myself. I was still puzzling over the lack of testimony concerning Texas buffalo stampede damage when I got into the chapter titled "White Man's Folklore" in Larry Barsness' great book on buffalo. Since he gave me the solution, I cannot do better than to quote his passage concerning it: "Myth tellers yarned about the all-destroying buffalo stampede, something that seems never to have trampled anyone or destroyed any wagon train. . . . Stampede yarns told by professional Western Adventurers, the Buffalo Bills, and Buffalo jacks, and Buffalo Joneses, were designed to enhance their bravado. Buffalo Jones wrote of the stampede as 'this movement when the heart fluttered at the roots . . . the living cataract . . . woe unto any and all living creatures that chanced to be in its pathway. . . .' But those who'd actually stood in front of the stampeding herd reported little danger. L. C. Fouquet, standing before 'herd after herd running into the wind' felt 'as if they would run over us, however they dodged us every time at the most skarish moment.' George Brown, hide hunter, 'never saw the time when they would not give way for a wagon or horseman.' He once stood in front of a running group but they gave him plenty of room and 'I never had any fear of being run over.' A camp cook lost on the prairies awoke at night to find a herd running right at him, but 'by his shouting and action they swerved and passed him without injury.' James

Willard Schultz, hiding behind a wagon from a stampede coming down through a Blackfeet encampment, saw them 'threading their way between the lodges, nimbly jumping from side to side to avoid them, kicking out wickedly at them as they passed.' After the herd had passed 'no one had been hurt, not a lodge had been overturned.' Men crossing the plains in wagon trains felt that the main danger of a buffalo stampede came from the stampede of their mules and oxen to join the herd. The running herds were less compact than imagined; the beasts were more agile than imagined. Furthermore, they were easily turned by firing shots. Today as a person watches a managed herd switch and turn, dodging horseback riders, corral gates, and footmen, he can see buffalo are wary of anything in their path and tend to run around it rather than over it. They seem not the most dangerous animal in North America as Ernest Thompson Seton believed."[91]

Frank Gilbert Roe summed up what is known about the subject by writing: "... it is remarkable that in all the material I have consulted on the species, I have not encountered one single instance of anyone being killed or even injured by buffalo from this cause [their stampeding]."[92]

So instead of being ashamed of my Texas explorers for not topping everybody else's stories of heroics in front of certain death in the form of buffalo stampedes or of being ashamed of our stampeding Texas buffaloes for not having trampled anyone to death, I am once again proud of my explorer reporters for their accuracy, and I want to point out to all that at least here the Texas braggadocio did not exaggerate the truth.

THE CREAM-PUFF THAT CAN TURN INTO A TIGER

Having met the challenge of stampeding buffaloes head on and found them less deadly than imagined, the next question which comes to mind is how dangerous was a buffalo when it was approached as it grazed or rested. Were these, the most huge bulls and most mammoth cows in their class, automatic attackers — or were they not?

The question is important. Our explorers, surveyors and early settlers tell of moving about all over the buffalo ranges, and we are wrong to imagine them all mounted. Many of them were afoot among the buffaloes. We have already noted Berlandier writing of almost literally bumping into buffaloes in a dense early-morning fog. Numbers of the described incidents of being literally surrounded on the prairies by buffaloes were experienced not from the safe advantage of fleet horses but from the ground, with no means for outdistancing a charging buffalo and often with no climbable trees at hand. Our concern for the safety of these ancestors is a little late, but they and their loved ones must have pondered the disposition of the buffaloes very seriously.

The fact that the explorers walked so freely among the giant ruminants lends much support to the idea that buffaloes were placid, and the ones who wrote about them often confirmed this. They often characterized them with one of two words, calling them either tame or timid. Don Juan de Onate used the first of these words to describe them. When in the future Texas Panhandle in 1601, he wrote: "God was pleased that we should begin to see those most monstrous cattle called *cibola*. Although they were very fleet of foot, on this day four or five of the bulls were killed, which caused great rejoicing. On the following day, continuing our journey, we now saw great droves of bulls and cows ... and they were so tame that nearly always, unless they were chased or frightened, they remained quiet and did not flee.... By experience we noted that they do not become angry like our cattle, and are never dangerous."[93] Pena wrote in 1772 that in their expedition in northwest Texas they had killed one hundred buffaloes, that even the governor had killed several, that they had also captured five young ones, and that in all this, "There were no accidents to the men."[94] In light of the inferior weapons that these early Spanish had, it becomes clear that the buffaloes must have been remarkably unwary and easily approached or every one of their expeditions could not have dined on quantities of buffaloes limited only by how many happened to be along their routes. How tame these animals could be is shown by a statement of Amangual. When in northwest Texas in 1808, he wrote, "Many buffaloes were sighted today.... Some of the buffalo came right into our camp."[95]

Various of our later explorers and settlers confirmed the usual imperturbability of these animals. Edwin James wrote in 1820, "The flesh of the bulls, in the months of August and September, is poor and ill flavoured; but these are much more easily killed than the cows, being less vigilant, and sometimes suffering themselves to be overtaken by the hunter, without attempting to escape."[96] An unnamed traveler to California, while passing through Texas in

1849, was turned off by the killing of such tame animals and wrote in a letter from Santa Fe, "Five days from leaving Little River we saw the first buffalo, and in three days afterwards were surrounded by countless thousands.... They are a large, unwieldy animal, easily overtaken by a horse or easily killed by still hunting. In fact, to me, hunting them has few charms. It seems too much like barn-door slaughter."[97] But there is a contradiction in the explorers' reports. The same animal, just described as tame and timid, could also be described very differently, as for instance, by Pena in 1772: "It's [the buffalo's] feet are cloven, and its fore head is armed as that of the bull, which it imitates in ferocity, although it is much more powerful and swift."[98] How is this disparity to be explained?

The first reason for different estimates of the buffalo's ferocity probably depended upon the courage of the observers. The peculiar bluffing actions of the bulls probably scared off the less courageous who told ever after of their ferocity, while those who stood and called the bluffs could laugh from then on about the huge animal's incongruous timidity.

Once again the great hunter Richard Dodge explains the details for us. He wrote, "When feeding, the herd is more or less scattered; but on the approach of danger it closes and rounds into a tolerably compact circular mass. Although there is not a particle of danger in approaching such a herd, it requires in a novice an extraordinary amount of nerve. When he gets within 300 yards, the bulls on that side, with heads erect, tails cocked in air, nostrils expanded, and eyes that seem to flash fire, even at that distance, walk uneasily to and fro, menacing the intruder by pawing the earth and tossings of their huge heads. The enemy still approaching, some bull will face him, lower his head, and start on a most furious charge. But alas for brute courage! When he has gone twenty or thirty yards Mr. Bull thinks better of it, stops, stares an instant, and then trots back to the herd. Another and another will try the same game, with the same result, and if, in spite of these ferocious demonstrations, the hunter still approaches, the whole herd will incontinently take to its heels."[99]

Another reason for contradictory ideas of the buffalo's ferocity is the fact that its disposition changed radically with the seasons. Since most of the explorers whose writings we read were among these animals for only short periods in single seasons, each usually saw only one aspect of this seasonally changeable animal.

For instance, a given observer may have been in the wilderness and experienced the buffaloes only in late summer or fall when, as Edwin James explained, the bulls were in poor condition and so easily killed as to sometimes allow the hunters to take them standing. Or he might have been among them during most any time during the rest of the year except during the height of the summer, in which case he might describe as did Dodge their exaggerated bluffing but actual timidity or tell of almost patting them as he passed them with Berlandier. But his estimate of their disposition would be most radically different if he approached them in the summer season.

This would be because the rutting season of the buffaloes was in July and August, and at this time the bulls became transformed into fearless engines of destruction. Alexander Ross, a fur trader, wrote: "There is perhaps not an animal that roams in this or any other country more fierce and forbidding than a buffalo bull during the rutting season. Neither the polar bear nor the Bengal tiger surpasses that animal in ferocity."[100] Nuttall, the well-known naturalist, seconded this, writing in 1819 that "The male, infuriate and jealous in his amours, gores every thing which falls in his way, and becomes totally unmanageable."[101] Woe to the explorer who approached this sexually inflamed monster. It might cost his life. So the contradiction is not a flaw in the accounts of the explorers, but taken together, a very accurate depiction of the major contradiction which existed in the seasonally varying disposition of the buffalo.

And there was yet another remarkable inconsistency in the behavior of the buffalo. The most timid, harmless of them could be turned by being wounded into a murdering monster stoppable only by its death. The Talon brothers, survivors of the La Salle expedition, testified at their official interrogation in 1698 about witnessing such a transformation. "One must... be on one's guard against the fury of these buffalo. When one has been wounded, it chased the hunters, even lying in wait with determination at the foot of the trees that they were obliged to climb and trying to uproot them with their feet until they had received the fatal shot."[102]

Joutel, another seventeenth-century explorer, described a typical reaction of a wounded buffalo and its sad result, the event having taken place in present Victoria or Calhoun County, Texas: "Father Anastasius, being a-hunting Bullocks with me, and coming too near one I had shot, and [which] was fallen, the Beast, as much hurt as he was, started up, attack'd and threw him down; he had much ado to get off, and I to rescue him, because I durst not shoot for Fear of killing him. The Bullock being weak, fell again; the Father was deliver'd but lay ill some Months."¹⁰³

General Wavel summed up the ferocity of the wounded buffalo, writing in 1835: ". . . it [the buffalo] is timid until wounded, but then its impetuosity is irrestible, and its attacks are repeated until it falls. . . . Should it discover and throw down its antagonist, it gores and tramples upon him until (if desperately wounded) it falls dead by his side."¹⁰⁴

Josiah Gregg commented in 1840 upon a peculiarity of the buffalo's behavior when it is wounded which may have contributed to many unfortunate happenings. Prompted by an episode probably occurring in Roberts County, Texas, he wrote, ". . . the wounded [buffalo] . . . though mortally wounded, stand sullenly as though unhurt. (This is a peculiarity of these animals.). . . . A buffalo bull, though mortally wounded, if chased will run miles, when if left quiet, would lie down and die in a few minutes. When irritated, they are extraordinarily tenacious of life. I have seen more than 20 balls (well directed) shot into an irritated buffalo bull, and yet he would not die for some time afterwards, whilst with one shot only, when quiet, they will frequently fall dead."¹⁰⁵

The buffalo which emerges from the totality of the explorers' accounts was an awesomely powerful beast which, fortunately, was so stupidly instinctive that, against humans, it never made full use of its power, either as a group or individually, unless wounded. Faced by men, the herd could only stampede — and this was not dangerous because it was always running away — or else stand and gaze stupidly at its shot relatives who had fallen without any visible predator's attack. Individuals could react to men by the same bluffing on the part of the bulls as they used against wolves, but would no more carry this to a completed charge against men than against wolves, probably because protected by instinct from charging out where they could be cut off from the security of the herd and from wasting their efforts upon enemies assumed to be as agile at dodging them as the wolves. But unfortunately, when actually cornered or injured, the animal's instinct was to abandon all caution and exert all its power, even to its dying breath, in either fleeing or else destroying the enemy. This instinctive switch in attitude when cornered probably explains most of the modern instances of buffaloes, necessarily fenced in and with the instinctive herd organization broken down, attacking people.

WHAT DID THE BUFFALO DO TO ITS ENVIRONMENT?

One of the most interesting and probably most important points concerning the buffalo in Texas is the question of this animal's effect upon the countryside. Surely the millions of these mammoth beasts which were part of the state's original living community extracted a huge toll from the environment. Did they make any contributions in return? Various aspects of this have been mentioned here and there, but little has been done to combine them into the total picture. We need to try to pull together evidence concerning this left by our explorers into a general view.

Millions of buffaloes obviously ate a lot of vegetation. The effect of their grazing, especially in the semi-arid regions of northwest Texas, could be catastrophic, at least in the short run. For any who need to be convinced of this, I include here the description by Amangual of a stretch of either present Randall or Armstrong County in the Texas Panhandle. Note that the time was May 25, 1808, which should have been a fine spring day in a verdant setting as yet ungrazed by domestic cattle, but Amangual wrote: ". . . we continued on our way, traveling over plains so extensive that the horizon was tiring to the eye. . . . It could be seen that there is usually much grass during the rainy season, but at this time it has been trampled by a large number of buffaloes, which in time, have exhausted the grass. Furthermore, there has been such a severe drouth that today the plains are so burned up and clean that we have not found in all our route the least blade of dry grass or weed. This condition was so noticeable that it caused great astonishment."¹⁰⁶

That this was not an unusual situation in the high plains and that the same thing occurred often, right up to the elimination of the buffaloes, is made clear by Thadis W. Box, formerly professor of range management at Texas Technological College, in his discussion of the history of the Texas range. He refers to one Rollie Burns' estimation that he had seen one million buffaloes in two days, and says, "That the large numbers of animals caused severe overgrazing in areas cannot be disputed. Burns reported that in the early Spring of 1873 the northwestern Texas Panhandle was almost devoid of grass. 'Large areas had been nipped clean by the buffaloes. We often had trouble finding sufficient grass for our horses.'"[107]

The buffaloes reduced the vegetation even in the wooded parts of the state. This is attested to by various reporters. An example is the observation of Edwin James when he was apparently in what is now Robertson County in 1820: "Since bisons had recently occupied the shade of the tree" under which he slept, "the place afforded as little refreshment for the horse," as for himself."[108]

Even though the extent of the buffaloes grazing is an uncontested fact, practically from the very beginning of modern ecology there has been discussion of and often argument over the effects of it. Some, such as Clements, minimized it as having had little long-term effect at all on the plant community. Others, such as Larson, Vestal and Carpenter, argued that the buffaloes, by their grazing, not only produced but maintained the short grass prairie, which without them would have grown on into taller grasses. The opinions of modern ecologists seem to lean toward the latter view, since they often speak of a "short grass disclimax" and of the buffalo as an almost unique example of a natural animal dominant in a terrestrial living community. This latter opinion would seem only logical, because if the hordes of domestic cattle turned loose upon the high plains reduced the grass cover to the pathetic minimum found on the ranches of that area around the end of the nineteenth century, what must have been as many or more buffaloes surely had their effect before.

Our explorers show that there was only one big difference between the two situations. While the cattle have been fenced and kept more or less continually on their pastures, the buffaloes were free and constantly moving. This was the most emphasized thing concerning their behavior. This day they were present in a given area and grazed everything down, then they promptly moved on and the next day were doing the same somewhere else, while the first area was free of them for often whole seasons in which to regrow. Isn't this the perfect model of the intensive, intermittent, "graze it all and move on till it grows back" pasture maintenance touted today? Who knows but that we could have produced all of the meat needed for Indians as well as for ourselves, kept the country verdant with its native grasses, and not fenced any of us in if we had left the buffalo to roam over an unapportioned country and harvested them with half the wisdom we claim we possess?

So the buffalo herds roamed about the wilderness, stripping great swaths clean and moving on—not migrating regularly in and out of any area to the detriment of any one grass or forb, but chopping off one species in its prime this season and then being absent when it seeded the next time, only to happen by and nip some other species the next time around—all getting their turns and the balance being maintained by this strangest of community dominants. Should the term overgrazing really be applied to such a natural management?

The buffalo had further effects upon the landscape. One such resulted directly from their constant movement. Traveling in such huge numbers from pasture to pasture and back and forth to water, they produced distinct trails. Espinosa mentioned such tracks when in eastern Bastrop or western Fayette County in 1709, as follows: "We recrossed the [Colorado] river to investigate the smoke, but there was no trace of it nor a footprint of man or beast, only deep tracks and pathways of the buffalo that crossed the river."[109]

In rough country the buffaloes would have found and followed many times the same routes of least resistance, and so their trails could be valuable aids to explorers working their ways through unknown and confusing areas. Mares tells of his having used such paths to get through rough spots of the Texas Hill Country when in present Mills County in 1787: "The paths that are sometimes found in these valleys are made by the buffalo herds. If you follow them and take care not to leave it, it sometimes lasts for a long time, as happened to me today, for I descended into a valley, and the path lasted until I left the valley."[110]

In open country, where no advantage kept the animals in any one path, the buffalo tracks would not be so deep and certain, but would apparently be the constantly intersecting trails of animals traveling capriciously. Dr. Roemer described a prairie still covered with such aimless trails in Central Texas in 1849: "After leaving this wooded bottom [the site of present Waco] behind us, we entered a sparse oak forest which led us to an open, undulating prairie extending toward the north and east in an immeasurable distance.... The whole prairie was covered with countless buffalo trails, crossing in all directions, reminding one of a European grazing ground."[111]

Besides such tracks, the buffaloes often left the surface of the country cratered with the peculiar depressions called "buffalo wallows." The pioneers never confused these depressions with similar features of some prairies, which they called "hog-wallows." They never connected those other wallows, which are dealt with in the first volume of this work,[112] with buffaloes in any way.

While our Texas explorers did mention buffalo wallows a few times, they did not report them often or ever describe any part of Texas "pocked like the moon" with them, as some regions farther north were reported to have been. From this and from the fact that much of Texas would have been too rocky for the animals to dig them, we may conclude that buffalo wallows were not as common here as in some places.

This may be the reason why I have found not one Texas explorer telling how or why buffaloes made these remarkable hollows. But since there were some of them in Texas, since these strange scars on the land are so fascinating, and since otherwise it may never be found by interested readers, I copy here from a very obscure source the most graphic description of the how and why of buffalo wallows I have read. It is told this way: "In the immediate foreground . . . there was a group of about half a dozen buffalo cows feeding quietly, and in the midst of them an enormous old bull was enjoying himself in his wallow. . . . The wallowing is a luxury usually indulged in during the hot months of summer, when the buffaloes are tormented by flies, and heat, and drought. At this season they seek the low grounds in the prairies where there is a little stagnant water lying amongst the grass, and the ground underneath, being saturated, is soft. The leader of the herd, a shaggy old bull, usually takes upon himself to prepare the wallow. It was a rugged monster of the largest size that did so on the present occasion. . . . Coming up to the swampy spot the old bull gave a grunt of satisfaction, and, going down on one knee, plunged his short thick horns into the mud, tore it up, and cast it aside. Having repeated this several times he plunged his head in, and brought it forth saturated with dirty water, and bedaubed with lumps of mud. . . . The old fellow did try it again, and again, and again, plunging, and ramming, and tearing up the earth, until he formed an excavation large enough to contain his huge body. In this bath he laid himself comfortably down, and began to roll and wallow about until he mixed up a trough full of thin soft mud, which completely covered him. When he came out of the hole there was scarcely an atom of his former self visible! The coat of mud thus put on by bulls is usually permitted by them to dry, and is not finally got rid of until long after, when oft-repeated rollings on the grass and washings by rain at length clear it away. When the old bull vacated this delectable bath, another bull, scarcely if at all less ferocious-looking, stepped forward to take his turn. . . ."[113]

Wallows — the above passage shows why they were buffalo wallows, not hollows — found along draws were started by such mud baths, but they were also found on upper, sandy ridges where water could not have been standing. These were made in a similar way, by gouging and pawing up dust, which, when thrown up into the coat, also helped insulate the skin from insects. Either type of wallow, once the grassy sod had been broken and the bare soil exposed, would not heal again for a long time, and in the meantime the buffaloes might use it again and again, enlarging it and carrying off more and more of the soil, while the powerful winds of those regions might scoop out, in dry weather, more and more of the loosened material. The wallow might thus persist as a puzzling, saucer-shaped depression in the prairie up to more than an acre in size, ringed with special plants, somewhere around a foot deep with water after hard rains, then bottomed with drying mud and finally loose dust as the weather became drier. Such wallows have constituted a legacy of the buffalo much appreciated by everything from ferns to water birds and fairy shrimp (appreciated too by me when I was a boy in western Kansas because two of these wallows were the only places where any water ever stood and any of those special things ever existed on my father's farm).

THE BIGGEST FALLS FIRST

Such was the buffalo — one of the most important, fascinating and saddest enigmas of original Texas — and such were some of its effects. Awesome, massive and powerful, the animal was at the same time remarkably stupid, defenseless and weak before its enemies, as its nearly complete demise shows. How can one explain the contradictions embodied in this animal?

I propose that both the buffalo and its history can be explained by its occupying the same niche as the other large-sized grazers of the world. Whether these be the elephants, giraffes, rhinos and other large herbivores of the African savannahs, the giant elk, bison, wild oxen and ponies of Europe, the majestic mountain sheep and goats, the hippos and dugongs of swampy rivers or the walruses, sea lions and large grazing whales of the seas, the same generalizations seem to apply to them as to the buffalo.

All of these large grazers are more or less gregarious, and this, with their large individual sizes, makes it impractical for them to hide. Left without the option of concealment, they must rely upon flight or some form of standing defense. The great development of the ability and the propensity of the buffalo to flee is legendary and explains their famous stampedes. It apparently worked well to save their lives in most natural situations thrust upon them.

But in situations where flight could not be resorted to and the buffalo had to stand and face foes, he was at a distinct disadvantage, as are all of the other large herbivores. It seems one just can't possess stabbing canines and the grazing herbivores' necessary grinders, or fighting claws and their supportive hooves at the same time, so the big herbivore is left with only comparatively ineffectual horns, hooves, the sheer force of his bulk, a thick skin and some form of communal defense for protection. From dire necessity, then, arise the communal defense strategies seen in some degree in all of these large grazers and taken to perhaps their extreme development in the buffaloes. Faced with their natural enemies, such as wolves, the buffaloes were almost totally safe when in their herds, where their practice of placing cow and calf in the center of the ring of bulls, and other strategies, worked well. An individual was only in great danger when separated from the herd, and many observers have left us testimony that even a massive bull would be torn to pieces by a pack of wolves when isolated from his kind.

But communal defense, even if it is only a positioning of the stronger around the weaker, demands a cooperation on the part of all individuals involved. And such complete cooperation as seen in the buffalo herd's remarkable defenses could only be achieved by such dumb beasts at the direction of unvarying instincts. The buffaloes were thus perhaps some of the most instinct-directed animals of any that existed, and this could work against them. While their instincts directed and protected them almost providentially in their natural environment, when new enemies they had never seen before appeared before them they could only react with the same old instinctive behavior patterns or not react at all. They could, therefore, not even use the power they had, often stood stupid and indecisively or ran for little cause, and were easy targets for the new enemies to kill.

Add to this that a new dominant can only take over a biotic community and change it into his own by first eliminating the previous dominant. Perhaps we can see from this why, from the unseen realm of the subconscious or somewhere, there arose the consuming motivation seeming to exceed mere greed in the settlers to exterminate the buffalo. The age-old dominant of the wilderness plains had to completely go, every bit as surely as the Indians, before the new, upstart humans could overrun, own, dominate and change to their own liking this Texas.

It is with a sense of relief that, with the buffaloes of Texas a little restricted in their range by the encroachment of settlements but still majestic in their numbers as well as in their instinctive travelings and in their individual might, we come upon 1860, the cutoff date for our study. How fortunate to leave the magnificent beasts this way, instead of having to wade through the blood and guts of their destruction in the following fifteen short years of mayhem and having to detail the plight of the few token ones allowed to survive in such small numbers and such restricted situations that their magnificent proportions look all out of scale and their fine-tuned instincts can't be expressed in action. We can only thank our early explorers for leaving us such fine pictures of these lost monarchs of wilderness Texas in their prime.

2

The Deer Story in Early Texas

There is no doubt that the deer is the most important of our state's remaining game animals. It still exists because it has achieved something of a truce with the all-pervading humans. To be sure this is a very desperate hide-and-seek arrangement, and one can hear all sorts of arguments about whether it is actually a truce or a limited war of attrition. It is not our purpose to settle that question here. However, the emotions generated by disagreements concerning the deer prompt numerous very categorical statements about the deer of history on the part of those who — no matter how well they know today's deer — weren't here in the beginning and know nothing directly about the naturally ranging deer of Texas' early history. Only the explorers and pioneers who were here then really knew the details about the make-up of the deer's original population and about their truly natural behavior. It might defuse some of the argued flash points and enable us to relate more intelligently to our brothers, the deer — as the Indians would say it — if we take time to see the deer as our ancestors saw them. With this as a goal, may we look at what the explorers of Texas tell us about the deer?

We have 265 different statements about deer written down immediately upon observing them between the first traceable seventeenth-century exploration of Texas and 1860. From these we may get our only truly valid pictures of the undisturbed deer in their natural wilderness. This is because, as we shall soon see, by 1860 the way of life of the buffalo, the elk and the antelope were being disrupted no more than that of the deer. Because of this the conclusions of even the earliest scientific studies of deer and the reminiscences of later Texans often yield a picture of deer almost totally different from that of the explorers because it is of deer already forced out of their natural haunts and into new survival strategies.

On one point everyone happily agrees. Discussions of deer usually begin by statements that these animals have always been throughout the whole of Texas. The explorers enthusiastically confirm this. Every region of the state has the mention of deer on the part of its early observers. There is only one statement by anyone early on the Texas scene about there being an absence of deer anywhere in the state. It was James G. Bell who wrote when he was traveling northwest through what is now Pecos County in 1854, "Those who have travelled this rout before, say . . . there is no deer. . . ."[1] That Bell was repeating a patently untrue rumor is shown by the fact that several other travelers on the same western route both before and after him reported finding deer there.

However, there are some parts of Texas where the explorers took the trouble to state that they found fewer deer than in others. Fortunately, they give us their opinions of the reasons for the animal's scarcity in these places.

The earliest statement about deer being scarce is a quite general statement by Fray Gaspar Jose Solis, surviving from 1767: "Now, in these places (those which are to the east of the Rio de la Trinidad), there are few deer, no buffaloes, some turkeys, and many bears."[2] That this was still true at least in certain parts of East Texas seventy years later was confirmed as well as explained by Friedrich W. von Wrede, who wrote in 1838, ". . . we arrived in Nacogdoces. . . . Larger game such as the Virginia deer seldom found near the town because the Indians, who come here almost daily to sell hides and game, eagerly hunt this animal."[3]

The responsibility for the reduction of game in East Texas was not put so completely upon the Indians by all. Edward Smith, writing in 1849, and reporting the verbal communications of one "Judge English, of Bonham," said, "He is well acquainted with all the changes through which this country has passed. . . . Many persons have settled in the country during the last few years, expecting to be able to live by their rifle after the manner of the early pioneers, but they cannot do so since the buffalo are gone, the deer are diminished in number, and the bear is become a stranger."[4]

There is evidence that deer were numerous east and northeast of Texas, so it seems clear that the large numbers of settled Indians in East Texas had already reduced the numbers of deer in their region, as we have seen they had the buffalo, by the time the settlers came, and that the new settlers immediately continued and amplified the assault upon them.

The same Edward Smith, writing at the same time, but quoting a "Mr. Dess, near to sulphur Bottom, Lamar county," shows that the unsportsmanlike massacre of deer by night hunting is not a recent development dependent on the invention of the spotlight. He writes, "Deer are very plentiful, and afford them much sport on dark nights by fire hunting."[5] John C. Reid, writing in 1857, expanded upon the various strategies used by the pioneers to kill off the deer, even as he retold of their huge original numbers in his own way. He wrote: "A few of the members of our party, occasionally, sallied out into the prairie and woods, skirting the road [from Goliad to San Antonio] with the design of killing some of the countless deer always to be seen. I use the word countless, because of the vast droves or herds, whose numbers would have defied the skill of the man who counted the litter of pigs, including the spotted runt. . . . Various modes are adopted, by the citizens here, for killing the wild animals. Game is ever in season. Thousands of deer are slain by the light of the fire pan; by snares and pitfalls, by the laying concealed near holes of water or 'licks'; stooping in the tall grass and attracting those in sight by occasionally tossing in the air an unfurled red handkerchief; or shooting those gentle enough to allow you to approach. They are often beguiled by the docility of others already domesticated; by driving them towards standers in waiting; by chasing upon fleet horses and lassooing them. The most approved mode, however is that of yoking a very gentle ox to a low sled or truck, squatting upon it, and with a guideline drive in the direction of the game — when within the vicinity of the game the ox is allowed to graze, as he moves through the grass (which latter conceals the vehicle), till within shooting distance."[6]

That this wholesale early slaughter of deer was not entirely limited to East Texas is attested to by the statement of Dr. Roemer, one of the most credible of pioneer observers. In 1849, he wrote, "The deer also disappeared quickly in the immediate vicinity [of New Braunfels] since they were hunted extensively by the settlers and in addition to this a band of Lepan Indians and other tribes appeared from time to time who waged a veritable war of extermination against them."[7]

Down in present Fort Bend County when he wrote it in 1837, but speaking generally about the situation, an anonymous traveler wrote: "Great havoc has been made among the deer of Texas, within a few years, by the settlers, as many depend upon this source for the principal part of their living. I have heard of some who made hunting a business that have killed as high as fifteen hundred during one year."[8]

If the picture is not yet vivid enough, Viktor Bracht makes it all too clear by writing from near New Braunfels in 1846, "It is a shame the way hundreds of deer are killed and left lying."[9]

The conclusion is inescapable that the deer were already, by the 1840s, greatly reduced in number in East Texas and near the principal settlements farther west. It is obvious that the problem of their overkill is as old as the settlement of Texas itself and that they were on the way, even by the time of the organization of the Republic of Texas, toward the extermination wreaked upon the buffalo. That they survived shows them to have been more adaptable than the buffalo, but any close look at what the explorers said about the deer before they had been disturbed shows much more similarity to the buffalo than modern theories allow or than we could imagine today.

The deer of Texas were like other large herbivores in being gregarious animals. Those who saw them undisturbed in their primeval wilderness saw not the magnificent lone buck posing cautiously in the vacant scene of our romantic pictures, but whole herds of deer grazing carelessly as cattle almost everywhere in swarming prairies.

Deer in herds? Can we take that literally? It seems we must. Deer not in the small family groups we find in these days of our supposed surfeit of them, but in masses, is what our early observers insist they saw. Look at the words they used to describe this: "large herds," "vast herds," "immense herds," "herds of great many," "droves," etc. And it is not just a few irresponsible travelers who use these terms to express the numbers of deer they found. I have the statements of forty-nine different pre-1860 pioneers describing Texas deer in herds, among them such hard to discount individuals as George Kendall, Dr. Roemer, F. L. Olmsted, Abbe Domenech, William Kennedy, H. Yoakum, Stephen F. Austin, Jean Louis Berlandier, Mary Austin Holley, Pierre Francois de Pages, Juan Antonio de la Pena, and even Audubon and Bachman.

Those who tried to estimate the numbers in these herds challenge our usual conceptions of the prairie scenes. In 1722, when in southern Medina County, Pena reported, "During the remainder of the day we passed through a flat country and found a great many deer. We saw around us, almost at the same time, as many as three or four hundred of these animals."[10] Somewhere in Houston, Cherokee or Madison County in 1767, Pages reported, "Here the hent-deer grazed in such numbers, that I mistook them at a distance for a company of our horses broken loose from their keepers."[11] Concerning what is now Fort Bend County in 1846, Josiah Pancoast wrote of the scene from his cabin, ". . . the land is as level as the salt Marsh you may stand in the door and see as far as your eyes can let you see and nothing to obstruct the view except herds of deer and cattle you can stand in the door most any time and see twenty or thirty deer and if you ride out a little ways in the preary you can see often a Hundred or more at a glance."[12] About St. Joseph's and Matagorda island in 1845, Lt. John James Peck wrote, "It is common in going from six to ten miles on any part of the island to see from one hundred to two hundred deer grazing. They are quite tame. . . ."[13] After moving through parts of Burleson, Lee and Bastrop counties in 1835, Charles B. Shain wrote, "From Tinoxticlan to Brasstrop, 80 miles, we did not see a house, but it certainly is the finest country in the world. [I]t has more deer and turkeys than any other region I have ever seen. I am confident, that I saw not less than three hundred deer in one drove."[14] This is echoed by Viktor Bracht. In 1847, he wrote, "I recently returned from Bexar [to New Braunfels] by cutting straight across the Cibolo hills. . . . I saw game in large numbers . . . many herds of deer, one that I counted contained three hundred."[15] Concerning the state in general, Arthur Ikin wrote in 1841, "Deer of about the size of our largest fallow deer, and in herds of from ten to a thousand, are common in every part of the country."[16] And Francis Moore, Jr., wrote in 1840, "The deer are so numerous, that they are often found in herds of several thousands. . . ."[17]

Before we surrender to the skeptics or to the wildlife biologists who discount these statements as wildly inflated and set the carrying capacity of the country at the paltry numbers of deer allowed today, it would be prudent for us to listen to Audubon himself. In their great work, *The Quadrupeds of North America*, Audubon and Bachman's entry on them says: "*Cervus virginianus*, Pennant, Common American Deer. The common Deer is a gregarious animal, being found on our western prairies in immense scattered herds of several hundred."[18] If you are surprised by this idea of so many deer in such concentrations, you are not alone. An anonymous traveler through Fort Bend County of 1837, wrote, ". . . the country here, as well as everywhere else, was alive with deer. The great abundance of this kind of game has been a subject of wonder to all those who have traveled through Texas. They start up around the traveler in droves, and he may see as many as fifty or a hundred at once, scampering over the plain."[19]

So how many deer were there in Texas before the assault upon them with modern arms? Anyone may speculate, and some have, but the opinions we are interested in here are those of persons who were here at the time. Many of them pronounced the deer "innumerable," but none put a figure to it. Instead they said things like A. A. Parker, who wrote in 1836: "And then, there is plenty of game. [F]irst in the list, is the deer. I hardly supposed there were as many deer on the continent, as I saw in Texas."[20] The most specific as well as the most startling statement on the subject is that of Mary Austin Holley, who wrote in about 1836, "Deer are still more numerous than the buffalo."[21]

We have seen that the estimates of the number of buffalo in Texas at that time range between 30 and 125 million. Could there actually have been that many or more deer here as well? Of course, we will never establish the answer on any scientific grounds, but something can be ventured. The number of deer in the United States at or near its lowest ebb in 1900 has been estimated to have been only 500,000.[22] But with some protection their U.S. population by 1976 was estimated by the same authority to have risen to 12.5 million. With about 361,111 estimated to have been taken in Texas in the typical year of 1972,[23] it seems clear that the deer have the reproductive potential, even with some hunting pressure, to produce untold millions.

But what about the country's carrying capacity? Could Texas have supported millions of deer? Along with the deer grazing Texas in the 1970s there were about 17 million cattle and 2.5 million sheep. That the state could support all those millions of grazing units on just the land not occupied by the homes, cities, highways and other developments of the millions of humans present then or their fields reserved to produce cotton, wheat, rice, vegetables, fruits and other products, seems to me to show that it could, and that Mrs. Holley may well have been right.

I know that the preceding is a very provocative statement because it flies in the face of our present ideas of carrying capacities, but it only shows that the problem we have is much larger than just the matter of how many deer to shoot each year. That our wildlife biologists are willing to chart the carrying capacity of today's Texas in terms of so few deer (or so little other wildlife, for that matter), accepting starvation-induced die-offs as the inevitable result every few years if we don't keep the relentless hunting pressure on, is a sad measure of the decrease we have allowed in our plant communities from what they once were. When the 1987 white-tail population of Texas was down to around 4 million, of which approximately 500,000 were killed in the 1987-88 hunting season, and yet our best observers of the situation could only come up with such statements as, "Texas habitat is supporting peak numbers of deer in most areas," and, "success [in managing our deer] requires the spilling of more blood — more selective killing,"[24] can there be any hope for rebuilding our plundered plant communities or even maintaining what we have as the producer base for all Texas life? How far down will we allow the wildlife carrying capacity of Texas to be pushed? And do we honestly think that our galloping developments will never reduce the carrying capacity of the once lush lands of Texas for cattle, and even for humans as well as for deer?

The early Texans noticed not only the numbers but also the kinds of deer they found and hunted here, and this gives us opportunity to learn more about the original ranges of the deer species in the state.

Numbers of them reported on what different ones called the "red deer," "Mustang deer," "Virginia deer," "American deer," "Pennant," or "white-tailed deer." Audubon and Bachman used the scientific name *Cervus virginianus* for this in 1851,[25] but Baird used *Cervus leucurus* for it in 1857.[26] We're supposed to call it *Odocoileus viginianus* now. By any of these names, it was our common white-tailed deer which made up the prodigious herds so often reported by our explorers.

They reported this animal in at least some numbers almost everywhere in Texas. The only question about its original range in this state is therefore exactly how far it ranged west, and our explorers give a clue to this. The westernmost report from before 1860 of specifically the white-tailed deer is that of Baird in his report on the survey for the western railway in 1857, just cited. His record is from "Pecos River, Texas." We have already seen that deer seemed to be scarce in the Pecos Valley at that time, and our explorers' many accounts of them ending at that river does not prove, but seems to indicate strongly, that it marked the western terminus of their range at that time.

Honesty requires me to add that one early traveler did say that a white-tailed deer was taken west of the Pecos, but the details of the incident make me think that this was one of those rare cases of an explorer being in error. When out in Hudspeth County in 1854, James G. Bell wrote, "Some hunters from the other camp brought in the largest white tailed deer I have ever seen; He was very old and so confounded tough, that a square inch would have been sufficient for breakfast, dinner and supper. I commenced on a mouthful, found it was no go but thought perseverance would master it as I had been told that perseverance would conquer anything, and I am able to say that, if no one else has, I have found an exception to the rule."[27]

Since this episode took place in their known territory it seems possible to explain what he called the extra large white-tail as perhaps an unrecognized mule deer, which would in turn explain its large size. It would seem that Bell was no expert on deer, because this would be his second mistake concerning them.

Be that as it may, there apparently is no other mention before 1860 of any white-tails in the trans-Pecos. This does not prove, but lends some support to the opinion that white-tails did not originally range west of the Pecos, and this in turn supports the idea, advanced by earlier biologists such as Bailey, that the Pecos River watershed marked a general dividing line between eastern and western forms of animals.[28] The Virginia deer may have joined other eastern animals in traveling little if any farther west than this.

Before we leave the white-tails, a word must be added about the size of deer. There is a special modern myth about this. We are continually conditioned with statements similar to the following: "White-tailed deer on the Edwards Plateau once were big of body and antlers. There weren't as many deer as there are today but what they lacked in number, they made up for in size."[29] This sort of thing has been said so often that it seems everyone actually has come to believe the double-pronged story that there were originally fewer deer than we generously allow to live today, but that they were therefore much larger. I assemble here only three of the clear statements on the subject by those who were here and saw the original animals, but it is evidence for us to use in judging these recent claims.

Writing in 1838, Friedrich W. von Wrede said, "The Virginia deer is more slender and somewhat smaller than the red deer. . . . It seldom appears in settled regions while in the west it travels in whole herds."[30]

In 1846, a different anonymous traveler than the one already quoted in this chapter wrote, "The American deer is slimmer and somewhat smaller than the European counterpart, and has become rare in the inhabited areas. However, in the less populated sections one can find these deer in large herds."[31]

In 1848, Viktor Bracht wrote down the most specific picture: "Texas abounds in game animals beyond any other country in the world. The most common game is the small American deer *(cervus virginianus)* which resembles very much the European fallow deer, and which originally weigh about eighty pounds or more. . . . This deer is present in all parts of the country, and in the West it is at times so numerous that one or two thousand may be counted on a ride of twenty miles through the wilderness."[32]

There is absolutely no hint in the hundreds of white-tail accounts, surviving from before 1860, of the 150- to 200-pound specimens imagined to have gamboled commonly on the prairies in the good old days — or of any earlier existence of a larger average size of the animals. Of course, modern selective breeding experiments can produce larger deer and grander antler racks, but this no more proves that the white-tails in their undisturbed state were larger than the breeding of a huge hereford proves that the wild oxen he came from were originally as large as he. Even as it is the exceptional racks and not the little spike antlers that survive in our Hall of Horns to prompt our imaginations, it is the rare extra-large individuals instead of the 80-pound little fellows which our grandparents remember and reminisce about so graphically that tend to color our whole philosophy. Why do we insist upon basing our opinions on the statements of these "old-timers" who saw only the situation around 1900, when of course there were fewer deer than today since they were at their all-time low ebb then, instead of basing our understanding, our statements and our management policies upon the clear pictures left us by the explorers of the white-tails? They saw the deer as naturally gregarious creatures existing originally as the smallest of Texas' native cervids but in herds perhaps as numerous — if not as spectacular — as the buffalo.

The white-tail deer have survived all of our assaults by becoming the furtive shadows in the thickets, but they were not always these timid creatures hiding all day in the solitude of the deepest brush. Our explorers found them ranging all day in the "immense herds" throughout the prairies. They were numerous and bold enough to at least share that court as lords of the prairies. And, incidentally, since they browse instead of graze on grass, they help prove that the original prairies were not totally brushless, all grass expanses like some imagine them to have been. Our white-tails have survived where the buffaloes succumbed, but they managed it by becoming pitiable shadows sulking about the edges of our shattered wilderness.

Another deer was reported by Texas explorers. Various ones of them called it the "black-tail deer," "mule deer," "mountain deer," or "those of New Mexico." Only Audubon-Bachman and Baird gave it scientific names, and both of them called it *Cervus Macrotis*.[33][34] All of these names clearly apply to today's *Odocoileus hemionus*, our West Texas mule deer.

These mule deer were never encountered widely in Texas. They were specifically reported before 1860 in only seven present counties. Four of these counties were in the trans-Pecos, being Terrell, Jeff

Davis, Culberson, and Hudspeth. Since these counties span the region and the deer was then common in both adjoining Mexico and New Mexico, it seems clear that the animal ranged over most, if not all, of trans-Pecos Texas.

The mule deer seems to have ranged into very little more of Texas. Michler's 1852 account of it seems to place it as far east as at least the Pecos River in Val Verde County, where it would have been the western species meeting its eastern counterpart in the white-tail, which was also reported from that county.

The only other place where the mule deer entered Texas was up on the very western edge of the Panhandle. They were reported in what are now Parmer and Deaf Smith counties.

In all of these places mule deer were apparently far from numerous. In present Terrell and western Val Verde counties, Michler reported only "some few deer — the latter of the black-tail species."[35] In 1850, in western Jeff Davis County, William Miles reported, "a black-tailed deer shot"[36] and in 1854, James G. Bell's cattle drivers succeeded in bagging one there, which Bell called, "something new to me."[37] In that same year, J. H. Byrne's group got one black-tail in present Culberson County, which, "was shot, skinned and stuffed."[38] Our one early record for Hudspeth County comes from assuming that Bell's over-large and out-of-range white-tail already noted was really a mule deer. There were only two individuals taken by LeGrand to establish the species up in Parmer and Deaf Smith counties.[39] So there were clearly no herds of these deer in far West Texas, even in the beginning.

The mule deer are the big ones, and apparently always were. Several of the explorers remark about that. In fact, going by one explorer's statement, it would have been the mule deer instead of the white-tail which would have been larger originally than now. Don Pedro Alonso O'Crouley wrote in 1774, "Deer are very common but are ugly. Those of New Mexico are larger than the biggest mule."[40]

There are some very large mules, and therefore this statement seems impossible, but several rationalizations of it have been suggested. O'Crouley wrote in Spanish after observations of only early Spanish domestic animals. If he meant to compare the deer to their burros, he could have been right, but his word seems to clearly translate as mules instead of burros. However, it has also been pointed out to me that our large mules are obtained by crosses with very large draft horses, and that the only mules the early Spanish would have had would have been obtained from small Spanish or Indian ponies, and so would have been small and light mules. The mule deers may have approximated actual mules of that time in more ways than we imagine.

These two, the white-tailed and the mule deer, seem to be all the deer native to Texas. The only other ones mentioned in the early writings are best explained not as separate species, but as the usual variations found within the two species already outlined.

One short passage covers both of the remaining deer variations described as seen in the early Texas wilderness. In a newspaper article of 1819, an unknown author said, "Some of the deer [of Texas] are perfectly white, and some are red and white, like our cattle."[41] Albinos are well known in deer as in many other animals, and this easily explains the white ones. At first thought the red and white ones present a difficulty, but this need not be. An unknowing writer might easily refer in this way to the white-spotted fawns so spectacular and beautiful in any scene.

So once again our explorers seem to have touched upon most of the important aspects of a wonderful animal encountered in the Texas wilderness. We may be big enough to applaud them for their thoroughness, but will we be courageous enough to let their statements limit our wild guesses about how deer figured in the unmodified natural communities and our wishful thinking about what is good for them — and for us — today?

3

Antelopes: The Texas Speedsters

Imagine, once again, that you are an explorer pushing through a Texas wilderness vast and diverse beyond all prediction. You are constantly having to take in stride things beyond all imagination. If you happen to feel any responsibility to name and describe these things for those back home, you really have a job, one almost as difficult as Adam's in Eden.

Somewhere, if you have pushed any distance into primeval Texas, you will be very literally confronted by a herd of most remarkable animals. They will stand stock still, staring you down with huge eyes, but if you move toward them, they will instantly wheel and speed away with a fleetness that you find almost unbelievable. What would you call these animals, and how would you describe them?

The earliest explorer to have this experience and to write about it was apparently Henri Joutel. In 1687, when probably in or very near present Morris County, Texas,[1] he states that they saw many strange animals which he called "wild goats."[2] In 1722, when in or near present Frio County, Don Juan Antonio de la Pena reported encountering there "deer, wild goats, turkeys, rabbits and quail in large numbers."[3] And in 1846, when in what is now Coryell County, Elijah Hicks wrote, "At Camp two Kickapoos arrived ... Venison, mountain goat, & turkey for supper, no bread."[4]

What in the world could these animals which reminded these explorers of goats have been? Fortunately, we don't have to speculate. George Kendall wrote the answer for us when he saw them in 1844. He explained it thus: "We had already, and with no inconsiderable difficulty, crossed one branch of the Bosque, and on the evening of the 5th arrived at another fork of the same stream, where we encamped for the night.... This day, for the first time, we saw an animal somewhat resembling both the deer and the goat, but with flesh preferable to that of either."[5]

So from the very first the explorers in Texas encountered these animals which the earliest called some sort of goats. We may think that less logical on their parts than it would have been to consider the pronghorns some sort of deer, but actually this shows the remarkable powers of observation of those explorers. Out there, even under the stress of the expeditions, they sensed correctly the distinctiveness of the pronghorns which has caused scientists to separate these animals from the deer by creating a separate family, about as close to that of goats as to that of the deer, just for them.

But they couldn't keep on merely calling these animals goats. Juan Almonte, writing in 1835 in Spanish, listed among the animals he said were on "the higher portion" of the Brazos some creatures called *"berrendos."*[6] In translating Almonte's work C. E. Castaneda left this word untranslated, but added a note: "native animal of Mexico similar to the deer." This gives us, of course, a Spanish name for the pronghorn, but one apparently not used again in Texas literature. Instead, Texas writers apparently noticed that these animals lacked deers' antlers and instead grew horns in some ways like those of a group of Old World ruminants including the gazelle, also noted for its fleetness. To those animals had been applied an ancient term, "antelope," traceable clear back through Old French and Latin to a Greek word for some mysterious, savage and very fleet beast of the Euphrates Valley. So our explorers started applying this term "antelope" to this strange speedster of the New World. The distinction of being the first to use this name for these animals in writing may go to Peter Custis in his 1806 catalogue of Red River animals.[7]

It should be noted that while some in other parts of the continent were calling this animal the pronghorn antelope, the pronghorn or the prongbuck from at least 1815 on, in our search of early Texas literature we found not one instance of any Texas writer using those terms. So the term "pronghorn," which seems to have become the preferred name for them, was apparently not in use in Texas in the antebellum period we are considering.

The animal all these names refer to is a remarkable speed demon. The explorers were greatly impressed by this. George Kendall, whose mention of his first meeting with it we have just quoted, continues his account by stating: "It [the antelope] runs with great speed, and has a stride like a horse. How fast the animal can run when in possession of four legs is a question I am at a loss to answer, but one with a fore leg broken by a rifle ball made out to escape from one of our best horses after a long chase."[5]

The scribe of the 1857 Leach wagon train journey across Texas wrote of their testing of this speed: "We saw in the early front of the morning several antelope, the first that we have met with. A few hot headed Nimrods gave chase to them, but they might, with as much chance of overtaking it, as well have chased the North Wind."[8]

We found no record of any explorer's horse having overtaken a pronghorn, but this is not surprising, since it is considered the fastest North American mammal. There is individual variation, of course, but it is estimated that some pronghorns can run up to a speed of 45 miles per hour. And it is a most graceful running. William Preston Johnston expressed its beauty when he wrote in 1855, "Here [in Lampasas and/or Mills County] I first saw the antelope. We saw several herds of half a dozen or more. The escort tried to get a shot at them in vain. [T]heir flight is the poetry of motion. They trot and gallop and sometimes seem to skim along the prairie like birds. . . ."[9]

This fleetness of the antelope clearly led to great frustration for the hunters among the pioneers. There are numerous notes about this in which one can sense the disappointment — and sometimes the resulting hunger — because of their elusiveness. An example was written by Bartlett when in present Pecos County in 1850: "The only living creatures seen to-day were a few blackbirds sitting on the mezquit bushes . . . and a herd of antelopes. The latter bounded before us, and were lost to view before our hunters could surround them."[10] A. W. Moore doesn't sound quite so hungry, but was obviously disappointed by the antelope's elusiveness when he wrote, in present Ellis County in 1846, "This evening saw a gang of antilopes they are about the size of deer, shorter and whiter tails, more white under the belly and run like a horse and very fleet they scampered before us within ½ mile for several hours but not near enough to shoot or to describe them correctly."[11]

The problem to be solved in hunting antelopes was clearly how to get them to stand still or, better yet, venture close to one's stand. Otherwise there was no chance to bag one. And apparently, since several of them mention it, some explorers soon discovered the stratagem with which to accomplish this. It depended upon making use of a strange weakness possessed by these animals. This failing and how to use it was succinctly outlined by Frederick Marryat in his 1843 work as follows: "Though of a very timid nature, they [antelopes] are superlatively inquisitive, and can be easily attracted within rifle range, by agitating, from behind a tree, a white or red handkerchief."[12]

Such a procedure carried out successfully, the source from which the pioneers learned it, and its results were graphically described by R. M. Ballantyne: "They [the antelopes] are so fleet that not one horse in a hundred can overtake them, and their sight and sense of smell are so acute, that it would be next to impossible to kill them, were it not for the inordinate curiosity which we have before referred to. The Indians manage to attract these simple little creatures by merely lying down on their backs and kicking their heels in the air, or by waving any white object on the point of an arrow, while the hunter keeps concealed by lying flat in the grass. By these means a herd of antelopes may be induced to wheel round and round an object in timid, but intense surprise, gradually approaching until they come near enough to enable the hunter to make sure of his mark. Thus the animals, which of all others *ought* to be the most difficult to slay, are, in consequence of their insatiable curiosity, more easily shot than any other deer of the plains."[13]

Attempts to bring off this stratagem must not have worked as infallibly as Ballantyne implies and must have resulted in many frontier comedies. Julius Froebel described one such which took place in the Texas Big Bend in 1853. It is dramatic enough to be worth repeating here. He writes, "In hunting these animals, both Mexicans and Indians disguise themselves with an antelope's head. A Virginian, who had joined our caravan at the Presidio, carried one with him for this purpose, and made the first trial of it here. Although he did not succeed in his attempt, he amused us excessively by his pantomime. While, with the horned head above his own, he endeavoured to act his part correctly, by making the most extraordinary jumps, which he evidently thought were inimitably true to nature, hundreds of antelopes stood, in a large semicircle, watching the actions of this strange mongrel figure, but never lessening a wide distance between themselves and him; so that, in spite of his dramatic talent, our friend did not accomplish his purpose."[14]

Perhaps the unnamed Virginian's antics failed to attract the antelopes within range because he failed to understand one of the behavioral differences which separates this animal from deer. It is mentioned that he made "extraordinary jumps" to try to entice them. But these animals, speedy as they are, are reluctant to leap. A modern student of these large animals states it this way: "Another peculiar trait [of the antelopes] is their disinclination to jump over fences or other objects. A low brush fence no more than three feet high will ordinarily turn the animals, and it is not uncommon for small bands to be reduced almost to the point of starvation within a fenced enclosure while plenty of food is available on the outside. They can jump over moderately high obstructions, however, when hard pressed. Ordinarily they crawl under or between the wires of barbed-wire fences."[15]

I began this chapter by saying that if you had been an explorer in early Texas you wouldn't have gone far without discovering antelopes. It remains for us to survey the evidence that these animals ranged very widely over the state.

My file of on-the-spot accounts contains explorers' reports of having encountered antelopes in locations which would now be in 109 of the state's counties. This places the animals, during the exploratory period, in a vast part of Texas. Not only is the huge area of Texas thus indicated as colonized by the antelopes significant, but their having been found live in certain of the places where the explorers put them is important because it forces us to reconsider some of our accepted assumptions about these animals. So it requires us to look more closely at the locations of the early antelope sightings.

We are not surprised that there are numerous accounts of antelopes in early trans-Pecos Texas, where they still run today, so it is not necessary to list the explorers who mention meeting them there. They include such as Albert James Myer, father of the U.S. Army signal corps and the U.S. weather service, Capt. S. G. French, and other persons of reputation.[16] However, the quantities of these animals once seen out there may surprise us and so require some details.

When in what is now Brewster County in 1860, Lt. W. H. Echols described them this way: "July 8. — Set out early this morning, as usual, about sunrise [from Willow Springs], and left the Camanche trail at camp for Fort Davis . . . found large herds of antelope on our route to-day, killed one. . . . July 9 . . . Antelopes very numerous. . . ."[17] After working through territory now in Jeff Davis, Culberson and Hudspeth counties in 1857, John C. Reid wrote, "Here, like the minutes of the day, we beheld coyotes (prairie wolf), deer, and antelope. The last named were often in herds of such size, that when reposing, we mistook them for cattle."[18] Even further east they saw them in masses. In present Pecos County in 1854, Froebel wrote, ". . . first proceeded to a desolate plateau, covered with grey bushes and scanty grass, where we saw large herds of antelopes."[19]

It shouldn't surprise us that various early explorers of the Panhandle reported antelopes there. Among them were such believable observers as Captain Marcy and Lieutenant Michler.[20] A. B. Gray summed up the place of these animals in that area by writing in 1854, "The Llano Estacado . . . is by no means a desert or barren waste; for, with exceptions of narrow belts less prepossessing, there are vast fields of fine grazing-lands, where antelope, deer and other game are seldom out of sight."[21]

Neither should it be too surprising that antelopes were found farther east in extreme North Texas. When probably in present Baylor County in 1844, George Kendall reported, "Deer and antelope were seen in every direction. . . ."[22] They were also seen in the area of present Clay and Jack counties.[23] They were still listed as part of the natural fauna as far east as Cooke County,[24] and Lawrie described them as "very numerous" in Denton and Tarrant counties in 1855.[25]

Now we have covered most of Texas usually thought of today as antelope country. But our explorers found them much beyond this. How far are we willing to follow their reports of them down through the state?

They were found in Jones County in 1852,[26] and in Callahan County in 1855.[27] They were reported in large numbers in present Upton and Reagan counties in 1850 and 1858 respectively.[28] And it is not too hard to imagine them, as reported, out in Concho, Tom Green and Irion County territory in 1850.[29] It may be a little more surprising to find them down in what now makes up Crockett and Val Verde counties, but numerous explorers testify that they were there. For instance, Lieutenant Echols, when traveling up the east bank of the lower Pecos, reported them.[30] The previously mentioned Albert Myer stated, concerning traveling up along the lower part of the Devil's River in 1855, "So we ride all day with arms in our hands, shooting now and then at deer or antelope that cross our path. . . . Flocks of deer and antelopes raise their heads, look at us for an instant, and then rush crazy away into the distance."[31]

But now we must follow the early reports of antelopes down into very different territory. Cox says that they found them in present Schleicher and Menard counties in 1849,[32] and Juan Dominguez de Mendoza had seen them in what is probably now McCulloch County in 1684.[33] Dr. Ferdinand Roemer saw them in the Hill Country in 1849,[34] Alex. W. Terrell claimed they were in the Travis County region,[35] and Ullrich had them in that of Comal County in 1860.[36] Concerning the area around San Antonio, there are two especially explicit passages. In 1848, Bracht wrote, ". . . there are flocks of antelope on the upper Cibolo and Salado,"[37] and Bollaert wrote, "SAN ANTONIO TO HEAD WATERS OF THE LEONA RIVER. — Passing the Leon and Medio Creeks, the country seen is prairie, covered with flowers and rich pastures, alive with deer and antelope."[38] The conclusion seems inescapable: If the antelopes were not normal residents of the Hill Country, then our explorers have misinformed us with a consistency which would surpass what such a diverse group could have accomplished if they had tried.

Could antelopes have originally ranged even east of the Hill Country? Those who were there say they did.

The poetic description by William Preston Johnston of the antelopes' running motion, quoted earlier, was inspired by his viewing them in present Lampasas and Mills counties in 1855.[39] James Buckner Barry managed to kill a couple of them in Bosque County in 1860.[40] Note that George Kendall's passage about them, which assured us that the antelope and the mountain goat were the same animal, was written after he had seen them in future McLennan County. And Elijah Hicks reports both seeing and eating antelopes in future Coryell and McLennan counties.[41]

Martin Austin Gauldin traveled through what became Ellis, Hill, McLennan and Falls counties in 1845, and wrote, "We then traveled through the wilderness a distance of sixty five miles . . . in traveling through this strech we saw many herds of Buffalo . . . we also saw many herds of dear and antelope in large numbers but did not kill any . . . we persued our Jorney from this place [the Falls of the Brazos]. . . . We saw some Bufalo also many mustang deer and antelope in great abundance. . . ."[42]

If the fact that antelopes gamboled all over north central Texas is not made clear enough by these specifically located sightings, there may be added the general statement of Symon Redfield made after he had traversed the whole region in 1846: "On the 13th. day of Aug. I was left at Red River by orders of our captain to take care of sick messurate. . . . From that point to San Antonio there was no chance to get a letter conveyed except by the wild beast. My friend and myself ascertained that there was a shorter and much pleasanter route to San Antonio than that which the Regiment had taken. Accordingly as soon as he was able to ride we mounted our horses and provided with one rifle and a few charges of ammunition commenced our journey of nearly 500 miles through a wild country. . . . I would not attempt in a letter to tell or describe scenes so strange and new and numerous as we witnessed on our way to San Antonio. . . . Our journey required nearly six weeks. Our spirits were kept constantly bouyant by the strange scenes of the country, mostly consisting of extensive prairies on which rove wild and free deer, antelope and buffalo on which prey the whole family of carniverous animals but still their number is almost incalculable."[43]

But we have still far from exhausted the antelope's range. We must follow them farther south — yes, even south from San Antonio. There are more pre-1860 accounts of antelopes from South Texas than from any other part of the state!

Starting from San Antonio and following the antelopes of the unharvested wilderness through the explorers' records, we are led first southeast toward the central Texas coast. A. Suthron, writing as Frederic B. Page, in an 1845 publication, described antelopes seen when going from Columbus to Gonzalez, Texas, after having forded the LaVaca River.[44] And J. C. Duval, in an account written just a few years after our period of study, in 1864, wrote, "Continuing our course, we passed through a heavily timbered bottom more than a mile wide, and then came to a large prairie in which we saw many herds of deer and some antelopes."[45] This sighting was in present Victoria County, east of the Guadalupe River, and places these animals on the coastal plain, essentially completing their range to the coast.

We are also led by the antelopes southwest of San Antonio. In 1772, when apparently in present Frio County, Pena listed them as among the game animals met.[46] Over a hundred years later, Olmsted reported encountering them on his trip from San Antonio to the Rio Grande through future Bexar, Medina, Zavala and Maverick counties.[47]

The South Texas reports of antelopes take us all the way to the south edge of the state. The military expeditions into the area at the time of the Mexican War encountered them in quantity. Lt. John James Peck reported "droves" of them in future Nueces and Kleberg counties in 1845,[48] and Maj. John Pollard Gaines "countless numbers" of them in the same area in 1846.[49] John Russell Bartlett, who was important in the work of the U.S.–Mexican Boundary Commission, when traveling through what was to become southwest Nueces County and part of Kleberg County, on the first day of 1853, wrote, ". . . the party was in motion [from San Francisco Creek] at the break of day. The prairie was now a dead level, the grass short, and the road very good. Not a bush or a tree was to be seen, yet there was no lack of prominent objects; for thousands of deer and antelope were scattered over it. Never before had we seen such numbers."[50] When going through present Brooks and Starr counties, the same author noted, "Large numbers of deer, antelope, and wild horses were seen during the day. . . ."[51] The Pereda title of 1807, in its description of the land which was in today's Zapata County, lists the antelope as among the inhabitants.[52]

That even this was not the end of the antelope's territory is shown by the fact that Baird stated in 1857 that its distribution "reaches the Rio Grande at its mouth, and probably extends some distance into Mexico, at least throughout the State of Tamaulipas, according to Dr. Berlandier."[53]

Another sort of evidence about where the antelopes were in quantity can come from information about where they managed to hold out the longest under the assault of civilization. Vernon Bailey, in his "Biological Survey of Texas," wrote, "in 1900 ranchmen told me that a few antelopes still remained on the prairies west of Alice, where they were once numerous; a few were reported to Oberholser 40 miles northwest of San Diego, a few 20 miles west and a few 25 miles southwest of Cotulla, a small herd 30 to 40 miles northwest of Rock Springs, and another small herd 35 miles northwest and another 50 miles southwest of Henrietta; while they were said to have entirely disappeared about Laredo and from the big valley in which Alpine is located."[54]

These should be enough references to establish that the pronghorn was not merely a resident of the wide-open spaces in West Texas, but lived, before our interference, over at least all of the state west of a line from the Red River approximately past Dallas and Waco down to the coast near Victoria. Doughty is probably right in stating its early range to have been east to about the 97th meridian,[55] but that was during the early settlement period. Joutel's strange wild goats, which he says he saw when somewhere near present Daingerfield in the northeast corner of the state, were well beyond this range. That sighting, which we mentioned at the beginning of this history, took place in an entirely different era, way back in 1687. If Joutel is granted any credence, he must be regarded as telling us that, like the elk and several other animals, the antelope evacuated the eastern outposts of its distribution before our broad frontal attack — so early that only the very first of our scouts found it still at home in those far reaches.

One significance of the fact that antelopes once lived over practically the whole of Texas is that we must rethink our assumptions that it is adapted for only the most open plains. And if it once lived successfully in most regions of our state, a question about our wildlife policies arises. Why, we proud Texans should ask ourselves, don't we, who are supposed to love our own so much, put these beautiful native creatures on more of our ranches throughout the state instead of spreading all sorts of strange foreign beasts over our prairies? If we so love to look at speedy horses, why don't we stock our pastures with our only native animals which can stay up with our steeds?

An illustration from Harper's Weekly *(May 29, 1875) of a typical attempt upon the lives of antelopes.*

We have seen that the explorers used terms like "herds," "droves," and "incalculable numbers," in speaking of the quantities of antelopes they found. I have found no explorers' estimate of the total antelope population they found in Texas. They just intimated that they were extremely numerous and did not hesitate to link them with the buffaloes and deer, which we have seen were here in the millions. Is this supposed to mean that antelopes — which are now only apparitions a few thousand strong in the whole of Texas — were once in bold herds of millions on these prairies? It certainly does, and modern scholars admit it.

Witness the statements in some standard works on North American mammals. The National Geographic Society's volume, *Wild Animals of North America*, states, "Early explorers discovered antelope in great abundance over a vast territory extending from near the present location of Edmonton, Alberta, south to near the Valley of Mexico, and from central Iowa west to the Pacific coast in California. . . . So abundant were they that it has been estimated that on the Great Plains they equaled the buffalo in numbers."[56] Another popular book on North American mammals says, "It is estimated that there once were between forty and fifty million [pronghorns] in the U.S."[57]

So what happened to these millions of beautiful speedsters? Dr. Doughty sums up their demise in the light of the most up-to-date knowledge, writing, "Perhaps as many as sixty million antelope in the United States had been whittled down to less than thirty thousand in the 1920's because of commercial hunting, which had delivered large shipments of meat for sale in urban markets after the Civil War. Antelope associated with buffalo. Between 1874 and 1884 the bison and antelope were almost exterminated."[58]

Stanley Paul Young, once senior biologist for the U.S. Fish and Wildlife Service, describes one ugly detail of this senseless slaughter: "During this time [approx. 1870-1885] antelope were also much in demand, but only the choice portions of this animal were saved for meat. For instance, the so-called 'antelope saddle,' or backstrap, which is the tenderloin, sold by the thousands for twenty-five cents a 'saddle.' The rest of the carcass was thrown away after butchering out this cut. Hence, the diminution in the numbers of antelope began almost simultaneously with that of the buffalo."[59]

The conclusion is unavoidable. The few thousand antelopes we allow to eke out an existence in unusurped corners of our state appear ghostly not just because of their elusiveness, but because they are phantoms of the millions of antelopes which once graced the expanses of Texas and were murdered by our forebears.

The only question today is: Can the explorers' statements about this profusion of life gamboling in original Texas even register on our modern consciousness? Dare we allow such hordes of antelope to become real in some reconstruction of a natural Texas, or will our guilt together with our greed keep them always phantoms?

4

Texas Elk

Suppose you were out in the wilderness and came across some animals like deer but as big as cattle, with their bodies ungainly, paunchy and lacking the sleek streamlining of typical deer. What would you call them? You might call them elk and you might call them moose. If you were an early-day explorer either term might have sufficed, but not today. People have always had trouble with these terms. So our first task is to unsnarl the confusing history of these words and learn how our explorers in Texas used them.

The name "elk" is an ancient European one, traceable back to an Old Norman word, and possibly even to an ancient Teutonic name for some animals of northern Europe. But what were the animals thus named? Passages from a thousand years ago up until only a hundred years ago give no good clues about whether they refer to some European deer, their moose, or even reindeer. The 1877 edition of the *Encyclopedia Brittanica* does not draw any distinction, referring to "The Elk or Moose Deer." Only by 1884 was the name unequivocally applied in print to the majestic but already extinct Irish elk. Historically, then, the elk included all the large northern deer-like animals, including the moose.

It was the North American pioneers who added to the confusion by adopting the northeast Indian name, "moose," for all these animals. At first, as in a 1637 passage by T. Morton, it was "The Elke, which the savages call a Mose" and in 1672, it was Josselyn's "The Moose Deer."[1] In North America, as in Europe, it is therefore only by indirect evidence that we can know whether any early references are to *Cervus elaphas*, our American elk, or to *Alces alces*, today's moose. This is why two of our well-regarded pioneers in Texas having left statements about moose being in Texas cause us no problems. We know that they were merely using the Indian term for the elk they were seeing. Everyone in Texas apparently always understood that. Even Spencer F. Baird, in writing up the section on mammals in the official report of the surveys for a railroad to the Pacific published in 1857, after using the name "moose" entered a note: "European name for the moose is 'elk.' But that does not cause confusion for us in Texas, since we have no moose."[2] In the north, pioneers also further confused things by calling the American elk the wapiti, another Indian name, but this name does not appear in early Texas writings.

The explorers did leave clear testimony of elk in Texas, and if you had been an early pioneer you might have seen them, for they were certainly here. They were *Cervus elaphas canadensis* Erxleben (the American elk) and/or *Cervus elaphas merriami* Nelson (Merriam's elk), and they must appear as impressive natives in any complete picture of original Texas.

"Impressive" is the proper word for the elk. Weighing up to 700 pounds, a bull elk stands as tall as a small horse and very well approximates it in bulk. Without his antlers he is formidable, and in the season when he is crowned by a rack of antlers spreading three or four feet, he intimidates by just looking at you. This writer can attest to that from the personal experience of once having risen up over the edge of a West Texas mesa to find himself facing several of these animals silently staring at him from only yards away. They couldn't have looked much more ominous if they had been brahma cattle.

American Elk
— by Audubon

And they preserved their intimidation by ambling slowly away with alert dignity instead of bounding off in fright like ordinary deer.

Elk are certainly deer. Their fleetness and jumping ability — they are said to be able to clear fences up to about seven feet high — attest to that. But they noticcably lack the deer's appearance of fleetness. When several elk escaped from an exotic game ranch near my farm in Central Texas, some neighbors reported "some sort of strange cows loose down by the river." This echoes the graphic description of the elk's size and appearance left by Don Juan de Onate from his observance of them as he moved across the Texas Panhandle along the Canadian River in 1601. He wrote: "This river is thickly covered on all sides with these cattle [buffalo] and with another not less wonderful, consisting of deer which are as large as large horses. They travel in droves of two and three hundred and their deformity causes one to wonder whether they are deer or some other animals."[3] The editor added a note concerning this passage: "The viceroy rather contemptuously remarks that besides buffalo Onate saw 'naught else but some birds and animals, particularly some deer out of all proportion in size.'"

The male's antlers, the largest of any American animal except those of the moose, weigh 35 to 50 pounds, and these huge structures are shed annually in early spring, to be regrown by September. The possession of these, together with their bugling, a remarkably loud and carrying bellowing uttered during their breeding season from August to about November, must have made it hard to miss these major game stags wherever they existed. So where and when were our explorers conscious of elk in early Texas?

Onate's is the best description of elk left by any Texas pioneer. Although some have tried to avoid its implications by imagining that Onate was seeing antelopes, it is impossible to pretend that we are taking this explorer seriously if we maintain that his animals "as large as large horses" were antelopes, whose old bucks do not usually exceed 125 pounds in weight. His statement actually possesses the most internal evidence of its author's having experienced these animals in quantity of any Texas report we have. And this is significant because it is also the earliest account of elk which remains to us. Even more than that, it is the only report of elk ever to come out of the Texas Panhandle. Of the score or so expeditions which have left accounts of crossing the Panhandle before 1860 — all of them except Onate's since 1800 — not one other reports having encountered an elk out there. So if the testimony of this explorer means anything, the picture is clear and consistent. Elk in herds of several hundred roamed the Panhandle, or at least followed the streams through it, up to sometime since 400 years ago. But by 150 years ago these great deer were apparently gone, their kind avoiding the Panhandle from then on. What new factor could have entered those great silent expanses to either destroy those herds of elk or cause them to flee even before the buffaloes were disturbed?

There were developments which could have caused this, but they seem to be some of the least known of any in Texas history. We should not forget that the Spanish had very early come up out of Mexico, moved along the Rio Grande and on into the pueblo country of New Mexico, where they established their major bases headed by Santa Fe. After Onate's — and who knows what other very early expeditions east into the grasslands — the venturesome Spanish moved out into the plains with the first modern attempts to exploit them.

First to enter our Panhandle were the *pastores*. The idea of these ancient sheepherders trekking with their herds into primeval Texas from the west, setting up residences and even establishing villages there before the cattlemen were even born, is so foreign to orthodox history of Texas that I turn here to the description of that era by one who has researched it exhaustively: "Driving thousands of sheep, carrying their worldly goods in crude carretas and on pack burros, the sheepmen and their families drifted along as their flocks grazed, settled along streams and in sheltered coves, establishing permanent homes. . . . Now little is left of the numerous *plazas,* which bore such musical names as Tecolote, Chavez, Salinas, Gallinas, Juan Domingo, Joaquin, Ortega, Sandoval, Mariano Montoya, Valdez and Ventura. . . . The sod roofs sifted down to the floor; rabbits and ground squirrels burrowed under the foundations. Shifting sands of streams, long years in the sun and wind, have wrapped the *plazas* in silence and ruin. Ironically, these little towns, having been built and occupied by sheepmen, were soon enclosed in big cattle ranches."[4]

Following these *pastores* there came into the Texas Panhandle a wave of entrepreneurs called the *Comancheros,* who were still out there trading with the Indians when the first of the rest of us got there. And by then, Amangual and other Spaniards were crisscrossing the region, linking Santa Fe with San Antonio by passing through it.

Back east, it was written in 1784 that "elk are decreasing as population gains ground in the Colonies,"[5] and this experience was repeated elsewhere. So the point is that when Tascosa was flourishing as one sheepmen's *plaza* among many along the Canadian River, opportunistic Indian traders were working the area, and caravans between the great capitols of the regions were crossing the Panhandle, the natural herds of elk there were possibly hunted out and driven away. At any rate, by the time Marcy and the nineteenth-century explorers and buffalo hunters entered the Texas Panhandle they never mentioned elk because there apparently weren't any left. This may therefore have the distinction of having been the first removal by man of a major animal species from any region of the state in historical times. If it seems strange that this occurred far out in what we think of as the most remote wilderness instead of in eastern Texas, remember that we are talking about events that commenced out in West Texas long before either the French or the Spanish entered Texas from the east at all.

Tracing the elk further southeast into Texas is not easy, but their tracks are present in the few really early accounts we have. For instance, they are placed as abundant in all of North Texas along the Red River from about Fannin County into the Panhandle in the time around 1765, by Juan Brebel, who traveled to Santa Fe in about that year. John Sibley's reporting of Brebel's catalogue of the animals of the area includes them in the following terms: "I asked him [Brebel] also what animals were found in the great prairies. He told me that from the Rio Azul [Blue River] upwards, on both sides of the Red River, there were innumerable quantities of wild horses, buffaloes or bison, bears, wolves, elk, deer, foxes, javalines, or wild hogs, fallow deer, wild goats, white hares, rabbits, etc."[6] That elk were present in North Texas at that time is perfectly logical, since they were well documented not far away in Arkansas, Missouri and Oklahoma.[7]

The next early adventurer into the wilderness of North Texas, which we must remember had still been practically unpenetrated from the east, was Col. Ellis P. Bean. Traveling out there in 1800 or 1801, he said, "In about six days' journey [from the Red River] we came to Trinity river, and, crossing it, we found the big, open prairies of that country. . . . For about nine days we were compelled to eat horseflesh, when we arrived at a river called the Brazos. Here we found elk and deer plenty, some buffalo, and wild horses by the thousands."[8] This places the elk at that turn of the century in the area roughly between present Throckmorton and Garza counties.

The evidence for elk farther on south in Texas and in later years is even move elusive, but it is still present. Taking the reports in chronological order we must start with the striking painting entitled "Elk and Buffalo Making Acquaintance on the Texas Prairie." This picture was used as the frontispiece and on the cover of the first volume of *The Explorers' Texas*. It was painted around 1834, by George Catlin, and constitutes his testimony that elk were present in what surely does not look like a Panhandle plain, but is a masterful rendering of north central Texas prairies.

In 1841, Arthur Ikin published the following statement: "Among and beyond the mountains, moose, a species of antelope, and wild sheep, are said to be common."[9] Remembering that in that day the known mountains were the heights of the Hill Country, and that beyond them was, to the east Texan pioneers, the still virtually unknown wilderness of the high prairies, this places what we know were actually elk all over the area northwest of San Antonio.

From 1852, Capt. R. B. Marcy, the great military explorer, left a note which confirms the presence of elk in the vicinity of North Texas, but at the same time shows their retreat by that time. He wrote from what is now southwest Oklahoma, just north of Wilbarger County, Texas, "From the circumstance of having seen elk tracks upon the stream we passed in our march today, I have called it 'Elk creek.' I am informed by our guide that five years since elk were frequently seen in the Witchita mountains; but now they are seldom met with in this part of the country."[10]

The last evidence in point of time of elk in North Texas is in a note by an editorial correspondent of the *Clarksville Standard*, Charles De Morse, published in that paper's May 28, 1853 issue. It reads, "At Worth we found in the line of curiosities a wild cat, a pet bear, some stone coal from Belknap, and an immense pair of Deer's antlers picked up on the Grand Prairie, probably four feet in length."[11] As far as we know, this pair of antlers, which from their huge size had to have been elk's, lay on the prairie as a last sad memorial to the herds of elk which were eliminated from North Texas long before the buffaloes, and whose passing was, most shameful of all, hardly noted and never mourned.

None other than George Kendall, the famous sheepman who should certainly have known his animals, said only about a decade earlier that there were many elk down farther toward Central Texas. He wrote that in 1814, when in what is now eastern Bosque County and on land now possibly under Lake Whitney, "the woods and prairies about us not only afforded excellent grazing for our cattle and horses, but teemed with every species of game — elk, deer, bears, wild turkeys, and, at the proper season, buffalo and mustang."[12]

Having traced elk down into Texas as far as Bosque County and as late as 1844, we reach a hiatus. There is no account of them from anywhere in the whole belt of Texas' central latitudes — from the trans-Pecos, from across the Edwards Plateau, the lower prairies and lower East Texas, early or late. What is to be made of this? Does it mean that the elk's range ended somewhere in northern Texas?

This might seem to be the answer, but we must not jump to conclusions too quickly. There exist two more passages listing elk as native residents of Texas, and these from a most unexpected region. In 1839, William Kennedy published the following statement: "About two miles south of this desert [the so-called Wild Horse Desert], on the margin of a beautiful and fertile prairie, is the celebrated Salt Lake. . . . The lake is surrounded by tracts of the best pasturage, the resort of wild horses and cattle, deer and elk."[13] The very next year, Bonnell published his book on Texas, in which he echoes, too closely for comfort, Kennedy's statement with his own: "About two miles south of this desert, and in the edge of one of the most beautiful and fertile prairies in Texas is the celebrated salt lake, which has for more than a century supplied the northern Mexican states with salt. . . . This lake is surrounded by the best stock raising country in the world, and the wild cattle, horses, deer and elk resort to it in thousands."[14]

These are only two statements, and they appear to have both originated from the same source, but they place elk in the area around the junction of Willacy, Hidalgo and Kenedy counties, with the implication that they abounded there. These elk, appearing in deep South Texas, apparently cut off by hundreds of miles from all their northern kind, look strange enough that we might want to deny their actual existence, and say, as some of our modern writers do, that the elk's range terminated at or near the Red River. But we want to be fair to our explorers who ventured these statements, so we look back into the works of some of the best scholars of earlier times. And we find statements such as the following: Audubon and Bachman, in their masterpiece on the quadrupeds of America published in 1851, "We have every reason to believe, that the Elk once was found on nearly every portion of the temperate latitudes of North America. It has never advanced as far north as the mouse deer, but it ranges much farther to the south. . . . It is found on the western prairies, and ranges along the eastern sides of the mountains in Texas and New Mexico."[15]

John Dean Caton, in his volume *The Antelope and Deer of America*, published in 1877, wrote, "But few quadrupeds in our country have occupied a wider range than the American Elk. He is found in every part of the present U.S. and in northern Mexico."[16] Such statements make it appear that those elk in deep South Texas were neither phantoms nor out of place.

Granting that elk were actual parts of the game animal mix on the prairies of deep South Texas only brings us face to face with another dilemma. Were these southern animals really isolated by hundreds of miles from any of their kin in North Texas, there being no elk at all on central-latitude Texas, or did our explorers entirely miss at least sparse elk populations which would have linked the whole of Texas into the one almost continent-wide range of these animals? All that can be said is this: Since one cannot prove a negative, the fact that the explorers did not mention elk in Central Texas does not prove they were never there. And just as the existence of those in South Texas and Mexico argues for the existence of elk in Central Texas, the sightings and killing of elk in Louisiana in 1829 and 1842[17] argues that they should also have been in lower East Texas in at least early historical times.

A major factor to be considered here is that no one explored any other part of Texas and left us any account of the country's animals at or even near the time when, according to Onate, elk in herds were roaming the Panhandle. They could have been as abundant in the rest of Texas as he found them out there, and we could not know. Similarly, they could have been eliminated somehow in the nearly 100 years before even La Salle arrived in Texas, the Spanish came looking for him and the numerous accounts of Texas began to appear, even as they were in the Panhandle, and we would have no record of it at all.

It is clear that elk were native Texas animals, numerous in hundred-fold herds at very early dates in at least two places — the extreme northern and extreme southern ends of the state — but absent even in those places before any widespread exploration took place. This leaves no real evidence of how many there once were or exactly where they ranged. That they were probably the first of the large herbivores exterminated from Texas is tragic, but not illogical or unexplainable. Elk have been among the first to go in other places — witness the great Irish elk — and the group's vulnerability before hunters is proverbial. The great hunter Richard Irving Dodge wrote, "They [elk] are not prolific, and, though cautious and difficult to approach by the novice, are easily killed by the skilled hunter. Moreover, they have many foolish traits, which oftentimes puts it in the power of the hunter to kill a great many at one time."[18] This the earliest great hunters in Texas probably did, and the large herds of these gregarious native animals, once too trusting of man on the prairies, are gone, replaced by the individuals of an imported breed protected on some reserves and special ranches for today's big game hunters to bag.

Any clear summary of all this would seem to reinforce our earlier statement that if you had been an early enough pioneer in Texas you might have seen elk. If you were a *pastor* or a *Comanchero* in early North Texas you would have. If you were in deep South Texas before it became the state, you would have. And from this it seems to me at least possible — though I can't prove it — that if you had been anywhere across the central belt of Texas before the Indians had horses to hunt them with and the settlers arrived with their guns to shoot them with, you would have seen these huge, awkward-appearing, stupid-enough-to-be-easily-duped beasts before they were gone.

This prospect should put us of a mind to ponder the musings of an early visitor to our continent. Prompted by his described adventures bagging our elk, he published in 1874 the following opinions which still seem all too applicable: "In Scotland the red deer is vaunted and his praises sung, for he is truly a noble beast, alike trying the hunter's courage and endurance; but if Caledonia's rocky glens and heath-covered mountains boast of possessing such a hero, the far distant plains and central plateaus of America have a right to glory, for they feed and shelter a nobler quarry, if size and power constitute such. The New Land surpasses us in the magnitude of its rivers, mountains, waterfalls, and trees; in her animal creation, also, she is ahead.... But a thought arises in my mind, will the western world long possess those representatives of animal life of which she has a just right to be proud? I say no, if the work of destruction continues as now, for every border ruffian, every squatter, is allowed to slaughter at his will, and at all seasons, creatures, the possession of which any land has a right to be proud."[19]

5

The Texas Bighorn Mountain Sheep

It caused quite a stir when explorers reported finding a new kind of animal in the high mountains of western America. This creature intrigued everyone who came across it, but it also puzzled them. Duncan McGillivray, the first to report taking these animals, found interest in them so great that he published a detailed account of them in the popular press, but he also stated, "in short, this animal appears to be a compound of the deer and the sheep, having the body and hair of the former, with the head and horns of the latter."[1] He himself seemed to prefer a translation of a French name for the animal which came out as the "mountain ram." This term might have come about due to the circumstance that the females of the species as well as the males grow conspicuous horns, but it seems, in the face of today's feminist feelings, it can hardly be used as the appellation for the species.

McGillivray took his specimens far up in Canada in the year 1800, but the existence of these animals in Texas was reported from back around 1765, and they were named by Texas writers five times between then and 1854. In these accounts Texans showed their uncertainty about the species' relationships, twice calling them wild or mountain goats and three times calling them wild or mountain sheep. The general modern decision to call them sheep may be correct, but it is backed by only a three-to-two opinion of the explorers. And the term "bighorn" does not appear in the literature of Texas exploration at all.

Scientists have also had their difficulties relating the Texas bighorns to others. In 1902, C. M. Barber called the animals in Texas and southeastern New Mexico *Ovis mexicanus*,[2] implying that they were the same as those already described in Mexico by Merriam. A decade later Vernon Bailey concluded that these were not the same, and christened the Texas and southeastern New Mexican population as a subspecies of the species described far to the north, his name coming out to be *O. canadensis texianus*.[3] But Texans' pride at having their mountain sheep named for their state was quashed when Cowan, in 1940, decided that the Texas and Mexican animals were actually the same, and dropped *texianus* into the synonymy. Since then the Texas-New Mexico population has been a nonentity. Most have been calling them *O. canadensis mexicana,* or commonly the desert bighorn sheep.[4] On the other hand, is it an unconscious expression of wounded Texas pride which has prompted some Texas scholars to avoid the subspecies rank entirely and use only *Ovis canadensis* for our bighorns?[5] The situation is probably worse than such a tongue-in-cheek suggestion may indicate. All native Texas mountain sheep having been extirpated long ago, nothing more definite can ever be determined on the matter. Texas members of the species may have been hounded out of existence without even a name to reflect a solid understanding of their place in the scheme of taxonomic things remaining as a memorial.

We are way beyond ourselves in telling the explorers' story of these animals. However, their account of them is not very complete. Not one of them left an iota of description of them — or even a comment on their numbers or the situations they occupied. There is not even one mention of their behavior or even of their remarkable horns. Except for one author they just remarked that these animals were supposed to be present here. In fact, we have found only five pre-1860 Texas writers mentioning these animals at all. These are easy to summarize.

In about 1765, one Juan Brebel made a heroic trip from the east all the way to Santa Fe. He recounted what he found in the wilderness to John Sibley, who wrote down the substance of his statements. In these, among the various animals he lists as being at that time "on both sides" of the Red River "from the Rio Azul [Blue River] upwards" he includes elk, deer, something we presume to be antelopes, and "wild goats."[6] This would seem to have placed bighorns somewhere in far northwest Texas. However unlikely a possibility this seems to be, none other than the careful governmental observer, Captain Marcy, wrote in 1849, when he was among the breaks which begin in extreme western Oldham County and continue on into New Mexico, that one of his trusted guides told him mountain sheep resorted there.[7] It is only an assumption that Brebel meant to include Texas in his statement, and Marcy did not claim to have seen the sheep here himself, so these two statements are not actual evidence of bighorns in the Texas Panhandle, but are they not hints of a possibility not usually even remembered that they might have survived there up into the earliest part of the historical period?

In 1841, Arthur Ikin wrote in his famous guide to the Texas of that day: "Among and beyond the mountains, moose [elk], a species of antelope, and wild sheep, are said to be common."[8]

In 1853, Brad C. Fowler wrote that Captain Reed, after two trips through West Texas, told him that mountain goats inhabited the Guadalupe Mountains.[9]

Finally, in 1854, Julius Froebel wrote, "As I was riding in advance of the caravan, I saw three mountain-sheep, one of which I might have killed if I had ventured to follow them; but, at a distance, I mistook the animals for bears, and confess that I had no desire to encounter three of these beasts alone. When I discovered my error they were too high up between the rocks. We had now entered the Limpia Mountains, from which the Limpia Valley opens upon the plain."[10]

That seems to be all the early Texans left us concerning our mountain sheep. It's not much, but maybe it tells us a few things. Most importantly, it reassures us that our explorers didn't miss much. That they mention at all such an elusive animal occupying such inaccessible portions of a mere corner of Texas is valuable evidence of not only the completeness but the accuracy of their observations. And the paucity of their accounts seems to bear upon one of the points concerning the bighorns which is still debated.

This is the question of just how numerous these animals were before their rapid decrease began with the coming of the Europeans. We find two schools of thought on this. One of these opinions is summarized by Helmut Buechner, who wrote in 1960, ". . . it seems that [Ernest Thompson] Seton's estimate of one and one-half to two million individuals for the whole species, including populations in Canada, United States, and Mexico, is entirely possible as a pristine level of abundance."[11] We will let W. B. Davis and W. P. Taylor represent the opposite opinion. In 1939, they stated, "Although the number of bighorns in the Guadalupes is doubtless decreasing, it probably never was very high. Mearns reported that in 1878 Lieut. Charles H. Grierson killed three adult males, all that he saw in these mountains. . . . We have no definite information that the population of bighorns in trans-Pecos Texas was ever large."[12]

The scarcity of early Texas references to these animals clearly weighs on the side of those who think the mountain sheep were always rare. Buechner realized this and attempted to explain the few Texas sightings of his supposedly abundant animals with two assumptions: first, that these animals kept to high elevations where early travelers would not have ventured, and second, that the large parties of the western expeditions were noisy and would have frightened these animals away so that they never even guessed they had been present. However, each of these assumptions faces difficulty.

The first of them is countered by the fact that mountain sheep do not spend all of their time on the pinnacles of mountains. The same J. A. Allen before quoted wrote of this animal, "It is only to be met with in the rocky mountains, and it generally frequents the highest regions, which produce any vegetation, though sometimes it descends to feed to the bottom of the valleys."[13] Not only this vertical travel is indulged in, but these animals were originally overland travelers. Barber mentioned this in 1902, writing that "a small band live on this range of mountains [the Guadalupes] and they pass up and down the range from New Mexico to Texas."[14] In 1939, Davis and Taylor wrote: "There is ample proof that the bighorns go down into the valleys and cross from one mountain mass to another. Bailey saw tracks in several valleys showing where sheep had crossed from one range to another. In May 1938, Snow observed three mountain sheep near Highway 54 in the valley between the Beach and the Baylor mountains. Stubblefield and others reported seeing bighorns cross U.S. Highway 80 near the rock crusher west of Van Horn. C. R. Landon, of the Biological Survey, using a powerful field glass on the porch of the hotel in Sierra Blanca, has seen mountain sheep on the hills of the Yates Ranch north of that town."[15] George Bird Grinnell is very explicit about this, writing: "In the early days of the cattle business it was not very unusual for cowboys to come on sheep in the flat country and to overtake them and catch them with their ropes. . . . It is not intended to imply that the sheep were ever actually a prairie animal or permanently left the general neighborhood of the rough land to which they might retreat. But they often resorted to and were killed on the flat country. . . . Many years ago I saw sheep feeding on the prairie with the antelope."[16]

That bighorns could in the past have been seen down in the valleys along the overland routes, plus one explanation of why they have not been thus seen more recently, is evidenced by Ben Tinker. Writing in 1978, he stated, "In former years these sheep [populations in Chihuahua] traveled back and forth to the Big Hatchet mountains in southwestern New Mexico, and others came south from these mountains into Mexico. Today, their travel is restricted by highways, fences, and ranches, and their numbers in Mexico cannot be augmented from this northern source, which is now rigidly protected and increasing."[17]

Literally dozens of expeditions crossed trans-Pecos Texas. Many skirted the very prow of the Guadalupes and then snaked down to the Rio Grande through the very heart of the bighorn's favorite Texas range. Some passed back and forth through the Davis Mountains, and more moved out from the Presidio area when there was actually a presidio there. And although the main bodies of these parties necessarily threaded through the valleys, they had expert lookouts, hunters and stalkers who ranged far and wide from the trails with eyes peeled for anything that moved. That almost none of them, from early Spanish explorers to California-bound settlers, left any evidence of having run into mountain sheep belies any opinion that the western Texas mountains were crawling with bighorns.

While the mountain sheep were seen and reported enough to assure us that they were definitely part of the explorers' Texas and may actually have ranged over a much larger part of northwest Texas than we can now either prove or disprove, they were always indistinct shadows in the wilderness mountains which provided the backdrop before which the drama of the taming of Texas was played out. Among the most untamable of animals, all of the original Texan bighorns have long since perished, and the prospect of even keeping introduced relatives of those once here alive does not appear at all certain. It may be that there is no place left in the "don't fence me in" state for such high ranging individuals as these sheep which don't take to shepherds.

6

The Bears of the Texas Hills

Turning from the large herbivores of natural Texas toward the carnivores, our attention is captured by an animal so strangely positioned between these antagonistic groups that you can still get arguments about where its relationships lie. This hard to catalogue animal is none other than the bear, which looms so large in bodily bulk, usefulness to the settlers, exciting object in the wilderness and sheer numbers of individuals in historic Texas that its existence cannot be ignored, even though it is very hard to fully imagine today.

Justification of giving the bear this large place in the early Texas scene can come first of all from the almost unbelievable numbers of them which were in the undisturbed natural communities of the state. And I don't ask that you take my word for this. Marin de Porras, making a general statement about the state, wrote in 1805, "Bear, wild boar, deer and buffalo are found in such abundance that it is incredible to one who has not seen them."[1]

If such a statement is too general and the linking of bears with deer and buffalo, the champions of prodigious numbers, seems too glib, there are statements giving actual numbers for specific locations. For instance, F. L. Olmsted gives us an idea about the number of bears once in an area now being invaded by suburbs of San Antonio and running on up into Kendall County when he wrote in 1854, "There was still, at a spot near Currie's Creek, a man who made his livelihood by hunting. He kept a pack of trained hounds and had killed 60 bears in the course of two years."[2] There is no doubt that bears were once very numerous in some parts of the state.

Only a couple of surviving accounts can be included here to give us glimpses of how the bears figured in the wilderness scene and how the settlers related to them. Perhaps the most clues to both occur in the briefest space in a passage by the Abbe Domenech. In describing an incident taking place in 1848, in the newly founded settlement of San Marcos, the good abbe wrote: "Bears are very numerous in this lonely spot; and here, for the first time in my life, I tasted of their flesh, and found it excellent. We met at the inn another passenger for San Antonio. He was a Frenchman, who had come to San Marcos to hunt bears, and was taking back with him two of those animals. Whilst at dinner, we were startled by a deep growling near us. At once the Frenchman seized his double-barrel gun, and left the room without a word. I asked our host what was the matter. 'Only a bear,' he replied, with the greatest possible composure; but seeing my astonishment, he added: 'Oh! no doubt, these animals sometimes commit depredations, but they rarely attack us. As soon as they catch a glimpse of us, they scamper off. It is even said that the farm of a Mr. Mosenbach [Meusebach], on the road as you go to Fredericksburg, is not guarded by dogs, but by tame bears. When one arrives there after sunset—' The double report of a gun cut short the conversation; and a minute or two afterwards the Frenchman reappeared, and took his place at the table, assuring me that he had certainly wounded the bear, but fearing lest he should lose his place in the wagon, he had refrained from pursuing the animal into the forest."[3]

Bears were clearly very common in many settlements, causing the settlers some inconvenience, but not actually being any great threat to their lives or successes in the land. On the contrary, bruins provided various things — meat for food, grease for various uses and skins of some value — all of which could have been available on a continuing basis if the bear population had been harvested with restraint while being managed so as to sustain it on a long term basis. But the settlers had no conception of such restraint. Instead they showed a ruling passion to exterminate all the bears possible, even when, like the Frenchman in the abbe's story, they had no goal but to waste the creatures. To this was added a hilarious frenzy which made the successful bear hunt famous beyond most other sports for its crude excesses.

The best way to show this bear hunt madness is to include the whole of F. L. Olmsted's description of one such as it took place in the Texas Hill Country around 1854. Olmsted's version of it goes like this: "The settlers told us with fresh excitement the story of a great bear-hunt which had but recently come off. The hero was one of the German hermits named P———, a famous sportsman. . . . On the last occasion he had wounded a bear, who took to his heels and disappeared in a pile of rocks. Following with all his speed, P——— found a hole down which the bear seemed to have dropped. Convinced that his shot had been fatal, yet unable to enter the cavity, he pried a large stone over the mouth and went for assistance. His hut-companion returned with him, and they at first attempted to smoke the bear out. Not succeeding in this, they battered the edges of the aperture till it was large enough to enter. Then, held by the heel, P——— went on his hands in search of his booty. After some not very pleasant groping, he found the carcass, and attaching a rope, it was hauled out, a magnificent he-bear, worth a good deal in cash, and much more in glory. But while half-smothered in the cave, he had heard an indistinct growl at no great distance, which indicated that more fun was to be had if properly applied for. It was a hazardous experiment, but one that exactly suited P———'s humor, to enter and have a hand-to-hand fight in the dark with the growler, whoever he was.

"Arming himself with a freshly capped and cocked Colt and placing a knife between his teeth, he crept cautiously in again. The passage shortly became narrow, and he soon reached a turn which he could only pass feet foremost. Retreating a bit, he turned himself, and pushed on. On clearing the obstacle, he found himself free and heard now close before him the steady breathing of a bear. . . . Aiming deliberately at the sound, he fired two barrels, then took himself out as fast as hands and knees would carry him. . . .

"Piling the rocks again over the aperture, the two returned to their hut, manufactured torches of wax from a bee-tree, and calling a neighbor or two to see the sport, went again to the den. Armed now with a torch, P——— forced himself to where he had been before and saw his bear lying dead. It was dragged out.

"After a congratulatory and recuperative draught of whisky all round, P——— resolved on further explorations. He found beyond the scene of his last adventure, a narrow cleft in the rocks. He had hardly squeezed himself into this, when he suddenly found his hand in contact with a third bear — dead. It had probably been smothered by their smoke. This, too, was got out amid an excitement that made the woods ring with echoes."[4]

The Texas bears were not hunted so strenuously because they posed a real threat to human life. In fact, the settlers belittled their fierceness. Von Wrede wrote in 1841 that they are not dangerous "because they flee from children."[5] And Edward Smith recorded in 1849 the "verbal communication of Dr. Matthews . . . residing upon colonel Reily's land, and a most intelligent man and farmer," as follows: "Nobody feared them [bears] and they annoyed the settlers less than in Tennessee."[6] But they probably justified killing them because they posed hazards to their livestock.

This brings up the question of the black bear's diet, which is apparently a difficult one since we can find contradictory statements about what they do or do not eat all the way to the present.

Many of our reporters on the early scene concern themselves with this question, and there is even some discrepancy between their opinions. All who discuss it agree that the bears eat much plant material, and most state that acorns form a major staple for them, with berries and other fruits also important. For instance, J. C. Clopper wrote when in present Colorado County in 1828, "Camp the second night three miles West of Scull Creek — hear bear in the night gathering mast from the live-Oak."[7] And Berlandier wrote in the same year, "It is these small forests of oak trees that contain bear. Sometimes they are found in groups eating acorns. The bear is not carnivorous. Its favorite food is the fruit of the oak tree and the berries of a type of *caprifoliacea* which is very common in this wilderness."[8]

But Berlandier apparently did not know the whole truth about the matter. No other early writer states the bear to be obligately herbivorous. In fact, they state otherwise. Nuttall is the most specific, in his 1819 statement based upon his experiences in what is now Oklahoma, writing: "Perhaps no animal employs a greater diversity of diet than the bear; the common American species feeds upon fruits, honey, wasps, and bees; they will turn over large logs in quest of other insects, and are also destructive to pigs and fawns. . . ."[9] Concerning the early Texas situation, A. A. Parker wrote in 1836, "The bears, generally, take to the dense forest of trees and canebrake. They catch the full grown hogs, and the wolves take the pigs."[10] Audubon and Bachman met the problem head-on and made what appears to be the most definitive statement, writing in their 1854 work, as follows: "Most writers on the habits of this animal have stated that the Black Bear does not eat animal food from choice, and never unless pressed by hunger. This we consider a great mistake, for in our experience we have found the reverse to be the case, and it is well known to our frontier farmers that this animal is a great destroyer of pigs, hogs, calves, and sheep, for the sake of which we have even known it to desert the pecan groves of Texas."[11]

So besides hunting the Texas bears for food, fat, fur and fun, the settlers had as an excuse for killing them the protection of the so-called domestic but not usually even penned hogs and calves they considered they owned. This meant that the large and hard to hide bruins were not long for existence in a Texas where it has been said that everyone had a gun and few ever missed with it. It is true that they were soon gone. But we can't forget them without satisfying our curiosity about the details of what bears were once in Texas and exactly where they lived, so we look for information about this.

From the very beginning the classification of the Texas bears and the outlining of the different forms' distributions within the state present difficulties all out of proportion to the few kinds of bears there were. This appears to be another situation where the subjects were eliminated so early that it was before the scientists got to do definitive studies. This makes the explorers' reports take on even more than usual importance because they were the only ones present early enough to tell us anything.

Take, for instance, the question of grizzly bears in Texas. Were they here, and if so where and in what numbers? What scientist can tell us, and back his statement up with scientific evidence? One would have had to say, speaking scientifically up until 1890, that the grizzly was not a Texas bear at all since none had ever been officially recorded as taken within the state. This is strange, and not what scientists would have had to predict, since the grizzly was common just outside Texas, both in New Mexico and in Mexico. Then a single grizzly bear was shot in the Davis Mountains of West Texas in 1890. It was seen by scientists, and so entered as an official record. But this only confused things further. Was the grizzly now to be entered as a Texas native or not? Since no other individual of that species was ever taken in Texas, most authorities do not list the grizzly as a Texas resident, apparently considering the old male of 1890 as a lost maverick or merely a tourist.

The question of the grizzly in Texas still stands, but it should not be ignored, because it could have important consequences. For instance, should the species be stocked in our West Texas parks because of having been as much a native there as in Yellowstone? Who can tell?

If we would really like to know whether there were ever grizzlies living in Texas, why don't we look to our explorers for what they can tell us?

Brad C. Fowler, in his account of the Rhine Party's 1853 trek west, wrote about going up Delaware Creek to the base of the Guadalupe Mountains. When at Pine Springs, in the process of working around the base of the mountains, he wrote that he "learned from Capt. Reed who is now performing his second trip through here to California, that the country is inhabited only by the Indian, Grizzly Bear, Mountain Goat, Antelope, and the Black Tailed Deer."[12] Now this is not an eyewitness sighting of grizzlies in Texas, but it is an incidental report of one explorer who had been over the route before informing a first-timer that the bears were there in "the country," which could surely be taken as including that edge of Texas where those men then were. It was tantamount to saying that grizzlies ranged down out of New Mexico at least as far as the Guadalupe Mountains extended into Texas.

Another statement arising out of the early accounts is that of the early Texas publicist, Viktor Bracht. He wrote point blank in 1848, "There are three kinds of bear in Texas. The dangerous grizzly bear is found in the northern mountains. . . ."[13]

The only difficulty with this statement is in determining what Bracht meant by his term, "northern mountains." This is because there are no mountains in North Texas at all. The only formations in Texas to be considered mountains are the hills of the Hill Country, the mountains of the trans-Pecos and several buttes in the high prairies. It may be an example of our Texian overstatement to call the Hill Country ridges mountains, and besides, Bracht made it clear that he didn't mean the Hill Country in this statement when he went on to refer to that area as follows: "The American or black bear *(barribal)* is found in the hilly section and near the coast. . . ." So logic turns us to the trans-Pecos for Bracht's mountains with grizzlies, and there we are pointed straight toward the Guadalupes. After all, they are our highest mountains, they are the only ones near a northern border of Texas and they are the northern mountains of that region. Furthermore, if you place yourself in the Galveston to San Antonio corridor, which was the part of Texas where Bracht spent the most time and which was thought of as the center of Texas in 1848, the Guadalupes are actually somewhat north of you, and certainly seem even more so than they are. Bracht's statement therefore seems to be a clear one from that time period that grizzlies inhabited at least the Guadalupe Mountains of West Texas.

Captain Marcy, in reporting his 1849 explorations, described the bluffs of the caprock in Oldham County of the western Panhandle and on into New Mexico, and stated that "it is to such places as this that the grizzly bear and mountain sheep resort."[14] This is no eyewitness report of grizzlies seen in Texas, but an intimation that there were habitats in the Panhandle such as they occupied within their range. Since they were known to exist in the mountains just west of this, it is a statement requiring a presumption that they be expected there.

But were they ever actually there? Numerous bears were reported in that area, as well as in the lower part of the Big Bend. Some of them were described as "large bears," but none were specifically said to have been grizzlies, and so we have no actual explorer-provided evidence from beyond the Guadalupes for that species. Also, Jean Louis Berlandier, while contrasting the common bears of Texas and the more dangerous grizzly, placed the grizzly out beyond Texas: "These black bears [of Texas] do not attack men unless they are closely pursued. The savages say that in the mountain range of New Mexico, they also meet bears. However, they are so ferocious that they chase a man even if he does not attack them."[15]

I would put all this together this way: Since grizzlies were common in the mountains of New Mexico on the north of West Texas and since some explorers intimated as much, it seems logical that these bears followed the New Mexican mountains down to their terminus, which is in Texas, and so ranged into Texas as far as the Guadalupe Mountains extended. They may also have strayed into the breaks of the Texas Panhandle, as Marcy speculates, but there is no real evidence of this. Since they were also common in the mountains of Coahuila and Chihuahua just south of West Texas, in might be expected that the grizzlies also ranged north through the mountains of the Big Bend to link the two ranges. This may not have been so, however, because none of the numerous expeditions of whose crossings through these mountains over a period of more than 200 years we have records ever mentions encountering a grizzly in them. This creates a reason for presuming that they were not there. But what about the 1890 record in the Davis Mountains? We will probably never know whether that individual was the last of a totally unmentioned population, was just a tourist after all, or was a pitiful refugee on the prowl, searching for new territory after his normal range had been rendered untenable, like the big cats often do. If I were to go out on a limb, I'd say that we should probably put grizzlies in the Guadalupe Mountains National Park as true original residents of that area, but that, at the same time, there is no evidence to support introducing them into the Big Bend National Park. They were, at best, very peripheral residents of Texas.

The situation with the black bears is entirely different. Almost everyone who explored in Texas before 1860 reported that they experienced these bears either directly in the field or indirectly by partaking of or using some parts of their carcasses. Many went into detail in describing them and their adventures with them.

These bears were clearly all of one species, *Ursus americanus*. The explorers called them "black bears," "American black bears," "mountain bears," or "black mountain bears." There is no mystery about any of these names except that it seems we should have to look to experiences of earlier times in other places for any explanation of why they associated this bear with mountains. In Texas they often found them in low riverine forests and sometimes even stated that such places were where they most abounded.

But how is it, then, that Bracht, in his statement which we have just considered, said that there were "three kinds of bear in Texas"? One was the grizzly in his "northern mountains." Then he went on to write, "The American or black bear *(barribal)* is found in the hilly section and near the coast. Its color varies from a dark brown to black with a yellowish brown-spotted snout. It is very shy and agile. It hibernates in hollow trees or in caves during the months of December and January. There is still another kind in the West, namely (near Fredericksburg) on the Pedernales, the real paradise for bears. This one is taller, more slender and much fleeter than the common bear; wherefore it is called 'racer' by the Americans. It has a heart-shaped white spot on its breast. It is uncommon."

Nor is Bracht the only explorer to differentiate between what he considered two kinds of Texas bears. Berlandier, after making his statement which we have seen about grizzlies, went on to write, "In Texas, there are two types and variations of black bears. One is completely black and not too fierce. The other is more intrepid, and the hair around its mouth is yellowish. For this reason, the inhabitants of Texas call it *ceibayo*."

We seem to have had here two types or at least races of bears. Bracht's American or black bear, also apparently called barribal, was dark brown to black with a yellowish snout and no white spot on its chest, was not especially active, was an eastern form and was common. He then had a western form which was more slender and active, with a white spot on its chest and which was uncommon in the Hill Country. It was simply called the "racer."

These two forms seem to coincide acceptably with Berlandier's two variations, Bracht's eastern one with his more black and not very fierce one, and Bracht's western one with the one called *ceibayo*, which was more fierce and with parts of it yellowish in color. Berlandier's important contribution here is the recognition that these were merely variations within the one black bear species. That the species is large enough to contain these different forms, as well as that Bracht was correct in stating that it was the western form which had a white spot on its chest, is vouched for by the description of the black bear in the *Audubon Society Field Guide to North American Mammals*, which includes the following: "In the East, nearly black; in the West, black to cinnamon with white blaze on chest."[16] But did anyone else see these as consistent enough variations in Texas native bears to warrant setting up categories for them?

Some expert mammologists have shown even greater "splitter" tendencies than our two explorers by dividing classification of the black bear. First they have *Ursus americanus americanus* Pallas. Then they have an *Ursus americanus luteolus* Griffith, which is usually called the Louisiana black bear. Some have also set up *Ursus americanus amblyceps* Baird, the New Mexican black bear. Do our explorers' related experiences show any clues as to which of these three bears, if not all of them, originally ranged into Texas, and if so what parts of the state they occupied?

To answer this question we need to have some way to synthesize all of the ninety-eight pre-1860 reports of Texas bears which we have collected in such a way that they give us the explorers' overall picture of the species. By painstaking research into the location of each eyewitness when he saw each bear he reported, we derive the accompanying map (Map 6). Each present county in which at least one bear was reported in those days (before they were eliminated over any large area) is marked on this map.

The result is one of the strangest distribution maps rising out of the explorers' accounts, and one hard to interpret. To me, it shows bears concentrated in two regions of the state — in North Texas and in Central Texas. There are scatterings of them in West Texas, in the Panhandle and in southeastern Texas. Strangely, there were none at all reported in South Texas, and while the valleys of two rivers, the Red and the Brazos, are almost completely occupied by bears, the valleys of four major streams, the Trinity, the Colorado, the Nueces and the Pecos are shown as almost bearless over most of their lengths. What could this distribution mean in terms of the three subspecies the scientists give us?

The black bears of far West Texas were declared by Bailey to have been *U. a. amblyceps*, the New Mexican black bear.[17] How far east that race once ranged is problematic. Bailey did not think that they got as far east as the Pecos River, but in 1938, a skull of a bear which was determined to have been that form was found in a cave in southern Edwards County. On the strength of that skull, William B. Davis maintained that all of the bears of Central Texas were New Mexican black bears.[18] I venture the opinion that this western bear was the more active and ferocious bear with the white spot on its chest, described by Bracht and Berlandier, which was present but uncommon in the Hill Country and called the racer or *ceibayo*.

But there was a much more common form of

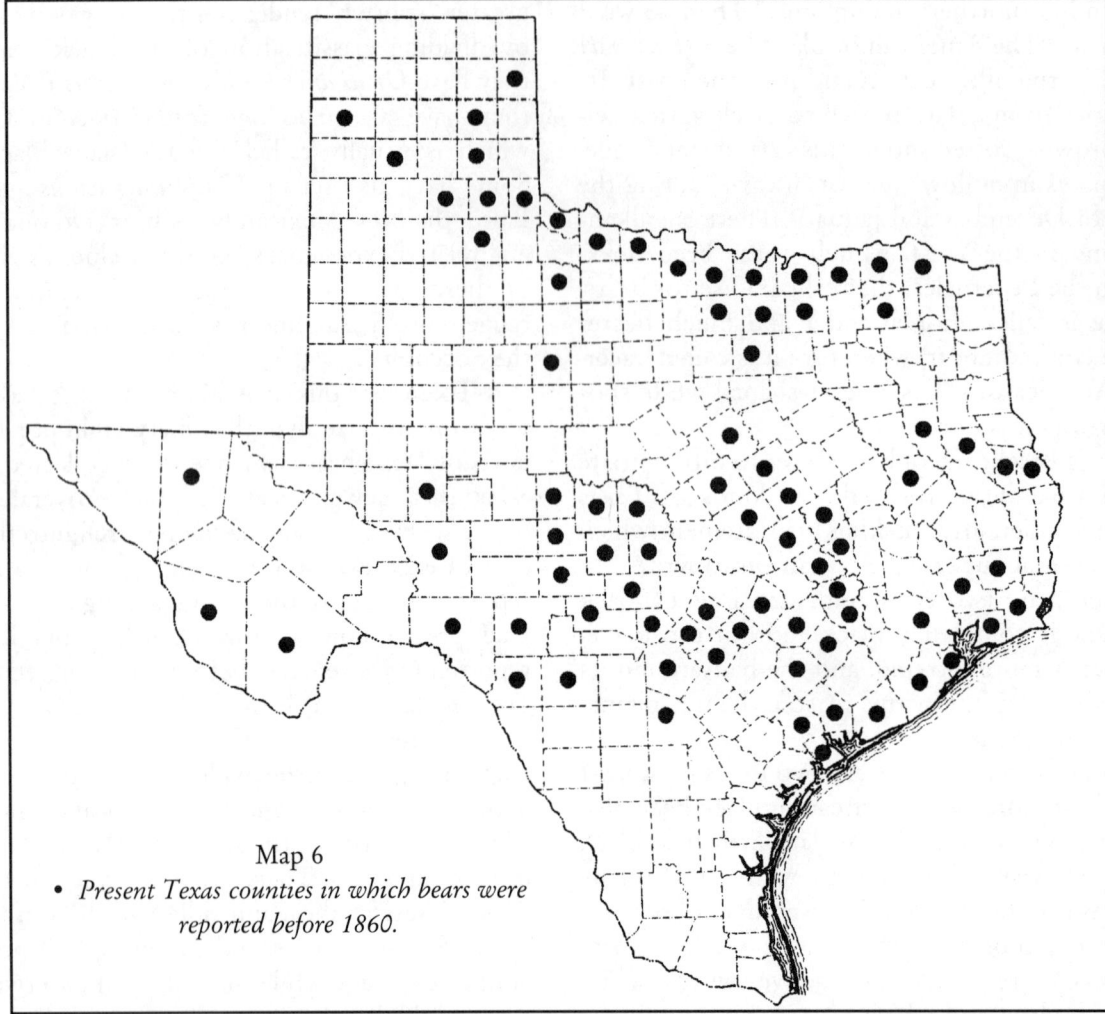

Map 6
• *Present Texas counties in which bears were reported before 1860.*

bear present in the Hill Country. "On the basis of geographic probability," Bailey, who came too late to see them alive at all, called these bears the typical northeastern black bear, *U. a. americanus*.[19] The bears so plentiful all along the Red River were certainly this northeastern black, but to have them in the Hill Country would be a major extension of its range, which some maintain did not go south of 33° latitude.[20] If this bear did spill through Central Texas in huge numbers, it only came down the Brazos Valley, since there were no bears reported on the upper Colorado or middle Trinity.

The reason for the lack of bear records over most of the Panhandle and for bears having been present in precisely the Panhandle counties where explorers reported finding them is clear when we consider the lay of the land. The great lumbering bear eschews open spaces where it is vulnerable because of no trees to climb or rocks to hide in. It also loves fruits, nuts and acorns, none of which are abundant on grasslands. So the only bear described as having been found on the flat openness of the Llano Estacado was a single one surprised and killed on the flat in Briscoe County by Marryat and company in 1843, but that happened within about half a mile of the breaks of Tule Canyon and the Prairie Dog Town Fork of the Brazos River.[21] The one seen by Edwin James in 1820, in Oldham County, was by the stream of the Canadian River among grapevines "loaded with fruit."[22] Abert's "mother and her cubs," reported in 1845, were actually in the channel of the Red River in Gray County.[23] Marcy reported seeing and killing several bears in 1852, but all of them were when he was in the breaks of the Prairie Dog Town Fork in or near what is now Palo Duro Canyon Park.[24]

The records show that bears were distributed in the Panhandle only in the canyons and breaks of the streams and were apparently not very numerous even there. As to which subspecies of the black bear these were, since all of the canyons of the Panhandle are extensions of the valleys of rivers flowing through the typical northeastern black bear's known range, it would be logical that they were that form. However, one could also argue that it is only a short distance on the west to areas once teeming with the New Mexico black bear. Unfortunately, not one of the explorers described a Panhandle bear, and they killed them so early that it seems no one else saw them, so we can probably never know which they were. We can only thank the explorers of that region for bothering to tell us that the bears were there at all, or we might never have known.

The matter of South Texas bears in the explorers' accounts in unequivocal. They just don't report having found any down there. The accounts of them stop abruptly as early travelers who have reported them in the Hill Country descend, like Berlandier, from the Edwards Escarpment. The only report of bears south of that step-off into a different bioregion is one describing a very localized South Texas habitat. Sanchez wrote concerning an 1828 experience as follows: "Rio de Medina, uninhabited, February 29. — The ground over which we had to travel the following day is almost all loose sand for seven or eight leagues. It is tiresome and hinders rapid travel, but though without verdure, lacking grass entirely, it is very picturesque, consisting throughout the whole extent of woods, not very thick, walnuts and evergreen oaks with acorns that serve as food for the bears and wild turkeys that live here in great numbers."[25]

This passage is describing the Carrizo Sands in extreme southern Bexar and northern Atascosa counties as they were when pristine. This unique outcrop, with its also unique living community, occurs as a giant arc only a few miles wide, cutting almost completely across the northern edge of South Texas. Sanchez's statement is good evidence that bears inhabited at least the Atascosa-Bexar part of it.

We must not argue any more strongly from the negative than scientists do when they draw their lines cutting off the ranges of organisms where their reports stop, but the total lack of any bear accounts from any of the many expeditions traveling up and down the several roads between various points in Mexico and San Antonio during the whole period of the Spanish explorations, the mission period, the various Mexican wars and the settlement of the Rio Grande Valley create the presumption that there were no bears in Texas south of the Edwards Escarpment in the west, the Carrizo Sands in Central Texas and the Guadalupe River on the coastal plains in Texas' early days.

The matter of bears in East Texas is not such an obvious one. It is usually assumed that the deep forests of this region were the paradise of Texas bears and their last refuge, but this is contradicted by the explorers' accounts. A glance at our map shows that bears were actually met with in relatively few parts of that region. It should also be remembered that Bracht told us that the "real paradise for bears" was on the Pedernales in the Hill Country. The big question is why the explorers found so few bears in East Texas.

Details of the reported sightings of bears there give us some possible clues. Most importantly, most of those reports come from eighteenth-century Spanish explorers. For instance, Espinosa, writing sometime between 1715 and 1721 about the area occupied by the Tejas Indians, which was the central part of East Texas, said: "At this time, which is usually in the winter, they [the Tejas] are accustomed to kill a great number of bears toward the north and they bring home a great deal of bear fat rolled up in moss and loaded on their horses.... These bears live on nuts and acorns which abound in this country. They are not seen in the Tejas country and the region thereabouts except when the crop of nuts and acorns to the northward has been short on account of the ice and the snow, as happened in the year '22, which was the first time I saw them alive so near the mission."[26] Lafora, when down at the Presidio Orcoquizac in 1767, writing about the Indians then in what is now Chambers and southern Liberty counties, said, "those unhappy people are compelled to live the greater part of the year on roots... and wild fruits. This is the customary diet of those natives whose laziness makes them content with it rather than trouble to hunt deer and bear, of which there is an abundance."[27] And Don Jose de Evis wrote in 1785, "The whole peninsula from the Rio Sabina to San Bernardo [Matagorda Bay] abounds in deer and bear."[28]

We thus are told that in the eighteenth century there were two distinct populations of bears in southeastern Texas: an overflow of northern bears, presumably *U. a. americanus,* coming down from the northeast corner of the state a ways at times, but apparently not remaining there, and a large, permanent coastal population, the two apparently separated by the whole of what we now call the Big Thicket, in which not one of the early observers reported any bears at all.

What I am calling the coastal population of bears was obviously far from a small one and clearly not made up of transient visitors from the north. The Talons listed them as generally present there in 1685.[29] Stephen F. Austin[30] and Mary Austin Holley[31] reported them as common in what is now Brazoria County in 1821 and 1831 respectively. An anonymous traveler reported them numerous in present Chambers County in 1831,[32] and Cushing tells of "bear's meat" being provided him for breakfast at a plantation there in 1835.[33] James Morgan wrote in 1838 about shooting bears "within less than half mile of my door" where he lived at New Washington. This would have been in the La Porte, Shoreacres area of Harris County. He explained this by saying, "in consequence of a great scarcity of means in the river bottoms the Bears are roaming through the Country in search of something to subsist on & have & still Come close to my Home — and kill hogs within hearing."[34] It may well be that these coastal bears made up a separate population of *U. a. luteolus*, the Louisiana black bear, which was supposed to inhabit East Texas, Louisiana and southern Mississippi.

The reports of bears in the whole of East Texas drop off drastically with the passage of time. There is only one more report of any bear in central East Texas after 1767. The many who wrote about the country around Nacogdoches during the nineteenth century are otherwise completely silent concerning bruins. We have seen several mentionings of bears down in Chambers, Harris and Brazoria counties in the early part of the nineteenth century, but Morgan's account of breakfasting on bear in 1838 is the last one.

We can probably never know the entire scenario of bears in East Texas, but a possible outline arises from these accounts and their timing. There may have once been many bears throughout the whole region, but if so that was apparently very long ago. They may have been forced north out of the interior forests by the many settled Tejas Indians who were there even before the first explorers came in the eighteenth century. If the Indians killed and made use of them to the extent Espinosa states, this would seem plausible. However, both the bears of the interior forests as described by Espinosa and those of the coastal river bottoms as stated by Morgan were pictured as creatures under dire stress from natural causes — specifically the failure of food sources. This sort of thing may have been at least partially instrumental in forcing them out of the region. At least, it seems clear that they were less common there by settlement times and that the newcomers quickly reduced those which still existed. What are taken to have been the last two sightings of native bears in East Texas occurred down in Hardin and Matagorda counties instead of farther north.[35] This seems significant as indirect confirmation of the explorers' testimony that bears were more numerous toward the coast than up in middle eastern Texas.

And the sad scenario ends there, because there are no native bears left in Texas. They were wiped out. And the worst of it is, such was done knowingly in a spirit of vengeance tinged with the sick gaiety of vandals wrecking wonderful things. The few reports of bears in East Texas in recent decades have been of individuals wandering over from Louisiana, where some Minnesota bears were released in the 1960s. And occasionally a poor Mexican bear fords the Rio Grande looking for the good life in the Big Bend of Texas, only to be dispatched to whatever bears' paradise there is by some modern Texan continuing the exterminating tradition of earlier Texans.

7

Wolves at the Door

One of the greatest certainties about the world our explorers say they found here in Texas is that there were wolves in it — and these not just scattered individuals but packs of them everywhere. We may as well get this matter of their presence in quantities which tax our imaginations straight before we try to learn what this meant to the other animals of natural Texas or to the pioneers.

One way to visualize the wolves of Texas as they were is to bracket the state with word pictures left by our explorers of these animals as they found them. Starting with the southeast corner, we can still experience a scene from 1835 through the eyes and ears of S. W. Cushing, who, in telling of a ride east of Galveston Bay in what is now Chambers County, wrote: ". . . mounting our horses, my new acquaintance taking the lead, we galloped off, taking a south-west direction, so as to strike the part of Galveston Bay at its intersection by Redfish bar, some eighteen or twenty miles from the island of Galveston. Nothing disturbed our midnight march save the howling of the wolves, who, startled from their propriety, made the welkin ring as they hurried away at our approach. . . . At the time of which I write they roamed the prairies in herds of thousands, judging from the uproar they made."[1]

Down the coast in present Calhoun and Victoria counties, Carl Hilmar Guenther drew the word-picture of wolves as they were there in 1851, as follows: "For thirty or forty miles [from Indianola] we saw nothing but the prairie — no water — no tree, nothing but tall grass two feet high growing out of fine black soil. . . . Deer were so wild no one could get nearer than 100 paces — but, so many wolves! The wolves are as numerous here as people in Germany. Any hour of the day you would meet a pack of from 200 to 300, and when night came they howled so no one could sleep."[2]

All the way down at the southern tip of Texas, Thomas D. Tennery wrote in his 1846 wartime diary, "September 16. — Today Mr. Hite rode up the river [from Camp Belknap] to see the country, and was much pleased with the trip though he found nothing but sandy ridges and wet overgrown prairie inhabited by wolves, armadillos and a large species of hare, besides cranes and countless numbers of the heron kind; also a species of eagle like the bald eagle but not so large."[3]

Going west along the southern border we pause for an 1857 word snapshot of canine things as they were in present Val Verde County in 1857, when John C. Reid wrote, "This was the favorite range of all kinds of Texas game: deer, antelope, wolf, prairie dogs, and mute rabbit, in the greatest abundance. . . . The third (wolf), of the several varieties, were always on hand, so that, when we could find nothing else, we fired at a wolf."[4]

Having made the very long trek out to old El Paso, we would have found wolves figuring quite largely in things at that outpost. John T. Hughes captured an 1846 episode, giving us the picture so graphically that we are able to not only see and hear it, but perhaps also to smell it 150 years later. He wrote: "Now, there are a great many wolves, which come down from the neighboring mountains, into the suburbs of El Paso, and kill the flocks when not penned in their folds, and also feed upon the offal about the shambles, and slaughter-pens. They kept up a dolorous serenade during the nights, and in many instances were so bold as almost to drive the sentinels from their posts. Oftentimes the sentinels were compelled to shoot them, in self-defense, as they would a prowling enemy. This would usually create a false alarm. On one occasion several beeves had been slaughtered in a fold, or corral, for the use of the army. During the night the scent of the offal attracted the wolves. A considerable number of them coming down from their lairs among the rocks, leaped into the corral, and feasted sumptuously. The walls of the corral were many feet higher on the inside than on the outside, so, at daydawn, when the wolves wished to retire, they could not repass the walls. The soldiers, therefore, in the morning, taking their sabers, went in amongst them, and, after much sport, killed them all. In such amusements did the soldiers delight."[5]

Edwin James was almost as far northwest as he could get and still be in what is now Texas when he found plenty of wolves and was kind enough to write about it. It was 1820, and he was apparently in what would now be extreme western Potter County when, as he put it, "We were glad to observe considerable numbers of wolves . . . as they afforded an almost certain indication of the proximity of herds of bisons."[6]

When cataloguing the animals his Red River expedition of 1806 encountered in northeast Texas and in adjacent Louisiana, Peter Custis wrote, "White wolves (I suppose the *Canis Mexicanus*) are said to be very numerous — They are perfectly white, except the feet and half of the legs. They are seen in large herds."[7]

So many wolves in all corners of the state should mean wolves overrunning all of it, and so, according to the pioneers, they were. Concerning south-central Texas, Fray Jose de Solis wrote way back in 1767, "In the woods between La Bahia and San Antonio there are a few lions and a great number of cattle, horses, deer, wolves, coyotes, rabbits, wildcats and boars."[8] Concerning the country along the lower Colorado River, Dr. Ferdinand Roemer wrote in 1849 that wolves were "very plentiful,"[9] and Bollaert wrote about the same time of "droves of wolves" in the same general area.[10]

Up in what is now Falls County in 1846, William McClintock reported "a gang of wolves,"[11] while A. W. Moore "saw many wolves," on up in present Ellis County in the same year.[12] Juan Brebel, who traveled up the Red River and on to Santa Fe in about 1765, was quoted by John Sibley as stating that, "there were innumerable quantities" of wolves in the whole area drained by the Red River.[13]

After traveling through parts of present Jeff Davis, Culberson and Hudspeth counties in 1857, John C. Reid equated the wolf population of trans-Pecos Texas with its most numerous species by writing, "Here, like the minutes of the day, we beheld coyotes (prairie wolf,) deer, and antelope."[14]

But perhaps the best way to indicate the huge numbers of wolves in early Texas is to note how they persisted and made themselves obvious around the early villages and towns. First hear them with Tennery when his unit was encamped just outside of the Mexican town of Camargo, directly across the Rio Grande from Rio Grande City, Texas, in 1846: "October 28. — As we have to be up all times of these nights we can hear the yelping of hundreds of prairie wolves in every direction, even in the very suburbs of the town, wolves, dogs and the crowing of cocks all forming a mingled noise not uncommon in the western villages of America."[15]

Now listen with Sister Mary Patrick and Sister Mary Joseph. It is February 1853, and the good sisters are not out in the wilderness but safe in their dormitory in the Ursaline Convent in the very heart of San Antonio. Here they write, "Now, we enjoy the company of some hundreds of wolves, who come from the interior to try if they can get anything good to eat, & such a funny noise as they make: one commencing, & all the others taking up the tone. Monseigneur told us that a poor Irishman being sent out by his master to seek for some of his cattle, had not gone far from the house when he heard a number of hoarse voices crying out: 'Catch him! catch him!' Such cries in a wild country, & at night terrified the poor man; but when he heard others in quite a different tone exclaim: 'Whip him well!' he ran back to his master, saying that he would never again be caught out of doors at night."[16]

Summaries of all this were made in the form of general statements by some early explorers. We look at two of them. Viktor Bracht wrote in 1848, "Every part of Texas has wolves in smaller or greater abundance, and I think that there are not less than six different kinds. . . . At night they approach in large packs near towns, close to the houses. . . ."[17] And A. A. Parker, as a result of his experiences on his trip through Texas, wrote in 1836 undoubtedly the most remarkable statement about wolves of all: "The wolves are the most numerous [of the animals of Texas]."[18]

I interject here an explorer's account of a happening which took place far north of Texas. It seems necessary to include it lest anyone think that statements about such huge numbers of wolves in the wilderness were limited to Texas and so were just Texas exaggerations. This is James Ohio Pattie writing in 1833, about an episode transpiring on the plains of the Platte River region in 1824. He says, "The following morning, we took a S.S.W. course, which led us from the stream, during this day's journey. Nothing occurred worthy of mention, except that we saw a great number of wolves, which had surrounded a small herd of buffalo cows and calves, and killed and eaten several. We dispersed them by firing on them. We judged, that there were at least a thousand. They were large and as white as sheep."[19]

We may as well stop and face it right here. The picture the explorers leave us is of dozens to hundreds of wolves at a time and place, multiplied by the whole expanse of Texas, preying upon the literally millions of grazers, from rabbits to deer, antelope, elk and buffalo, which they describe in the Texas they found. According to them the whole was a gigantic spread of predators and prey as teeming and yet balanced as the savannahs of Africa once were. In fact, the millions of buffaloes and deer our reporters tell of require the existence of hordes of wolves and other predators as surely as the opposite is true. So it seems we have a choice between only two alternatives: Either Texas was this immense park stocked with these incalculable populations of creatures, or *all* of our pioneers were hallucinators, compulsive liars or scheming deceivers. My job as writer is only to outline the explorer's world as clearly as possible. It is the reader's privilege to decide for himself — and for himself only — how valid it was, which means at one and the same time how many wolves there were and how honest our forebears were.

Each of us having decided, according to his own predilections, how many wolves there once were in Texas, logic would lead us to consider next the various kinds of wolves the explorers say they found here. We have seen that Bracht thought there were no less than six different kinds. This turns out to be conservative. All together those actually seeing them described more nearly a dozen different variations — white, red, black, gray and yellow ones, plus lobo, buffalo, timber, prairie wolves and coyotes. The task falls upon us to try to relate all of these and see how they square with scientists' categories.

The most impressive of the Texas wolves were clearly the white ones. And often these must have really been white. We have seen Custis saying that they were "perfectly white, except the feet and half the legs." Pattie put it: "They were large and as white as sheep." For a more detailed description of this animal we have Jean Louis Berlandier to thank. Writing up the story of his 1828 hunting expedition into the Hill Country, he said, ". . . a Comanche had killed a white lobo. . . . The white lobo (*Canis albescens*) of which we had spoken earlier was already in pieces by the time we saw it. The sole objective of the description which follows is for the knowledge of the travelers: The lobo's fur was completely white with patches of gray. The whiskers were also white. The ears were pointed and pure white. The vocal membrane, the extremity of the paws, and the palms of the feet were black. This leads one to believe it was not an albino. However, the eyes were not seen. The gray spots on the white tail were darker than on other parts of the body. This lobo is called *isa* by the Comanche. They believe it to be very fierce. The savages put much value on its fur."[20] Other writers stressed the huge size of this wolf.

For the most graphic account of these white wolves and their way of life I bring in R. M. Ballantyne and quote him at length. Although he does not specifically state his episodes took place in Texas — or where and when they did occur — and even though the form of his book is that of fiction, we know he spent some years in North America before 1848, and no one else has described these wolves in action so vividly. I include his words here even though they are gory, for three reasons: first because our imaginations, fed on televisions of friendly wolves, probably need for balance the shocks of the scenes, second because they are in such an obscure book that the chances of their being read otherwise are almost nil and third, because, as we shall see, other eyewitnesses confirm most of his observations.

He writes: ". . . the travelers came upon a wounded old buffalo which had evidently escaped from the Indians (for a couple of arrows were sticking in its side), only to fall a prey to his deadly enemies, the white wolves. These savage brutes hang on the skirts of the herds of buffaloes to attack and devour any one that may chance, from old age, or from being wounded, to linger behind the rest. The buffalo is tough and fierce, however, and fights so desperately that although surrounded by fifty or a hundred wolves, he keeps up the unequal combat for several days before he finally succumbs. The old bull that our travelers discovered had evidently been

An early illustration of wolves attacking a buffalo.

long engaged with his ferocious adversaries, for his limbs and flesh were torn in shreds in many places, and blood was streaming from his sides. Yet he had fought so gallantly that he had tossed and stamped to death dozens of the enemy. There could not have been fewer than fifty wolves round him; and they had just concluded another of many futile attacks, when the hunters came up, for they were ranged in a circle round their huge adversary — some lying down, some sitting on their haunches to rest, and others sneaking about, lolling out their red tongues and licking their chops as if impatient to renew the combat. The poor buffalo was nearly spent, and it was clear that a few hours more would see him torn to shreds and his bones picked clean."

If that scene isn't enough, our author adds another: "White wolves are quite distinct from the ordinary wolves that prowl through woods and plains in large packs. They are much larger, weighing sometimes as much as a hundred and thirty pounds; but they are comparatively scarce.... Their method of killing horses is very deliberate. Two wolves generally undertake the cold-blooded murder. They approach their victim with the most innocent-looking and frolicsome gambols, lying down and rolling about, and frisking playfully, until they think themselves near enough, when they make a simultaneous rush. The wolf which approaches in rear is the true assailant; the rush of the other is a mere feint; then both fasten on the poor horse's haunches and never let go till the sinews are cut and he is rolling on his side."[21]

To satisfy any who may doubt the veracity of Ballantyne's stories, and begging the pardon of sensitive readers, I include here a second description of the same predatory activity by these wolves. Although it is also describing an event seen north of Texas, it is by a very credible writer, was published in 1855, and the same animals as well as episodes were mentioned — although not so well described — in Texas.

David H. Coyner wrote: "June 5th. This afternoon something in motion was discovered on the prairie ahead of the company, but so far off, they were not able to determine what it was. As they approached it, Captain Williams, by the aid of a glass, ascertained that it was a band of wolves in full chase after a buffalo coming directly towards the party. As all were anxious to see the race, and how it would terminate, they placed themselves in a position not to be noticed very readily by the wolves, and, in a few minutes, they had a fair view of the whole affair. The buffalo proved to be a well grown young bull, in fine condition. There were about twelve wolves of the largest kind, and [they] must have had a long and tight race, as they seemed (both wolves and buffalo) very much fatigued. As they ran the wolves were close around the buffalo, snapping and snatching all the time; but they were observed not to seize and hold on like a dog. Their mode of taking the buffalo is to run them down; and when they are completely out of breath, by a constant worrying and snatching kept up by all hands, they drag their victim to the ground, and then fill themselves with his flesh, sometimes before he is entirely dead.

"Indeed in this case they seemed to feed upon their victim as they ran, for every thrust they made at him they took away a mouthful of his flesh, which they gulped as they ran, and by the time they had brought him to the ground, the flesh of his hind quarters was taken away to the bone. So eager were they in the chase, and so fierce was the contest, that they did not observe the company until they rode up within ten steps from them, and even then they did not appear to be much frightened, but scampered off a short distance and sat down and licked their lips, and waited with much impatience to be permitted to return to their hard-earned feast. The buffalo had suffered violence in every part. The tendons of his hind legs were cut asunder; the tuft of hair at the end of the tail was taken away, with part of the tail; pieces of hide and flesh, as large as a man's hand, were jerked out of his sides in several places; his ears were much torn, and in the battle he lost one of his eyes. Just before they succeeded in bringing him to the ground, one of the pack, a very large gray wolf, was seen to spring upon his back, tear out a mouthful of his hump, and then bound off. Having gratified their curiosity, the men withdrew, and the hungry pack in a moment set in, with fresh rapacity, tearing away and gulping the bloody flesh of their victim, that still faintly struggled for life.

"Captain Williams represents the wolves as being very numerous, and always to be seen hanging about the outskirts of a buffalo herd. They kill a great many calves, and any that are unable, from any untoward circumstances, to resist successfully their attacks, are sure to fall victims to their rapacity."[22]

These engines of destruction were the white wolves. We have seen that Custis called them *Canis Mexicanus*, while Berlandier called them *Canis albescens*. Audubon and Bachman, in their 1851-63 *Quadrupeds of North America*, wrote, "*Canus Lupus* Linn. White American Wolf. . . . The White Wolf is far the most common variety of the wolf tribe to be met with around Fort Union, on the prairies, and on the plains bordering the Yellow Stone river. . . . It is found along both sides of the Rocky mountains, to California on the west side and Arkansas on the east."[23]

What about the white wolves in Texas? Accounts of them are scattered across the northern part of the state. The most southerly one is that included in the "Report of the Post Surgeon at Fort Phantom Hill for 1852," which placed them at that time in present Jones County.[24]

In his summary of western American wolves, that champion of hunters, Richard Irving Dodge, wrote, "There is scarcely a portion of the prairie that can be traversed by the hunter on which he will not see wolves. These are of two kinds — The buffalo wolf, as tall as an ordinary greyhound, lean, gaunt, and hungry-looking; the prairie wolf (miscalled coyote on the middle and northern plains), about half-way in size between the fox and the buffalo wolf. The coyote proper I have never seen except in Texas and Mexico. It is a miserable little cur of an animal, scarcely larger than a fox."[25] After the bloody descriptions we have read of the large white wolves dragging down buffaloes and literally camping around their herds, can anyone doubt that the white and the buffalo wolves were the same large animals?

They had another name for a wolf in early Texas — the single word, "lobo." This is a harsh word, well-chosen to excite, even as the presence of the animals must have made the pioneers' skin crawl. Read the following, written by J. C. Duval in 1836, and watch for goose-bumps: "Audubon, who is a recognized authority upon the subject of birds, if not of beasts, told me that the lobo was the largest known species of wolf in the world, and certainly they are much larger than any [other] on the American continent. They resemble the hyena in form as much or more than they do that of the common wolf. Their howl is also very different, and when camping out alone on the prairies, it always seemed to me to be the most mournful, doleful and 'lonesome' sound I ever heard."[26]

It is a reminiscence written after our exploratory period and so not the direct evidence we like, but the following seems to further our understanding of the wolves. It was written by O. C. Fisher in his telling of the early days in the northern part of the Hill Country. He says, "The Llano valley settler of the sixties found the territory seething with big lobo wolves, as well as the smaller species of timber wolves and coyotes. A coarse, stentorian voice distinguished the lobo's howling from that of the smaller species of the same family. . . . The lobo feasted upon smaller animals, especially the rabbit, but fortified by a few of his brethren he took special delight in hamstringing a steer, or, single-handed, laying waste to a half-grown calf. One frontiersman tells of witnessing a huge steer being pulled down by four lobos. The victim bawled and fought furiously, but his attackers had weakened him by cutting into his ham-strings, and he was soon torn to pieces."[27]

Doesn't this sound like the same white wolves which had the same massive size and downed buffaloes with the same techniques? Remember also that we found Berlandier calling this animal "the white lobo," and that our records show the white wolf a northwestern form, with Audubon placing it as common around Yellowstone. Then read Bailey, who listed for Texas: "*Canis griseus* Gray wolf. Loafer; Lobo. Plains and mountains, mainly west of 100th meridian. Same as Colorado and Wyoming animals."[28] It seems clear that the explorers knew the huge, light-colored wolf which was the only one strong enough to down buffaloes and cattle by several names, among them white wolves, buffalo wolves, lobos and loafers. Under one or another of these names this wolf was reported down in Gillespie, Kerr and Kendall counties, placing it with certainty throughout the Hill Country, but no farther southeast into Texas.

Reported the most times in early Texas of any wolf was what the explorers usually called the black wolf. This would lead us to think that this was the most common wolf in the state. We are encouraged to believe this, for instance, by Fisher and by Colt, each of whom stated in the 1840s that this wolf "abounds in the country."[29] What was this dark wolf, and what was its role in the early scene?

We have seen that Bracht contrasted three main types of Texas wolves: "the very large ones with yellowish pelts, black ones of medium size," and "several small kinds." Mary Austin Holley wrote of the "large black wolf,"[30] as did both Colt and Fisher. It would appear that this dark wolf was intermediate between the little coyote and the massive northwestern white or lobo wolves. It was reported quite generally previous to 1860 throughout eastern Texas, the most westerly account of it being

An early artist's conception of various wolves, illustrating the difficulty when relying upon color for classification of wolves.

Prairie Wolf by Audubon

that of 1849 by Dr. Ferdinand Roemer from Comal County, west of New Braunfels.[31] Audubon and Bachman listed it as "*Canis Lupus* Linn Black American Wolf. We have heard of this variety in the northern part of Missouri, Louisiana, and the northern parts of Texas."[32]

Bailey, in his great 1905 work, gives us some clues which broaden our understanding of this but can also confuse us. He lists the black wolf, says it was found, "in timbered regions of east Texas," was reported as the "Large gray wolf" or "timber wolf," that, "only a minority were really black," that it, "may be the same as the wolf of Kentucky to North Carolina to Florida," and that although, "common years ago, now [in 1905] very rare or quite extinct," in Texas."[33]

This naturally turned me back to our explorers to see what they tell us about gray or timber wolves, and I met with surprises. Hasson, in his surgeon's report on Fort Phantom Hill cited before, calls the huge northwestern buffalo wolf the "big white or grey wolf." This identifying of the gray wolf with the white one was seconded by Dr. Roemer when he wrote from Fredericksburg in 1849, "During the night a large gray wolf (*Canis occidentalis* Richardson), called loafer by the American settler was killed by a settler. This wolf was so bold as to come up to the house to steal a piece of meat. Such wolves were found frequently near the city, but proved harmless to human beings here as well as in other parts of Texas."[34] And Bailey himself, only two pages from the passage quoted above where he said the black wolf of the timbered regions of East Texas was called the gray wolf wrote, "*Canis griseus* Gray wolf; loafer, Lobo. Plains and mountains mainly west of 100th meridian, same as Colorado and Wyoming animals."

Certainly the pioneers were often referring to the lobo or buffalo wolf when they wrote of gray ones. Dr. Roemer made that clear at Fredericksburg. Yet this same explorer wrote of a gray wolf far southeast of that northwestern wolf's range, and in so doing gave us the answer to wolf identification by color. He wrote from near present Columbus, Texas, on the lower Colorado River in 1849, "According to a custom of the country, viz. to sell or trade anything one possesses, the owner of the farm offered several wolf skins for sale. He had taken them from wolves recently caught in steel traps. The pelts were of various colors, one black, the other yellow, and still another grayish brown. The farmer informed us that such variation in color was quite common among the larger wolves. They were very plentiful in the forest surrounding his house and a number of hogs had been killed by them."[35]

There it is. The humble pioneer farmer should put everyone depending on wolf color to identify them to shame. The truth is that all wolves varied in color at that time, probably much more than today's few surviving wolves, based as they are on a narrow genetic base, do. The most that should be said about it is that there were trends. The explorers' picture seen in totality yields a huge northwestern wolf tending to be light in color, with individuals from almost pure white with only gray tips through yellowish — a natural color or from long-time effect of blood contact, who now knows? — to some darker ones. It then presents a slightly smaller eastern wolf tending to be dark-colored, with a few individuals really black, but with most varying through gray and brownish to some unknown limit of lightness. Then there were the small coyotes with their own variations. In all of these there were gray individuals, and no mention of a gray wolf should be taken to identify the individual as to which of the above forms it was unless accompanied by other characteristics.

The term "timber wolf" serves us no better, because the pioneers just didn't use it — at least not in their writing. I have found not one account of anything called a timber wolf in Texas before 1860. This is definitely an eastern term in no general use in the southwest until later.

But we have to deal with another term used often by the Texas pioneers. It is the term "prairie wolf," and it brings its own confusion, fatal as we shall see.

To jump right into it, we have already seen that the good authority, Richard Irving Dodge, states that in wolf kinds there were first the big buffalo wolf, second the "prairie wolf (mis-called coyote on the middle and northern plains), about half way in size between the fox and the buffalo wolf," and third, "the coyote proper, which I have never seen except in Texas and Mexico... a miserable little cur of an animal scarcely larger than a fox." This makes Dodge's prairie wolf seem to be the black wolf of the Texas explorers and the timber wolf of farther east. It is clearly stated not to be the coyote.

But no sooner have we read that than we notice Mary Austin Holley's 1836 statement, also already quoted, that, "The prairie wolf is common. This is a very small species of the wolf, very mischievous, but not so much to be feared as the large black wolf." Her prairie wolf is obviously not the same animal as Dodge's. What is it?

First in point of time to enlighten us is Josiah Gregg. Writing in his diary during September 1846, he says "Wolves abound, especially the *COYOTE* or *Prairie wolf;* and their almost continual howl heard at night even in the center of the town of San Antonio, strongly impresses us with the wilderness state of the country which surrounds us."[36] The term "prairie wolf" can also mean the coyote.

Audubon and Bachman made it more official, listing: "*Canis latrans* Say., Prairie wolf, Barking Wolf...."[37] The scientific name they use is that of the coyote. And Baird makes it perfectly clear in 1857, writing, "*Canis latrans* Say., Prairie Wolf, Coyote."[38]

The use of the term "prairie wolf" for both the large black or timber wolf and the little coyote can be cited over and over, so the point is that the term is an ambiguous one used to refer to at least two different forms, and that it is therefore a term useless unless accompanied by specific identifying characters or names. In the composite explorers' world there just wasn't a separate, identifiable prairie wolf.

With that out of the way we are left with only one more large Texas wolf, and it is one of the curiosities of history that this, a very elusive and really doubtful one, is the only one of them all for whose survival in Texas there are efforts being made today. This wolf still in question is the red wolf.

Audubon started it all by publishing the following in 1851: "*Canis lupus* Linn. Red Texan Wolf. In shape the red Texan Wolf resembles the common gray variety. It is more slender and lighter than the white wolf of the North West, and has a more cunning fox-like appearance.... This variety is by no means the only one found in Texas, where Wolves, black, white and gray are to be met with from time to time. We do not think, however, that this Red Wolf is an inhabitant of the more northerly prairies, or even of the lower Mississippi bottoms, and have, therefore, called him the Red Texas Wolf.... This variety of Wolf is traced from the northern parts of the State of Arkansas, southerly through Texas into Mexico."[39] Baird picked up on Audubon's statements, amplified them a little, and came out in 1857 with the following: "*Canis occidentalis* var. *rufus,* Red Wolf. According to the above authority [Audubon and Bachman], this is the most common variety of wolf in Texas. Its color is mixed red and black above, lighter beneath."[40]

And believe it or not, that's all there is from exploratory times concerning the famed Texas red wolf! This seems so significant, I repeat it. I have found no other mention of it by any explorer, pioneer or settler before 1860. In spite of all their accounts of white, black, gray and yellow wolves, no early Texan claimed to have seen a red one. And I am not the first to notice such an omission. Dan L. Flores, in his very thorough annotation of Peter Custis' 1806 accounts of his Red River expedition through Louisiana and Texas (in which Custis describes the very numerous white wolves he found there) remarks, "Interestingly, no mention is made of the only wolf now native to the area covered by the exploration, today's endangered red wolf (*C. niger gregoryi* Goldman). Evidently none were seen."[41]

I ask it cautiously because I do not know the answer, but if Custis' not mentioning the red wolf meant that his party did not see it, then does the fact that all of the several hundred Texas pioneers who wrote before 1860 did not mention this animal mean they never saw it — and does this mean it wasn't originally in Texas at all?

Parker Gillmore, as a result of his own experience hunting wolves in early times, summarized what he found in almost exactly the words we would use to express the essence of the explorers' pooled observations, so we quote him here: "There are certainly three distinct species of wolves on the American continent, many persons say more, but I am inclined to believe that from a desire to increase the fauna of a country, varieties are frequently transferred to the responsible places of species. My opportunities of studying the habits and appearance of the wolf have been very great; still although my ideas are not in accordance with Audubon and Bachman and other accepted naturalists, I have no hesitation in stating them.

"First, on account of the greater size and nearer resemblance of the animal to the European race, we will take the common familiarly called grey wolf. At one time it was scattered all over the North American continent to the Gulf of Mexico; but now, with few exceptions, is not to be found until the great prairies of the West or the slopes of the Rocky Mountains are reached, or the immense timber lands to the north of Canada entered. But still, although their habitat has become restricted, owing doubtless to difference of latitude — great varieties of colour are to be found among this species — but neither in habits, voice, nor shape are they in the least dissimilar; I am aware that at one time I possessed a different idea, but further experience and study of the subject caused me to change. . . . Thus what is generally called the grey wolf is one and the same race with the black, brown and white. . . . The two other species are the coyote and prairie wolf, both much smaller than the aforementioned species, in fact bearing the same relative position to the new world as the jackal does to the old. They are essentially prairie animals and invariably live in burrows, while the larger race, although found in the open country, is partial to forest, and generally sleeps in a nest or den upon the surface of the soil or in a crevice of the rocks."[42]

It is my aim here to gather, before all of their words are forgotten, the actual explorers' impressions of the Texas they found, to focus these into a coherent picture and to set this forth for any to see. It is not necessary for me to bring this image in line with "official" scientific nomenclature, nor could I ever be knowledgeable enough to do this across the whole spectrum of plants and animals. However, may I venture that authorities who list *Canis lupus* as America's one homogeneous large wolf have failed to recognize the two larger wolves insisted upon by the explorers? These would seem to match well with the two forms sometimes proposed, *C. lupus nubilus*, the Great Plains wolf, and *C. lupus lycaon*, the eastern timber wolf. On the other hand, *C. rufus* or *C. niger gregoryi*, the so-called red wolf, does not appear in the explorers' scene at all. But lurking just out of sight — which is typical for this most elusive animal — in the early accounts has been *C. latrans*, the coyote.

Now we must try to get this coyote to sit for its portrait as sketched in the explorers' word-pictures. And I think we are in for surprises played upon us by the coyote. At least I was. Before compiling my sources I had assumed that most of the wolves in early Texas were little coyotes, with a sprinkling of big, bad wolves as rarities here and there in the wildest places. But according to our exploring fathers, I had it dead wrong.

To begin with, I have 101 references written before 1860 to wolves in early Texas, and only 13 of these turn out to be coyotes. Some more of them may have been coyotes loosely called wolves, but by any sophisticated manipulation of statistics anyone has shown me, a majority of the packs and herds and bunches of wolves our pioneers reported in wilderness Texas still turn out to be made up of large wolves instead of coyotes.

Not only that, our explorers did not report coyotes over all of Texas. Most of the pre-1860 reports of them were from deep South Texas, and incidentally, many of these list wolves and coyotes as both present, showing that their authors were being very specific in their reports.[43]

Looking northward, we have seen that Gregg placed coyotes in quantity almost in the heart of San Antonio. Ehrenberg, describing the military camps just outside San Antonio in 1835, wrote: "When we walked beyond the fields adjacent to the two camps, we came upon large flocks of blackbirds seeking food on the ground. . . . Large bands of buzzards hovered also over the fields where we killed our cattle. These birds, as well as wolves and coyotes, came to feed on the offal of the slaughtered animals."[44]

When probably in northern Guadalupe County in that same year, Ehrenberg placed coyotes there, confirmed that large wolves could be present at the same time, and described the contrasting sounds made by the two in terms any who have ever heard them would have to affirm: "Suddenly, piercing the unbroken silence of the night, a clear sound like a dog's bark rang out, striking at times so hideous a note that it sent cold shivers down our spines. A second and some what deeper voice broke in. After a few moments a third, then a fourth, a hollow bass, was heard. Several minutes later thousands of them mingled in a deafening chorus. The performers of this frightful serenade were the coyotes. Soon the wolves took their turn and swelled with their deep howls the shrill dog-like clamor of the coyotes."[45]

The next surprise is that there is not one pre-1860 report of a coyote in north-central Texas! Even Audubon and Bachman state that the specimen they used for their description was obtained at San Antonio.[46] In order to find more coyotes — if we trust the failure of our explorers to mention them there to mean they weren't in north-central Texas — we would have had to go either east or west from San Antonio.

There are several accounts of coyotes in southeast Texas. The earliest and most northerly of these is that written by Captain Pages in describing the country encountered in what would now be Nacogdoches, San Augustine and Sabine counties of Texas and on into adjacent Louisiana. He wrote in 1767, "In our progress through this country we frequently met with a species of roe-buck, and a meager race of wolves, or wild dogs, whose barking, however, is very different from that of the same kind of animal in Europe."[47] On the west, there are early accounts of coyotes into trans-Pecos Texas, as witness the passage already quoted from John C. Reid about the numerous coyotes they found in Jeff Davis, southwest Culberson and southeast Hudspeth counties in 1857.

The complete absence of the coyote from all of the surviving written accounts left by the many pioneers who criss-crossed early North Texas which I can locate stands as one of the most surprising findings to come out of my readings. To have to assume that the coyote was not in North Texas before some post-1860 date is difficult, particularly since Audubon and Bachman stated that they had seen the species up on the Missouri and Yellowstone rivers and Lewis and Clark had found in that north country what they called foxes until they shot one and decided it was some kind of little wolf — which sounds like a coyote. Is this a case where all of our explorers omitted a significant animal species from a whole region where it actually ranged in numbers?

But wait — there is more to be said. Col. Richard Dodge, who hunted over most of the Great Plains in early times and is considered to be perhaps the top authority on the game of that region in that time, wrote, "The coyote proper I have never seen except in Texas and Mexico."[48]

That this great hunter, after pursuing everything huntable through Santa Fe Trail country and in future Oklahoma, states that he had never seen a coyote there is most remarkable. But it makes more plausible the testimony — admittedly only an unprovable negative — of our Texas explorers that the coyote wasn't originally in north-central Texas.

Doesn't this mesh with other facts as well? For instance, the coyote is in a special sense a Mexican animal. Even its name is a Spanish corruption of *coyotl*, the Aztec name for it. Isn't the fact that this animal, of all the significant species, is the one carrying a Spanish name an indication that explorers met with it only after they had gotten down into Spanish territory?

On the other side, there is evidence that the coyote has been, along with such as the armadillo, moving north and east since the exploratory period, which would explain its current widespread presence.[49] The extension of its range is best seen on its edge and where the movement has been most recent. For instance, prior to 1930 coyotes were absent from most of Arkansas. Paradiso was able to use this fact to guarantee that wolf specimens collected in that state before 1930 were not hybrids. But by 1967 coyotes had spread farther over Arkansas.[50] It may be too late for anyone to find direct evidence to confirm or deny the intimations of those who were there at the time that while you could be anywhere from the Sabine to the Rio Grande you had to be in Spanish South Texas to see or hear the entertaining little coyote in its original range, but that is the gist of the early accounts.

Entertaining is perhaps the best word to use in describing the coyote, and it also appears to be the kindest, since most pioneers spoke of this animal in deprecatory terms. Colonel Dodge, for instance, called it "a miserable little cur of an animal."

I do not think the piece called "The Coyote" comes from as far back as our exploratory period, nor do I know the identity of its author. It only appeared in 1949 as copied from something called "The Texas Siftings." But I quote from it here not only to rescue from oblivion undoubtedly the wittiest description of the coyote, but to let the reader enjoy one passage giving us an actual sense of the animal's spirit as well as of his appearance: "The cayotte is about two-thirds the size of a yellow dog and looks like a second-hand wolf in straightened circumstances. He bears about the same relation to the genuine wolf that the buzzard does to the eagle, or that a chicken thief does to a modern bank cashier. He has a perpetual air of being ashamed of himself, or of something he has done. As you catch a glimpse of him, trotting away from one mott of timber to another, looking back over his ears, and with his tail curled around his left leg, he looks as if he were aware that the police had a clue to his whereabouts, and were working up his case. No one ever saw a fat cayotte. You may catch a young one, civilize him as much as you can, feed him on canned groceries, and put a brass collar on him, but his ribs will still be his most prominent feature, and at the first favorable opportunity he will voluntarily and ungratefully leave your hospitable roof, and from choice, become a roving vagabond on the prairie, living on carrion and sharing his meal with the buzzard."[51]

The coyote's most famed accomplishment, endearing or infuriating according to how you react to it, is its singing — if you choose to call it that. There must be nothing else in the world quite like it. Reread the passage by the Ursaline sisters, already quoted, about the sound of this in old San Antonio and seriously imagine the effect. Then let your imagination be led along by the humorous description of the coyote's concert written by the unknown author of "The Cayotte," and the combination should give you who have never heard it some conception of the coyote's tragicomic audio production. This strongly Texas author says, "The cayotte has a small head and fox-like ears, but the biggest end of him is his voice. The mellifluous silvertoned euphony of one of his nocturnal overtures would scare a monkey off a hand organ, and make an Italian opera singer hang himself with envy.... When he slinks up, and, seating himself in the twilight of a campfire on the prairie, opens out with a canticle and runs up the scale — starting with a diminuendo whine, throwing in a staccato howl — the sonorific outburst terrifies the Genus of Acoustice, and makes the welkin ring until it cracks itself and has to be carried off and repaired.... Suddenly the air is alive with direful yells, shrieks and howls, as if all the Indians on the American continent had been turned loose.... One coyote at night can make enough noise to induce the inexperienced traveler to believe that there are at least fifty of them in the immediate neighborhood. If a cayotte were assayed, we venture to predict that he would be found to consist of one part wolf and nine parts vocal ability. The only time when the voice of the cayotte, as one of the resources of Texas, has any value, is when it is used to take the conceit out of some smart stranger from the Eastern States. The acclimated Texan induces the stranger to go with him in pursuit of game, and to camp out on the prairie or in the woods, and he enjoys the stranger's fear when he hears the cayottes for the first time as they howl around the camp-fire in 'the dead waste and middle of the night.' It is difficult to convince a stranger that the cayotte will not make a meal of him and eat his horse and baggage for desert. In fact, it is not the policy of the Texan to convince the stranger."

This lands us squarely in the middle of the battlefield where the no-holds-barred fight between humans over the benign versus rapacious role of the coyote — and wolves in general — has been going on for 300 years at least while coyotes cheer us on with their grins and yelps. I don't know which side this will make happiest, but concerning the coyote singled out from the wolves and regarded separately there is no pioneer's stated opinion. We have found not one pre-1860 word in which any Texan either condemned coyotes as predators on domestic animals or lauded them as not. They were only marveled at for their cunning, derided for their cowardice, praised or berated for their music, mentioned in passing, but they were never granted enough importance to be called either friend of man or branded as enemy of him or his domestic animals. The explorers did not stand for either side of the love-hate coyote battle.

What the early Texans did concern themselves with was wolves. But here we have an ambiguity. When a pioneer makes a general statement about wolves, we can never know whether he is including coyotes or not except indirectly by checking whether the location of his experience falls within the otherwise indicated range of the coyote. Actions attributed to Texas wolves in general may have been perpetrated by any of the wolf races but can be pinned on no one of them. For instance, when Steinert writes in 1849, "Sheep raising has also started. In the western parts [of Texas] I only found some here and there, but in the east, in the country around Washington [on the Brazos], I saw a considerable flock of them. Here, too, wolves attack the sheep, and for that reason herdsmen are required,"[52] we have no clue as to which wolves were the killers. When A. A. Parker writes in 1836, "The bears catch the full grown hogs, and the wolves take the pigs,"[53] we learn that some wolves kill pigs, but not specifically whether the coyote does this or not. When Arthur Ikin writes in 1841, "Sheep in the upper country do very well, but require folding, not being so well able to protect themselves from the wolves and other beasts of prey, as are the horned cattle,"[54] we have a little more in the way of clues. Since Ikin is writing about sheep in the "upper country" of Texas and we have reason to doubt that there were coyotes in northern Texas, we can hardly use his statement to indict coyotes as sheep killers.

But these two statements bring up a more important point. It should be noticed that they give herding and folding the sheep as mandatory. No pioneer ever dreamed of ranching untended, unprotected sheep in the wilderness teeming with predators that was early Texas. The Spanish throughout the west always tended their sheep and taught the Indians to do the same. We have seen how the *Comancheros* came into the Panhandle of Texas and established their Spanish villages around their sheepfolds long before the modern ranching system

with untended cattle was begun there. George Kendall, the very father of sheepmen in Central Texas, who had over 2,000 ewes in what is now Kendall County by 1860, imported European shepherds especially to protect his sheep. And in that region, according to all evidence then overrun by droves of both large and small wolves, the use of expert herders paid off handsomely, for Kendall wrote after that winter, "Total number of deaths in my flocks, since 1st November, exactly fourteen: — five puny sheep killed by wolves; three drowned; two killed by accident; and four died from cold or poverty, call it what you will."[55]

The point is that Kendall didn't hire hunters to kill off all predators so his sheep could graze all day and laze all night unprotected in the farthest pasture while he and his hands did other things all day and slept at night. He and his protected sheep coexisted with the wildlife — predators included — instead of adopting the all too typical modern rancher's philosophy that anything which interferes with himself and his free-ranging animals should be exterminated. The modern rancher's vendetta against the coyote is just not in the early pioneer's pictures. Instead we have already seen Tennery describing the "large flocks of goats" at 1846 Camargo, where the night was at the same time full of "the yelping of hundreds of prairie wolves in every direction."

There is a very interesting factor which it would seem necessary to introduce here in order to properly evaluate the place of coyotes in pioneer affairs. The pioneers picture coyotes as very small, cowardly varmints fit to be the butts of their jokes but otherwise largely ignored, while more recent ranchers and farmers take them too seriously to joke about and as aggressive and powerful enough to be appropriate targets of real fear, anger and warfare measures. Are the pioneer and modern Texans relating to the same animal? It may be that they are not.

This idea comes directly from scientific studies. First we have Audubon and Bachman's statement which is ripe with possibilities. They wrote, "The common wolf is not unfrequently met with in company with the Prairie wolf.... We saw hybrids, the offspring of the wolf and the cur dog, and also their mixed broods."[56] With this to alert us we find very suggestive the opinions of a member of the U.S. Division of Wildlife Research published in 1968. John L. Paradiso wrote as a result of his research: "When the post-1960 series of canids from east Texas was compared with the pre-1930 sample of the red wolf and the sample of the coyote from west Texas, it was found that the post-1960 series from east Texas spanned the size gap between red wolf and coyote, with every intermediate size represented. . . . The east Texas canids discussed herein may tentatively be regarded in Goldman's taxonomic framework, as an interbreeding population of red wolf and coyote."[57]

This idea of hybridization bears fruit in important possibilities. If the coyote and a wolf could interbreed in East Texas to produce a whole population with intermediate characteristics, what could these hybrids be but super coyotes larger, more aggressively wolf-like and more dangerous to domestic animals than the original little coyote clown? And if this was possible, then why couldn't the coyote interbreed in other places and with other wolves or even with any others of the dog tribe genetically compatible with wolves? If any of this is correct then today's coyote hybrid would be a different, more worrisome predator than the pioneer's object of ridicule, and much would be explained.

With such encouragement, I do not hesitate to add my own experience. It is firsthand and eyewitness. Albeit not pioneer, I grew up on the western prairie. Many a night I was kept awake by coyotes' concerts — they often awakened me but never lulled me to sleep. On many of those same nights our neighbor had unprotected sheep in his pasture, these unharmed by the coyotes which must have been vocalizing near them. No one in our neighborhood entertained the idea of the coyotes being any danger to sheep. The only thing I knew of which feared the coyotes was our yard dog, which happened to be a large collie. On warm summer nights when they serenaded he would push against our screen door trying to get in, and it would rattle with his fearful trembling at the sound of the coyotes out there. But then he was replaced with another dog. This one was a male German shepherd. And he didn't quail at the sounds of the coyotes. In fact, as I grew older and began coming home late at night, several times my headlights, in sweeping across the yard, spotlighted our dog and coyotes socializing. We sometimes joked about our dog being more of a wolf than the coyotes were.

Not long after this our sheep-producing neighbor had some sheep killed by predators. This caused some consternation because it was a new thing for our community. When sheep continued to be killed over a period of time, there was much speculation about what could be attacking them. Before long the ever-present coyotes were blamed for going bad.

This prompted the hunters from far and near to organize a major coyote hunt complete with trained greyhounds and cross-country chases. This hunt yielded, together with several ordinary little coyotes, several animals larger, much more formidable than the coyotes, and most puzzling. Experienced coyote hunters were sure they weren't ordinary coyotes, and some thought they were young wolves. I remember an uncle of mine saying aside to my father that these things looked an awfully lot like our German shepherd, but nothing came of that. With those animals eliminated things went back to normal around there, with carefree sheep and an occasional coyote chorus. But I remembered our dog and the coyotes caught partying right in our yard, and I have always been fairly sure that those killer animals were a litter of dangerous half coyote-half German shepherds.

From such youthful experiences I have never been able to believe that actual, original little coyotes killed sheep. But neither did I have any explanation for my rancher friends who claimed modern coyotes do. However, now with scientific evidence that many if not all East Texas individuals are not true coyotes but larger, wolf-coyote hybrids to reinforce my own experiences, I have an explanation for the modern situation. I believe that the actual cur-like, scavenging little rascal that was the coyote our forefathers considered a joke is mostly — if not entirely — lost by hybridization with wolves and with the more wolf-like of domestic dogs. I believe that this has produced a larger, more aggressive set of animals — to which our German shepherd almost contributed some very powerful genes — now ranging widely, called coyotes by everyone, and perpetrating the atrocities the true coyotes our ancestors almost ignored could never have been capable of. If I am correct, our explorers' word-pictures of the animals are doubly important, for the true coyote may otherwise be as forever lost as the world's original dog.

When it came to predation then, settlers in the world of the Texas explorers faced the same three levels of wolves as we have already outlined. In at least the western part of the state they met with the huge lobo or buffalo wolves, predators *par excellence* which could, in groups, even pull down strong steers. Throughout at least the eastern half of the state there were the somewhat smaller timber wolves called everything else but that in Texas. These were death to deer fawns, some calves, many pigs, unprotected sheep and whatever else they could overpower. Then limited to South Texas was the coyote, small, furtive, living by stealth and scavenging instead of by assaulting anything of any size. All of these were actually scavengers as much as predators, classed with the buzzards in some accounts already quoted and for this reason sometimes called jackals by those experiencing them.[58]

The red wolf tries to creep into the primal Texas picture, but it is only on the strength of Audubon's one statement that it can claim even a dubious place there at all. His statement that it ranged into Mexico may mean that it was the so-called Mexican wolf, but even this has never been certain. When Baird picked up on this questionable form he did it very cautiously, and when he treated it as a valid scientific taxon he was very careful to credit his decision directly to Audubon, as though attempting to relieve himself of the primary responsibility for it. Audubon's picture of the red wolf may be a beautiful masterpiece to hang in Texas galleries, but it remains as dangerous to erect wolf species as it is petunia species on color alone.

Yet another question arises out of the wolves' predatory nature. How did the explorers who rode and walked all over the wilderness, camped in the open and often slept on the ground, protect themselves from these wolves which had to often be surrounding them in droves, usually shadowing them closely, with repeated opportunities to jump them? The answer does not go well with our imaginings of the horribly dangerous wolf, but it is an answer undisputed among the explorers.

Edward Smith, quoting the verbal communications of "Dr. Matthews . . . residing upon Colonel Reily's land, and a most intelligent man and farmer," wrote in 1849, "He has resided in Hopkins county during fourteen years. Bears and wolves exist there, and sometimes steal his hogs. . . . Nobody feared them and they annoyed the settlers less than in Tennessee."[59]

The unconcern with which knowing explorers regarded wolves is best shown by such accounts as the following. Imagine the plight of W. Steinert traveling alone through rain-soaked parts of future Guadalupe County in 1849, and his coolness which belied any fear of wolves. He wrote: "Soon I had traveled the six miles to Mill Creek, but here again I had a difficult problem. The creek was up higher and the current faster than it was in Natchez Creek. It was almost nighttime, and I had not taken along any food. I was discouraged, got off my horse and let him graze, then I wrapped myself up in my blanket and lay down on my saddle. It was cloudy and new rainstorms were threatening. Wolves, smaller than those in Poland, howled nearby incessantly, but I soon fell asleep."[60]

Such behavior was not unusual. Witness the lack of fear shown by Frederick Julius Conrad Tips and a companion. The two were traveling toward San Antonio, also in 1849, when they slept on the open prairie. Tips recounted, "During the night we were awakened several times by the howl of wolves. The first time we listened attentively to hear if the sound was coming nearer or going further. Later, we took no more notice." Some might argue that they feared the wolves so little because of being heavily armed and prepared to defend themselves, but the passage continues, "The country between Coleta and San Antonio is romantic but sparsely populated, and we often saw large herds of stags and deer. These animals were often so tame that they accompanied the wagon within a short distance and then stood still. Many times Louis and I had itchy fingers and were vexed that we did not have guns with us."[61]

Since the fact of American wolves being so harmless to man that travelers would sleep among them unprotected and unarmed is so opposed to our myths about them, here is another early statement to substantiate it. The author of this passage is anonymous, but he wrote a book on Texas in 1837, and he wrote of "the wolves, which prowl over the country in great numbers and whose howl is often the only sound to break the stillness of night, as the traveler rides over the prairie or lays himself down upon the green earth to sleep."[62]

David Coyner was writing about experiences north of Texas, but he wrote before 1855, and he reported an instance very significant here as an example of wolves not harming a human in the most favorable situation for an attack. Concerning the wolves in the ruthless wilderness, Coyner wrote, "They frequently get together in considerable gangs, and when emboldened by numbers, and espe-

Red Texas Wolf by Audubon

cially when infuriated by hunger, dreadful is the fate of anything that crosses their path." This is just the sort of unqualified and extreme statement which has probably prompted our fear of even extinct wolves. Yet the same author who wrote that wrote in detail about an episode which would prove that the human being should be excepted from such a statement.

He wrote about a hunter named Carson who left his party to ride off across the prairie in hot pursuit of a large buffalo. After they were several miles away from his party and out of their sight, the buffalo suddenly attacked, seriously injuring the horse, but then ran off. Carson was left alone and lost on the prairie. Coyner wrote, "His horse was so badly injured, that he abandoned him and wandered about, when he crept into a hazel patch, where he slept until morning without anything to disturb his rest except several bruises he received in the fall from his horse."

The man was found the next morning where he was sitting exhausted on the prairie. Coyner completed the account by writing, "As they returned to the camp, they passed his unfortunate house. He was dead, and a band of hungry wolves had already found his carcass and were greedily snatching and gulping his flesh. In fact, the men thought the wounded horse had been killed by the wolves, as they were very numerous and fierce, and would attack a horse as soon as anything else, especially if they were incited by the smell of blood. They had even committed violence upon Carson's saddle, which he had removed from his horse, and left on the prairie."[63] The point is that the wolves, present in numbers and hungry enough to attack a wounded horse and to attempt to eat the leather of a saddle, did not attack a lone, defenseless man, even when sleeping. Nor is there mentioned any surprise on the part of the company at their companion's immunity from attack.

The record is consistent. Although neophytes in the wilderness, such as the newly arrived in Texas Abbe Domenech, usually registered abject fear of wolves, if they stayed any length of time experience soon taught them freedom from this fear and, as did the seasoned wilderness-traveling Abbe, they came to ignore the wolves. This was part of becoming a real Texan instead of a tenderfoot. So doesn't it seem that the wolf-dread which even we who have never seen a wolf have is prompted by experiences of our forefathers with the wolves of northern Europe? Or that our hair automatically rising at the mere thought of wolves is a leftover from our ancient ancestors, experiences with the giant wolves of prehistoric times instead of from any bodily threat from American wolves?

Wolves were clearly everywhere in Texas from the beginning of the exploratory period to its end. There is no evidence in the explorers' writings of any important change in them or their numbers before 1860, but there is evidence of changes in the way people in Texas at the beginning and at the end of this period treated the wolves.

The Indians had obviously lived with wolves throughout their existence in Texas. While they undoubtedly hunted them to some extent, there is no evidence that they relied on wolves for any necessities or that they made any attempt to eliminate them from their surroundings. The only explorers' statement I have found detailing any relationship between Indians and wolves comes from the beginning of Texas' historical era. The Talon brothers testified in 1685 that, "There will be presently a quantity of runaway or wild pigs in all the country, the French having released some that had already marvelously reproduced by the time. . . . And the savages do not eat them, saying that they are the dogs of the French, which they imagined because they have not known other dogs than the wolves which they take when very small, tame them and raise them for the hunt."[64]

Throughout the main part of the 200 or so years of Texas exploration, wolves were recited to be almost ever-present, sometimes described or railed at as pests, but largely ignored except to be wondered at. However, by the end of the period a deadly new attitude toward them had developed. Not only do we have John C. Reid's account already quoted of an 1857 expedition shooting wolves merely because they could find nothing else to fire at, but we have him writing that by that time, "Wolves are often poisoned, the drug having first poisoned a piece of fresh meat, or a carcass, which is then placed in their path; hunted with dogs; caught in pits and dead-falls, and shot whenever opportunity offers. The chase is but little resorted to here. . . . A lover of this sport could enjoy himself no where better than here."[65]

The campaign of extermination is practically over. It is probable that the true Texas wolves are all gone forever. Certainly the Texas lobos and the timber wolves are long-gone. There are lots of creatures called coyotes in Texas, but we have already seen that many of them responsible for most of that species' horrible reputation are actually hybrids with dogs, which instead of being coyotes are much more vicious predators. David Schmidly recently stated this problem with the present-day coyotes very clearly, writing, "In eastern Texas, the coyote may be difficult to distinguish from the red wolf and certain breeds of dogs. Hybrids have been reported between the coyote and the red wolf as well as between each of these species and the domestic dog."[66] I think it would be hard to prove that there are any full-blooded coyotes in the state today.

That leaves us with perhaps a few animals called red wolves and a drive to protect them as our native wolves. But we have seen that the red wolf was always a doubtful species at best, and now it is further degraded. Over thirty years ago, William B. Davis wrote, "All of the so-called red wolves I have examined from eastern Texas have proven to be large coyotes. Consequently, it appears that in Texas, red wolves are now restricted to the Gulf Coast counties and are on the verge of extinction."[67] About ten years ago, Schmidly wrote, "The genetic integrity of red wolves has been seriously threatened by hybridization with coyotes. . . . Man also played a major role in bringing about the decline of the red wolf. . . . These factors, together with the expansion of the Houston metropolis, have virtually eliminated the last remaining red wolf populations."[68]

Whether we can assuage our guilt before wolves by allowing a few token wolf-dogs to survive in some unneeded corner of this state, which should be big enough for everything, is the question for today.

8

Texas Cats

Any picture of natural Texas making a claim to being realistic has to portray the state as having been the mother den of most U.S. cats. While it probably wasn't the primary birthplace of any of this hemisphere's cats, it surely functioned as a pleasant extension of their original ranges and an acceptable home for most of them. Not only that, its thickets and forests, swamps and mountains must have provided a broad and at the same time covert highway north for those tropical and subtropical felines which could tolerate the more temperate zones. Among the U.S. cats only the lynxes don't appear to trace back through Texas to the tropics. Thought to have been northern in origin, these, in the form of the bobcat, seem to have made a home of most of Texas and to have used it as their route on south into Mexico.

The claim of Texas to have originally had more species of cats, as well as more individual felines than any other state, therefore appears legitimate. However, it hardly behooves Texans to boast too loudly about members of their natural community which they extirpated so rapidly and so ruthlessly as we did these. It would be more becoming for us, while we are agitating for the salvation of another continent's cheetahs or leopards, to dwell upon the cats we once had — some of which could still be saved if we really valued them. So we turn to what our explorer-pioneers tell us about the cats in primeval Texas.

THE JAGUAR

Not common in any sense of the word, but certainly the most spectacular of Texas native cats was the beautiful and mighty jaguar. Attaining a record length of seven and a half feet from the tip of its nose to the tip of its rather short tail, the jaguar's body was more compact than those of the other Texas cats, enabling it to have attained a record weight of 251 pounds. Nor did this monster have any drabness in its appearance. It was one of the dandys of the wilderness, the ground color of its fine coat buff or tan shading to whitish on its chest, the whole body covered with blue-black spots, these solid on the extremities but larger and with light centers on the sides of the torso and forming irregular bulls-eyes along the back. Viktor Bracht stated in 1847, as though expecting no argument about it, that "the handsomest native animal is the spotted jaguar."[1]

With its short ears and massive, blocky head on a stocky body, the shape and bearing of this animal was closer to that of the old world's tigers than to other cats, while its spots reminded one more of the other hemisphere's leopards. It fell in between those two in size as well, being smaller than the Bengal tiger and larger than the true leopards. The result when explorers from that other hemisphere came upon this American cat was the usual confusion of names. Francis Moore, Jr., illustrates this, having written in 1840, "A species of tiger is found in the western part [of Texas], different from the cougar or catamount. It is spotted, and resembles the Bengal tiger in almost every respect, but is smaller. It is about the size of the catamount, and is probably allied to the Jaguar of South America."[2]

This Texas cat was not only related to the jaguar ranging all the way down to Patagonia, but was that same feline — Linnaeus' *Felis onca*. Subspecies of this wide-ranging species have been described, but we need not concern ourselves with

The Jaguar by Audubon

them. The original name for this American cat was the Indian word *jaguara*, said to mean "carnivore that overcomes its prey at a single bound."[3] We have seen that Bracht used this name, as did the anonymous writer of 1846,[4] Ullrich in 1860,[5] Audubon,[6] and others.

I must pause to mention here that some, doubting the wide range of the jaguars in early Texas, have interpreted all accounts of tigers in upper Texas as merely references to the common cougars. Dan Flores, for instance, goes so far as to state that "most American naturalists of the period routinely employed 'Tyger' to refer to the cougar."[7] It is true that Custis, whose catalogue of Red River animals Flores was annotating, did call *Felis concolor* the Tyger, but he may stand alone among Texas explorers in doing this. While there are some passages mentioning the tiger in which, for lack of detail, it is impossible to know what cat was meant, I have found no other Texas explorer who can actually be demonstrated to have been so illogical as to have called a Mexican lion a tiger.

I have been careful to base my conclusions on only the explorers' statements in which there can be no ambiguity on this point. For instance, we can know the Talon brothers, in their official report of 1685, did not mean mountain lions when they said tigers because they list lions and tigers in the same sentence as two different entities.[8] Moore, in his passage quoted above, says his tiger is spotted and contrasts its size with that of the catamount. We can be assured jaguars were present when the Abbe Domenech, camped just west of San Antonio in 1848, wrote of "panthers and tiger-cats" there,[9] or Dr. Joseph E. Field wrote in 1836 about, "A beast of prey, resembling the tiger of Africa."[10] Lindheimer made the distinction clear when he wrote from Mexico that "Lions (without mane) and tigers are not infrequent here (3 tigers were slain here the day before we arrived)."[11] Bracht was perfectly clear in writing about the two, using "the beautifully spotted American tiger, or jaguar," and "the American lion, puma, panther, or cougar," to describe them.[12] And Spencer Baird, in his 1857 Railroad Reports, listed "the American Panther" and "The Jaguar, or American Tiger," with no indecisiveness.[13]

The Texas explorers might be much more quickly pardoned if they confused things in the other direction by calling the spotted jaguar a leopard than for their confusing it with a drab-colored lion. If they did this it would leave us uncertain whether passages containing the term "leopard" meant the jaguar or the also spotted Texas cat we now call the ocelot. Audubon did venture that while the animal was known by Mexicans as the "Mexican tiger" it was known by the Americans as the "Leopard,"[14] but I have watched carefully for passages where this usage is proved by internal evidence, without finding any. Instead I have found such passages as Almonte's of 1835, in which his list of the animals of "the lower section of the Brazos" includes "tigers" and "leopards," the two recognized separately.[15] And the Pereda land title, written up and filed in 1807, lists as animals present on that part of present Zapata County as "tigers, leopards, wolves. . . ."[16] I believe that explorers who survived to write about their adventures could hardly have been so unobservant and careless that they misidentified the large animals they met up with in the forests. I have not used any passages concerning leopards as evidence about jaguars.

This leaves plenty of unequivocal accounts to give us a picture of the jaguar in early Texas. And the picture we get is of this magnificent animal appearing rarely, but when it did, fulfilling very well the refrain, "Tiger, tiger, burning bright . . ." in the shadowy forests of the Texas that was. This creature, spotted as though disdaining camouflage to broadcast sharp warnings and challenges, must have been an unforgettable vision to any who met up with it in its wilderness.

But apparently few saw this apparition materialize before them. One pioneer after another repeated that the jaguar was rare. Bracht, for instance, wrote in 1847, "unfortunately, it is very rare. I have seen only three skins, and high prices were paid for these."[17] But Audubon was not so certain of this, writing in 1854, "This species is known to exist in Texas, and in a few localities is not very rare, although it is far from being abundant throughout the state."[18] What appears to be a small discrepancy may well be explained by the retiring habits of this cat. Audubon described these as follows: ". . . it is owing, perhaps to his being nocturnal in his habits to a great extent, that he seldom issues from the deep swamps or the almost impenetrable thickets or jungles of thorny shrubs, vines, and tangled vegetation which compose the chaparrals of Texas and Mexico."[19] Ben Tinker confirmed this recently: "The jaguar is a nocturnal beast and spends the daylight hours among crags and caves or in vine-covered trees, where its keen sense of hearing and smell warns of danger."[20]

If the jaguar was secretly present wherever within its range there were daytime hiding places and nighttime prey, then where within Texas was its range? We know it still lives in Mexico, and there is no question that it used to come up into adjacent Texas. There are numerous testimonies to its presence all through the exploratory period in the Rio Grande Valley. There are also statements about its early presence on the coastal plains. Domenech, in the passage already cited, placed it in Bexar County, Bracht went on to say it was found "especially between the Medina and the Rio Grande," and Ullrich's statement, also already referred to, had it in Comal County as late as 1860. Did it go where the land rose from this lower semi-tropical region, and if so, how far afield did it live?

Northwest, Audubon stated that, "In a conversation with General Houston at Washington City, he informed us that he had found the jaguar . . . abundantly on the headwaters of some of the eastern tributaries of the Rio Grande, the Guadaloupe, etc.,"[21] and we have Audubon's own statement that it was "on the Nueces."[22] This placed the cat solidly throughout the western Hill Country, and this was confirmed more recently by O. C. Fisher, who wrote about its occurrence in Kimble County as late as 1910.[23]

Did these escarpments of the Edwards Plateau mark the extent of the jaguar's westward range? Not if we believe Audubon. He stated that, "Towards the west and southwest it extends to the mountainous country beyond El Paso."[24]

Do we find jaguars farther north? Baird, the official zoologist of the 1857 Railroad Surveys, covered all of North Texas at one stroke with his statement that they were found as far north as the Red River.[25] Vernon Bailey, in his 1905 "Biological Survey of Texas," accepted and repeated this.[26]

On the east, we have already seen that Almonte listed jaguars as found in 1835 on the lower Brazos. Audubon went on to quote General Houston that he had found the jaguar "east of the San Jacinto river." Baird placed it as far east as the Red River in Louisiana, and Bailey stated that it was "once reported as common over southern Texas and as occupying nearly the whole of the eastern part of the State to Louisiana."

Numerous statements by explorers reporting brushes with "tigers" and "leopards" in locations almost all over Texas are in my files, but are not used here due to the inability to be certain which cats they were reporting. If even a part of them were jaguars — and some of them surely were — this would fill in most of the large range outlined above. A final sad confirmation of jaguars once well north in Texas was the killing of one of the last surviving individuals at Goldthwaite, just north of the center of the state, in 1903.[27] There is also confirmation of Audubon's statement about the cat once occurring even beyond El Paso in the form of records of it from northern New Mexico.[28] The burden of proof would seem to be upon anyone who wishes to deny that there once were jaguars over most if not all of Texas.

If a jaguar might have been close by practically wherever in Texas a pioneer was, that must have prompted a concern. Our predecessors surely must have thought about the disposition and behavior of such awesome cats. Were they threats to humans and their domestic animals, or were they not? The answer to that question might have been critical.

There survive several statements about this written down at the time. They do not all agree, so we must try to discover why this is and distill the truth from them.

The anonymous writer of 1846 made a statement typical of several. He wrote: "The real beasts of prey, the jaguar, a member of the cat family, and the local wolf, small and fearful, do damage to the herds at times, but they fear man."[29] Bracht wrote that the jaguar "is very destructive to domestic hogs and red deer, and when harassed would probably attack man."[30] What appeared at first to be one unprovoked attack turned out not to be such at all and is reported as a comic mistake on the part of the jaguar involved. This illustration of the cat's fear of humans, found in the diary of Eliza (Mrs. Albert Sidney) Johnston, reads, "14th [of January 1856] Marched into Fort Mason and Camped near the Fort ... 15th Jan Went into quarters during the morning as Sid was shooting his arrows in camp a Tiger Cat sprang from the chaporral at his side, as he thought at him, but I suppose the creature did not see him until it made the leap, as it ran through the camp after seemingly frightened out of its wits."[31] I must note that Mrs. Johnston's tiger cat was not a mountain lion, since she mentions on the same page the killing of what she calls a "panther." She obviously knew the two apart from firsthand experience.

Against such statements as these must be ranged the remarkably strong opinion of Audubon. His remarks about the species are unqualified and extreme: "The Jaguar compares with the Asiatic tiger in size and in shape.... Alike beautiful and ferocious, the Jaguar is of all American animals unquestionably the most to be dreaded, on account of its combined strength, activity, and courage, which not only give it a vast physical power over other wild creatures, but enable it frequently to destroy man. Compared with this formidable beast, the cougar need hardly be dreaded more than the wild cat; and the grizzly bear, although often quite as ready to attack man, is inferior in swiftness and stealthy cunning. To the so much feared tiger of the East he is equal in fierceness." Noting that Buffon had already stated the jaguar to be timid, Audubon digresses to explain how he thinks that writer could have made what he considers a mistake: "Buffon, in describing the habits of the Jaguar, appears to have received his accounts of the timidity of this species from those who referred to the Ocelot, which is generally admitted to be a timid animal. He erroneously supposed that when full grown it did not exceed the size of an ordinary dog, in which he egregiously underrated its dimensions. It is certainly a third heavier than the Cougar, and is not only a more powerful, but a far more ferocious animal."[32]

This is something we have seldom seen — explorers expressing directly opposite opinions on a subject. Since these are irreconcilable statements, our only choice is to look for any existing records of jaguars mounting attacks upon humans which might confirm Audubon's view and to look beyond our explorer's accounts for other information on the subject.

A search back through all of our early Texas sources shows not one unprovoked attack upon a human by a jaguar. In the whole literature there is only a single report of a jaguar attack upon a person. In an 1836 publication Joseph E. Field wrote, "A beast of prey, resembling the tiger of Africa, infests some portions of the unsettled country, as appears from the following anecdote. A Mrs. More, at whose house I was residing, told me of a young lady, who after having made her a visit, sat out on horseback early in the afternoon to return home, a distance of five or six miles. In the midst of a forest through which the road lay, she heard a cry resembling that of the human voice. Listening, and hearing it repeated, until she was satisfied that some person was near, she answered it, and the call was repeated two or three times, until the animal came in sight, when she put her horse to his greatest speed, and was pursued by her collocutor, who soon overtook her, mounted behind, and began lacerating and tearing her neck and shoulders, and did not desist until she rode into the yard at home, and a gun was fired, which broke his hold and brought him to the ground."[33]

This is a remarkable report, but there is more than one questionable thing about it. First, it does not meet our criterion of being an eyewitness account. Field is merely recounting a story told to him by a woman to whom it had apparently been related earlier. This greatly lessens its strength as evidence of anything, since Field did not see the animal to verify its being a jaguar and he was twice removed from all of the events. Beyond that, even assuming that the attacker was a jaguar and that the event took place as described, the story does not describe an exactly unprovoked attack. Answering the caterwauling of an amorous tomcat is definitely provocative. So should the result in this case be considered an unprovoked attack on a human or the actions of a decoyed and tricked tomcat rutting?

No other attacks having been recorded, this being so doubtful, and with Mrs. Johnston's jaguar fleeing in such fright when it finds itself near a human, Audubon stands unsupported in his opinion by any early record.

For more recent information on the question we turn to Nelson and Goldman's exhaustive and technical work on all of the jaguars of the hemisphere. In it they make the following statements: "[Jaguars are] very destructive to large animals, but they are completely lacking in the ferocious aggressiveness sometimes shown by leopards in their encounters with man.... [Jaguars] so rarely attack man that reports of such occurrences are very difficult to verify.... [Jaguars] seem to have the same shyness and dread of man as is shown by the puma or mountain lion."[34] If these statements do not satisfy, I add one recently written by Tinker in his discussion of Mexican wildlife: "Jaguars are not truculent and ferocious like African leopards. They are cowardly and shy like mountain lions. Often natives who dwell in their tropical habitats fear 'el tigre' but admit they have never seen or heard of them attacking or harming humans." Tinker reduces to a minimum even the animal's propensity to attack when harassed by recounting the results when one of his own companions followed a jaguar up its tree. He wrote: "During a trip in Nayarit the dogs bayed a big male in a hardwood tree which had many low branches. The native guide (and his dogs) cautioned us to shoot quickly, but my companion wanted a 'close-up' action picture and was climbing up as the jaguar came around on his side climbing down. The big cat paused directly overhead with open jaws, so close that our photographer forgot his picture and leaped to the ground as the jaguar jumped and climbed another tree, where I was lucky to bag him."[35]

The remarkable forbearance of that jaguar is equaled or even surpassed by the action of one described by one of our explorers. A Capt. William Seaton Henry published the following account in 1847: "Col. C. of Texas told me that on the Bernard River while he was hunting coons with a friend, the dogs treed something in an immense live oak, over which they made an unusual commotion. Being the youngest, it was his fate to climb the tree and get, as they thought, the coon down. The tree was directly on the river bank, and its horizontal branches reached nearly across.... He climbed the tree and crawled out on one of those horizontal limbs. Expecting every moment to see the coon, what should present itself, upon his rising up to look around but an immense spotted tiger with eyes 'like balls of fire.' What to do was the question. He could not back out; he dared not drop into the river, for it was full of alligators. He fell upon this plan: he swung himself below the limb and hung on by his hands! The tiger walked over him, descended the tree, and went through a crowd of nine dogs — as fierce ones as there were in Texas — which never even growled at him."[36]

Audubon mentions the fact that jaguars had been known to follow humans for some distances. Although he does not state that any of these shadowed persons were actually attacked, he tells of this in such a way as to imply that the cats were plotting injury. Since we know of no such incident in which a person was actually jumped, it seems clear that the jaguars only indulge in the same harmless curiosity resulting in harm to no one that has so often been noted in the mountain lion. This will be discussed in connection with that species.

Call them tigers if you will, but it is clear the American tigers were no man-eating monsters grabbing either native Indians or pioneers from forest paths for dinner. This is but one of the ways in which the American wilderness was amazingly benign toward the explorers struggling through it.

This returns us to the same disturbing question that arises concerning every one of our large native animals. If the jaguars were such mild pussycats as far as humans were concerned, just why did our pioneers carry out such relentless search and destroy campaigns against them? Casting around for some possible answer reveals only one legitimate reason. Jaguars might have been real threats to the pioneers' domestic animals.

It is hard to determine just how much depredation the jaguars actually waged upon domestic animals. The whole subject of their behavior and diet must be known in order to find out. Our first aim is to search out what the explorers say about any subject, but they left us only very few and far from conclusive hints on this subject. The anonymous writer already cited merely said that jaguars "do damage to the herds at times." Bracht's statement, also already quoted, narrows the range of prey very much, saying that they are "very destructive to domestic hogs and red deer." That is all we learn from the early writers. None other even mentions the subject of the jaguar's taking domestic animals — not even Audubon in all his effort to make a case for its ferocity.

When we consider the whole range of statements on the subject chronologically we see the same trends so often evident in the history of man versus predators. Our earliest pioneer to leave a statement on the subject was noncommittal, saying merely that the cats do damage sometimes. Later, with more knowledge, another was able to be more specific, saying that the jaguar's prey were deer and hogs. Then there were no more statements about the subject for the rest of the settlement period at all, which implies that these cats were not enough of a problem for pioneers to mention.

Then strangely, later, even as the predators were largely exterminated, the stories of their horrible destructiveness tended to become spectacular. Nelson and Goldman wrote in 1933, when jaguars were essentially extinct in Texas and greatly reduced elsewhere, that they were "very destructive to large animals." And O. C. Fisher wrote in 1937, "This animal was never plentiful in Kimble County, but his presence was keenly felt by the early sheepman, as the snarling jaguar was fond of lamb chops and was most destructive when preying upon a flock of bedded sheep at nighttime."[37]

It takes much credulity to believe the stories of a predator's prowess which surface as this trend to antagonistic frenzy peaks, which is usually just as it becomes no real menace at all. As an example of this phase I cite an article published in 1947. It mentions a jaguar which apparently strayed from Mexico into Texas and was killed near San Benito, Texas, a few miles from the Rio Grande River in 1946. It states that this cat "was said to have killed 28 yearling cattle in a three week period."[38]

Then, after what seems to be excessive emotional magnification of the predator's evilness has dissipated and the fear is reduced because the animal is extinct or practically so, sober minds begin to look again at the real behavior of the predator. We have apparently entered that stage concerning the jaguar, since recent statements are much more conservative. Tinker, writing about jaguars in Mexico in 1978, said, "The jaguars are not numerous throughout their habitat, although their food, which largely consists of deer, peccaries, and wild turkeys, is fairly plentiful and there is sufficient water." He did then go on to say, "At present jaguars seldom kill livestock, but in the past this frequently occurred. . . ."[39] How much of his statement about the past is the result of accumulated reports from the period of exaggeration we do not know. The point is that in present, verifiable experience they were not major livestock killers. Coming right up to the latest word, a 1985 article says that the jaguar feeds upon "small animals from peccary to armadillos."[40]

Peccaries are wild hogs, and the cycle has come full circle in the case of the jaguar. We are back to our explorers' animal which was not very serious as a predator on settlers' animals except for perhaps their pigs. Why couldn't we have looked at the situation soberly before the jaguar was rendered extinct in Texas, before we lost the chance to again have the thrill of seeing our tigers lighting up our forests? The jaguars are indeed gone from Texas.

But would it have made any difference if the jaguar had eaten only grass? Is it possible that it was just too flamboyant even for Texas?

THE TEXAS LION

If Texas is looking for superlatives it has made a mistake, because it has blown one away. This state had not only one king of the jungle but two. If it had kept both of its royal cats, Texas could outdo most any oriental potentate or African chieftain, for few of them could boast tigers and lions in the same jungles. Texas could, because besides its tigers it had lions and had them wholesale. Texas lions were once competing strongly with the bears and wolves to be the state's most numerous predators.

That lions were almost universally present in original Texas is shown by both the many times our pioneers wrote of them and the variety of names they used for them. I have sixty-two separate reports written before 1860 of these animals, placing them in almost every part of the state. And the pioneers used an array of names for them, calling them Mexican lions, mountain lions, panthers, painters, cougars, pumas and catamounts.

That all these could legitimately be called lions is obvious. Of course, they lacked the long mane of the original king of beasts, but in color, shape and bearing they were practically small copies of Old World lionesses. And they were not so small at that.

Recent authors give their maximum attainment as about "7.8 feet from nose to tip of tail and a weight of 225 pounds."[41] But our pioneers insist that some of the specimens they bagged exceeded these measurements significantly. We owe our explorers at least a glance at their statements on this.

None less than F. L. Olmsted, the architect of New York's Central Park, wrote in 1854 about a panther killed near the Texas Hill Country settlement of Sisterdale which, according to him, "proved ... the largest that had been known in the settlement, measuring nine feet from nose to tip of tail and weighing, by estimate, 250 lbs."[42] Apparently almost identical was, "A large one ... killed by Lieut. Givens, of the U.S. army, near Fort Belknap, some eighteen months ago. It measured, if we remember right, upwards of nine feet from the tip of the nose to the end of the tail. This animal is unquestionably the Puma of naturalists."[43] What may have been an even heavier one was killed near Bonham, in North Texas, in 1853. As described at the time, "It had a round short head, with large dangerous looking tusks, was six feet long exclusive of the tail, which was two and a half feet in length. The color was that of a deer in the summer; its weight full 300, and it measured when killed 15 inches around the arm."[44] Capt. R. B. Marcy killed one in the Texas Panhandle in 1852, which he reported "measured 8 feet from his nose to the end of the tail."[45] And there are numerous more general statements about individuals of great size. Viktor Bracht, in writing about a trip he made across the hills between San Antonio and New Braunfels in 1847, stated, "I saw game in large numbers; a panther as large as a small cow. . . ."[46]

If there is any truth in these pioneers' statements, our more recent and scientific scholars have had only younger or less well-grown specimens than once existed to base their size generalizations upon. And with the merciless hunting eliminating the grizzled old monster cats and the decline of the prey species turning the whole cat population into gaunt survivors instead of fat cats, this might well be assumed. So what difference does it make how big we say these lions can grow? Isn't it an unkind slap at our forefathers for us to so arbitrarily discount their statements? And we may be unfair to the Texas lion also, because if we take the statements of our explorers at face value, Arthur Ikin's 1841 statement, "Here also is seen the cougar, or Mexican lion, the largest animal of the panther kind,"[47] would be correct, the lion would be larger than the jaguar and thus Texas' largest cat.

It is a welcome relief that since it is the only one of Texas' large cats lacking spots, this species can hardly be confused with any other Texas feline. The kittens do have indistinct blotches when very small, but lose these signs of their leopard connections very soon and spend the rest of their lives as chocolate, brown, gray, tawny or pale yellow lions which only otherwise betray their closeness to the leopards and jaguars by their tree climbing.

The confusion connected with this species lies not between it and other species, but within it. A nagging question has persisted throughout the study of this animal. Is it one single cat presence found the same everywhere in Texas, or do the many names the pioneers coined for it mean that there were lions here which the pioneers could tell apart and which they experienced as different entities?

Of course, some of the explorers appear not to have observed subtle differences or cared about details. To a few a lion was just a lion — or a panther or a cougar or a puma or a catamount. These tell us only general things. But many of the pioneers were more observant. These accompanied the use of the above terms with details about the animals so named, opposed two or more of these names in the same account, or otherwise pictured the forms meant when they used these terms so that we can characterize them. There is some overlapping in the pictures they draw of these forms, but since they

Cougar by Audubon

were perhaps at best only subspecies they should intergrade, and the synonymy in their common names is certainly no worse than that in the scientific terminology with which we must try to cross-reference them.

The most prestigious explorer who made no distinction between the lions was Audubon. Concerning *Felis concolor* he made the flat statement: "The Cougar is known all over the United States by the name of the panther or painter."[48] That was it, for him. He apparently looked no further, either in Texas or elsewhere. Dr. Ferdinand Roemer also did not bother with small distinctions. When traveling on the San Saba River in what is now Menard County in 1849, he reported, "On our journey one of the Shawnees shot a cougar (called panther by the American settler, and *leon* by the Mexican)."[49] Bracht did not discriminate either, writing in 1848, "The American lion, puma, panther, or cougar which is very common in the uninhabited regions. . . ."[50]

But these three are all of the Texas explorers whose words show that they had not seen any reason to subdivide this species. Many others show clearly that they used the various common names carefully because they meant to them different races or subspecies which they recognized.

We could not do better than to start the search for these different cats under the direction of that dean of hunters, Col. Richard Irving Dodge. Although his opus on western game and the hunting of it was published in 1877, much of his experience was within the period of our study. In his book he describes separately two forms of the American lion. Under the heading of "COUGAR OR PUMA," he writes, "This animal, called variously the 'Mexican lion,' 'Californian lion,' and 'mountain lion,' is an habitual resident of many rough and broken parts of the plains. . . . Except by the rarest accident the hunter cannot hope to bag him except by the aid of dogs. . . . When pursued by a pack, he runs well for a little distance, but soon tires, and will then take to a tree, selecting one that leans well to one side, for he is not a good climber. Out of reach of the dogs he stands upright on a horizontal branch, and calmly surveys his vociferous and baffled pursuers. Should a man appear on the scene, he ceases to watch the dogs, and dropping in a crouching position on the branch, prepares for a spring. Under such circumstances I would advise no one to approach within thirty or even forty feet. He is now, of course, easily bagged, but no bungler with the rifle should be allowed to shoot at him, as, when wounded, he is a desperate and most formidable antagonist...."

Dodge follows this with the heading, "PANTHER," and writes, "This is nearly the same animal on a smaller scale. The cougar is almost a lion. The panther is but a huge cat. It is much more plentiful than the cougar.... It is equally difficult to bag without dogs.... It is a good climber, and when pursued by dogs, goes up the first tree, however straight, and lies like a squirrel close to the trunk, with its head in a crotch, watching the dogs. It takes no notice whatever of the approach of a man, who might even pull its tail, with no more effect than to make it go higher up the tree. It is not at all dangerous to man, never attacking him even when wounded, though a poor shot may cause sad havoc among the dogs. One becomes accustomed, as he grows older, to having the illusions of his youth dispelled; but after having killed fifty or more panthers, under a variety of circumstances, without ever seeing one show fight, it is difficult to account for the respect, even terror, with which eastern professional hunters surround the 'painter' as they call it ... the animal is really very harmless to the hunter, and bagged with less danger than any other of the larger carnivora. In many years of panther hunting I have never known a person to be hurt by one; and I have myself seen a Mexican boy lay hold of the tail of a panther which had taken refuge from dogs in a small mesquite tree, and hold on lustily, while his brother shot the animal through the head."[51]

Dodge's cougar which "is almost a lion," approaches so closely to the African lioness in some early accounts that the descriptions are generally laughed out of court as being ridiculous on the face of it. But fairness to both our explorers and to all reading this requires that I lay out to be considered, along with the more reasonable-sounding, the most spectacular statements made at the time by those who actually saw the felines which were once here.

So without hesitation I bring onto the witness stand Mr. C. W. Webber, a personage usually discounted because of the very tall tales he tells. He does tell stories to strain our credulity, but he is a pioneer voice published in the 1850s, and our picture of early Texas would be incomplete without hearing him. He wrote: "In an excursion towards the Rocky Mountains, I have met all our most formidable animals under the most varied circumstances of sudden collision. On this expedition we saw several skins and two specimens in the flesh of the puma, which is yet unrecognized by any American Naturalist.... I once, while hunting around a camp on one of the head streams of the Red River, encountered a Puma, in manner much resembling the instance of the wild cat given above. ... After our surprise had subsided, I examined it coolly, and found it to be entirely distinct from the cougar, both in size, which I am convinced was considerably greater, (I took no measurement,) and color, which instead of tawny, was a light roan, or mingled red and dull white. Then the head was of greater size in proportion to the body, and the rudiments of a mane and tufted tail were sufficiently distinctive. I regret that I was not more careful at the time, for my measurement might have substantiated a new species.... We saw several skins of these creatures, which had been killed near San Antonio de Bexar, in Texas ... yet, on the most careful inquiry, we learned from the hunters, that they were quite as cowardly, and averse to attacking man as the cougars, which yet linger in the swamps of the Mississippi, the pine woods of the Carolinas, or along the course of our Western rivers, are known to be."[52]

The next witness called is known merely as J.M.C., who published his testimony in the *Dallas Herald* in 1856, as follows: "West-Brook, April 30th, 1856. You will not believe it when I tell you that I have twice chased a Mexican Lion in the Trinity bottom, not more than three miles from Dallas, in the last two months. Both times it was seen in full view in the open prairie, and has been seen once beside. On yesterday, just below the Cedar Springs ford, having my bull dog with me, I gave it a very close chase; one of my hounds coming off minus a considerable portion of one of his ears. This is a strange animal, and resembles a lion more than any other. It, of course, is not as large as the African lion, but we have many evidences that it is not a panther. Its form is not that of the panther, but of the lion; it will not tree, when pressed by dogs, as the panther; the extraordinary chest and muscular power of the shoulders and length of the tail is a subject of remark by all who have seen it. I have no doubt but it is a species of the lion. It is very fleet, and as cunning as a fox ... let sportsmen look out, it is a curiosity and worth hunting. Yours, etc., J.M.C."

An editor added his opinions at the end of J.M.C.'s letter, and may be considered our third witness, writing: "We have no reason to doubt the statement of our correspondent. An animal of the kind described certainly frequents our river bottoms. Several of them have been seen at different times from the first settlement of the country to the present. Another gentleman informs us that he got within about 50 feet of this same animal, some ten days ago, in a small prairie in the river bottom... he represents it as being a pale, yellow color, with a long flowing mane, a bunch of hair on the end of his tail, and very large."[53]

Did any others of our pioneers see Dodge's distinction between what were most often called cougars and the panther? William Kennedy must have, for he wrote in 1839, "There are some of the feline tribes in Texas, such as the Mexican cougar and panther, which commit depredations on the stock of the solitary settler, but are not formidable to man."[54] We have already seen Arthur Ikin's statement that Texas had in 1841, "the cougar, or Mexican lion, the largest animal of the panther kind," after which he went on to say that, "Leopards and panthers are more numerous, but by no means so formidable." It is clear that many persons on the scene distinguished between the same two forms as Dodge. It was quite common at the time for them to name the two forms separately in their lists of Texas animals, which would be meaningless duplications if the cougar and the panther were the same.

Then there were several who showed by their statements that while generally the cougar and the panther were considered to be different, they could be difficult to distinguish. For instance, Charles De Morse, writing as C. De M. in 1853, prefaced his description we have already quoted of the 300-pound cat killed near Bonham with the following statements: "We staid there [in Bonham] one day, observing nothing new pertaining to the locality except preparations for the new Court house, and the remains of a large animal killed near town, which we were requested to examine and identify. The skin had been stuffed and placed in the upper room of Mr. Doss' store. Going there, we found what I was at first disposed to call a Cougar, but which others believed to be a Panther. Having seen no Menagerie, for years, I yield the point."

It has to be admitted that, close as these two cats may have been, most pioneers recognized the cougar and the panther as separate entities. And this distinction came down through them to persist in the reminiscences about those days. Although, for reasons explained in the Introduction of this work, I don't base my arguments upon reminiscences, I wish to quote one here. It is because the clarity of its pictures forms a good framework upon which to hang our explorers' scattered reports.

O. C. Fisher has written: "Vying for a place of prominence in the wild animal kingdom of the Llano valleys was the crouching panther. That species of the cat family was quite plentiful in those parts, and rarely a night was spent by the early-day ranchmen without hearing the cat-like scream of the panther. One pioneer said the panther's scream was similar to that of a house cat, except a hundred times as loud, and was somewhat 'like unto that of a woman's.' This animal was not as ferocious as he has been pictured. He could be treed by a small dog, and would not make fight unless it was forced upon him. When a fight was in the offing, the shrewd panther would often nonchalantly climb a tree, and there crouched close to a bough would look down upon his foe with a purring growl.... Then, there was the mountain lion, with its defiant roar. Perhaps the loudest of the mountain creatures, on a still night his growling roar would echo a full mile across a mountain canyon. He was a wild, fighting animal — the terror of the animal kingdom."[55]

Fisher, perhaps all unbeknown to himself, here claims that a characteristic which has sometimes been used by students of anatomy for dividing the cat family into two main branches also distinguishes the mountain lion/cougar from the panther. Some categorize what they call "little cats" which have tightly connected bones within their voice boxes so they can only move with small and fast vibrations, yielding the high-pitched yowling scream fading at the low end into a purr, all of which the housecat makes so familiar. Opposite this they have the so-called "big cats" which have instead in their throats such long vocal cords that they can, like any longer band, only vibrate with longer, slower wave motion, producing only the low-pitched, deep but powerful tones of the roar, the African lion's being the classic example. The puma, panther or painter is said to be the largest "little cat" in the world, and its unforgettable, high-pitched caterwauling as well as its purring has been noted many times. But if Fisher is correct that the more western mountain lion/cougar roared instead of screaming, then it would not have been merely a different race of the same species, but a "big cat" as truly different from the "little cat" panther as the "big cat" leopard is from the actually larger in size but technically "little cat" snow leopard. Would that there were some of the mountain lion/cougars left and some way to find out whether they roared. Or why didn't someone look them closely in the eye to see whether the pupils of their eyes were round, as those of "big cats" are, or slit, as "little cats'" and the typical Florida panther's were said to have been?

Texas explorers did not leave much detailed information about this mountain lion or cougar. They reported this cat less than once for each ten times that they did panthers. When they did come across it they seem to have had only fleeting glimpses of it. For instance Julius Froebel, working his way through the Big Bend in 1853, reported when in present Presidio County, "The first watering-place eastwards from the Rio Grande is called Low Alamos.... The journey through the next night brought us into a well-watered valley of considerable extent and ramifications, opening towards the Rio Grande. It is bounded by hills of conglomerate, a few isolated and curiously formed mountains being only seen upon the horizon to the east. Where the road comes upon this spring, the place is called Punta del Agua. The road passes through this valley along a brook bordered with high reeds. The cougar, called by the Mexicans, leon, abounds here. We passed the haunt of one of these wild beasts disturbed by our vanguard, — the skeletons of several deer lay around...." Farther on, in what is now western Pecos County, he wrote, "The Lion's Spring — Ojo del Leon — was our next watering-place. This name also proved to be a correct one. The advance of our party drove a cougar from his breakfast, — a freshly-killed stag, which was yet warm."[56] We get here a picture of a cat not associated with trees at all and preying upon large animals. Friedrich von Wrede had written in 1838 about the cougar that "Frequently he jumps in great bounds; and though he flees from humans, he is bloodthirsty and eats all animals that he can subdue."[57]

No cat found in the Big Bend is called a panther by any pioneer. They only reported cougars out there. However, cougars were not limited to the southwest of the state. They told of what they call cougars as distinguished from panthers east through Val Verde and Kinny counties into Bexar County. In North Texas cougars distinguished from panthers were reported as far east as present Clay County. To the explorers the cougar was a large western cat robust in preying upon large animals, not necessarily associated with trees, not aggressive toward man but not quite to be trusted if pushed. Their name, cougar, for this cat is English for *couguar*, the Brazilian name for that country's form of this species. It was one of the western forms most aptly called mountain lions.

If we try to square this cat with the taxa set up by the official scientists, we have still another job ahead of us — that of sorting through their confusion. The cougar is, of course, part of Linnaeus' species, *Felis concolor*. But it can't be *F. concolor cougar*, because that name was given to something else called the "Adirondack or eastern cougar." The western mountain lion was designated *F. c. stanleyana* by Goldman, and specimens from as far east as Central Texas have been called this. However, Merriam named what he called the "Mountain Lion or Rocky Mountain Cougar" *Felis hippolestes*, and also set up *Felis Aztecus* for what he called the "Mexican cougar" from Chihuahua, and all of these names have been applied to West Texas cats. It is not required of us to unravel the scientists' synonymy, but the point should be clearly seen that they support our explorers by also seeing something in the west which is different from the eastern panther. The fact that recent field guides and popular books do not even mention any such distinction does not mean that it did not once exist, but more likely that so few of the animals survive that neither form still exists as a viable population, or that we just no longer really care.

But the explorers did care, and they found what they called panthers almost everywhere in Texas except in the trans-Pecos and on the Llano Estacado. Over all of the state east of about the hundredth meridian, this feline was so common that they encountered it almost anywhere they went even when not looking for it. It even entered the yards of their pioneer cabins, and sometimes it even intruded into their frontier villages.

This common cat may well have been an eastern form different from the cougar of the West, as Dodge and many others thought, but which form it was and what its scientific name should be may never be certain. Kerr called the panther of the northeast U.S. *Felis cougar* and Banks proposed *Felis coryi* for the panthers of Florida and the Gulf Coast. When both of these are thought of as subspecies of the one general species, they become *F. Concolor cougar* and *F. concolor coryi*. But whether the two were ever actually separate populations has been doubted by some, and this question may never be answered because the Florida panther may already be extinct. Nor may it ever be known with certainty whether the Texas panthers were separate from the eastern ones, because due to the elimination of the original East Texas population, escapes of pets and releases of cats from widely different regions into Texas, the original forms may not be recoverable at all.

Chance meeting with panthers in the wilderness were naturally exciting, and the accounts of them would sometimes be comic if the circumstances had not been so often life-threatening — due to other factors than the cats. For instance we have the incident, so dryly recounted by Charles B. Shain (who was one of a group of soldiers escaping from the Fannin massacre) of an 1836 brush with a panther which probably took place in present De Witt County: ". . . we came to the Guadalope shore. We were pursued by six or eight Mexicans; but we saw them first, and ran to the river and swam it. We thought we would hide in the bushes, but we found a very large Panther in the bushes. The Mexicans to our rear, and a large river before us; of the three dangers we took the latter, and all got over in safety."[58]

The good Abbe Domenech seemed to be particularly fated to meet with panthers in the travels necessary to his clerical duties in early Texas. In the year 1848 alone he reported several brushes with these cats. Imagine the young French priest only a short distance west of Houston on his first entrance into Texas suffering the episode which he reported as follows: "Suddenly the horses stop short, snort wildly, tremble all over, and plunge backwards. In their paroxysm they dash the waggon with violence against the trunk of a tree, and the pole is smashed. My companion alights with his carabine. At the same instant a panther of huge size crouches and springs on the foremost horse. Then a shot is fired, and this formidable denizen of the forest falls to the ground lifeless. As for myself, the shock sent me head over heels to the bottom of the waggon, whence I witnessed the scene from quite an extraordinary point of view *(a l'envers)*. The horse happily received but a few slight scratches, and the pole was soon put to rights by means of ropes. The panther was hoisted into the waggon alongside of me; and after half an hour's delay we were on our way again as though nothing had happened."

One wonders how composed the Abbe remained when later, down between Indianola and Victoria, he says, "I saw an enormous panther on the side of the road. . . . Our horse, in his onward career, only snorted twice or thrice at the presence of the monster, and dashed forward, without shying either to the right or left." He shows that these cats were ever near by recounting that when on his way from San Antonio to his charge at Castroville, "We bivouacked in a chapral of the Leona [Leon Creek]. . . . Larger animals prowled around us, and all night our ears were entertained with the barking of coyotes and the caterwaulings of panthers and tigercats." But most disturbing to his services, if not to his personal composure, must have been the event described as taking place when he was conducting mass in D'Hanis, Texas: "On one occasion during mass, which was celebrated in a wooden hut, the dogs commenced barking in a most terrible manner. My Alsacian seized his rifle, left the cabin, and went out to see the cause of the noise. It was an enormous panther, which chased by the dogs, had taken refuge in a tree near the cabin which served us as a chapel. To see the beast and shoot it dead, was for my friend the work of an instant."[59]

Travelers came across panthers in such widely separated places as opposite corners of the state. When walking between Sabine and Galveston Passes in 1860, an anonymous traveler had the experience he put into these words: "For miles to the right— the prairie was spotted with wild cattle. Whilst we were reclining upon the grass, this immense herd suddenly threw their heads up as if snuffing the air, and with a simultaneous start they rushed into one close and compact mass, trembling in every limb. This unusual movement attracted our attention. We were not long in suspense. A cry like that of a human in great distress drew our gaze to a quarter that had been vacated by the cattle. A panther, the largest I ever saw, walked out from the grass into the path, and walked leisurely toward us. He arrived within fifty-yards when he observed us — scanned us closely — and very much to our relief, turned in his path and disappeared."[60]

Clear across the state from the above sighting, when in what would now be extreme northwestern Briscoe or extreme southern Armstrong County just under the breaks of the Llano Estacado, Captain Marcy called up a panther he didn't know was there: "As Capt. McClellan and myself were passing to-day along under the bluffs, we saw in advance of us a herd of antelopes quietly feeding among some mezquite trees, when the idea occurred to me of attempting to call them with a deer-bleat, which one of the Delawares had made for me. I accordingly . . . commenced exercising my powers in imitating the cry of the fawn. I soon succeeded in attracting their attention, and in a short time decoyed one of the . . . animals within range of my rifle, which I raised to my shoulder, and, taking deliberate aim, was in the act of pulling trigger, when my attention was suddenly and most unexpectedly drawn aside by rustling which I heard in the grass to my left. Casting my eyes in that direction, to my no small astonishment, I saw a tremendous panther bounding at full speed directly towards me, and within the short distance of twenty steps. As may be imagined, I immediately abandoned the antelope, and directing my rifle at the panther, sent a ball through his chest, which stretched him out upon the grass about ten yards from where I had taken my position. . . . The panther had probably heard the bleat, and was coming towards it with the pleasant anticipation of making his breakfast from a tender fawn; but fortunately for me, I disappointed him."[61]

Pioneers didn't always have to travel to meet up with panthers. They often came into their farmyards. No doubt the livestock attracted them. Accounts of this are numerous. W. Steinert wrote in 1849, "His [Mr. Klappenbach's New Braunfels] property, consisting of fifty acres, makes a picturesque scene around the springs of Comal Creek. . . . A few days ago he shot two panthers that his wife encountered on the way to the garden."[62] Charles De Morse wrote very nonchalantly in 1853, "While on this subject, I may mention, that I hear that Mr. William Welsh, living four or five miles from Clarksville killed four panthers, near his residence a few days since."[63]

It is probably beyond us today to imagine how numerous these large predators were in the original Texas biotic communities. The herds of hundreds of deer which we have seen grazing so peacefully in the prairies must have been almost constantly shadowed by panthers. That we have difficulty believing such calmness could exist in the presence of such threat must show our own overdependence upon security, because the panthers were there in quantity, just in the wings of the peaceful scene. The pioneers asserted that over and over. For instance, Edward Smith, writing in 1849 and quoting "the verbal communications of the Judge English, of Bonham," said, ". . . his father had settled in Texas in 1816, being one of the first pioneers. He came with his father and . . . had never left the neighborhood of his first location. On his arrival, the country was in the possession of the Indians. . . . They eat the flesh of buffalo, which was then most abundant upon the prairie; of deer, which abounded on the high woodland; and of the bear, which they hunted in the river bottoms. . . . In one season he killed sixty panthers, having discovered their retreat and laid in wait for them."[64]

Explorers and settlers almost everywhere in Texas having had to count on panthers being everywhere around them, isn't it remarkable how little they let this affect their lives? Letters, diaries and journals repeatedly tell of unarmed adults and even young children walking miles through the deepest forests as unconcerned about panthers as they would be about housecats. Plainly, early Texans did not regard this cat as any direct physical danger to themselves. W. B. Conger was entirely right when he wrote, "In the early history of this country, when cougars were plentiful, children went to school through fields and forests unharmed and unalarmed. Those who have come in contact with this animal in its natural home, minus the desire to shed its blood, have found it not ferocious but friendly. Through all the centuries the cougar was untroubled by the North American Indian. It had no fear of squaw or brave; it harmed no papoose, nor did the Indian, in turn, have any dread of it. The Gauchos of the Pampas called it 'Amigo del cristiano'— man's friend. It does not naturally run from members of the human race, but learns to do so when continuously persecuted."[65]

It seems entirely relevant to add here testimony of an early-day naturalist concerning the pumas of South America and the far West. After all, what may properly have been the same magnificent species occupied an unbroken range from south of the Argentine pampas through Texas over much of the U.S., and the forms such as puma, cougar and panther may have been no more than subspecies or races sharing many traits. After years of experience with the animals in Argentina, W. H. Hudson wrote at length concerning the harmlessness — and even friendliness — toward humans of the animal he says the Gauchos called *amigo del cristiano* with good cause. He says: "How strange that this most cunning, bold, and bloodthirsty of the Felidae, the persecutor of the jaguar and the scourge of the ruminants in the regions it inhabits, able to kill its prey with the celerity of a rifle bullet, never attacks a human being!. . . . In places where the puma is the only large beast of prey, it is notorious that it is there perfectly safe for even a small child to go out and sleep on the plain."

Hudson then fills numerous pages with descriptions of episodes in which pumas ignored humans, reacted with curiosity at their presence, or even refrained from attacking them when assaulted. He sums this up by writing, "In encounters of this kind the most curious thing is that the puma steadfastly refuses to recognize an enemy in man...."

It is a mistake to think that Hudson was ignorant of the feline horror stories which exist in the folk tales and reminiscences of North America. I will quote him again here to let him take care of all such myths for us. He wrote, "Everyone is... familiar with the dreaded cougar, catamount, or panther — sometimes called 'painter' — of North American literature, thrilling descriptions of encounters with this imaginary man-eating monster being freely scattered through the backwoods or border romances, many of them written by authors who have the reputation of being true to nature.... It is now many years since Audubon and Bachman wrote, 'This animal, which has excited so much terror in the minds of the ignorant and timid, has been nearly exterminated in all the Atlantic States, and we do not recollect a single well-authenticated instance where any hunter's life fell a sacrifice in a cougar hunt.' It might be added, I believe, that no authentic instance has been recorded of the puma making an unprovoked attack on any human being."[66]

In fairness it must be added that Audubon and Bachman, in the same book quoted by Hudson also made the following statement: "... at long intervals, and under peculiar circumstances, when perhaps pinched with hunger, or in defense of its young, the cougar sometimes attacks men. These instances, however, are very rare."[67]

Stanley P. Young, in his exhaustive study of this species, tells of about a dozen cases in which pumas were said to have attacked humans or exhibited menacing behavior toward them and relates three of what appear to be confirmed accounts of fatal attacks. This is his harvest from all of the animal's practically western hemispheric range. Young sums it up by saying, "From field observations and recorded incidents in the literature there is no doubt but that the puma sometimes makes unprovoked attacks upon human beings. This trait is neither general nor common. [Theodore] Roosevelt summed up the situation well when he said, 'The cougar is as large, as powerful, and as formidably armed as the Indian panther, and quite as well able to attack man; yet the instances of its having done so are exceedingly rare.'"[68]

Probably contributing to the confusion over whether or not these animals menace humans is the remarkable curiosity about humans which they show and the strange behavior it promotes. Young discusses this and mentions several instances of it in his study just cited. Several of the Texas explorers mention it in passing, but give no detailed description of it or its results.

Since Young is emphatic, saying, "The puma is rarely seen by man. Even where it occurs in goodly numbers it is so elusive that the student must have good luck to observe it,"[69] I take the liberty to boast that I have seen one in the wild and observed its curiosity about a human. Some years ago a companion and I were working our ways along the opposite sides of a narrow but deep canyon high in the Franklin Mountains of West Texas, doing plant studies. There was not more than perhaps 100 feet of space directly across between us, but it would have been a large effort down and back up for one of us to cross to the other. Imagine my feelings to notice, sitting stiffly on its haunches not far ahead of him, silently watching my companion approach, a large mountain lion. My friend had not seen the animal and was moving slowly toward it, while it cocked its head and studied him intently. When I finally found breath for it I called out to my friend, at which the cat turned and gracefully bounded away. I saw all of the signs of curiosity in the animal, but realize how hopeless it would have been to devise whether it had any thoughts of attacking him or not. This could only be known after the fact.

But one fellow field biologist of mine did also have the good fortune to see a mountain lion in the wild, was the center of its curiosity, and did have the fortitude to allow the cat to carry through with its plans. This very experienced outdoorsman was hiking alone through an area with scattered thickets and open grassy spaces when he got that uncanny feeling of being followed which many sensitive outdoorsmen have felt. Watching behind himself, he finally caught glimpses of a mountain lion which was stalking him closely. Not too disconcerted by this because of what he knew about the harmlessness of these cats, he moved along, and soon the lion did not seem to be following him anymore. But then my colleague approached a fence gate through which he was to pass, and imagine his feelings upon seeing that the lion had circled around him, gotten ahead and was lying right by the gate, its chin on its paws, waiting for him to approach. He says that walking by that huge cat, opening that gate and passing through was one of the hardest things he ever did, but that, being a true explorer who often bets his life upon what experience has shown to be the expected behavior of natural things, he did it. He says the cat did not move a muscle as he passed within mere feet of it, and that he can explain its behavior only by assuming the animal anticipated where he had to pass and placed itself to indulge its curiosity by watching him at close range. I would only add that I think, when in the wild, we often are observed at much closer range than we ever imagine by curious animals of various kinds. The wise wildlife photographer and naturalist uses this to help him get his pictures and gain his insights of wild things.

Not even the great hunters maintained they were shooting panthers to save people's lives. In fact, the hunters who wrote often made statements about how cowardly the panther was. Read back over Dodge's statement quoted earlier about a boy holding a treed panther by the tail until his brother shot it. A. A. Parker wrote in 1836, "The panther is an animal of the size and color of a full grown lioness, but too cowardly to attack his prey in the open field. Like the Indian, he lies in ambush, or sits perched on the branch of a tree, and seizes his victim unawares. Even a small dog has been known to chase him into his favorite retreat on a tree."[70]

The harmlessness of such a powerful appearing feline led to incidents which test our sophisticated preconceptions today. I choose to repeat here, as the champion of these, the story of two Sisterdale boys who aspired to be panther killers. As told by the highly credible F. L. Olmsted in 1854, events developed like this: "Made aware at dusk one night by the dogs that something unusual was around the house, the two boys started with their guns to see what it might be. Light enough was left to show them a panther who retreated and, pressed by the dogs, took to a tree in the bottoms. He was ensconced in the branches of a cottonwood that hung obliquely over the stream. It was too dark to see his exact position, and taking places upon the bent trunk to prevent his descent, the boys agreed to keep guard till the moon rose. But they were tired with work and daylight found them both asleep where they were — the panther missing! He had either walked over their bodies or dropped into the river."[71]

There is no single account in early Texas on-the-spot descriptions to contradict such stories of the harmlessness of the panther to humans. On the other hand, there is a story too long to reproduce here about a Mexican lion which was the pet of a man in early Corpus Christi. It was supposedly cared for by a Mexican who is said to have led it around without a chain, taken naps with its body as a pillow, and let it ride with him in his cart pulled by oxen. The writer tells quite comically of having ridden up to this cart to be faced by this cat wearing its keeper's hat.[72] Whether this story is true as told cannot be determined. It is the only Texas account of the taming of the animal, although both Young and Hudson described several tamed pumas in early South America.

The diet of Samuel Augustus Maverick may be a surprise to most. He wrote in his journal: "OCT. 2 1848 To banks of Rio Grande, where we killed and ate a Panther."[73] Although there is no evidence that panther was a common item of food, several others reported eating these animals under dire necessity, but none express any particular relish of the cats and a couple write that they provided less than the best meat.

The lions themselves apparently had a varied diet dictated by circumstances. Deer provided a large part of their sustenance. There is no mention of any lion attack upon buffaloes. But we have seen one early Texan's statement about the cougar, that "he . . . eats all animals that he can subdue." This must literally include most anything that moves, since from his experiences tracing the Red River through Louisiana and along the Texas border in the years 1808 to 1816, Henry Kerr wrote that the catamounts of that area "destroy young alligators."[74]

Upon the introduction of horses, cattle and hogs into Texas the lions probably took quick advantage of the new food sources. Numerous statements of the times mention panthers taking pioneers' hogs, but surprisingly, there is little evidence that they were any problem for early sheepmen. Their damage to horses and cattle probably was limited to the young of these, since there are several statements written later than our exploratory period that Texas lions killed no adult horses or cattle. We have already seen that Abbe Domenech's panther was able to do no instantaneous damage when it jumped his horse. This inability to take really large animals may have been because of these large cats' unusual method of subduing their prey. Rather than raking the prey with its claws or biting the life out of it, "Darwin and others reported the lion killed by jumping on the back of the prey and turning the head back with its paw until the vertebrae of the neck were broken or dislocated. . . . Azara ascribes the same habit to the Jaguar."[75] Hudson confirms this by relating having examined the carcasses of many South American deer killed by pumas and telling of finding all with dislocated necks. He then suggests that the pumas' attacks "are successfully resisted by the ass, which does not, like the horse, lose his presence of mind, but when assaulted thrusts his head well down between its fore-legs and kicks violently until the enemy is thrown or driven off."[76] By checking for this sort of neck injury in victims, ranchers and others might be able to verify actual feline attacks and avoid blaming large cats for kills actually committed by other predators.

When all was said, Texas explorers pictured for us majestic cats first called *leons* by the Spanish, and so often Mexican or Texas lions by others. They almost never used "puma," the native Peruvian name, for them, seeming to have regarded this as the naturalists' fancy name for the animals. A few of them studied the species no further and applied the names cougar and panther to it indiscriminately, but most recognized a division within it. These usually applied the terms "cougar" and "mountain lion" to the larger, more aggressive, less tree-dependent, roaring western form. To the eastern, more retiring, definitely tree-dependent, screaming race of the species they applied the terms "panther," "painter" and "catamount." Once kings of the wilderness in at least some senses, these marvelous animals rule no part of Texas today. Whether the original races still exist as viable populations at all is doubtful, and the pitiable survivors still in Texas slink along, endangered refugees in their own realms. But Texas never did take to royalty — least of all to its own.

THE "DAINTY OCELOT"

There is a cat which has caused the Texan's feelings for cute kittens to war with his urge to kill all predators. This feline, just large enough to appear dangerous to the smaller domestic animals and yet small enough to seem little more than an overgrown tomcat, is generally known today as the ocelot. It is the *Felis pardalis* of Linnaeus, which once ranged all the way from Argentina into Arizona and through Texas into Louisiana and Arkansas. It is another of the beautifully striped and spotted cats which help decorate the world.

Some of Texas' early explorers were so fortu-

The Ocelot. From The Naturalist's Library, *by Sir William Jardine, published in Edinburgh, 1834. Original, steel engraving, hand-colored. Though not as easily seen in a reproduced version, the two color phases of the animal are indicated in this illustration and the one which follows on the next page.*

Ocelot, or Leopard Cat

nate as to know this elusive cat, but few of them seemed to know it by the name of "ocelot." That name appears to have been introduced by the more formal scientific community, first entering the Texas literature through Dr. Roemer in 1849, followed by Audubon and then Baird in the 1850s. Earlier explorers called this animal the leopard, leopard cat, tiger cat, striped tiger cat, or by the Mexican name which so aptly combines its formidable and its kittenish sides — *el Tigre Chiquito*.

That this cat existed in Texas and that the explorers could distinguish it from the other felines found here is clearly shown by passages such as the one left by Francis Moore, Jr. He wrote in 1840, "A species of tiger is found in the western part, different from the cougar or catamount, and is probably allied to the Jaguar of South America. . . ." Moore has thus described the two largest cat species of Texas, which we have already dealt with. Then he goes on to write, "A species of leopard is also found in the western forests. The skin of this animal is most beautifully spotted, and is highly prized by the Indians, as an article of ornament. This leopard is about as large as a wild-cat, and is commonly styled the leopard-cat."[77]

Moore's statement rings true in every respect. We now know that the ocelot reaches a maximum weight of about 35 pounds, the same as that of the bobcat. This is the "dainty ocelot" of Dr. Roemer.[78] And a most beautiful animal it is. We have just read Moore's statement that the Indians highly prized its skin for ornament. They were not the only ones decorating their trappings with ocelot spots, since Bracht wrote in 1848: "One of the most common of the cat family, found in almost all river bottoms, is the beautifully spotted leopard cat, whose fur makes a fine flap for a hunting bag." There must have been enough demand for ocelot hides for them to figure in the fur trade, because Francis Smith wrote from what would now be Burleson County in 1832, "My cart is now loaded with beef hides deer skins buffaloes hides and robes some leopard & beaver, my oxen are tyed to the wheels and are to start for Brassoria tomorrow morning."[79]

Bracht's note is exceptional in that it recognizes the two color phases found in the ocelot. We have seen that he calls the common one the "beautifully spotted leopard cat." He goes on to say, "the striped tiger-cat, equal in size to the leopard-cat, is rarely found; the habits of the two are the same."[80] Note on both ocelot illustrations the two color phases which were published in 1834, when these cats were still common over large parts of two continents and the variations could easily be compared.

When all of the names applied to this cat by the pioneers are combined and the places where they reported them plotted, we have a range for the ocelot blanketing practically the whole of Texas except the far northwest. They found it along the lower Brazos,[81,82] repeatedly throughout Central Texas, west into the Big Bend,[83] and north all the way to the Red River.[84] Even though it was apparently quite numerous in many places over this huge range, it was not as often reported as the larger cats because it was very retiring, staying almost totally in the deep lowland forests and dense chaparral where its small size enabled it to hide very successfully. In fact the ocelot so depends upon and restricts itself to dense cover that it is probably facing extinction in Texas more from brush and forest clearing than from direct hunting. I am told by biologists studying this cat that it absolutely requires for its habitat an area of at least four miles' width with a shrub canopy of at least 75 percent, and that an optimum situation for it is a larger area with a 95 percent or greater shrub covering. It is incidental evidence of the widespread occurrence of chaparral and other kinds of brush in natural Texas that this cat was once able to range almost the whole state. If Texas had been mostly open grassland, as many would like to imagine it once was, there wouldn't have been many ocelots here.

The fine studies of the ocelots carried on by scientists in which individual animals have been monitored by radio have shown how large a territory of unthinned brush a South Texas ocelot must have in which to survive. I still remember with sorrow their telling of one ocelot's fate whose large territory of dense South Texas brush was not eliminated, but only reduced a little by the clearing of one more plot on the edge of it. As a result the tagged animal's radio signal disappeared altogether. It was a mystery what had happened to it until some time later when its remains were found something like seventy miles away. Apparently that particular clearing had reduced the animal's territory of brush to below its tolerable limit and it had therefore struck out across what to it must have been unbearably clear South Texas, looking for another large enough tract of brush to sustain it, but finding instead some fatal situation. Nor was this a unique episode. It must have been another such displaced ocelot which was seen way out in the open country near Clarendon, Texas, in 1950, and killed in Donley County soon after.[85]

Is this terrible drama to be replayed until the last ocelot has embarked upon its fatal search across a scraped, coastal bermuda Texas? This beautiful cat doesn't ask much. It is not large enough to threaten our large grazers. It feeds, as Audubon stated, "upon the smaller quadrupeds, and on birds, eggs, etc., when they can be seized on the ground."[86] But it could not be much of a hazard to wild birds such as turkeys and quail, since these were in prodigious numbers when and where ocelots were numerous. And ocelots could hardly threaten today's chickens cooped as they are for their whole lives in tiny pens in secure houses. We have no imaginable reason for eliminating this beautiful animal, but it may be doomed simply because we want everything — every acre of brush along with every stretch of wetland or forest or desert — for our human uses. If so, Texas will have crowded out another Texan who couldn't be fenced in.

THE WILD BOBCAT

The most successful survivor of the Texas cats is not another southern species managing to colonize at least parts of Texas, but is instead a northern — actually an arctic — feline making itself at home throughout the state. This, the bobcat, is actually a lynx. Whether you call it *Lynx rufus* or *Lynx maculatus*, the Texas bobcat is a southern cousin of the marvelous cats of the northern forests. And this beautiful animal with the more or less mottled coat of thick fur, the pointed ears and the bobbed tail of the lynxes was definitely a part of the Texas explorers' world.

Yet the bobcat was apparently not very important to our pioneers. They almost always included it in their lists of the predators of the wilderness, but this was usually along with other creatures such as wild hogs, raccoons, foxes, etc., which were more pests than game. The only statement by any explorer attributing positive importance to the bobcat is the 1838 passing remark of von Wrede that "It is much sought after for its heavy pelt."[87] However, its pelts are so conspicuously absent from the fur traders' lists that they must have figured in no significant way in the trade.

It doesn't even seem that the bobcat was a very formidable pest for the pioneer. There is not one account of a bobcat raiding their domestic animals — not even chickens. This must be contrasted with the repeated stories of panthers in the farmyards. An anonymous traveler wrote in 1846, that they "present only a danger to wild fowl."[88] Jean Louis Berlandier did write in 1828 that "wild cats frequently steal the hunter's kill. We have been told that many times when a hunter kills a turkey, if he does not hurry to retrieve it, then the bobcat will snatch it and run into the forest."[89] If the pestering of the bobcat was limited to this, then it was hardly any major problem for the pioneers.

Berlandier's statement does tell us several other things about this animal. First, it tells us how numerous and ubiquitous they were in the original scene. Audubon remarked that they were "found even on the prairies."[90] Also, Berlandier shows us how cat-like they were, both in managing to be present though unobserved and in the quickness and daring of their forays when they did act.

The bobcats just don't show the sleek, regal bearing of lions, tigers and leopards. All they can ever be are big, bushy tabbies. Perhaps this is why the explorers almost always called them "wild cats," a term which confuses them with the old-world wild cat, an entirely different species. Ullrich did once call the species "the short-tailed cat,"[91] but bobcat, the only really specific term for this American feline, seems to have been unused, if not unknown in early Texas.

THE RARE RIO GRANDE CATS

There were two cats which crossed the Rio Grande into Texas. They came to hunt in and perhaps to remain living in the dense *galeria* forest which fringed the lower stretches of that river and filled much of its valley. They were always elusive, but they were occasionally met up with around the *resacas* and in the densest parts of those forests. Never common in Texas, with the uprooting of most of that tropical forest unique to the U.S. they have become so rare that a sighting of one of them today prompts newspaper expressions of wonder and new rephrasing of our lamentations over our lost wildlife.

One of these rare cats which flirts with Texas is *Felis yagouaroudi*, variously labeled the *jaguarundi*, the gray cat, the red cat, the black cat or black panther, and probably meant by the term, the long-tailed yellow lynx.

This is a smaller feline than any of those yet considered. At its largest it weighs only twenty pounds or so. It is often no larger than a big housecat, but it is very different from a housecat in shape, being a long-bodied, low-slung animal with a long tail, sometimes described as weasel-like in shape and bearing. The *jaguarundi* has no color markings on it at all beyond subtle shadings of the basic color. This occurs in two phases in the species, gray individuals being salt-and-pepper agouti and others being reddish, both of these shading into blackish on parts of the body. These variations account for most of the different color-descriptive names the cat has been saddled with.

Wildlife students say that the *jaguarundis* subsist upon rodents and other small animals, especially upon birds. There are reports that these cats are so expert in their sudden rushes for the prey that they sometimes succeed in leaping as much as five feet in the air to intercept late-flushing birds.[92]

Interesting as the *jaguarundi* is, it cannot be said that it figured with any importance in the world of the Texas explorers. It entered into so little of the geographical area of their travels that most of them could not have glimpsed it even with the best efforts. And even those who traveled in and wrote about the lower Rio Grande Valley during their exploring or warmaking, if they met with this cat, did not find it important enough to mention.

It was only an explorer formally engaged in zoological studies who met with this cat and considered it important enough to report. Berlandier had already collected an individual of the species at Matamoros, Mexico, and described it when Spencer Baird, in doing his great survey of the mammals encountered during the Mexican boundary survey of the 1850s, was introduced to it from a Texas collection made near present Brownsville. He included it in his report as a Texas animal,[93] and this is the *jaguarundi*'s only actual entry into the recorded consciousness of Texas' founding fathers. Deep in its thickets and probably always rare, this cat probably avoided the newcomers very skillfully, probably did not make enough attacks upon their domestic animals to attract their ire, and provided not enough attractive pelts to prompt their pursuit. So it apparently lived mostly unnoticed by anybody in that edge of Texas until the explorers were replaced by the developers of the Valley, and now this cat's survival or extinction has become a symbol of the saving or losing of the only tropical jungle we Texans have ever had.

The other rare cat of the Rio Grande is *Felis wiedii*, the margay. This is often called one of the exotic cats of Texas, and it may be true not only in the sense of its being colorful but because it may actually have been alien in Texas throughout historic times.

The margay is a small feline, hardly housecat size but rangy and very long-tailed. Its ground color is grayish or buff and it is marked with blackish spots and bars at least as distinct as the ocelot's. It lives in forests from Argentina through the American tropics up across Mexico.

This cat is claimed as Texan on the basis of one specimen from Eagle Pass recorded in Baird's 1850s boundary survey report as an ocelot, but identified later as actually a margay.[94] And that's all. There is no further record of this animal in Texas to this day. In order to place it any more securely in our state you have to go back 10,000 years or more to the ice ages. Fossils of the margay found in Pleistocene deposits near the Sabine River provide evidence that the species ranged at that distant time over much of at least South Texas. But apparently it had already retreated entirely — or almost entirely — from our state before our explorers arrived. It was definitely not a usual part of their world. So that single margay taken at Eagle Pass has special significance for our study. Whether that individual cat was one poor Mexican immigrant trying to come back to where its ancestors had lived during the ice ages or merely was a tourist, it is a credit to our explorers that this single cat — so rare and so unique — figures at all in their accounts of Texas as it was. They really didn't miss much.

9

Texas Little Foxes

So little space will be taken up here with the foxes of the explorers' Texas that they may seem to be slighted, but there are two reasons why they deserve only a small place in our reconstruction of that scene.

The first reason is that there simply weren't the foxes here which we usually imagine. Most of us, in thinking of Br'er Fox, see in our imaginations the red fox. So we imagine it playing its now-you-see-me-now-you-don't games with the explorers of Texas. It is usually only after supplementing our thinking with some outside knowledge that we realize that there are gray foxes as well as red ones and add them as minor actors to our reconstruction of the early Texas picture. In this we have things entirely reversed from reality.

The red fox is *Vulpes vulpes* or *fulva,* the nomenclature depending upon the guidebook in hand, but all agreeing that this species is originally an Old World animal. While its various races range over Europe, much of Asia and even down into north Africa, it just wasn't native to the western hemisphere.

It is fortunate for our faith in our explorers' accounts that they didn't say this fox was here during their times, because if they had it would have damaged their credibility tremendously. Far from that, one of them grudgingly admits that it must have been imported. Spencer Baird, in writing up the mammals encountered on the western railway surveys in 1857, noted that there had been seen no red fox in Texas, and wrote, "It is not a little remarkable that there have as yet been no remains of the red fox detected among the fossils derived from the Carlisle and other bone caves. The gray fox is abundantly represented, but not a trace of the other. This would almost give color to the impression somewhat prevalent that the red fox of Eastern America is the descendant of individuals of the European red fox imported many years ago, and allowed to run wild and overspread the country."[1]

So we must erase the red fox from our picture of the original Texas. It just wasn't here, even peering, mostly ears and grin, from any of the great cover the chaparral would have made for it. It is generally agreed that the species was imported from England by a group of Maryland planters in 1730, for the purpose of providing the sport of foxhunting in that colony.[2] Whether any of the descendants of those first individuals ever reached Texas is not known. Texas got its own infusion of the species later, at least 145 individuals being released in Central and East Texas in the 1890s.[3]

There were foxes in the Texas wilderness, but instead of red they were gray. Explorers called them either gray or silver foxes. In the scientific language they are *Urocyon cinereoargenteus,* which means something like "the gray-silver, tailed dog." Audubon and some other early students called them *Vulpes virginianus,* but they are so different from the red foxes that modern opinion has even put them in a different genus.

While early writers listing the animals of Texas usually included foxes, there are too few explorers' accounts of foxes in specific locations to outline any definite range for these animals within the state. Pre-1860 reports are very widely scattered over the whole eastern half of Texas, but are entirely absent from roughly the western half of the state.[4]

Nor do the pioneers leave us any clear idea of the quantity of foxes anywhere in the state. Only two early writers even mention how numerous they were. Concerning the region around Nacogdoches in 1841, Von Wrede wrote that "Foxes are few."[5] On the other hand, Mrs. Holley wrote in 1836, about the area down on the lower Brazos River, that, "The fox-hunter could find constant employment in this country, where Reynard peeps from every bush and brake."[6] Which of these opposing statements reflects reality it is hard to say, but one thing would seem to lead us toward a conclusion. The very few times that foxes were specifically said to have been seen — only nine times in the written accounts of the whole 200-plus years — should mean that they were not anywhere very common in Texas.

One would think, from all the metaphors, stories and even fables prompted by the actions of the red fox that the Texas gray fox would have generated some comments on the part of our pioneers. But no pioneer even bothered to describe our foxes beyond calling them gray or silver. Neither did anyone here take time to describe their behavior. In fact, there is only one comment from early-times Texas about what should have been a preeminent problem if there were many foxes around. An anonymous immigrant into Texas, in a work published in 1846, after describing the damage the "real beasts of prey" do to the herds, stated, "Fox and wildcats present only a danger to wild fowl."[7]

The few times the gray fox was mentioned by our pioneer reporters and the off-hand manner in which it was mentioned would seem to mean that this animal was an even less significant actor in the dramas of those times than its retiring habits would lead us to expect.

Not only that, we know that there are two smaller foxes which had to have been in Texas at those times. On the trans-Pecos mesas there are the little desert foxes, and on the high plains up through the Panhandle there are the still more tiny kit or swift foxes. Neither of these species figure even once in any of the pre-1860 Texas accounts we have seen. They apparently did not figure in the explorers' world in any way.

The native foxes of Texas had to have been those quiet, unobtrusive, yet worthwhile Texans which, believe it or not, did and still do exist behind the scenes.

10

Texas Hogs: Native and Naturalized

MEXICAN HOGS: THE ONLY NATIVE TEXAS ONES

If somewhere in Texas you come across a creature so uncomely as to appear gotten up for the ugliest Texan competition, so cantankerous as to outdo even the crustiest mustang and so pugnacious as to be considered by many in the running for Texas' most vicious native animal award, you have almost certainly met a peccary or javelina. If the situation is such that you can comfortably study this animal you should do it, for even though it is famous more for negative qualities than positive ones, it has always been here, and Texas is not completely comprehended without it.

The collared peccary figured much larger in the explorers' picture of early Texas than its diminutive size would justify. It was named or described over and over again by those early in our territory, from chroniclers of early Spanish expeditions to pioneers and their surveyors up to 200 years later.

Most of the pioneers show that they knew the animal to be the same peccary which ranges south over so much of this hemisphere. Anthony Ganilh, for instance, published in 1838 the description of a South Texas incident in the following words: "A boy killed a pecari, one of the most singular animals in nature, very abundant in the lowlands of Mexico."[1] Others took the precaution to add words indicating the Mexican connection, as for instance, Dr. Ferdinand Roemer, who wrote in 1849, "While crossing a small brook, one of the Shawnee Indians killed a pecari or Mexican hog."[2] Many more, such as Mrs. Holley[3] and George Ullrich,[4] simply called them Mexican hogs and were done with it.

The word "javelina" as name for this animal had been around for a long time. It is the name for this species which John Sibley used in writing down Juan Brebel's list of animals found on the upper Red River in 1765.[5] However, it was apparently not as commonly used by the Texas pioneers as it has come to be by their descendants. In my collection of several dozen pre-1860 references to the animal, the term appears only two more times. In 1822, W. B. Dewees wrote when in present Robertson County, near present Hearne, Texas: "Bears are very plenty, but we are obliged to use great care when hunting for them, lest the *havalenas* (meaning the peccary) kill our dogs."[6] It seems significant that he felt it necessary to add what must have been a better known name in parenthesis. The third and last appearance of this term is in Auguste Fretelliere's account of early Castroville written in 1844.[7]

The fact that Fretelliere was a Frenchman brings up some interesting speculations. The word "javelina" apparently is not Spanish in origin, as might be thought. It seems to be French, which may explain its less than general use by the early Texans. But there still remains the problem of the word's specific origin. Some would relate it to the word "javelin," meaning a spear or dart. The name would thus supposedly have been prompted by the darting swiftness with which this animal can move and fight, as there have been those called javelin-lizards and snakes, along with dart-snakes. However, some think the name originated instead from the word *javel* or *havel*, meaning slovenly or "low fellow," which certainly fits these inelegant creatures. Who can pick which it was? But why can't we have both of these derivations, crediting its originators with the genius required to coin a name combining two very different attributes of these strange animals?

Collared Peccary by Audubon

Scientifically inclined observers of this animal have had their own problems with naming it. For its genus various ones have come up with *Pecari, Tayassu, Dicotyles* and *Sus.* And for its specific name they have coined *tajacu, torquatus* and *angulatus.* Publications have appeared with almost every possible combination of these names, and within the present decade Texas academic circles have published studies using two different genus names for the animal.

By whatever name, the explorers knew exactly what creature they were writing about and could describe it. A. J. Pickett, for instance, wrote in 1856, "The most formidable animal, and one to be most dreaded is the Mexican hog. They have a grown one in a pen here. It is about the size of a half grown hog. Its back is covered with hair resembling porcupine quills, but much finer. It has enormous teeth & they come together like sheers & cut every thing in pieces."[8]

These animals are small for hogs. John C. Reid wrote in 1857, that grown ones averaged about seventy pounds.[9] This is larger than the fifty pounds most modern authorities find them, but still small for hogs. They are short-legged and close-coupled, looking, as one of my students once remarked aptly, something like constipated pigs. Their heads seem entirely too large for their bodies and their hindquarters slighted, so that they have the front-heavy look of the buffalo, and when they bristle in attack mode, as Audubon's rendering of one so beautifully shows, one seems to be faced with all head, jaws and teeth.

This is the actual peccary. Many erroneous things are said about this little fellow because it is so often confused with either the domestic hog, the wild European boar — both of which have been let loose upon Texas — or with all sorts of sports which have come out of the woods where all of these rut at will. Any animal you meet having noticeably curving and external tusks or any visible tail, which is followed by more than two offsprings or roots in the ground beyond merely stirring the loose surface debris, is not a peccary. Nor is it a native Texan, and anything it is or is not, does or does not do cannot be credited to Texas' account.

Peccaries are noted for being gregarious. Whenever numerous they are almost always met with in groups which may be large. The quantity of them in pristine Texas may be sensed by reading what the observers of the situation describe about this. Mrs. Holley wrote in 1836, "The Pecari or Mexican hog is even yet occasionally met with, on the frontiers, in considerable gangs."[10] Victor Bracht reported in 1846, "The entire hilly region of the West is infested by large herds of Mexican hogs, also called peccary or musk hogs. . . . I killed a musk-hog (out of a herd of thirty), about a hundred paces from the city limits [of New Braunfels] on the other side of the creek."[11] In 1849, Dr. Roemer wrote, "Mexican peccaries (Dicotyles torquatua L.) were encountered in small herds several times on the forested banks of the Comal and several were shot."[12] That the animals may have already begun to be depleted or to flee from the settlers by the time of the above writers and may have been much more numerous earlier would seem to be indicated. For instance, Bishop Marin de Porras appears to link them with the most numerous animals in the Texas wilderness when he wrote, back in 1805, "Bear, wild boar, deer and buffalo are found in such abundance that it is incredible to one who has not seen them."[13] It is only a hearsay report published seventy-five years after the fact, but O. C. Fisher wrote that javelinas were said to have been seen "in herds of fifty or even a hundred" in 1860, on out in Kimble County, which was settled later than Comal.[14] The evidence is all that these animals were once teeming in Texas.

In 1854, Audubon and Bachman credited the peccary with a very large range north to beyond Texas, stating that they based this upon Nuttall's having seen one on the Red River in Arkansas at north latitude 31°.[15] Baird repeated the same thing in 1857, placing Nuttall's record in Arkansas at latitude 34°.[16] Many later repeated that the animal's range goes to the Red River, or more recently, like Davis, said that it formerly did.[17] All of this seems based upon Nuttall's statement when he was in present Oklahoma, just north of the Red River, opposite present Lamar County, Texas (the Red River is not near either north latitude 31 or 34 degrees when in present Arkansas).[18] Most recent authorities have been following Davis in stating that the animals are now limited to southwest Texas. But more definite things can be said, based upon both the explorers' words and those of modern field biologists.

Of course, the Mexican hogs would be common in South Texas, and Lt. J. D. Webster, of the Topographical Engineers, reported them among the most noticeable animals in the chaparral along the lower part of the Rio Grande River in 1848.[19] Ganilh reported them near the junction of Atascosa, Bexar and Medina counties in 1838,[20] Fretelliere at Castroville in 1844,[21] and Josiah Gregg at San Antonio in 1846.[22] We have seen that Bracht killed one only paces from New Braunfels. J. DeCordova reported them "in great abundance," in what is now San Saba County in 1858.[23] We must agree with Bracht's statement which we have already seen that the whole of south-central Texas was "infested" with them.

Francis Moore, Jr., published in 1840 a blanket statement that "The peccary, or Mexican hog, frequents the forests of all the western streams."[24] Recent works usually have general statements that peccaries inhabit West Texas and on through southern New Mexico. Just how much do the early travelers west support this for the original situation?

We can follow by means of their journals the treks west of various early expeditions. Setting out with them, we have John C. Reid reporting in 1857, "While here (Camp Davis), we availed ourselves of the fine opportunities presented for killing small game, ducks, turkeys, and wild swine (peccary), in the [Devil's] river and its bottom. Each kind was abundant, though our success in taking them was but indifferent."[25] This put the javelinas solidly in Val Verde County, and Capt. S. G. French, in his 1849 report to the Congress of the U.S. confirmed that he found them there.[26]

But then we push up along the Pecos River, have to cross it sooner or later, and jump off into the expanses still awesome for auto drivers, let alone then for wagoneers, of the trans-Pecos. We can cross to El Paso high under the bosom of the Guadalupes with some California-bound pioneers, cut down through various mountain passes to the Rio Grande with others, even detour down through the Big Bend with a few government explorers or come up from Presidio with the really early Spanish expeditions, and in all of these journeyings over almost 200 years' time, we are told of the sighting of not one peccary out there. This must be evidential. Most of those expeditions had expert hunters ranging widely along their routes to provide food for the companies, and their scribes usually reported very happily whatever game they found. Since many times the parties were on the verge of starvation and you can feel the chroniclers' excitement in reporting even one bear taken or some venison to eat, it must be significant that they never reported a javelina or exulted over a pig on the spit. In the explorers' Texas the range of the peccary in southwest Texas stopped at the Devil's River.

In northwest Texas the story is very different. We have already seen that Juan Brebel listed wild hogs among the animals in "innumerable quantities" on the upper Red River. There is a partial confirmation of this idea, no doubt surprising to some of us. In Don Athanase de Mezieres' report to his superior on the situation of the Indian towns on the Red River. He wrote in 1778, "Firewood is at hand, being brought from that large woodland of which I have spoken [the Cross Timbers]. It is eighty leagues long [see the explanation in our first volume of this measurement], one, two and, in places, even more in breadth, and in it live bears and wild boars."[27] This puts javelinas in the whole swath of brush and forest running out of the Edwards Plateau, where we have already seen that these animals abounded, northeast across the Red River into Oklahoma, where we have seen that Nuttall found them.

There is some recent evidence showing that our explorers were once again accurate when they placed the Mexican hog up in the wooded parts of North Texas. Mezieres' statement concerning these hogs in the Cross Timbers is corroborated by Rupert Norval Richardson's writing in 1963, "The javelina, or Mexican wild hog was not common in the Cross Timbers but was not unknown."[28] And Mezieres' placing them farther down in the belt of brushy forestland once stretching across Texas from the Edwards Plateau to the Cross Timbers is validated by the taking of four javelinas in 1986 and 1987, in Coke County, Texas.[29]

If it came out of Mexico, as it seems it must have, the peccary must have run into something — or the lack of something — which stopped it from ranging far to the east. Mrs. Holley reported them near the mouth of the Brazos,[30] and A. J. Pickett's description of them, which we have already read, comes from his experiencing them in the Brazos and Colorado rivers' lowlands in the area of present Wharton County. But the early accounts of javelinas require us to follow the Brazos River lowlands northwest from these in delineating the eastern boundary of their range. When in what is now Bell County in 1844, George Kendall wrote: "The place where we encamped on Little River . . . is one of exceeding loveliness, healthy, and combining every advantage. . . . Bears and Mexican hogs, the latter a ferocious animal, are found in great numbers in the bottoms."[31] We have already quoted W. B. Dewees' statement about javelinas killing his dogs in present Robertson County in 1822. This is the easternmost record of these animals we have found until we come upon Nuttall's reference to them across the Red River approximately north of our Paris, Texas. For some reason this species just did not manage to colonize the eastern part of the state.

Is it possible to even hazard a guess about why the javelina did not prevail farther east where thickets suited other hogs so perfectly? The explorers don't shed any light upon this directly, but they do leave some indirect evidence which, when put with what modern field studies have taught us, seems to provide basis for at least an educated guess.

Javelinas are, like other hogs, omnivorous, but Davis says that they are "chiefly herbivorous and feed on various cacti, especially prickly pear, mesquite beans, sotol, lechuguilla and other succulent vegetation."[32] He relates that where the right cacti are abundant they do not even require drinking water, getting both their food and water from the cacti. Now remembering this, note that the eastern edge of the ranges of both the mesquite and the large prickly pears is not far from the edge of the javelina's territory. Could it be that they are as dependent upon such plants as some other wild hogs are upon oaks and their acorns?

Our explorers give us a range for the peccary rising out of Mexico and the Gulf between the Devil's River on the west and the Brazos on the east. Its western boundary curves northeast up to the Red River at the Cross Timbers and its eastern is the Brazos Valley until it abandons that to follow the blackland prairies to the Red River. This was a denizen of the Central Texas corridor, all the way from south to north.

The explorers did not bother to leave us much information about the javelina's behavior, except to stress two things. We have already seen that they made it very clear that when it was still present in quantity the species lived and moved in groups. And a quick review of this chapter will show that those early in Texas found the peccaries very vicious and dangerous animals. Because recent authors mostly echo Davis, who wrote just a score or so years ago, "Regarding their supposed vicious habits . . . wildlife observers, in general, consider the peccary absolutely harmless to the range, to livestock, and to other species,"[33] we must dwell on the reason for the discrepancy between early and recent experiences with this animal.

To review — we have already quoted Dewees, Pickett and George Kendall to the effect that peccaries were very vicious. Many more could be heard on this, as for instance, none other than Mary Austin

Holley, who wrote, "They [peccaries] will boldly attack a man, and are considered more dangerous than any other wild animal in Texas."[34] Bracht wrote in 1848, "Usually they flee when a person comes near them suddenly; but sometimes they attack the intruder of their wilderness, and are then unusually dangerous for dogs."[35] Arthur Ikin wrote in 1841 about, "The peccary, or Mexican hog, a ferocious and, when in herds, formidable little animal. . . ."[36] And we certainly must take seriously the quotation of a Mr. William P. Smith which Audubon and Bachman placed in their great 1851 work as their statement on the subject. It is as follows: "The Mexican hogs previous to the overflowing of the bottom lands in 1833, struck terror into the hearts of the settlers in their vicinity, oftentimes pursuing the planter whilst hunting or in search of the lost track of his wandering cattle — at which time they frequently killed his dogs, or even at times forced him to ascend a tree for safety, where he would sometimes be obliged to wait until the hogs got tired of dancing attendance at the foot of his place of security, or left him to go and feed. These animals appeared quite savage, and would, after coming to the tree in which the planter had ensconsed himself, snap their teeth and run about and then lie down at the root of the tree to wait for their enemy to come down."[37]

It is apparently a reminiscence and so not presented here as the same kind of evidence as the accounts written contemporaneously with the happenings, but a story told by Ann Raney Coleman seems useful to indicate the extent of the fear the settlers had of javelinas. The event described is purported to have occurred during the 1830s, near the lower Brazos.

Mrs. Coleman tells, "One day Mrs. Atkinson came to visit me and spent the day. I promised to return home with her in the evening and stay all night with her as my husband had gone to Brazoria. On going home with her in the evening and coming to a turn in the road, we heard a noise like the grunting of hogs. On hearing them Mrs. A said, 'What if they should be Mexican hogs?' 'Oh, no,' I said, 'I think they are some of ours or our neighbor's hogs. There are no Mexican hogs about at present.' 'Yes, but there are,' replied she, 'my husband saw a drove of them somewhere about here.' The words had hardly been spoken when we came up on seven of them. Mrs. A on seeing them said, 'Run! Run, Mrs. T. They are Mexican hogs!' She left me standing in the road, hardened with unbelief. I had not yet noticed the difference between them and our tame hogs. Having stood about three minutes looking at them, I noticed how small and short their legs were, when presently one or two bristled up at me, gnashed their tusks which were very long and large, and came after me. I took to my heels and ran as fast as I could. Looking back, I saw my pursuers close at my heels. I doubled my speed, and soon passed my friend Mrs. A on the road. She cried, 'Oh, do not leave me, Mrs. T, or I shall faint in the road. I have run until I can run no longer.' I told her I was going to the creek to get Mr. A to bring his gun to shoot the hogs. . . . She still cried after me, but I paid no attention to her cries, as I did not see the hogs anywhere, we having outrun them or either they got tired pursuing."[38]

Davis' term for all such statements is "legendary tales . . . [which] have caused inexperienced hunters to kill them [peccaries] through fear. . . ." But are we really going to have to brand all of these pioneers, some of them worthies in their own rights, as spinners of tales and tall talkers? Mustn't there be a logical explanation of the discrepancy between the earlier and recent opinions of javelina behavior?

I, myself, have met up with javelinas which ran from me, others which casually walked away from me, and I have backed as nonchalantly as possible out of a thicket where a couple stood their ground before me, but I have never been chased by any. I also have some South Texas friends whose outlets for their *machismo* are regular javelina hunts and barbecues and who assure me that they have never been challenged by an unprovoked one. So I am inclined to agree with those in the field in recent times that peccaries do not now-a-days viciously attack people. But I note one important factor: I have never met up with a herd or drove of these animals and I have been unable to find any present-day Texan who has. Four is the most I have seen in the wild at one time or know of anyone else meeting up with in one group in recent times. Both their numbers and their required habitats have been reduced so drastically that I seriously doubt that any large herds of them have built up here for many years past.

The other side of the coin is that I once had a student from Central America who told me of having been pursued and treed by a large, unprovoked group of peccaries, the literature of Central and South America abounds with such accounts, and our explorers insist that these animals once did such things in Texas. The important detail is that all of these attacks were by large groups of peccaries. There is no report of one or several little javelinas running at anyone anywhere, any time, while they apparently do just that when in larger groups.

So this seems to be the factor explaining why the vicious, aggressive little hog of early Texas is the reclusive, don't-bother-me-and-I-won't-bother-you little pig of today's thickets. Gang psychology turned the individuals of the large herds in which they once ran into the boldest of mass attackers, and the pioneers were wise to fear them. But pigs aren't dumb, and unable today to congregate in any significant numbers, today's nearly solitary peccary being no fool, retreats instead of attacks, and is vicious only when fighting for its or its offsprings' very lives.

And Mrs. Coleman's group of seven is no contradiction, but instead must have been just large enough a group to prove my point. They were probably just a big enough gang to be courageous enough to mount a pursuit of the women, but were probably so few that prudence prevailed over mass psychology and they broke off their attack early.

Once again I submit that our explorers present an accurate picture of pristine Texas' natural history and that when it is taken seriously and analyzed carefully it can often explain the differences between what was and what is now. And I think we can learn helpful things from it. The specific lesson to be learned in this instance would seem to be that while you can be guardedly unconcerned about meeting up with only one or several javelinas, you had better look for a tree if you come across a whole herd of them. But the larger lesson may be that our pioneers' recorded experiences may reveal instances where systematically inclined observers have erected taxa by overemphasizing trivialities or misinterpreting situation-induced behavior differences as based upon heredity.

For instance, consider the following passage: "There are two species, so nearly allied that they will breed together freely in captivity.... The Collared Peccary ... ranges from the Red River of Arkansas through the forest districts of Central and South America as far as the Rio Negro of Patagonia. Generally it is found singly or in pairs, or at most in small herds of from eight to ten, and is a comparatively harmless creature, not being inclined to attack other animals or human beings. Its colour is dark gray, with a white or whitish band passing across the chest from shoulder to shoulder. The length of the head and body is about 36 inches. The White-lipped Peccary ... is rather larger, being about 40 inches in length, of a blackish colour, with the lips and lower jaw white. Its range is less extensive, since it is not found farther north than British Honduras or south of Paraguay. It is generally met with in large herds of from fifty to a hundred or more individuals, and is of a more pugnacious disposition than the former species, and capable of inflicting severe wounds with its sharp tusks. Anyone who encounters a herd of them in a forest has often to take to a tree as his only chance of safety."[39]

Juxtapose to that C. W. Webber's eloquent passage which he put at the end of his 1854 account of a harrowing Texas peccary hunt: "[The peccary] seems to be entirely insensible to all those sudden influences, the unexpected supervention of which are sure to cause panic in other animals. Ungovernable rage seems to take the place of this panic — a rage quite as headlong and as blind.... It is yet, really, one of the most formidable animals belonging to our hemisphere. It is gregarious, and goes in droves of from ten to fifty. Its jaws are armed after the manner of the wild boar, with tushes, but they are of very different shape, and if possible, more to be dreaded. They stand straight in the jaws, instead of curving upwards, and have the form as well as keenness of the lancet blade. Their motions are as quick as lightning, and with shoulders, head and neck possessing extraordinary muscular power, they manage to slash and gash in the most horrible manner with these villainous little weapons, which are only about an inch and a half in length. As they do not hesitate to attack any thing or any body, big or little, provocation or no provocation, that may chance to cross their paths, men and animals very soon learn that their only safety is in flight."[40] It seems clear that anyone who sets up the peccaries of the tropics as more formidable than those which were in Texas must have closed his eyes to what the Texas explorers wrote — or else impugns their words offhand.

When they were yet present in quantity these animals must have presented problems for the early Central Texas settlers other than from the danger of their gang attacks. This was from their gang depredations. Audubon's Mr. Smith goes on to tell: "At this early period of the settlement of Texas (this refers to 1833) they used to hunt this animal in company. From five to fifteen planters together, and occasionally a larger number of hunters, would join in the pursuit of these ravagers of their corn-fields, in order to diminish their number and prevent their farther depredations, as at times they would nearly destroy a farmer's crop."[41]

But the javelinas were not entirely unprofitable scoundrels. They were, after all, pork, and pork free for the taking was surely often a pioneer's boon. Bracht wrote, "Those that I have killed weighed between sixty and eighty pounds and made a fine roast," but cautioned, "When the musk gland is not removed properly, the meat acquires an odious scent and taste."[42] Dr. Roemer tells of removing this gland and says, "If this precaution is taken, the flesh of these animals is palatable and similar to that of our domestic hogs, as we had occasion to find out that same night."[43] However, it stands to reason that the meat of any such a wild animal must be very much more lean and firm than that of our pampered domestic hogs, and any of us who have eaten javelina will give the highest marks for accuracy to William Miles, who wrote in 1850, "the meat tough but sweet."[44] While not exactly one of nature's delicacies or a staple in many pioneers' diets, peccary pork must have been a welcome part of original Texas' bounty for many a struggling settler.

Did such tough little characters as the peccaries, running around in their intimidating gangs, have the free range of the countryside without any challenges? Or was I being told the truth as a child when they told me the bully always meets a tougher guy sooner or later? Well, according to the explorers, the javelinas sometimes met more than their match. John C. Reid wrote, "Their most formidable enemy is the bear."[45] And A. A. Parker wrote in 1836, "The bears, generally, take to the dense forest of trees and canebrake. They catch the full grown hogs, and the wolves take the pigs."[46] It was a battlefield out there in natural Texas, and the peccaries were small, but they were well-armed, and their strength was in their gang organizations. They were survivors.

FERAL HOGS: THE DOGS OF THE FRENCH

There are many reports by explorers and settlers of hogs in early Texas which could in no way have been peccaries. Jose Enrique de la Pena's 1836 account would have to be one of these. He wrote, "Today we camped at Tejocote Creek, having traveled fourteen miles [from Gonzales]; the pigs found at this place were as big as a five or six month's calf."[47] D. B. Brooks also wrote in the same year from near Brazoria, "As to game there is no end to it of every kind there is 2 deer in this country for every hog in Georgia plenty of large fat wild hogs. . . . I took a file of men and went after meat a few days past we killed four wild hogs about 2 years old that averaged 250 pounds net."[48] These certainly weren't javelinas, which attain a maximum weight of fifty to seventy pounds or so.

We let Mrs. Holley enlighten us about what these large hogs were. After writing about the peccaries, as we have seen, she continued as follows: "The wild hog also is frequently met with, and, although it has never been known to make a voluntary attack upon a man, yet, when provoked, it is a very furious and formidable animal. These hogs are descended from the domestic swine, and have become wild by running at large in the woods."[49] So by the time of Texas independence the wilderness of at least its south and eastern parts was already overrun by the escaped descendants of domestic hogs brought into the country. This was the Texas version of what is commonly known farther east as the "razorback," although I have not found this word in the explorers' vocabulary.

There are many passages in the journals of those early in Texas which I have not used in this compilation because the writers just spoke of hogs, with no specific descriptions. All such accounts could, of course, be reporting peccaries, feral hogs or both, and so most of them are of little value to us at all. But there are enough accounts with clues that they indicate feral hogs to give us a picture — not always pleasant — of the place these introduced creatures carved for themselves in the primeval Texas scene.

W. Steinert may well have been including javelinas in his statement from Fredericksburg in 1849, but he is almost certainly reporting also on the price early farmers had to pay for having brought hogs with them to this land. He wrote, "Unfortunately we could not have our host with us this evening; he has to spend the night in the field in order to keep the raccoons and hogs out of the corn."[50] And since it is hard to imagine a skitterish and gregarious peccary venturing anywhere alone, let alone into a building full of people, it probably was a feral hog which prompted the following passage showing us how these animals must have infiltrated with their swinish attributes most every aspect of the settlers' lives. The Abbe Domenech was describing his services conducted in the new settlement of D'Hanis in 1848, when he wrote: "Another time an ill-advised boar, attracted no doubt by the chant entered the chapel whilst we were at vespers. His curiosity cost him dearly. He was killed on the spot, and eaten the next day."[51]

To point up the picture of these reverting-to-nature porkers as they were around the settlements, we follow the lead of Charles Hooton, who wrote in 1847, "Any gentleman who happens to be enthusiastic in natural history as displayed in the grunting genus of animals ought to go to Galveston forthwith, since no place can be named where greater facilities for study in that particular department of science may be enjoyed . . . since the pigs are not only amazingly numerous, but remarkably acute and sharp, and, in their industrious researches after the various edible delicacies of the island, display a degree of sagacity and discernment eminently calculated to redeem the character of their whole race from that odium of proverbial stupidity which, by the common consent of mankind, has been fixed upon it. Enjoying unchecked the republican freedom of going at large wherever they please, both town and prairie are overrun by numberless herds of them. Useful as aids and assistants to the turkey-buzzard in clearing away all descriptions of refuse and offal, they likewise exert all their powers of nose and teeth in smelling out and destroying snakes of all kinds, which they devour with surprising avidity; in fact, through their instrumentality mainly, is the eastern end of the island, upon which the city stands, indebted for its comparative freedom from those annoying and dangerous reptiles. The pig catches a serpent by placing his foot upon it, and pinning it to the ground in the division of his hoof. Both day and night do they hunt about over miles of ground, though most generally during the day. Early in the morning, almost before daylight, they may be seen setting out from the town in the greatest of all possible hurries. . . ."[52]

It is hard for us, living today in the Texas which is one of the most completely fenced of all the contiguous states, to realize the situation when there was no wire fencing of any kind and only the most closely held gardens could be protected by any sort of barrier. In the days we are talking about, there were ugly battles at San Antonio, for instance, between those purporting to own free-ranging stock and those trying to protect farmed fields from the marauding animals."[53] In many places feral hogs must have been a big part of the problem.

An illustration of how severe and how pervasive the problem must have been is shown by the plight in which F. L. Olmsted found himself. That well-known visitor to Texas, in his 1854 trip to San Antonio, reported: "The second day's camp was a few miles beyond the town of Crockett. . . . At this camp we were annoyed by hogs beyond all description. At almost every camp we were surrounded by them; but here they seemed perfectly frantic and delirious with hunger. They ran directly through the fire and even carried off a chicken which B. on a second excursion had been able to procure, after it was dressed and spitted. While the horses were feeding it required the constant attention of two of us to keep them at bay; and even then they secured more than half the corn. . . . For some minutes the fiercest of them would resist even a clubbing, eating and squealing on through the blows. . . . We made our camp on the edge of the bottom, and for safety against our dirty persecutors, the hogs, pitched our tent *within* [Olmsted's italics] a large hog-yard, putting up the bars to exclude them."[54]

There were obviously myriad big, tough old hogs and their swarming offspring let loose upon the countryside of at least southern and eastern Texas. Many of them must have been escapees from the best rail fences the settlers could put up, but many more were probably turned out on purpose to grow and fatten on the acorns and other fruits of the wilderness. Shooting your hogs in the woods was no doubt more fun than forever feeding them in the pen. It was the Spanish free-range ranching system applied to pork production.

So it is not hard to see how the feral hogs got started in Texas. But it will probably be a surprise to most of us to learn how early they got out and started multiplying. The Talon brothers were the survivors of La Salle's ill-fated settlement of the Gulf Coast of Texas. When they got back to France the Talons were subjected to an official interrogation which took place in 1698. In their replies to questions about the country of the settlement, which was to become Texas, they stated: "There will be presently a quantity of runaway or wild pigs all over the country, the French having released some that had already reproduced prodigiously by the time [the Talons] left there. The savages do not eat them, saying that they are the dogs of the French. . . ."[55]

This is testimony that feral hogs were already spreading before the end of the seventeenth century because the French brought hogs with them to their earliest settlements. And it may explain a confusing report of wild hogs in very early East Texas.

Concerning East Texas beyond the Trinity River, Fray Francisco Casanas de Jesus Maria wrote to the viceroy of Mexico in 1691: "This country contains various kinds of animals that are good to eat, such as wild hogs. They are quite large and savage like those in New Spain."[56]

This has been a puzzling report. It has been assumed that it had to refer to the only native hogs in Texas, the peccaries, but if it does, it has to mean some of several hard to accept things: either the peccaries were in seventeenth century beyond the Trinity — where they were never seen again, and were at that time as large as domestic hogs (after which they drastically shrank) — or else Maria was totally in error in his report to his viceroy. None of these are alternatives to be assumed without corroboration, which has not appeared. But the primary evidence supplied by the Talons provides a way to clear up the mystery. If the comparatively small French settlement of Fort St. Louis came equipped with hogs, it is much more likely that the more elaborate French colony of Champ de Aisle brought domestic hogs to East Texas. And if some of these had also escaped and multiplied (note: one of the Talon brothers had been for years in East Texas and may have been referring to those French-released hogs), then Maria's large wild hogs in East Texas would have been feral hogs already rooting there in the seventeenth century. Incidentally, is Maria's remark that those were "like those in New Spain," instead of a reference to peccaries, a hint that the Spanish had their domestic hogs as early also?

It is a scene pictured through the statements of many witnesses. Into the pristine wilderness which was Texas as discovered, the earliest explorers and settlers immediately released not only their horses and cattle to graze the marvelous verdure, but their hogs to consume the fruits, acorns and seeds, to root out the succulent roots, the wild potatoes and all, and to slash to bits whatever unfortunate Texas creatures could not escape them. Have the effects of the feral hog on Texas ever been calculated?

11

More Than Critters

I use the above word in this chapter title not only because it is familiar to us, but in order to point out that when we use such uncouth terms today with a sense of pride that we are speaking the language of our pioneers, we are probably kidding ourselves. So far as I can find, the term "critter" never appears in any pre-1860 Texas pioneer's writing. Those true explorers, from Spanish aristocrats to American army officers, to intelligentsia such as Dr. Roemer, the Abbe Domenech, Berlandier, Olmsted, Kendall, Austin and the rest, were far from uncouth and were knowledgeable enough that they named the animals they wrote about with specific, recognized names. When we speak of critters and such we ally ourselves not with the real heroes of our history, but with the undiscriminating masses who overran original Texas later, the effect of whose treating its animal life as nothing but "critters" is all too obvious now.

Since the explorers' world was the teeming wilderness before our depredations culled out so many forms, we will probably find the smaller animals figured less in it than we expect. There may have been any of several reasons for our pioneers reporting fewer small animals than we think they should have. Explorers, their attentions upon the large, valuable, dangerous or merely spectacular animals all around them, may have passed over the smaller ones as too unimportant to mention. Or, the wilderness possessing so many perfect hiding places as it did then, they actually may not have seen these little animals when present as we usually do in the scraped and scalped, so nearly bare environments we have produced today. Or, just possibly, when the large, powerful carnivores who must have often been the small animals' competitors and sometimes even predators upon them were still everywhere, might there not have been fewer of these little creatures in the untamed wilderness than we imagine? Lacking clues as to which if any of these conjectures may be true, we can only take the records left by those who were witnessing the scenes at face value and build our conceptions as best we can upon them.

THE RACCOON

The raccoon is too ubiquitous, its masked face and ringed tail too spectacular to require description here. And so it must have been in early Texas, for I find only one early Texas writer devoting any words to that purpose. Friederich W. von Wrede did write in 1838, "The raccoon is the size of a badger — gray brown with a white nose and a brown stripe over the eyes. There are five black stripes on the eight-to-ten-inch long tail."[1] It is as though all the rest assumed that everyone already knew this little outlaw from their own experiences.

They were probably right. The raccoon is one of the few animals which is thought to have ranged over absolutely the whole of Texas from the time of the first explorers even until today. Various explorers confirmed this by reporting it from very widely scattered locations,[2] and Viktor Bracht said simply in 1848, "Raccoons and opposum are found throughout the country."[3] The only difference in the various parts of the state was probably in the quantities of these animals present. Dr. Roemer was probably correct in noting in 1849 that while raccoons were common in eastern Texas, they were much less so in western Texas.[4]

Add to the wide range of the animal, which in totality comprises everything from the Atlantic to the Pacific and from Canada to Panama, the fact that it may be surprised foraging in almost any situation from beaches to rocky ledges, and we can see why it must have been so well-known. They are known to eat almost anything organic, from plant material such as persimmons, acorns, grapes, blackberries, holly berries and soft, unripened corn through animals such as birds, snakes, fish, mussels and snails to crayfish, beetles, grasshoppers, wasps, spiders and probably most anything else that moves — except they seem to seldom if ever eat other mammals or carrion. Von Wrede put it this way: "He [the raccoon] exists on sugar cane, corn, birds, eggs, and worms." This almost omnivorous food habit explains why the animal is found through so many different habitats. Audubon and Bachman give us an example of how unusual a place it may be found in because of its strange food habits, writing, "There exists a species of oyster in the Southern States of inferior quality which bears the name of Raccoon Oyster: it lies imbedded in masses in the shallow waters of the rivers. These oysters are covered by high tides, but are exposed at low water. On these the Raccoons are fond of feeding, and we have on several occasions seen them on the oyster banks."[5]

Most of the pioneers only bothered to write about raccoons when the animals affected them, but their food habits often led to this. We have seen von Wrede accusing the animals of eating sugar cane and corn, and this would make them serious enemies of the settlers. Bracht, after his statement already quoted about the raccoon's range, confirms their depredations in the fields, writing about raccoons and opossums, "The latter are destructive to chickens; the former injure the cornfields." And we must feel sympathy for the settler who was the host of W. Steinert when he visited Fredericksburg in 1849 and wrote that passage best showing the extent of our masked creature's villainy: "Unfortunately we could not have our host with us this evening; he has to spend the night in the field in order to keep the raccoons and hogs out of the corn."[6]

It must be a small portion of this world's justice that this bothersome raccoon is featured in the explorers' accounts as their victim as well. It may surprise us, but the raccoon is mentioned by early Texans more often as a game animal taken to be eaten than for any other reason. Among the authors already quoted, von Wrede goes on to say, "His [the raccoon's] meat is edible." Bracht ventures, "The raccoon makes a juicy roast." Gustav Dresel wrote in 1839, "Walker had provided again for a roast on the way. The bullet of his good gun had killed a raccoon, which, spread out on poles like a bat, was roasted on the fire."[7]

Since raccoons have in more recent times become the most valuable fur bearers in eastern Texas, producing in the 1976 to 1981 seasons almost $21 million income — which is about 70 percent of the income of East Texas trappers for that time —[8] it is interesting to note that no pre-1860 Texas writer we have found mentioned the use of the raccoon's fur in any way. Nor does any one of them remark about the animal's courage and fighting ability, which has been so often noted since.

So the raccoon was found throughout Texas. Few of the explorers bothered about any scientific name for him, but Baird, ever the scientist, ventured to call those of southern and western Texas *Procyon hernandezii*, the Mexican raccoon, and admitted he did not know where the line between this and the eastern raccoon, *P. lotor*, fell.[9] Later, the Texas raccoons were called *P. lotor fuscipes*. Generally, our explorers merely noted this animal as a creature that was here, a pest to the settler but compensating for this by being an acceptable item of diet.

THE RINGTAIL

It's been called the ringtail cat, the civet-cat and the raccoon-fox, but don't call it a cat, because even though it has cat-like features, it isn't a cat at all. And you can't logically call it a fox, even though its face and attitude are often fox-like and its genus name is *Bassariscus*, meaning "little fox," because it isn't one. Its tail outdoes those of the raccoons in both number and contrast of its rings, but it isn't a raccoon. It is sort of weasel-like and it climbs almost as well as a squirrel, with its species name, *astutus* meaning "adroit" and "cunning," but it isn't either of these. It is unique among the creatures of Texas, and you had best just call it the ringtail and let it go at that, or use the Indian name, *cacomistle*, for it.

If we are surprised that the explorers mentioned the almost ever-present raccoon as seldom as they did, we should be more surprised that they were at all conscious of the ringtail or ever bothered to mention it. Since it is a small animal hardly as large as a housecat, strictly nocturnal and most furtive even then, most Texans have never seen a ringtail and don't know that they are still around. I,

Ring-Tailed Bassaris *by Audubon*

myself, have only come across one in over thirty years of pretty active field work in Texas, although once I learned to recognize them, I found their lairs rather often, and trappers show that they are fairly common. The only one I have actually handled was an immature one which fell out of a nest in a niche high on a building on the edge of San Antonio. Those of us who were in and out of that building both day and night did not even know there had been any such animals there at all, and never did see the adult even though she presumably matured the rest of her family near us.

The only early Texas reports of this animal which we have found are all from the central part of the state. Dr. Ferdinand Roemer was in present Menard County, at the site of the old Spanish fort in 1849, when he wrote: "When we returned to our camp, one of the Shawnee Indians had just shot an animal about the size of a marten with a long tail, ringed grey and black. I had not seen it in the lower coastal region, but it does not seem to be uncommon in the higher, hilly country. The Texas settler calls it civet cat, but the scientific name is *Bassaris Astuta* Lichtenstein. It had previously only been reported from Mexico."[10]

At about the same time Audubon and Bachman were publishing the following: "The general features of the State of Texas . . . do not indicate a country where many tree-climbing animals could be found, and the present beautiful species, which Professor Lichtenstein most appropriately named *Bassaris astuta*, is by no means common. It is a lively, playful and nimble creature, leaps about on the trees, and has very much the same actions as the squirrel . . . always having a hole in the tree upon which it resides, and betaking itself to that secure re-treat at once if alarmed. . . . As far as we could ascertain, the northern limit of the range of this species is somewhere in the neighborhood of the southern branches of Red River. As you travel south they are more abundant. . . . We were informed by our friend, the celebrated Col. Hays, the Ranger, that he saw them more abundant in the mountainous region near the head-waters of the San Saba river than at any other place."[11]

No explorer reports having found a ringtail east of the Texas Hill Country. Although we cannot argue from a negative and it would be easy to imagine our observers missing such a fugitive animal as this, the fact that the animal is now being found almost throughout East Texas makes us wonder if this is another species which has been increasing its range north and east in modern times.

Here again, as with the raccoon, we have the peculiar circumstance of not one of the pioneers mentioning that they used the coat of the ringtail at all, while it is said to have become in recent years the most important furbearer on the Edwards Plateau.[12]

There is another way in which the ringtail might be thought to have affected the lives of the pioneers. These animals are about as omnivorous as the raccoons, but they eat proportionally less plant material and more animals. Insects and other small creatures make up a large part of their diet, but they eat birds and mammals, both those they kill and those found as carrion. Among birds they are known to sometimes take large species such as jays, doves, flickers and quail. Rats and mice, squirrels, bats and rabbits are eaten by them, and investigators have found in their stomachs remains of deer, sheep, cows and skunks which they no doubt found as carrion. Taylor points out that, "It is a mystery how the ringtail catches some of its prey."[13] The animal must be a very aggressive hunter, and it would seem that it would have posed a very definite threat to the pioneers' poultry, if not to their other small or young animals. So we go to their writings looking for their stories of ringtail's depredations in their farmyards, and the surprise is that there is not one such account and not even a hint of any early Texan worrying about such happening. The ringtail must have been one wild predator which behaved itself around domestic stock.

This leaves the ringtail as an aborigine of at least Central Texas which rarely crossed paths with the explorers, even though it was usually near them, which they did not seem to hunt for any reason, and which did not figure in their lives at all. Probably as elusive and mysterious to the pioneers as it is to most Texans still, it was a fascinating part of the explorers' Texas.

THE BADGER: TEXAS UNDERGROUND FIGHTER

There is yet another Texas animal with startling black and white markings, dangerous teeth and an unlovable disposition. However, this one's sharply contrasting colors are not displayed on its short tail, but on its face, which is almost as much an outlaw's as that of the raccoon; and this one is too short-legged and broad to climb anything, so it lives in underground burrows instead of trees or ledges. It is the curious creature called the badger.

This animal was definitely present in pristine Texas, but the explorers apparently took very little notice of it, only three of them even mentioning it before 1860. It appears as often in early traders' lists of furs handled as in pioneers' accounts.

Brad C. Fowler, who was on one of the earliest expeditions through West Texas, met up with the animal and left a brief description of it which hits upon some of its important characteristics, even though his syntax is confusing. He wrote in 1853, "The Mexican Badger, the body of which will weigh about forty pounds, of a brindled color and made fight with the energy of a Tiger; our boys killed and brought one into camp at Salt Creek, one of the tributaries of the Colorado."[14]

Fowler's estimate of the badger's weight seems too heavy, most of them weighing in at about 25 pounds, but his word for its color is well-chosen, and he expresses very well the most obvious thing about its behavior. The "badger" is an implacable fighter. Many a hunter has learned this to his sorrow and to that of his whipped and torn dog. William B. Davis says, "In one recorded instance a badger successfully defended itself in fight with two coyotes."[15] It is an unforgettable experience, well pictured by Audubon, to be faced by a broad, squat, snarling badger at bay. To "badger" is a very meaningful action. Has anyone ever seen one break and run?

The incident with the badger which was reported by Fowler occurred in or near present Young County, in North Texas, yet notice that he called the animal the "Mexican Badger." Baird, in writing the animal up for the 1857 Railroad Surveys, also called it the Mexican Badger and notes that in his report for the earlier Mexican boundary survey he had named it *Taxidea Berlandieri*, separating it from the northern *T. taxus*.[16] They were both correct in that the species does range deep into Mexico. Lindheimer, in his 1835 letter from near Vera Cruz, Mexico, had already listed the badger as one of the animals he found down there, making that clear.[17] However, we now know that the species is found all the way into Alberta, Canada, and its closest relative is the badger of the British Isles and northern parts of that other hemisphere. So this is not another species venturing out of Mexico into Texas, but one of the far fewer species which ventures through Texas into Mexico from the north. The only question remaining is whether our Texas-Mexican population is a separate race from the northern ones or not, and some scholars are still subdividing ours, variously proposing *Taxidea taxus berlandieri* and *T. t. littoralis* for those in different parts of Texas.[18]

The explorers' records of badgers are too few to help establish much about their range. However, the one Fowler reports from the vicinity of Young County, the one Baird reports that Captain Pope brought in from the Llano Estacado, and his own recorded down on the Mexican boundary make it clear that they ranged generally over much, if not all, of western Texas.

There is more than one opinion about the badger in East Texas. Schmidly, in his discussion of East Texas mammals, noting only recent records of badgers taken in East Texas, states, ". . . it has only recently been recorded in eastern Texas," and concludes, ". . . it appears that the badger represents another example of a western species that has recently expanded its range eastward as a result of land-clearing operations."[19] This conclusion appears false if the evidence in the census reports of the Department of Nacogdoches for the years 1828 to 1834 is considered. Furs traded in those years in that place and presumably trapped somewhere in that East Texas region included badger.[20] They must have been there at that early time. It is true, as Schmidly points out, that badgers need open, sandy country and avoid heavily wooded areas, but as we have learned in the first volume of this study, East Texas was not an unbroken forest and there were always prairies and sandy ridges in it. In fact, the presence of badgers in early East Texas constitutes an additional argument for the existence of prairies in East Texas as originally found.

It would be pleasant to ramble on about the badger, how it lives, how it can fight and how remarkably it can dig, but the explorers did not concern themselves with all this — or at least did not choose to enlighten us about their experiences with the animal — and most of it has been told elsewhere.

Only one thing concerning these animals needs to be dealt with when trying to picture badgers in the explorers' world. This is the fact that they dig large burrows wherever they live. These are tunnels usually about eight to ten inches in diameter leading into the ground at an oblique angle. It is said that these tunnels sometimes extend as much as thirty-two feet in length, down to a depth of ten feet, and are so effortlessly dug that when the animal makes a big kill, such as a rabbit, it sometimes digs a burrow on the spot, drags the prey into it and stays secluded there, eating for days.[21] I grew up in a country of sandy soil with many badgers, and although I never saw it tried, it was commonly remarked that it would be useless to try to dig out a badger because the animal could dig down faster than several men could excavate after it. The openings into these slanting holes are not abrupt, but broadening near the surface. There is little dirt left piled near the entrances to these burrows. It is as though the animals scatter their excavated material so widely that there is at most the slightest suggestion of any mound nearby. These burrows are always completely in the open, away from any woody growth or from any ledges.

It should occur to anyone riding across any prairie where there were badgers that these holes might be horrible pitfalls for any horse galloping across the area. This did occur to me in my youthful horseback days on the plains, and there are various harrowing stories scattered through the western literature of the past 100 years of riders being thrown when horses stepped into such holes. So what about the explorers and this hazard? With all of the early horsemen who rode pell-mall across unfamiliar prairies for any old reason, hell-for-leather after game, or blinded by dark nights at the horse's leading, shouldn't the explorers have reported some gruesome instances where someone's horse tripped in a badger burrow, or shouldn't they have issued at least some warning about the possibility? It would seem so.

The point is that we have found not one such incident reported or even any mention of the possibility from the exploratory period. It is just as though it never happened and was not even considered a danger.

Of course, we can no more reason from a negative here than elsewhere, but this made me rethink my fears and examine the evidence a bit. I soon remembered that my father's horses, as those of all our neighbors, often raced wildly about their pastures where badger holes were scattered — with no accidents. And I realized that none of the ranchers I had known had ever voiced any concern about this matter. Only in what might be considered fictionalized turn-of-the-century and later literature did I find horses thrown by stepping into holes. Is it possible that mavericks thundering madly across the prairies in closely bunched stampedes as well as

Texas Skunk by Audubon

horses propelling their riders across country at break-neck speed could react quickly enough to avoid those holes or else compensate for a hoof which descended into the space of a burrow opening instead of onto solid ground so as not to fall? The fact that our explorers never recount an accident from a horse stumbling over a badger's burrow — or that of a skunk or prairie dog either — while not proving that all horses are that sure-footed, might at least argue that range-wise horses could take such animal burrows in stride.

This leaves the badgers in very obscure burrows in the Texas explorers' world. The pioneers seem to have been hardly conscious of him, he seemed to bother them little if at all, and they apparently bothered the badger only in the taking of some of his pelts for the fur trade.

THE POLE CATS WHICH WERE SKUNKS

Other omnivorous marauders in the Texas wilderness were the skunks. And the explorers are not oblivious to skunks. They were very conscious of these animals and left us good records of their brushes with them. Skunks may well be the most disliked wild animals still with us, so we will probably be surprised to learn that some of the pioneers were happy to find skunks and shocked to find out why they were.

Before we can deal with the skunks of the Texas wilderness we have to sort out some names and worry about distinguishing between some different species of them. First of all, in writing about these animals the pioneers were about equally divided between those calling them skunks and those calling them pole cats. This application of the term, "pole cat," to them is especially curious, but there should be logical explanations of it.

Pole cat is a European term widely used there for any weasels. Its use in America may therefore be a reflection of the European background of the early settlers. But what would prompt them to apply a name for a brown European weasel to a spectacularly black-and-white American animal which is not a weasel? This inconsistency was early recognized. In 1718, in his *History of Connecticut*, S. Peters wrote, "The skunk is . . . very different from the Pole-Cat, which he is sometimes called."[22]

Further investigation gives us our first clue to this enigma in a note published in 1688, by J. Clayton, who wrote, "There are [in Virginia] several sorts of Wild Cats, and Poll-Cats."[23] This sounds as if "pole cat" is a general term covering a number of animals. So what were they, and what characteristic held in common placed them, in the minds of the colonists, under the umbrella of this term?

A venture into etymology shows us that the first half of this name, pole, probably is from the Old French *pole* or *poule*, which means chicken or fowl, and hence poultry.[24] The term would therefore mean the chicken, fowl or poultry cat, a European term for weasels notorious for attacking poultry. And it would make it entirely logical for those recently come from Europe to apply this name to whatever American skunks they found after their poultry. If this is the explanation back of the name, it provides a damning indictment of the skunks, but one which any chicken farmer knows is entirely justified. Skunks are as truly pole cats as anything in either hemisphere. A second explanation for the hanging of the pole cat alias on our skunks arises from the existence of an African animal, *Ictonys striatus,* called there the Zorilla, but in most English publications the striped pole cat. This animal is in appearance almost identical to our spotted skunk and ejects musk in exactly the same way. It even has the same strange white temple-spots as our spotted skunk. If things actually did come to be by evolution, then this is a prime example of parallel evolution, with animals of two different families developing essentially the same appearance, glandular equipment and behavior. Look up a good picture of a Zorilla and see if you can tell it isn't a spotted skunk. Reverse this, and it becomes entirely understandable that some explorer who knew the African Zorilla as the pole cat, seeing an American skunk, called it polecat and started the whole thing. From such convergences do nicknames arise.

Whether called pole cats or skunks, these animals were with the settlers from the first. They were often said to have been numerous, and they were everywhere from the Atlantic to the Pacific and from Hudson Bay through most of South America. Of course, explorers could find them virtually anywhere within Texas, and so their surviving accounts inform us.

But it can't remain that simple. There are at least four kinds of skunks in Texas — and they are apparently not merely different races or subspecies. These are four different species, placed by modern students in three separate genera. Rarely are such closely similar forms dispersed so widely in taxonomy.

To their credit, several of the early explorers observed the differences prompting some of these divisions, and noted them down. Jean Louis Berlandier, for instance, wrote in 1848, "There are two distinct types of this animal known in Texas. Their difference is found in the position of their black and white spots as well as the size of their heads."[25]

By the Texas explorers' times there were some ventures into naming these animals scientifically, and several explorers attempted to be scientifically proper. Lt. J. W. Abert, the leader of governmental expeditions, found a skunk in the breaks of Minneosa Creek just north of the Canadian River in the Texas Panhandle, and tried to name it correctly, writing in 1845, "In one of the crevices of the rocks we found a polecat, 'mephitis Americana.'"[26]

Lieutenant Abert's skunk would now be called *Mephitis mephitis.* The word emphasized by double usage here means, literally, "bad odor," so the animal's name means "bad, bad odor" or "very bad odor." This is the common or striped skunk dreaded over practically our whole continent for its pungent perfume. It is certainly common enough throughout Texas, and was in the explorers' times as well. Audubon and Bachman wrote of this species, "There is no quadruped on the continent of North America the approach of which is more generally detested than that of the skunk."[27]

Audubon and Bachman also wrote about another skunk: "*Mephitis mesoleuca* Licht. Texas Skunk. This odoriferous animal is found in Texas and Mexico, and is very similar in its habits to the common skunk of the Eastern, Middle and Southwestern States."[28]

This would be the hog-nosed or white-backed skunk. It is now known officially as *Conepatus mesoleucus.* The genus name is from the Mexican word, *conepatl,* and the species name is a combination of "middle" and "white." Both the words of this name are especially well-chosen. It is a venturer into Texas, New Mexico and Arizona out of Mexico, coming through Central America from South America, where members of this genus are the only skunks found. The species name is also apt because this skunk has the whole dorsal surface pure white from the head to the tip of the tail, the lower parts of the body and the limbs being the black parts. The nickname "hog-nosed skunks" also is appropriate, as the members of this genus have large snouts bare of fur. This is no doubt the feature noticed by Berlandier which caused him to state that there were in Texas skunks differing in "the size of their heads."

How far the hog-nosed skunks ranged into Texas in the undisturbed natural community is an interesting question which should have a straightforward answer, but it leads us into unfortunate confusion.

The explorers and pioneers noticed white versus striped backs, naked, hog-like noses versus neat furry ones, and a few other characters observable from a distance, but for reasons easily guessed at, they had no inclination to measure ear lengths, hind feet, zygomatics or mastoids, so the hog-nosed skunk was, to them, just one entity, species *mesoleuca*, ranging over most of Texas. Audubon and Bachman put it thus: "The *Mephitis Mesoleuca* is found on the brown, broomy, sedgy plains, as well as in the woods, and the cultivated districts of Texas and Mexico.... The long and beautiful tail of this skunk makes it conspicuous among the thickets or in the musquit bushes of Texas.... [It] is not met with in any portion of the U.S. eastward and northward of Texas."

But this is not good enough for modern scholars, and they have divided this apparent entity up into two supposedly distinct species and various races. The southwestern part of the Texas population is now separated off and designated *Conepatus leuconotes*, which is sometimes further reduced to *C. leuconotes texensis*. This leaves the explorers' *C. mesoleucus* restricted to only the eastern part of Texas, with the hottest debate right now being whether this form's southwestern limit is Bexar or Atascosa County.[29] Eastward, this species is further divided into *C. mesoleuca mearnsi* and *C. m. telmalestes*, the latter apparently surviving only as an isolated population in the Big Thicket area.[30] There has also been an attempt to designate those specimens taken down on the coast in Atascosa County as still another species, *D. maperito*.[31]

Putting all of these back together to equate the one hog-nosed skunk of the explorers, we get a modern, recognized version of its range which includes all of the trans-Pecos, whose northern limit then drops down across the Edwards Plateau to Mason County, from which it arcs down through Travis County, jumps over to San Jacinto County and ends in Hardin County — except for two strange records for the animal. There is one record from McLennan County, near Waco, and another from Collin County, north of Dallas.

The citing of such completely isolated records as these latter two if done by explorers would be grasped at once as evidence of their making mistakes — but these are no mistakes. They are recognized by recent authors — which fact makes it necessary to agree with Audubon and Bachman's intimation that the hog-nosed skunks ranged over most of Texas. It might still be possible to argue that these skunks didn't frequent northwest Texas, but if we are required to accept the two isolated modern records from North Texas, then may our pioneer observers not fairly ask us to accept the record of Spencer Baird, the government's scientific observer, who described in 1857 a specimen of this species "collected by Captain Pope on the Staked Plains"? This puts the animal at that time near the northwest corner of the state and goes together with the other explorers' statements to make it appear that the hog-nosed skunk (or skunks) were at the time of Texas' discovery more widely ranging northward than they are now. This may be another southern animal whose range is more recently being pushed back toward its base in Mexico. And this, in turn, might mean that the presently found relict populations are of much more recent isolation than usually imagined.

There is another skunk which ventures only marginally into Texas. It is *Mephitis macroura*, the hooded skunk. It is similar to the striped skunk, but has longer fur, particularly about the neck — hence the hood — and an even finer tail. It is also a Mexican species, and it has been in recent times found only in the Big Bend part of far West Texas.

It is not surprising that this skunk figured very little in the world of the earliest Texans. There were few pioneers in the Big Bend before 1860, and those who trekked through that region had little time or energy left from their exertions to reflect upon or write about slightly different kinds of skunks.

It was only the great Audubon and Bachman, with their genius for observing the finest distinctions between animals, who recognized, pictured and wrote about this skunk for us. In their great work on animals it is stated: "The specimen figured by John Woodhouse Audubon was obtained near San Antonio, and he describes it as common in western Texas. Its superb tail is now and then used by the country folks as a plume or feather for their hats."[32]

Most noteworthy here is that the specimen used by Audubon as a model for his illustration came from near San Antonio. This puts the animal in the 1840s and 1850s far outside of the Big Bend, to which it seems more recently restricted. Not only that, but it is stated that the "country folks," by whom we assume is meant the pioneer settlers, decorated their hats with the especially fine tails of this skunk. There having been few if any settlers in the Big Bend that early, this seems to presuppose that the animal was at that time found much more widely in Texas than it has been more recently. Apparently this is another of the southern species for which settled and developed modern Texas is not as hospitable a country as the original Texas was.

There is what must be considered yet another skunk in Texas. This one is so different from those already listed that in scientific parlance it has its own separate genus, and it is often called by different and confusing common names. It is *Spilogale putorius*. The genus name says "spotted" and the species *nomen* cries out "stench" or "bad smell."

This is certainly a spotted skunk. A confrontation with one of these has one looking at a triangular black head with a startlingly white spot in the center of the forehead and with two black ears standing over very white temples. The beady black eyes are lost in the black background so that there hardly seems to be a face. This confusing head is the prow from which four rows of sometimes more or less confluent white spots run back over a broad, jet-black back. There are usually more white spots scattered on the thighs and rump, and the long hairs of the lower part of the tail are totally black while those of the upper tail are tipped with or sometimes totally white.

This is the pygmy of the skunk tribe. An adult is hardly larger than a large fox squirrel and is surpassed in size by any adult housecat. Only the relative broadness of its body and its having long hair, which it elevates at any provocation, make it appear any more formidable than a large rat. But the animal lives up to its species name, the odor of its defense spray seeming to be every bit as bad as that of its relatives, and some insist it is worse.

The common names for this little skunk plunge us into mazes of confusion. Besides the spotted skunk, this creature had been saddled with such names as the little striped skunk, the civet cat and the hydrophobic cat.

Baird, in 1857, gave a very accurate description of this species, based on specimens from Indianola, Texas, but did not set it off so completely from other skunks, and so called it "*Mephitis bicolor*, the little striped skunk."[33] But once set off in its own separate genus, it can hardly be maintained to be a diminutive of the striped skunk — so drop Baird's common name along with his scientific one.

Calling it the "civet cat" is a much more serious error, but for many this is all the animal has ever been. This is serious because it leaves us in the midst of uncertainty. For instance, Viktor Bracht, in his 1848 volume, writes: "Several specimens of the civet cat have been killed in the hilly section, but two killed on the banks of the Llano River were especially fine ones. Several kinds of skunks live in hollow trees along the banks of the larger rivers."[34] Now who will tell us whether Bracht's civet cats were these little skunks, as might be thought from the following sentence, or were actually ringtails, which are also often called civet cats and whose stronghold is the very region mentioned? The passage is rendered ambiguous because of this unfortunate name. Worse than this, the name is false and leads to other errors when applied to either the ringtail or the spotted skunk, because neither belongs to the cat family and there are no actual civets in this hemisphere at all. The civets are four species of African and Asian animals which, together with mongooses and others, have their own family, *Viverridae*.

How the name of these Old World creatures got transferred to two different American animals belonging to two different and separate families of mammals is hard to imagine.

Practically the only reason even conjectured for bringing the Old World name to America and applying it to our little spotted skunk is that the skunks and civets share the feature of having a pair of musk glands located at the anus. It is true that they share this feature. They share the possession of musk glands with very many other mammals. The deer have them on their legs, the peccaries on their backs, etc. And each group has its own brand of musk. It is by means of this diversity that these glands fulfill their first function, that of identifying and attracting the opposite sex. So the musk of the true civets is chemically different from that of the skunks, is not so radically malodorous as theirs, and is not ejected across distances as a defense against enemies. The only thing uniquely shared between civets and skunks is the position of the musk glands. Everything else is different. This seems very little reason for calling them by the same name.

Still, some would ask what difference it makes if skunks are called civets. The answer is that such minor inaccuracies in naming lead to major fallacies. In this case the fallacy has followed the wrong name around the world. Most of us have been told all our lives that skunk scent is used to make perfume, but this is not true. How did this remarkable error get started? Simply because civet, the secretion of true

Old World civets' musk glands, has long been collected and used as a carrier for the scents of fine perfumes. The skunk's musk contains no civet and is not so used, but their having been dubbed "civet cats," the idea that they contributed to perfumes was transferred to them as well. This is a perfect example of the principles that appropriate naming is not only a high art, but one of the most important accomplishments of science, and that careless use of names can have as misleading results as willful falsification.

There is one remaining common name for this skunk, and it is the most unkind of all. They like to call this the "hydrophobic cat." I hasten to say that no explorer does this. The term never appears in any pre-1860 Texas writings I have been privileged to examine. But most recent accounts of the animal persist in including this very derogatory name, and so we must deal with it to at least see whether the explorers missed something important or not.

The term "hydrophobia" is an old name for the disease rabies. The applying of this name to the spotted skunk is an attempt at linking this animal very closely and specifically to rabies as a reservoir of this infectious organism and as its main vector. It turns this species into a feared and hated pariah and the scapegoat whose existence is supposed to explain one of our most feared infections.

There is no denying how strongly the case for this animal being the primary carrier of rabies is stated today. You see news releases cautioning about it regularly in the media. And the concern has spilled over to include all skunks, condemning them all at once. The popular *Encyclopedia of Mammals* recently stated that skunks are said to be "major vectors" of rabies, that over 4,000 cases have been diagnosed in them in some years, which amounts to "over two-thirds of all cases in wildlife."[35]

We have here an interesting progression from over 200 years of explorers tramping all over Texas, sitting and sleeping all over the open ground of that wilderness, casually reporting skunks around them lots of the time, yet none of them ever hinting at any rabies, any fear of the disease or any dread of the skunks, all the way to modern health professionals scaring us about the deadly skunks and even at times organizing skunk extermination drives in order to save even urbanites from rabies. It is a curious shift of attitudes which must be based upon something factual and which deserves at least a stab at explanation.

If the early explorers did not report skunk-related rabies — or rabies at all, for that matter — when did these reports first appear and what prompted them? She does not give any of her sources, but that great historian of the plains, Mari Sandoz, places the first outbreak of rabies in skunks in the year 1872. The location of the phenomenon is the plains of Kansas, and her description is most graphic: "It was the year of the mad skunks. In addition to the Indians and in summer the tarantulas, rattlesnakes and an occasional copperhead in the south, there were the skunks to watch too now, skunks that came out boldly in daylight. The men might be attacked as they crept up on a herd or pegged out the hides, while they sat around the big supper frying pan sopping their sore-finger bread into the gravy or while asleep, even up in the wagons. Usually the skunks were harmless, even sociable creatures, moving in under corn cribs or under houses in the settlements. They were always hanging around the buffalo camps like stray dogs, eating the beetles around the hide piles, showing up for the supper bones, perhaps a mother marching in out of the dusk with a row of the striped little kittens following, hoping not to be driven away with thrown firebrands or a splash of hot grease. *But now suddenly* [italics mine] the neat black and white, plume-tailed animals were ragged and drooling as they came charging in, snapping at everything, the small teeth sharp and deadly."[36] Ms. Sandoz tells how the hunters tried unsuccessfully to exterminate all skunks, but that the scourge didn't last long because, "Finally the skunks disappeared, a dead one found here and there...."[37]

If this seems to be the first remembered occurrence of rabies in plains skunks, epidemilogical principles would seem to confirm that it might have been. A strong, new infectious disease moving into a population previously unexposed to it typically wreaks havoc during a short time of terrible mortality and then just as suddenly calms to remain endemic in the small number of surviving individuals. Witness the pattern of smallpox and other diseases among the Indian populations of the same period.

So isn't it possible that the 1872 phenomenon marked the first entrance into the western skunk population of rabies brought out somehow by the huge flood of men and animals surging over the plains at this time? If so, then our Texas explorers' complete silence about this disease — while it doesn't prove it — may mean that the infection had not gotten into Texas any earlier.

There is just a hint of this, but also of something leading to an entirely different interpretation in Sandoz' further statements. She goes on to tell about an instance when Colonel Dodge was on an expedition up the Arkansas River. A skunk entered a tent one night and bit one of his men. She says that Colonel Dodge was very uneasy about the possibility of hydrophobia developing, but that, "This case, however, turned out to be the only non-fatal skunk bite that Dodge heard about in all the Arkansas River region while he was there, although in Texas and up north along the Platte he had known of many men bitten without a serious consequence."

That is a remarkable statement. Is there any possible explanation for many men being bitten by skunks in the first place, and then for none of them developing rabies when they were? A search of the literature on the spotted skunk reveals just such an explanation. It needs to be remembered in order to help balance our attitudes toward these animals as well as toward the disease, so I take the opportunity to resurrect it from the dusty tomes of old scientific journals.

It begins with a remarkable article published in 1923, in the prestigious *Journal of Mammology*.[38] Its author was Joseph D. Mitchell, a resident of Victoria, Texas. He was a naturalist, and his article was granted the unusual recognition of an introduction by the great biologist Vernon Bailey of the U.S. Biological Survey, in which Bailey says of Mitchell, "His conclusions may be fallible but his facts are first hand, carefully selected, and valuable."[39] So whether or not you choose to accept his conclusions, at least note the facts in Mitchell's words: "The common idea that the bite of this little skunk will give hydrophobia is erroneous. It is true, there is a time in its life, when it is mad, but not with rabies. During the mating season, the male sometimes has spells of 'temporary insanity,' and runs amuck. During these spells he travels usually in a gallop, and will attack anything in his path. Several times I have met one under these conditions, and have given him the road. I have known four persons to be bitten by these little animals while under these mad fits. In every case they were sleeping in open camps, and the moon was shining bright. Three of the cats were killed and the fourth was identified, but escaped after a second attack."

Mitchell goes on to give details about how the four persons were attacked, where on their bodies they were bitten, the persistent aggressiveness of most of the skunks after the bites, and then writes, "I knew all four of these people for from ten to twenty-five years after their being bitten and no evil effects followed in any of the cases."

He then tells of witnessing the attack of a spotted skunk upon a full-grown bull and of an instance when he literally pulled one of them loose from a wolf pup upon whose ear its teeth were clamped after it had bitten three other pups in the den. He concludes by writing, "Many cowboys, whites, negroes and Mexicans, have told me their observations on this audacious habit, of this otherwise timid little animal. The general opinion was that they were afflicted with rabies, and they were always slaughtered without mercy. My opinion, from my experience and observation, does not agree with the rabid theory. I believe it is a species of violent frenzy, brought on by unsatisfied sexual desires, or by being whipped by a rival. *All that were examined by myself or by others after death were males* [italics mine]."

This article was followed in the very next year by an article on the striped skunk in which the author, W. K. Cuyler, wrote on the same subject as follows: "There is a widespread notion that rabies is endemic among skunks, especially in the genus *Spilogale*, hence the names 'hydrophobia skunk,' 'hydrophoby cat,' and 'phoby cat' applied to them. It is even said that the skunks occurring west of the Mississippi River are 'sure death,' while those east of the river are of a milder type. There is no truth in this additional accusation against the much maligned skunk. I have been bitten several times by skunks and even now have wounds from the bites of two skunks on my fingers. The only precaution I ever use is to rub crystals of potassium permanganate into the abrasions.... If skunks carry hydrophobia chronically, the hunting dogs should be more often infected. I know of one dog fourteen years old which has been bitten on an average of four times a month for five months of the year for the last eleven years. That makes two hundred twenty bites in eleven years. She is a healthy animal today. In this connection, Dr. J. T. Wilhite, head of the Texas Pasteur Institute, stated to me that rabies is not more prevalent among skunks than among other species of carnivorous animals.... The fear that the skunk tribe constitutes a reservoir of hydrophobia seems to be not well founded. In this I am in full agreement with J. D. Mitchell (this Journal, February 1923)."[40]

The idea of the spotted skunk being the Typhoid Mary of rabies seems to have persisted and grown in spite of such articles as the above. Soon many authors were routinely writing as though these animals were always infected and lunging about just looking for victims to inoculate. But throughout the years there have always been more rational voices, and these often among the most authoritative. Some of these have even restated the obvious reason why this particular animal has been falsely maligned. William B. Davis, former head of the Texas A&M University Department of Wildlife Science and one of the grand old men of Texas biology, wrote it this way: "In certain regions they are known as 'hydrophobia cats' and feared as carriers of rabies. This fear is largely unfounded, although during the mating season the males appear to be rabid, run amuck, and may attack humans sleeping on the ground. Nevertheless, they should be no more feared on this account than any of the carnivores, and certainly less so than the domestic dog."[41]

The little spotted skunk is a very agile animal. It is the only skunk which climbs trees, and when pursued closely by dogs can often be treed. Many have noted its playful, excitable and even nervous manner. Many have also observed its aggressive behavior during whatever sort of frenzy it sometimes lapses into. I have myself seen such an individual pursuing domestic animals so much larger than itself so persistently that it was ludicrous, and I have been chased by one in broad daylight. Before very much of this headlong running around the little thing looks bedraggled and it is very easy to imagine it is sickly. It is not the most pleasant experience for one of these apparently crazy things to lock onto you and chase you around. Thoughts of hydrophobia come very easily to your mind at such a time. It is easy to see how a full-blown rabies-skunk phobia has gotten started. It is paralleled by the dread which has needlessly doomed so many bats to eradication projects.

I am certainly not denying that there is rabies now present in most if not all populations of carnivorous animals, both wild and domestic, and I am most emphatically not recommending that anyone ignore and fail to treat any animal bite. I am only pointing out that the apparent absence of references to rabies or even the fear of it during the exploratory period together with the curious pattern of the disease's later appearance might make it worthwhile to investigate a hypothesis that this disease was brought to the West — or at least south to Texas — at the time of the buffalo hunters and the opening up of the frontier by the railroads. More specifically, I am only pointing out that the earliest Texans left no evidence of any fear of the antics of skunks and that the spotted skunk often shows behavior which is easily mistaken for rabid action and which may very well explain a more recently developed irrational fear of the animal. I must add that the wildlife biologists actually working in the field whom I have happened to query about this problem, although they won't allow me to quote them directly, tend to be skeptical about the rabies tests conducted on long-dead animals upon which many of the terror-promoting statistics concerning rabies-infected skunks, as well as bats and other animals, are based. The conclusion seems plausible that the spotted skunk has been unjustly defamed and that your chances of getting rabies from its bite are about the same as those of getting it from the teeth of your free-ranging dog or cat.

Roast skunk, anybody? It will no doubt be a major effort, but we must now put our concept of the skunks as evil, foul-smelling, disease-carrying attackers aside and consider them as luscious servings to deck our dinner tables. Many early Texans ate them.

To show how commonly the skunk was used as food by different groups in early Texas, I reproduce here several statements of explorers about the practice. In 1828, Jean Louis Berlandier wrote, "The skunk (a type of polecat) is commonly eaten by the soldiers and residents of the presidios in spite of its disagreeable odor. After carefully removing the anal glands and burning off its fur, the Comanches eat it with relish."[42] In the same year, J. C. Clopper wrote as follows: "[Leave San Antonio] next day reach the Seawully [Cibolo] — meet two or three Mexican families moving to San Antonio with a small stock of horses cattle and hogs — they were making a part of their supper from a polecat — which caused a considerable space between their camp and ours. . . ."[43] We have already cited Lieutenant Abert's account of finding a striped skunk among the breaks of the Canadian River in the Texas Panhandle in 1845. He goes on to relate what happened to that unfortunate skunk: "The French people who were with us caught it, and ate it. The odor, however, was too pungent to suit everyone's olfactories."[44]

That the use of skunks for food was not limited to the earliest Texans is attested to by W. K. Cuyler, who wrote in his 1924 article already cited,

An engraving of the otter made, hand colored and published by William Daniell, in London, 1809.

"Skunk meat, if not contaminated with its own musk, is most palatable." And that skunks have been eaten in places far removed from Texas, as well as that Texans have not been the only ones sometimes reduced to such a diet, is shown by the South American naturalist W. H. Hudson, who wrote, "I was told in Patagonia by a man named Molinos, who was frequently employed by the Government as guide to expeditions in the desert, that . . . some years ago he was sent with two other men to find and treat with an Indian chief whose whereabouts was not known. Far in the interior Molinos was overtaken by a severe winter, his horses died of thirst and fatigue, and during the three bitterest months of the year he kept himself and his followers alive by eating the flesh of skunks, the only wild animal that never failed them."[45]

Perhaps a fitting prayer for Texans might be, may I never be hungry enough to have to eat skunk. But perhaps the skunks are here to remind us there is some good in the worst critter.

THE AQUATIC CARNIVORES IN TEXAS

There were two of these in Texas as found, the otter and the mink. Since they equal any creatures in streamlined grace, daring speed and devil-may-care maneuvers in water or on land and are swathed in some of the most luxurious furs in the world, it would seem that our pioneers would have treated them like animal royalty and we would at least have them sharing the center tanks of our present-day water worlds. But these animals did not figure large in the Texas explorers' world. They were apparently only appreciated by the commercial hunters and trappers. So our account of them here is not long.

First the otter. And we take a new tack this time by beginning at the present and working back through time to the earliest accounts of the animal in Texas. The species here is *Lutra canadensis*, and mercifully for us it seems to have always been called this, due to the fact that, as Audubon and Bachman observed and stated in 1851, "The form is precisely similar to the otters of Canada and those existing in various intermediate States."[46]

So the river otter found over so much of North America was Texas-bred also. And it still manages to exist in East Texas, although it is so fugitive today that few of even the outdoors people in the region have had the thrill of seeing one in the wild.

Audubon and Bachman's conclusion about the animal already quoted was based upon an otter taken on the Colorado River near LaGrange, Texas, in 1846.[47] Viktor Bracht published in 1848 that the species was found on the Guadalupe River, this placing the otter not only in southeast Texas, but into the Hill Country and toward South Texas at that time.[48]

In 1847, David G. Burnet wrote in a letter: "The Comanche take no furs, and but few deer-skins, the most of which they consume at home. There are very few beavers or otters in their country, and they know nothing of the art of trapping." This is evidence that otters were less common to the north and west in the Texas of that time, and it attempts to remove the responsibility from the Indians. Then Burnet introduced a new factor into the situation, adding, "The American trappers have nearly extirpated these valuable animals from the waters of Texas."[49] Is he serious? Can it be that the fur traders had already affected these furbearers that seriously by the 1840s?

A clear picture of the situation of the otters in northeast Texas during the 1830s emerges when we put together the following elements. The otter is one of only six wild animals whose furs were reported as traded in the commercial fur market at Nacogdoches in 1832,[50] and around this time Berlandier says that up to 1,200 otter skins were traded there in less than a year.[51] In 1838, von Wrede wrote: "Fishing in the small brooks around Nacogdoches is nothing extraordinary, probably on account of the numerous turtles and otters which do much damage."[52] And William Kennedy wrote in 1839, "In the list of amphibious animals are the otter and beaver, which formerly abounded in the district of Nacogdoches, but have been greatly thinned by the hunters and trappers."[53] It is clear that by that pivotal pre-statehood decade the otter population in Texas was nothing but a crop being harvested, with its numbers already being diminished.

But we can go back beyond any possible American hunters and trappers ambushing otters in Texas, and as soon as we get beyond the grim reapers, we find these animals not only numerous but widespread beyond anything usually considered. For instance, Custis, after his remarkable expedition up the Red River in 1806, listed the otter in his catalog of animals encountered, and stated that they were "Abundant on the tributary streams of Red River."[54] It may be hard for us to realize today, but this puts them generally throughout northwest Texas before our interference.

However, there is a more beautiful picture farther back in the more remote past. Fray Jose de Solis pushed his way almost entirely across the future state in 1767, and afterwards wrote: "In all the rivers of Texas beaver and otter can be found in large numbers."[55] It is an idyllic picture we get of these animals gamboling in and out of most — if not all — of the waters of the undisturbed Texas wilderness, but it is the picture the earliest explorers have left us.

We can accept it or leave it, but the dwindling numbers of otters under the assault of the fur trade is well documented. Added here as one more seal on the fate of these animals is testimony of an anonymous Texas traveler, who wrote in 1846, "Beaver and otter were frequent in the past, but now they have become rare because of the hunters."[56]

We can hardly leave the otters with only this dismal history to represent them, so we turn to Audubon and Bachman's masterful description of the delightful nature of these animals.

They wrote: "This species has a peculiar habit of sliding off the wet sloping banks into the water. The Otters ascend the bank at a place suitable for their diversion. They slide down in rapid succession, and there are many at a sliding place. On one occasion we were resting ourself on the bank of Canoe Creek near Henderson when a pair of Otters appeared, and not seeing our proximity began to enjoy their sliding pastime. They glided down the soap-like muddy surface of the slide with the rapidity of an arrow from a bow, and we counted each one making twenty-two slides before we disturbed their sportive occupation. We are inclined to the belief that this propensity may be traced to those instincts which lead the sexes to their periodical associations. . . . The Otter is a very expert swimmer and can overtake almost any fish. . . . Otters when caught young are easily tamed, and although their gait is ungainly they will follow their owner about, and at times are quite playful. We have twice domesticated the Otter. They became so attached to us that the moment they entered our study they began crawling into our lap — mounting our table, romping among our books and not infrequently upsetting our inkstand and deranging our papers."[57]

Would that these interesting animals remained more widespread in Texas as they once were.

The other amphibious carnivore in Texas is the mink, but it is difficult to find it in the explorers' picture of Texas. In fact, this animal is almost missing from the early accounts of this state. There is only one Texas mention of it before 1860, and even the indefatigable Audubon and Bachman do not record having seen any Texas mink specimens at all. Perhaps the most telling indication of the mink's poor showing in original Texas is the fact that even

An eighteenth-century conception of the opossum. The background is clearly not Texas or even Mexico, but a stylized, imaginary scene typical of art work of the time.

in the early years when otters were so numerous that we have seen up to 1,200 of their pelts coming into Nacogdoches within a year, not one mink is mentioned in the Texas fur trade. This is a complete reversal of the recent situation where as many as ten mink pelts were harvested in East Texas during the 1970s for each otter.[58]

This absence of mink in the state's early records is most significant in the light of facts that these animals are larger, more conspicuous animals than otters, are more valued and therefore are more hunted for their wonderful furs. If they were present in early Texas in any worthwhile numbers it is certain that they would have been widely discussed, many efforts would have been made to capture them, and their pelts would have made up an important part of the fur trade here as it did in other places. It is hard to escape the conclusion that they must have then been rare animals in any part of this state.

It is Viktor Bracht who leaves us the one testimony that mink were originally in Texas. It is in his 1848 statement already mentioned, where he said, "On the Guadalupe and probably elsewhere are found the common otter and a small predacious animal called mink by the Indians."[59]

This places the mink as then in the south central part of Texas. Presumably this means that the species existed from there eastward to meet its wider range, which would mean it then ranged over approximately the eastern half of the state. This duplicates rather nicely the recent known range of the species. But the almost total lack of any further reference to mink in early Texas can hardly mean anything but that this attractive animal was so rare and reclusive in the Texas wilderness that even the wiliest hunters and trappers seldom took it, and that to the rest of the explorers and pioneers it was no more real than it is to most Texans today.

Is the inference that seems to rise out of this — that the mink is one of the very few animals which have actually thrived with the changes in the Texas environment and even increased under the pressure of all the hunters and trappers of the last 150 years — actually true? The history of the Texas mink remains something of an enigma.

THE RAT OF THE TREES

If this heading seems outlandish you are only experiencing the same shock the earliest explorers in the New World suffered upon meeting with this strange creature. The French actually dubbed it the *rat-de-bois*, and on the surface it is a plausible name. Captain Smith of the colonies wrote aptly in 1612 that this animal "hath a head like a Swine, and a taile like a Rat, and is of the bigness of a Cat."

Have you figured out what it is? If you haven't Captain Smith's next sentence should enlighten you, because he continued: "Under her belly she hath a bagge, where shee lodgeth, carrieth, and sucketh her young." Of course! It's the only American animal with a marsupium in which to rear its prematurely delivered fetuses. But what name should really be used for this pig-like, rat-like, climbing thing? Captain Smith, not being as inventive as the French, gave up and merely used the Virginia Indians' name for the animal, thus introducing the word "opossum" into the English written vocabulary. This explains the strangeness to us of the word. The initial "o" of opossum stands, not for our "o" sound, but is an attempt to indicate the peculiar grunt-like sound which the Indian languages often use in association with their pronounced words. So perhaps the pronunciation "opossum" is not more correct than a simple "possum." It should actually be an Indian "grunt-possum," if you can manage it.

Texas appears to constitute a territorial bridge for the opossum, as it does for so many creatures, and this has once again posed problems for taxonomists. If you are an Easterner, you have had the opossum with you all the way from the Atlantic, have long ago christened it *Didelphis virginiana,* and will find what seems this same animal over most of Texas west to at least the Pecos River. However, if you should have come into Texas from the south, you would have been accompanied along the eastern coasts of central America from at least as far as Guatemala by opossums which you would have known as *D. marsupialis* or *D. mesamericana,* and you would want to call the Texas opossums one of these names. But then, if you were a native Texan, or after you became an adopted one, you would very likely insist upon a uniquely Texas opossum, as did Allen in 1901, calling certain South Texas specimens *D. marsupialis* var. *texensis.*[60] But later opinions have tended to regard all these as one entity after all. W. B. Davis, for instance, says to put them all back together, since he sees "no good argument for maintaining [them] as distinct species."[61] So most recent writings call our Texas opossums *D. marsupialis,* some *D. virginiana,* and some a combination of these two names.

Taken as this one species, Texas opossums have been very common throughout eastern Texas in recent times. W. B. Davis, once head of the Texas A&M University Department of Wildlife Science, calculated and published in 1966 that the opossum population of East Texas could be one animal to each thirty-one acres, and quoted a researcher who estimated that in "good opossum country" the number could be one opossum to four acres.[62] They have apparently continued to be very numerous throughout South Texas, less so in North Texas, and scarce but present in the Panhandle and to the Pecos River. Beyond that river there have been only a very few records of the animal. It is distinctly an eastern species.

But the many opossums in modern Texas make their meager appearance in the early Texas accounts surprising. I have only found eight reports of the animals in all of the pre-1860 Texas writings. Does this mean that they were rare before settlement times or that they were not significant enough to those then here to be mentioned? We may not be able to settle that question with certainty here, but perhaps there are some clues pointing to one answer or the other.

It seems that just the strangeness of this animal should have dictated its mention by any explorer who met up with it, if he wrote of anything at all. Such uniqueness seems to have prompted Joutel to describe it when he passes over many more commonplace species. He wrote in 1687, "Our Hunters kill'd Beeves, wild Goats, Turkeys and other Wild-Fowl, and among the rest some Creatures as big as an indifferent Cat, very like a Rat, having a Bag under their Throat, in which they carry their Young. They feed upon Nuts and Acorns, are very fat, and their Flesh is much like Pig."[63] This very early account establishes that the opossum was in Texas at the beginning of our historical period and before us.

Little can be established about the range of the opossum at that time from the explorers' reports. Baird lists early collections of it from Matamoros and the lower Rio Grande.[64] Moore lists it as one of the animals "found in all the forests [of Texas in 1840],"[65] and Bracht says it was "found throughout the country" in 1848.[66] Ullrich has it in his list of animals found in 1860 in Comal County,[67] and von Wrede in his lists for the Nacogdoches environs in 1836, and again in 1841.[68] These are all of the statements left to us about where the opossums were, and they distribute them across East, Central and South Texas, as we would expect, but they surely spread them thinly.

There remains only one more early reference to opossums in Texas, and it may be the one which gives us the best clue to why the animal wasn't mentioned more often. The same von Wrede just mentioned, when writing about his 1836 trip through present Sabine, San Augustine and Nacogdoches counties, said, "During our journey we occasionally saw some of the creatures of the wilderness; wild turkeys and gray squirrels were the most plentiful. Seldom though did we see an opossum...."[69]

Is this perhaps the hint we need? Von Wrede

has said that the opossum was present in this far East Texas area, and so we may be thinking of them having been as abundant as they are found now. But here he implies that though present they were not numerous. What other explanation do we need for the fact that though found practically across the future state, they were reported only eight times by only six different pioneers? If it means anything, doesn't the absence of mention of this strange animal by the over 200 other explorers and pioneers who went to considerable pains to report the animals and plants they found in Texas probably mean that the opossum was relatively rare in the primeval wilderness community of Texas?

Once we start to think in this way it seems very logical. If the pioneers were surrounded by numerous opossums, besides mentioning them because of their peculiarities, wouldn't at least some of them have experienced and so recorded, along with their stories of chicken losses to raccoons, skunks, wildcats, foxes and even panthers, the depredations upon their poultry which most farmers know all too well the more recent populations of opossums commit?

And if we look for reasons why opossums might have been more scarce in those early times, several come to mind whose causal validity may not have been demonstrated experimentally, but which seem logical. First, the rat-of-the-trees was usually in the trees because it was vulnerable on the forest floor or prairie surface, because it does not dig its own burrows and because there must have been intense competition for any hollow trees in the wilderness. But up-a-tree, it must have been easy prey for the climbing predators such as the larger cats. So the species may have been severely limited until we came along and built all sorts of buildings with attics for it to live in and floors to hide under. The opossum has today to a great extent left the trees to become probably the most numerous of our native wild animals living within our cities.

Second, since there were in pioneer days large populations of predators which must have relished opossums and since these have been mostly removed, this must have held the species to a minimum then, but freed the species to increase since. I myself only appreciated the effect of predators upon such animals as this when I was involved in a biological survey of a heavily wooded Central Texas tract standing apart from any similar area. In it we found numerous raccoons, some armadillos and a few ringtails and squirrels, but no other fauna, not even opossums. We were mystified by the imbalance of the animal populations until we discovered that this forest was the hunting ground of a large set of hounds kept half-starved by their owners with the aim of increasing their deadliness in the chase. These dogs were allowed to run free in these woods at almost all times, and they were so desperate that there were scary moments when they actually stalked us. Under this extreme predation pressure almost all animals, including opossums and even deer, had been wiped out. Only the raccoon and the armadillo could stand up to — or in the case of the armadillo lie down and curl up to — the onslaught of large dogs with any chance of survival on the ground, and only the ringtail and the squirrel were usually quick enough to scale a tree. In situations like this, and, I think in the original wilderness situation with wolves, foxes, cats large and small, peccaries and other swift and deadly predators almost everywhere, I would expect to find the wily and formidable raccoon successful and the slow, stupid opossum held to a minimum. So I see the accuracy of the explorers' accounts reflected once more in the paucity of their opossum references alongside more numerous accounts of raccoons.

I must mention a third possible reason for a significant increase in opossums from the unaltered wilderness Texas to the settled post-Civil War state only tentatively as a tantalizing possibility, but one which might deserve questioning at least. Opossums are about as omnivorous as any animal. Besides fruits — their weakness for persimmons, for instance — and other vegetable matter, they eat most sorts of invertebrates, amphibians, small reptiles, birds and mammals whenever any of these are the food available. In winter seasons, with tender vegetation and many animals unavailable, they must make do with whatever small animals are still active. These would be mostly mammals and birds. Carl G. Hartman, in his volume, *Possums*, points out that in some such situations almost one-fourth of an opossum's diet has been found to be made up of rats.[70] Of course, there were various field and woodland rats and mice in the original Texas wilderness, but other predators on these were very numerous as well, and the food supply from these little mammals may have been limiting for the opossums. But then maybe we did the struggling opossums a major favor when we imported the house mouse, the roof rat and the Norway rat. Maybe the opossums' more recent abundance, as well as their coming to town,

Nine-Banded Armadillo by Audubon

is not only the result of our building them fine hiding places, but of our providing them just the prey they need, scurrying in the very recesses which give our modern opossums refuge.

There is one more reason why we would expect opossums to figure more in Texas pioneer's writings if they were present in any significant numbers. Anyone familiar with common folks' diets in the southeast U.S. knows that opossum has been, and to an extent still is, a human food item. And it hasn't been only a stopgap when starvation looms. According to Hartman in the volume just cited, opossum has the distinction of having been the main course in feasts served to two U.S. presidents — to President Taft in 1909 and later to President Franklin D. Roosevelt.

Even the early writings from the first American colonies tell of eating opossums. For instance, W. Strachey wrote from Virginia in 1615, "*Aposon*, a beast in bignes like a pig and in test alike," and in 1763, Wesley wrote, "the tender Young of the Opossum are delicate morsels."[71]

But the only hint that the animal was ever eaten in early Texas is Joutel's presettlement remark already seen, that "their flesh is much like Pig." All through the rest of the exploratory period, when both very daring and very hungry pioneers were telling of eating every Texas thing around them from raccoons, and peccaries, and skunks to turtles and rattlesnakes, and it must have been generally known from experiences back East that these animals were edible, none of them reported dining on opossum.

There were some opossums in primeval Texas, and they were distributed over much of the state. Our explorers tell us that. But these animals figured very little in the world of the Texas pioneers, only being shadows glimpsed too rarely to be important sources of food or fur and too few to even be hated as predators around the pioneers' chicken coops. The burden of proof would seem to be upon anyone who would maintain otherwise.

TEXAS ARMADILLOS

They were in the Texas explorers' world all right. Those who have said that the armadillos were not present in early Texas at all are wrong. But that doesn't mean that they were everywhere. They were just barely present. A few were fidgeting in the chaparral in one small corner of that world, but that was all, and any explorer who saw one had to be in just the right place at the right time, and was even then a lucky one.

So far as I can find, only six travelers have left testimony of having come across armadillos in Texas before 1860. This is very few, but still it is important because it is practically our only evidence concerning where these animals were at that time.

One of those familiar with the armadillo from actual contact was the "esteemed friend" of Audubon and Bachman, Capt. J. P. McCown. Since it appears that they were not fortunate enough to ever see one in the wild themselves, these authors quote him on this animal as follows: "The Armadillo is to be found in the chaparrals on the Rio Grande. I have seen their shells or coat-of mail on the prairies; whether carried there by larger animals, or birds, or whether they inhabit the prairies, I cannot say." [72]

Another familiar with the armadillo was Lt. J. D. Webster. In his 1848 official report of his work surveying the area around the mouth of the Rio Grande River, he wrote, "Along the banks of the river [below Matamoros] there is a narrow belt of chaparral, consisting mainly of species of acacia. . . . Of the wild animals the most noticeable are the deer, *(C. Virginianus,)* the armadillo, the tiger cat, and the peccary or wild hog."[73]

Baird, in 1857, lists Berlandier as having collected an armadillo at Matamoros and a certain J. H. Clark as taking one on the "Lower Rio Grande."[74] Bracht wrote in 1848, "Armadillos are found east of the Rio Grande, close to Mexico. Their meat is eatable."[75] Thomas D. Tennery, a soldier brought to the encampment near the mouth of the Rio Grande by the Mexican War, wrote in his 1846 diary: "September 16. — Today Mr. Hite rode up the river to see the country, and was much pleased with the trip though he found nothing but sandy ridges and wet overgrown prairie inhabited by wolves, armadillos and a large species of hare, besides cranes and countless numbers of the heron kind: also a species of the eagle like the bald eagle but not so large."[76] And that completes the list of the armadillos actually reported in Texas before 1860.

Audubon and Bachman give their summary of this by writing that at that time the armadillo "is common in Mexico, and is found in the southern portions of Texas. It is not very uncommon near the lower shores of the Rio Grande."[77] Just what their "not very uncommon" means is anyone's guess. It is such an artificial construction that it seems they may have been trying to bridge over a gap in their knowledge.

At any rate, when we think of the paucity of the explorers' reports of armadillos it seems that the animals must have been far from common, even in that tip of Texas. There were several early Spanish expeditions which went through that area with their chroniclers listing whatever animals they came across — with no mention of any armadillo. There were several official reports, some diaries, and numerous letters of both officers and enlisted men who deployed over the very same armadillo range, fought at Palo Alto and Resaca de la Palma, took time to describe coyotes, wolves, several cats, peccaries and even such things as rabbits and skunks, but who never even hinted at knowing armadillos existed. Surely the Abbe Domenech that we have seen showing such fascination with the animals of his previous Texas mission field, when he was serving in the lower Rio Grande Valley and telling of his day and night journeys through the chaparral forest, would have had very quaint and exuberant descriptions to add to his volume on Texas if he had seen such a bizarre creature as an armadillo.

And the complete silence of every explorer north or west of this very lowermost tip of the Valley must mean that the armadillos had not, before 1860, begun their movement out of that semitropical pocket. If they had, surely William A. McClintock, that soldier who so graphically described whatever creatures his large army unit scared up on their long march from Corpus Christi to Fort Brown and the Mexican War, would have delighted in telling it. Others, traveling here and there over South Texas, just didn't report seeing them either. If it is reasoning from a negative to say that the armadillos must not have been coming north yet before 1860, make the most of it. But I have found no evidence that they were, and I am following a very good precedent in saying it. John K. Strecker, in an article on the range of the armadillo, wrote: "In the large collection of Texas books in Baylor University library are several volumes relating to hunting in Texas in early times. I have carefully read these but fail to find mention of armadillos in any part of the state except the extreme southern portion. As other quadrupeds of as little importance (and of less striking appearance) were mentioned in these works, had the animal been at all well known, much would have been made of it and more or less wonderful tales related of its habits and peculiarities."[78]

If the armadillo was still bottled up in the southern tip of Texas in 1860, its escape and movement north after that was so sudden and rapid as to be one of the most remarkable migration phenomena we have seen. In only twenty years, by 1880, the animal was ranging over all of South Texas bounded by a line from the mouth of the Pecos River northeast through Gillespie County and from there southeast past Victoria to the head of Matagorda Bay. In merely another twenty-five or thirty years it had scurried all the way up the Pecos Valley to the

New Mexico border and over most everything up to about Abilene and Dallas, with the Brazos River being the edge of its range on the east. By 1914, armadillos first reached the lower Sabine River and by 1925 they were found over most of East Texas. From this they have gone on, not only over most of Texas, but into many other states.[79]

The story of all this migration came too late to be within the scope of this study. But the interesting question, and the one still not answered with certainty today, is: What caused — or allowed — the armadillos to so suddenly go blundering all over where they apparently could not go before? In other words, what changed in either the animals or their environment to prompt, or at least allow, this migration?

It is clear that there was no basic change in the armadillo itself. It isn't a newly adapted creature we have here now, but the same old nine-banded armadillo christened *Dasypus novemcinctus* long ago by Linnaeus. Even if you want to be so correct as to deal with subspecies, this great traveler is not a new U.S. variety, but subspecies *mexicanus,* with its type locality in Mexico. There hasn't even been any argument over naming this creature. It was the same old animal which suddenly went north.

It is interesting that the change — whatever it was — must have taken place almost exactly at the end of the period we are studying, for that is when the armadillos started to move north. It is also clear that it was no basic change in Mexico or any sudden bad times for armadillos in the Rio Grande Valley which prompted them to embark upon the northward migration. The change must have been up here in Texas.

And this seems to give us a special opportunity. Our gathering and systematic studying of the Texas explorers' surviving accounts should have given us a surpassing knowledge of any changes in either the Texas physical environment or its biological communities which would have climaxed around 1860 in any new ecological situation which might allow the armadillo to succeed where it hadn't been able to before. Perhaps it is our responsibility to point out any of these we can recognize so that they may be evaluated more formally by others.

Some have been so puzzled by the animal's sudden travel that they have looked for former barriers to that which might have been eliminated around 1860. But we can point to no alteration of forest or prairie which took place to explain the phenomenon simply because we can point to no landform or biotic community short of full-blown desert which would even delay its migration after that.

In about sixty years the armadillo traveled almost to the north edge of Arkansas, all across Louisiana and somehow even crossed the Mississippi River to make its first appearance in the state of Mississippi, and in achieving this it had proceeded with remarkable speed through practically every kind of forest, prairie, swamp and thicket, as well as over good examples of almost every landform this region ever displayed. Nothing new or old stopped it. Some have even theorized that it walked across rivers on their bottoms, while others have seen it as able to bloat its body with trapped gasses so as to float for long distances, it moved so unconcernedly over what looked to observers like formidable barriers for it. Fortunately, no one ever reported it walking on water, but it makes no difference anyway. However it crossed the rivers it did not do it by any newly acquired ability, for it had long before anyone remembers crossed the lower Rio Grande without any fanfare. And it certainly wasn't any river which had kept it bottled up until the post-1860 move within the very tip of southmost Texas, because all that lay north of it there was no river, but instead scores of miles of Mustang Desert. When they were released, these animals crossed any unchanged wilderness areas, newly cleared forests, settlers' fields, as well as the largest rivers as though no physical barrier had ever existed they couldn't surmount, other things being cleared for them. So what else could have held them in check so completely only to be so suddenly eliminated as an armadillo deterrent?

It would seem that sometimes animals are restricted to one area and kept from invading another by something essential to their diets present in one and absent from the other. So some have looked very carefully at the armadillo's food habits to see if some such special food item's presence or absence might have controlled it.

But such a food factor is especially difficult to imagine here because the animal is virtually omnivorous. The overall staple in the armadillo's diet is insects, these most commonly making up around 75 percent of what it eats. Apparently most any kind of insects will do, but beetles are favorite, adults and theirs grubs together sometimes comprising up to 98 percent of the diet. Also, since the armadillo belongs to the same group as the anteaters, it should not be surprising that their stomachs often contain thousands of ants. To these and other insects are added a dash of spider, scorpion, sowbug, centipede, millipede, snail or slug and earthworm, as circumstances allow.

Vertebrate material is sometimes a side dish for these animals' mostly in the form of small amphibians or reptiles or reptile eggs. Birds' eggs are occasionally eaten, but armadillos are not considered any major threat to groundnesting birds. One study concluded that they "may occasionally raid quail nests, but not enough to affect the population."[80] Another study kept track of the fate of ninety-three quail nests laid in territories foraged over by armadillos, and found that only two of those nests were destroyed by these animals.[81]

Armadillos also eat plant material, but the selection of this is very restricted and therefore the amount very variable. They eat whatever soft or overripe fruits or seeds they come across. In the harvest seasons these may temporarily make up as much as 80 percent of their food, but for the bulk of the year there are few if any soft vegetable parts lying around, so plant material makes up scarcely more than 2 percent of their overall diet. This is so low because of a simple anatomical matter. The armadillo is a member of Order *Edentata,* and is very little better off than its relatives, the toothless anteaters. Its teeth are simply too few and too weak to grind up green vegetation or roots. It is one of the cruel ironies of our supposedly enlightened stewardship of nature that the armadillos which we killed for supposedly destroying the roots of our plants did not eat the plant roots at all and were really digging in our lawns and gardens after the enemy grubs and worms and slugs which we have to poison the whole tract to get rid of once we have shot our armadillos.

The point is that the armadillo's insect-centered but omnivorous appetite would seem to require nothing which wasn't available almost anywhere except where the soil remained frozen for long periods of time. Neither is there any evidence of any wave of additions to the invertebrate fauna beginning around 1860 which could have prompted the armadillo to follow it north.

The possibility of armadillos having difficulty in northern climes where their invertebrate prey might be unavailable to them because of freezing conditions suggests another factor possibly limiting them — the direct action upon them of cold itself. Since they have gone north so far, various authors have pointed to well-attested instances where armadillos have been found dead or dying after very severe cold spells and their numbers in the affected areas were greatly reduced. The facts that these animals are cold sensitive and that their populations suffer declines sometimes approaching collapses after record cold spells are well established. But on the other hand, while each cold-devastated population suffers a blow, in each case kept track of, during only a short time of normal weather the armadillos are back as before, and in most cases marching on to new territories.

It is certain that somewhere the armadillos will come up to the latitude where cold severe enough to decimate them comes so regularly that they cannot recover and colonize. They may already have met this edge of their possible range in some places. But to get back down to the original population homes based in the southern tip of Texas — such a cold-dictated limitation could hardly have kept them until the proper time cowering in the Rio Grande Valley and then with startling suddenness allowed them to spurt northward, for the simple reason that this would have taken such a climatic change throughout Texas and at least the whole southeast U.S. as there is no evidence has occurred since the ice ages. The weather may have been a little less stable in exploratory times, but the greenhouse effect had not started by 1860. The armadillos did not ride north then upon any new outburst of balmy tropical breezes. Exactly the opposite: they went north then to challenge the cold as they had not before because some other constraint upon them was lifted then.

Searching the records for any changes which might have been far enough along by 1860 and important enough to the armadillo to have facilitated its bursting out of its valley starting about then yields one change possibly qualifying. Even though modern ecologists dislike ascribing any great influence upon an organism's range to the factor involved, it is all we find.

The present situation for the armadillo is an enviable one. It can go groping blindly along, concentrating upon sensing its beloved but buried grubs, because no creature it blunders near is likely to hurt it. It is hilarious to watch even a large dog trying to bite into a curled-up and inert armadillo until he gives up in disgust. As one authority recently put it, "The armadillo's only serious predator appears to be man."[82] This leaves it very free to go where it wishes, as long as it avoids our jealously guarded gardens and our highways upon which nothing has a right to be except automobiles.

Things probably were not so congenial for armadillos in the presettlement wilderness. It appears there lurked some very formidable predators upon them in the original Texas wilderness communities. We get a clue to this when we learn that in Central America the jaguar feeds on armadillos.[83] But even more important, cougars prey upon armadillos.[84] Apparently, the claws of the large cats can rip apart armadillos' hard shells where those of the dog family can't.

Don't we have here something which may explain the changing range of the armadillos? Look back into the chapter on the Texas cats and recall how jaguars were in the thickets practically throughout early Texas. Then read again the stories of the Texas lions called cougars, panthers, etc., which were once so numerous that pioneers killed them around their early cabins and one North Texas settler claimed to have killed sixty in one season. After refreshing your memory with that picture of the primeval wilderness teeming with these large cats, then imagine a rash armadillo straggling north from its ancestral homeland. It would be meandering into the very jaws of death! Perhaps the shells of some of those incautious explorers were the ones Captain McCown told Audubon of seeing on the prairies just north of the Rio Grande galaria forests.

So we may have an explanation in the myriad large cat predators patrolling the bulk of Texas for the armadillos' original containment in the southern tip of Texas. And we have ample evidence of the wholesale slaughter of the large Texas cats beginning to affect their populations seriously by the 1840s and reducing their numbers to a pitiful survivor here and there by 1860. Isn't this the change we have been looking for? Can't we imagine the roving armadillo, after this decimation of its cat enemies was far enough along, shuffling unconcernedly north, blindly colonizing whole states which had very fat untouched grubs? Didn't we invite the armadillo on up when we eradicated our feline security guards who had so faithfully kept them out?

With the armadillo present in so tiny a portion of Texas, it certainly had little importance in early Texas. The animal could be significant to only the small minority of pioneers who found themselves near the mouth of the Rio Grande. But what importance did it have there?

Lieutenant Webster, already quoted, was not a resident of the lower Rio Grande Valley, but merely an explorer temporarily there while doing his job surveying the area. But in his short time there he had already learned about one of the armadillo's values. He noted that "their meat is eatable."

We do not know how Lieutenant Webster learned this. It is hardly likely that he or his men from the north tried cooking and eating any animal so bizarre and strange to them as this without prompting. It would seem that he must have learned of this exotic food source from someone more familiar with these animals. I have found no evidence of whether the Indians with which the Rio Grande Valley had long been populated made use of armadillos for food or of whether this was a custom brought out of Mexico by the Spanish. However, it is clear that as the armadillos went north the custom of eating them followed to become a commonplace among the rural poor and a gustatory adventure for the gourmets of game, at least in South Texas. But it is clear that the pioneers of most of Texas did not have armadillo to calm their hunger or armadillo-shell baskets to decorate their cabins.

12

The Rodents as They Were in Texas

These may be varmints to us and called that in the language of the pioneers we imagine, but they seem to have been more than that to the actual explorers. The word "varmint" is an American variation of the Old French word "vermin" meaning obnoxious or offensive animals. The *Oxford Dictionary* points out that the term is "rare before 1825," and that one of its early appearances is Washington Irving's use of the word in 1835, when he was in territory which became Oklahoma and was referring to beavers.[1] However, I have found no Texas explorer writing before 1860 who used the word at all. This may be explained by the lateness of the term's origin, but I would like to imagine it is because of our pioneers having higher regard for all creatures small as well as great than to label them "varmints." Would that the nice sensibility with which our explorers speak of these humble animals might prompt something similar in us.

Loved or hated, these furry, gnawing animals had the Texas our scouts found very well populated. And they were such ubiquitous creatures — different ones of them scurrying, hopping, jumping, climbing, even tunneling, swimming and flying all over Texas — that they could hardly be ignored. So our explorers tell of them. And the only significant bias in their accounts seems to be that the number of times and the extent to which they describe them seems to be more an indication of how useful or pestering they found them than of how relatively numerous they were. But perhaps this is just as important, for it is the way these animals figure in the explorers' Texas that we want to discover.

TEXAS BEAVERS

Is the remembrance of Texas' first stream-flow experts and dam-builders — its first engineers, if you will — still with us? Can we or will your children be able to picture at all adequately our beavers and the expert, precise beauty of their work which was once to be seen practically all over our state? Or were these beaver monuments lost — not lost, but sacked and the inhabitants massacred, like some of history's human engineer builders' proudest cities — too completely and too early for anything capable of giving us a real conception of their wonders to remain?

Since the Texas beavers' works were almost all destroyed before there were any preservationists around, we don't have much physical left to build our conception of their work upon, but fortunately we do have the word-pictures of a few pioneers to turn our minds' eyes upon. Since this is about all most of us will ever have, our explorers' descriptions of beavers' works are especially precious.

One beavers' dam was so perfect that it moved a hard-bitten military officer in the midst of an expedition in very unfamiliar and quite risky country to wax eloquent in describing it and rendering tribute to its builders. The officer was Capt. R. B. Marcy, and he was in what would someday become the Texas Panhandle (specifically in what would today be Wheeler County, near where Mobeetie would later come to be) when, in 1852, he wrote the following: "Our course to-day was very nearly due west, up the left bank of Sweetwater creek, until, within about three miles of our present position, we turned with the course of the stream more northwardly.... A community of beavers have also selected a spot upon the creek near our camp, for their interesting labors and habitations.... In the selection of a suitable site, and in the erection of the structure, they appear to have been guided by something more than mere animal instinct, and have exhibited as correct a knowledge of hydrostatics, and the action of forces resulting from currents of water, as the most scientific millwright would have done. Having chosen a spot where the banks on each side of the creek were narrow and sufficiently high to raise a head of about five feet, they selected two cotton-wood trees about fifteen inches in diameter, situated above this point, and having an inclination towards the stream: these they cut down with their teeth, (as the marks upon the stumps plainly showed,) and floating them down to the position chosen for the dam, they were placed across the stream with an inclination downward, uniting the centre. This formed the foundation upon which the superstructure of brush and earth was placed, in precisely the same manner as a brush dam is made by our millwrights, with the bushes and earth alternating and packed closely, the butts in all cases turned down the stream. After this is raised to a sufficient height, the top is covered with earth, except in the centre, where there is a sluice or waste-wier, which lets off the superfluous water when it rises so high as to endanger the structure.... I observed one place above the pond where they had commenced another dam, and had progressed so far as to cut down two trees on opposite sides of the creek; but as they did not fall in the right direction to suit their purposes, the work was abandoned."[2]

The animals which were the authors of these stream development projects, the engineers of their planning, as well as the artisans who brought them to reality, were *Castor canadensis,* the beavers. There was little ambiguity here and no competing names to confuse us were yet coined.

Apparently everyone in early Texas knew what a beaver was so well that it appears no Texas writer before 1860 thought it necessary to describe the animals themselves. Or else, most of the chroniclers, even though they observed the beavers' handiwork closely and could describe their dams in detail, may never have actually seen the animals themselves, so could not describe them. As an instance of this, Captain Marcy, after writing up the fine description of the beaver dam just quoted, added the following terse sentence: "I watched for some time upon the banks of the pond, but could see none of the animals."

Once having thought of the way these animals move around under water and hide inside their houses, it is possible to read the explorers' journals and see their problem stemming from this elusiveness. Froebel, for instance, wrote in 1854, "I observed the marks of beavers' teeth on the trees upon the banks of the [Devil's] river; a large sycamore-tree had been thrown down by these animals and the bark was stript from many of its branches,"[3] but he never says he saw a beaver. And Ruxton, when traveling up the Rio Grande out of El Paso in 1846, wrote, "On the banks of the river I saw some fresh beaver 'sign,'"[4] but that's all. No doubt it is significant that this term, "sign," is so often attached to beavers. That is probably all most explorers saw of them.

Trappers must have observed these animals very closely, but few trappers wrote anything for us. So only one explorer left any description of beavers. This was Fray Jose de Solis, who left us only one phrase concerning one feature of them which must have particularly impressed him. In 1767, he wrote, "With their sharp teeth, that look like awls, they gnaw...."[5] Maybe this is an appropriate guide for us. Imagine a set of the most formidable gnawing teeth ever, surround this with the picture of the furry animal with the fat, naked tail traced over and over for us in every wildlife publication because we will probably never see more of these animals, and that is probably the best we can do.

If beavers were elusive, that does not mean they were scarce or that they didn't have a wide original range in Texas. But it is not easy to arrive at either their original numbers or range through the explorers' accounts. This is because before the nineteenth century was half over, the trappers' assaults upon the beavers had already diminished both their numbers and their range greatly. Because of this the pioneers' statements about beavers change as time goes by.

The statements of the earliest explorers were very general, intimating that beavers were everywhere in the region. Typical is that of Solis, who, continuing the passage already referred to, stated boldly in 1767, that, "In all the rivers of Texas beaver and otter can be found in large numbers." Concerning northeastern Mexico and Texas south and west of the Nueces River in 1795, Calleja wrote, "In the margins of the smaller rivers that join the larger ones, beavers, birds, and animals of many known species are produced...."[6] Marin de Porras was able to write about "the province" of Texas that, "The woods end in great streams filled with beavers."[7] And Custis, in his catalog of the animals encountered on his remarkable 1806 expedition up the Red

River, covered a lot of northwest Texas when he noted that beavers were then "Abundant on the tributary streams of Red River."[8] Any fair summary of eighteenth century and the earliest nineteenth century accounts of beavers has to admit that the explorers of that early time lead us to believe that these animals ranged over the entire state, including northwestern parts where it is not usually remembered that they ever existed.

This picture changed so suddenly in the first part of the nineteenth century that it taxes our ideas of the effects of hunting and trapping. This is because beavers were among the first of the Texas wild animals taken in quantity for the fur trade. They were the first of only six wild animal species mentioned in the census reports of the Nacogdoches 1830s fur trade.[9] And the result was swift and inexorable. William Kennedy stated it in 1839, writing, "In the list of amphibious animals are the otter and beaver, which formerly abounded in the district of Nacogdoches, but have been greatly thinned by the hunters and trappers."[10]

It may be hard for us to believe the swiftness with which the jaws of the traps harvested our beavers, but we must if we credit our exploring forebears with any honesty at all. In 1846, an anonymous traveler wrote concerning Texas as a whole, "Beaver and otter were frequent in the past, but now they have become rare because of the hunters."[11] And none less than David G. Burnet, the first president of independent Texas, wrote in 1847, "The American trappers have nearly extirpated these valuable animals [the beavers] from the waters of Texas."[12]

These animals apparently were able to survive best on the remote streams of the upper and western Hill Country where they were protected longer by the wildness of the country and the marauding Indians. Bracht and his companions found them still in what was to become Blanco, Gillespie, Llano and Mason counties in 1848, but from what he wrote they were taking care of that as fast as they could, since he wrote: "Several beavers have been shot in the upper hill country, especially along the Chimal, Llano and Pedernales."[13] The Devil's River must have been their best refuge. Samuel Augustus Maverick found them still near the mouth of that river in 1848.[14] Capt. S. G. French found them near the head of that stream in the next year,[15] and Froebel found them still on the Devil's River in 1854.[16]

The statements which we have seen about the virtual elimination of the beavers over most of Texas by the 1840s receive oblique confirmation from the absence of travelers' reports of any beaver signs in most of Texas as they crisscrossed it between 1840 and 1860. Of all of them, only the three just mentioned in the upper Hill Country, Captain Marcy up on the edge of the Panhandle and Ruxton on the river way out above El Paso, report finding any beavers still existing. Except in such remote places, they must already have been almost totally removed from the explorers' Texas.

Wrapped in some of the thickest, softest fur ever, the beavers early paid the price with their lives when we coveted that fur to brush our cheeks and make the hats on our brows. Aristocrats of the rodent tribes and possessors of skills almost unbelievable, Texas still has no place for more than a few token beavers. Even though our explorers show little remorse at their taking, maybe their accounts of them will at least enable us to remember these lost engineers with respect.

PRAIRIE DOGS: THE ORIGINAL URBAN TEXANS

If the beavers were the aristocrats of the rodents, living on their exclusive country-club lake developments, the prairie dogs were the commoners of that tribe, swarming in the urban sprawl of their monotonous towns. And the prairie dogs did swarm. Their unbelievable numbers in nature's original scheme of things is clearly the most significant thing about them.

We can do no better than to start with the matter of their numbers, and we can find no better statement about that than the one written down in 1852, by Captain Marcy after that military officer's company had passed through territory later to become Donley and Armstrong counties just southeast of Amarillo. He wrote: "Our road during the whole day has passed through a continuous dog-town . . . and we were often obliged to turn out of our course to avoid the little mounds around their burrows. In passing along through these villages the little animals are seen in countless numbers sitting upright at the mouths of their domicile, presenting much the appearance of stumps of small trees; and so incessant is the chatter of their barking, that it requires but little effort of the imagination to fancy oneself surrounded by the busy hum of a city. The immense number of animals in some of these towns, or warrens, may be conjectured from the large space which they sometimes cover. The one at this place is about twenty-five miles in the direction through which we have passed it. Supposing its dimensions in other directions to be the same, it would embrace an area of six hundred and twenty-five square miles, or eight hundred and ninety-six thousand acres. Estimating the holes to be at the usual distances of about twenty yards apart, and each burrow occupied by a family of four or five dogs, I fancy that the aggregate population would be greater than any other city in the universe."[17]

That seems a rash statement, especially remarkable for having been included in the journal of a sober military man. Can it be confirmed, or was the captain exaggerating?

There have been various ways of estimating the populations of Texas prairie dogs throughout the century and a half since Marcy, and different authors have come up with different estimates. No one can give an absolute figure, but some numbers have been proposed to indicate the probable range of their populations. Such a number was once proposed by W. R. Long, an officer of the Texas Parks and Wildlife Commission, in the publication of that agency. He wrote, "The mounded burrows stretched for almost endless miles in some areas." He then singled out one "colony" north of San Angelo, and wrote that it had been estimated "to harbor as many as 800 million prairie dogs."[18] Another was estimated by Merriam to have 400,000,000.[19]

Does anything more need to be said in defense of Marcy's statement? When the social insects (the bees and ants whose swarms impress us so) have in the range of only 50,000 individuals to a colony-city, Texas total human population (Dallas, Houston, San Antonio and all the rest of its towns together) is somewhere around only 16 or 17 million people, and the greatest human cities in the world are only beginning to crowd populations of 30 million, the prairie dogs' towns had clearly bested all others that have yet existed by several orders or magnitude, and Marcy was literally correct.

When we turn to the question of where in Texas these prairie dogs were, the explorers' many reports of them give us some definite answers. Beginning on the west, I have found no account placing the animals specifically within present El Paso County, although Baird, in his 1857 work, lists among his specimens those secured by Major Emory from "San Antonio to El Paso."[20] The westernmost specifically located reports of them in Texas are two from the years 1849 and 1850 in northern Hudspeth County.[21] At the same time they were encountered in either extreme northeastern Culberson or Reeves County.[22] There are eight pre-1860 reports of them from various parts of what would become Jeff Davis County, one from Presidio, and one from Brewster County. They were also seen in present Pecos County, this rounding out their presence in most of the trans-Pecos.

From the Panhandle we have numerous explorers' reports placing these animals both on and below the Llano Estacado, but usually near its breaks and edges. They come from present Oldham, Potter, Hemphill, Armstrong, Donley and Briscoe counties.

In 1842, Falconer described prairie dogs from what is now Cottle County northwest for an unknown but quite great distance: "We ascended a very steep side of a hill near us, and came to perhaps the first true range of table-land. The ground was flat, and sprinkled with misquite trees, and there was excellent pasture for the cattle. For four days we continued to traverse it to the N.W. Throughout the whole distance was an almost endless 'dog village,' or mounds at the mouths of the burrows of the prairie-dog, a species of marmot."[23]

On down in either present Floyd or Crosby County, George Kendall related: "We had proceeded but a short distance, after reaching this beautiful prairie [the Llano Estacado] before we came up on the outskirts of the commonwealth. A few scattering dogs were seen scampering in, their short, sharp yelps giving a general alarm to the whole community. The first brief cry of danger from the outskirts was soon taken up in the centre of the city, and now nothing was to be heard or seen in any direction but barking, dashing, and scampering of the mercurial and excitable denizens of the place, each to his burrow. Far as the eye could reach the city extended, and all over it the scene was the same."[24]

These animals were found generally south of the counties mentioned all the way to the Rio Grande. The accounts of them seem to become the most numerous in the Concho River region, but this may be merely a reflection of the fact that more expeditions west traversed that section than any other. It is interesting, however, that "large dog towns" were encountered down in Crockett County, and that James G. Bell said, when down in what is now northeastern Val Verde County in 1854, "We passed through a dog town; not very extensive however. We did not see any of the inhabitants; when we get in to the country where they are more plenty I will endeavor to give a description."[25] This would seem to indicate that Val Verde County marked the southeastern edge of the species' range.

From there the eastern edge of the prairie dog's range in Texas, as drawn from the explorers' accounts, ran northeast through Mason and either McCulloch or San Saba counties. The most northeastern specific peg on which to anchor it is Captain Marcy's talking of the prairie dog at Fort Belknap in Young County, which is just south of Wichita Falls, as reported by Baird in his list of specimens already cited.

Two significant things arise out of this explorer-drawn original range of the prairie dog in the wilderness. The first is that the animal's range in the unaltered environment was almost identical to the recent maps drawn of its range since practically everything has been changed. This places a cloud upon the many — and still forthcoming — statements that the effects of agricultural and other practices upon the land have caused the prairie dog to invade new regions. This means that the use of this false premise as an excuse for eliminating the little fellows wherever they are in our way is animal pseudoscience. But happily, the evidence from the explorers' accounts backs the often-stated theory of biogeographers that the region of the 100th parallel is a major dividing line between eastern and western life forms. The prairie dog becomes a perfect example of a western form with its natural eastern range ending almost exactly upon the 100th meridian.

The explorers having given us such a well defined range for the prairie dog in their days, together with the persistence of this range over the more recent century of change, gives us a standard by which to evaluate any reports of the animals from any time period. And I don't hesitate to point out where one explorer appears to have mistakenly reported these animals. Anthony Glass left a journal of an exploration up the Red River and into parts of East Texas in 1808 and 1809.[26] In it he claims he encountered prairie dogs in a location which would be just east of present Paris, Texas, in Lamar County. This is approximately 200 miles east of the eastern limit of range otherwise drawn by the rest of the Texas explorers, and it is rendered suspect otherwise by the failure of all other travelers or settlers in northeast Texas or anyone since then to report the species there, as well as by being east of all known occurrences of these animals in Oklahoma, Kansas or Nebraska. This is an example of the way the occasional erroneous report of an explorer usually becomes glaringly obvious in the light of his fellows' general picture.

The example of Glass' questionable report becomes the vehicle for a further lesson when we trace a use recently made of it. Dan L. Flores, in his excellent book on the Freeman and Custis accounts of their Red River expedition, refers to Glass' prairie dog report and uses it as an indicator of "rapid ecological change in the region."[27] The lesson is that an explorer's single out-of-general-range report should not be credited on its own and certainly not used as a basis for any generalizations. It is the whole picture emerging from the total gathered host of explorers' accounts that must be used this way if we are to capture reality. And that is what we are trying to arrive at here.

There is yet another lesson in the accounts of prairie dogs of the caution with which early reports must be used. We have seen the clear evidence that these rodents lived only from the Devil's River country north and west of a line through the upper Hill Country and then on past present Wichita Falls into Indian Territory. This leaves San Antonio and all of South Texas without them. And there is some confirmation of this, it being stated in Audubon and Bachman's 1851 work that, "None of these animals were seen by J. W. Audubon in his journey through that part of Texas lying between Galveston and San Antonio."[28]

What then do we do with a statement made by Herman Ehrenberg as he was marching to Mexico in 1836? When in deep South Texas he wrote: "A few days' tramp through the wilderness brought us to the Mission del Refugio. . . . The southern climate displayed its colorful luxuriance here more abundantly than elsewhere. . . . The dimly lit groves of the forest led on to prairies where numerous flocks of wild geese waddled quite unconcernedly among droves of horses, oxen, and red deer that roamed at liberty in these open spaces; prairie dogs and large wolves also abounded." Can it be that this man actually found our gregarious little rodents way down there almost to Corpus Christi? This would require a total realignment of their range. Was Ehrenberg a totally misguided and misleading witness, or is there another explanation for this passage?

Before we decide this, we must read Ehrenberg's second statement about his prairie dogs. He went on to write: "The luxuriant vegetation which flourished in the neighborhood of the mission grew scantier and coarser as we drew nearer the coast. A flat arid country, covered with tall, reedlike grass, stretched around us.... This featureless plain was dotted with thickets of mesquite trees, under which lurked the prairie dogs which are so numerous in this region. Our small caravan did not in the least frighten them away, for leaving their hiding places, they ran in file at a short distance from us, keeping their odd-looking faces constantly in our direction."[29]

Don't we see the clues in this second statement which make it clear that this explorer did not see the rodents we are studying, and yet was not writing a false report? First note that he speaks of "thickets of mesquite trees, under which lurked the prairie dogs." Who can imagine prairie dogs in thickets, lounging in the shade of trees? This is the very opposite of the typical dog town with the little fellows standing in the full sun on their mounds scattered over the almost table-clear expanse. A modern technical study of these animals concludes: "To summarize, the characteristic vegetation of dog towns consists of an abundance of short perennial grass, a large variety of forbs, annual and perennial, and a scarcity of shrubs.... Mid grasses, tall grasses, and shrubs are more common around a dog town than on it."[30] Doesn't the suspicion arise that Ehrenberg's prairie dogs must have been something different from our West Texas rodents?

There is a second clue that something is not consistent here. Note that Ehrenberg says that his group "did not in the least frighten these animals away," but that on the contrary they actually, "leaving their hiding places ... ran in file," along beside the group, observing them. This is exactly opposite the behavior every other explorer describes in actual prairie dogs. Lt. A. W. Whipple's statement, made when he was in Hemphill County of the Texas Panhandle in 1853, shows their typical actions upon being approached: "Prairie dogs were numerous, and barked with great energy to warn us away from their villages. They were, however, very cautious, dropping into their holes whenever danger approached."[31]

One more small caveat: Ehrenberg especially notes his animals' "odd-looking faces." Now who, upon observing actual prairie dogs, notes their faces, which are even more homely than those of most rodents and without any emphasizing marks, color or otherwise, at all? It may be the barking, the bolt-upright posture so often assumed or the short, jerking tail which is noticed, but not the nondescript faces.

So what were Ehrenberg's prairie dogs anyway? A new reading of his first statement gives me an answer which satisfies me. He wrote in it "prairie dogs and large wolves also abounded." If I read this as: prairie dogs and *large* [larger] wolves also abounded, the shift in emphasis makes me think that he is saying clumsily that little wolves and also large wolves abounded. Little wolves would be coyotes, often called prairie wolves, and prairie wolves are, like all wolves, really dogs — prairie dogs, if you please, and we have arrived at Ehrenberg's term with no more permutations than every translator uses every day. And the coyote fits the description very well. It would be entirely in character for coyotes to live in thickets and to dog the group of travelers because of curiosity and in hopes of food. The big-eyed, alert, foxy faces of coyotes have been emphasized before, and these animals were very numerous in South Texas. If we are correct that Ehrenberg's animals were coyotes, then they are in the right place acting as they should, what has been told us of actual prairie dog rodents is still credible, and we have hopefully learned the lesson that we must not take every explorer's term for what he sees uncritically; but also that if we apply some analysis to what is said in the light of what is otherwise known, we can usually determine its true meaning and find the explorers' total picture remarkably consistent.

In dealing with the prairie dog's populations and ranges we have probably made the all too common mistake of not looking at the individual. We must get a close-up look at this creature from our explorers, for most of us may never actually see it. But this is not going to be easy. With Dr. Ferdinand Roemer in Menard County near the San Saba River in 1849, we can see the difficulty. He reports the problem as follows: "Toward evening we descended from the high plateau into a beautiful prairie in which tender grass and mesquite trees grew.... It was on this prairie where most of us saw for the first time a colony of prairie dogs. A number of mounds, two to three feet high, covering an area of about a half mile in diameter, were scattered about. The grass round about them was destroyed. On the top of each elevation was a round opening which served as an entrance to the subterranean passages, connecting the homes. On each mound sat a little yellowish grey animal, the size of a rabbit, which on closer approach emitted a whistling sound and disappeared quickly in the hole of each mound. The entire company immediately felt the urge to kill a prairie dog, in order to learn a little more about them. But this proved to be more difficult than it appeared on the face of it, for the animals were so wary that we could hope to shoot them only with a rifle. Furthermore, they usually had time, even when mortally wounded, to withdraw into the depth of their houses to prevent their dead bodies from falling into the hands of the enemy. Finally one of the Shawnee Indians, spurred on by an offer of a reward, managed to kill one of these animals, and we now had an opportunity to satisfy our curiosity."[32]

Neither Dr. Roemer nor any other explorer goes on to describe the animals for us in any detail. Perhaps it would have been difficult to do from specimens mutilated by long-distance rifle bullets. We must be satisfied by hints written in passing. John C. Reid, for instance, wrote in 1857, that prairie dogs "are about trebel the size, and have much the shape, in limb and body, of a full grown rat — have a brown color, and short tail, resembling that of the ground squirrel."[33] And James G. Bell wrote in 1854 that "the claws are sharp, and always uncovered for the purpose of digging; the tail like a dog, hair between a Grey and Fox squirrel; the head resembles the Chewawah dog with his ears cropped, are about the size of a grown fox squirrel."[34]

Captain Marcy showed the most interest in these animals of any explorer, and he is the only one of them who reports having examined a live prairie dog. When out in northwest Potter County, just northwest of present Amarillo, in 1849, he reported: "Our road has for a good portion of the day been passing through a continuous dog-town. One of the animals was brought alive into camp this evening, and having an opportunity to examine it, I was at a loss to conceive why it should ever have been called 'prairie dog.' It is a very timid animal; but when irritated, bites severely, as one of our young gentleman can testify. It is but little larger than the gray squirrel, of a reddish brown color, with head, teeth, and feet, very similar to that animal, and a more appropriate name, in my opinion, would be 'prairie squirrel.'"[35]

Hopefully something of the appearance of these animals may be gained from the combination of those descriptions. The idea that they should better be called prairie squirrels than dogs would be a good one if it is realized that these creatures do not present the streamlined, graceful shape of squirrels, as ground squirrels do. Sitting upright on their haunches as they so often do, they present the pot-bellied, broad-hipped appearance of overweight old-timers, and when walking on all fours they actually waddle. Reid was correct when he wrote that they were in shape more like fat rats. Perhaps the stumpy and hairy tail is all that keep them from being called prairie rats.

Little more than this can be gleaned from the explorers' accounts about these animals themselves. Our pioneers were much better at leaving us word pictures of the prairie dogs' towns with their countless mounds. We even have one bird's-eye view of such a scene. James G. Bell was in the Davis Mountains of the Texas Big Bend in 1854 when he wrote, "Around us at the head of Limpia canyon are thousands of dogs who singly appear, give a few barks and slip into their underground houses . . . some of the men are engaged digging out Dogs. . . . Mr. James and myself went to a point on the mountain to watch for a signal within one hour of sun set. . . . Looking down upon the plain small circular blazes could be distinctly seen, and very numerous. This was caused by the little mounds thrown up by the dogs, for hundreds of acres these blazes could be seen; on the places where there is no grass, small pits — large as a dollar — cover the ground. Almost certainly, my ideas induce me to believe, these are caused by dogs digging out the roots of grass etc."[36]

Bell has done us a service by giving us this picture of a dog town from such a unique perspective, and he performs another service by turning our thoughts, through his speculating upon these animals digging out grass, to the subject of prairie dogs and their environment. The millions which existed must have had important interrelationships with almost everything else in West Texas. What do the explorers tell us about these?

The prairie dogs' most important effect must have been upon the vegetation in the areas occupied by their towns. First, they built mounds, as we have already seen mentioned. The throwing out of the soil excavated in digging their tunnels formed very much flattened heaps occasionally up to two feet high around the central opening and sloping to their edges so gradually that they could be up to six or seven feet across. These were kept packed so firmly in place that all vegetation over that area was, as Dr.

Roemer put it, "destroyed." How significant the amount of acreage removed from production by the millions of these mounds which existed in early Texas I have never seen even guessed at by any explorer or anyone else

But there has been much speculation — and even argumentation — about the effects of these animals beyond the immediate edges of their mounds. This is because they are to a great degree herbivorous, and their existence in such high concentrations as they maintained must have resulted in the removal of much vegetation.

The result of this on the original wilderness was described by various explorers. John Russell Bartlett is typical. He wrote in 1850, "The ground occupied by this fraternity was distinctly marked by the shortness of the grass, which these little creatures feed on. . . ."[37] Capt. S. G. French made it clear that this was general, but that the grass was not actually killed out, writing in his 1849 report, ". . . over the whole country they inhabit the herbage is kept closely cropped by those little animals, and the fresh grass springing up gives it the appearance of a bright lawn."[38]

The hundreds of millions of these little fellows which were gnawing away at the West Texas vegetation are said to have been the equivalent of millions of grazing cattle.[39] It is said that, "Prairie dogs disturb the soil near their burrows and thus favor the establishment of pioneer forbs, which they eat. And by cutting down tall plants on the town . . . [they] favor the dominance of two short perennial grasses, their staple foods, buffalo grass and blue gramma."[40] And the grazing of the prairie dogs was continuous and permanent, unlike that of the herds of buffaloes which constantly moved on and probably didn't return to again graze down the same area for a season or two. Students of such things have said that, "Prairie dogs are characteristic of the short-grass plains, and the eastern limit of their distribution corresponds fairly well with the western edge of the tall-grass association."[41] So it seems strange that these little rodents aren't usually given credit, at least along with the buffaloes, for the existence of the short grass prairies as they were discovered.

Prairie dogs have been maligned not only for competing with domestic animals by grazing, but for supposedly damaging the soil with their digging. But the latter charge must be pure slander. They live and dig their burrows only on very slightly sloping terrain with little potential for erosion, and erosion channels are not normally observed originating in their towns. In fact, they should be regarded as soil builders rather than destroyers, because their burrowing goes down very deep and subsoil material is continually deposited upon the surface. This is the best soil producing technique, and Kofort quotes Bailey in saying, "There is no doubt that the prairie dogs have done great good in deepening and enriching the soil."[42]

There may have been one more interesting way in which prairie dogs had at least a small part in maintaining the original balance of nature. Although primarily herbivorous, they also ate insects. They have been especially observed working to capture grasshoppers. L. C. Whitehead reported a time, during a grasshopper invasion in the Panhandle, when, "Swarms [of grasshoppers] in passing over and alighting in a prairie-dog town provided a great feast for the animals. The prairie-dog population was out in full force chasing after, catching, and eating the grasshoppers. Numbers of the animals were successful in 'fielding' the low flying and dropping grasshoppers as they passed."[43] Wouldn't the hundreds of millions of prairie dogs originally on the plains have been some check upon the grasshopper populations? Of course they could hardly have prevented them, but might not the grasshopper plagues which devastated — and still from time to time threaten to overrun — the regions from which the prairie dogs were eradicated have been at least delayed in forming by so many prairie dog predators?

Most of the early travelers who wrote about prairie dogs agreed in reporting that these animals had some special relationships with two other animals — a small owl and the rattlesnake. This was because they repeatedly observed these other animals around about and even entering the prairie dogs' burrows. Bartlett told it this way: "In one instance I saw a rattlesnake enter one of the habitations: but whether he belonged there or was an interloper it was impossible to tell. Small brown owls flitted about, and lit on the little hillocks in the midst of the prairie dogs, with which they seemed to be upon good terms."[44] The chronicler of the 1857 Leach wagon train trip across Texas, thought to have been James B. Leach himself, wrote, "We have seen enough of the facts in the case in our 'Prairie Dog Experience' to warrant us in accepting as true what may seem to many the apocryphal tradition to the effect that rattlesnakes and owls make common quarters with Prairie dogs in their burrows. Several of these venomous reptiles escaped death by taking refuge in the underground habitations of their guests. One snake over six feet long was killed when half way in the earth."[45]

There is no doubt that these three species frequented the dog towns at the same time. Many since the explorers have documented this. But it has been difficult to determine whether they actually occupy the same underground passages at the same time or not, as well as who are guests and who are invaders — or whether it is really a matter of predator and prey.

The explorers, showing their great curiosity which played a part in bringing them out into the wilderness, speculated upon these relationships. John C. Reid, for instance, observed well, but concluded entirely without evidence: "Their [prairie dogs'] towns are often found twenty miles from visible water, or other vegetation than grass; they burrow at great depths in the ground; their holes are within a few yards of each other, and each seems to contain a half dozen animals. Indeed the inmates are not alone — these animals; but rattlesnakes, owls, and ground squirrels, mate with them in perfect harmony."[46] William Preston Johnston wrote of observing these animals in 1855, but fell back on hearsay when it came to this point, writing, "Numbers of owls were seen watching at their holes, two of which my father shot. I am told the owls and rattlesnakes live all together in these holes. The rattlesnakes feed on the prairie dogs, the owls on the rattlesnakes, making a harmonious set equal to Barnum's Happy Family."[47]

Baseless speculation and hearsay, as we already know and these two pioneers have illustrated once again, lead to contradictory and often false conclusions. But fortunately other explorers did not rely on such, going on instead to augment their observations with real, if rudimentary, experimentation.

Edwin James was already on the right track in 1820, and wrote up his investigation as follows: "In passing through a village of prairie dogs, of which we saw great numbers, Mr. Peale killed a burrowing owl. The bird, though killed instantly, had fallen into one of the marmot's burrows but had luckily lodged within the reach of the arm. On opening it, the intestines were found filled with the fragments of grasshoppers' wings, and the hard parts of other insects. We have never been able, from examination, to discover any evidence that these owls prey upon the marmots, whose villages they infest."[48] James G. Bell had expanded the research in 1854, when he wrote: "This morning found a beautiful piece of watered cornelian; lost it again in rooting a rattlesnake out of his hole. He could not get all in on account of a great bunch about the middle of his body. I cut the *gent* open and disclosed a small owl, such as go into the nest of the Prairie Dog."[49] Captain Marcy carried on, writing, "The rattlesnake and a small species of owl are found in the same holes with the dogs. At first I was doubtful whether this domestic arrangement was in accordance with the wishes of the owner of the premises, but a short time since, I was satisfied no such friendly relations existed between them, for on killing a rattlesnake at one of the dog holes, it was found that he had swallowed a young dog, thereby establishing the fact that the snake is an intruder, and preys upon the dogs."[50]

Need it be more firmly established that the explorers had abolished the happy family theory of the three species? That they were exactly right in showing up the rattlesnake as the predatory invader of the towns is clear from statements of later animal scientists, such as the following: "Another popular belief is that the rattlesnakes and burrowing owls living in prairie-dog towns unite as a kind of happy family in the burrows of the dogs. The truth is, the owls live and breed in deserted dog holes, while the rattlesnakes visit the occupied holes to feed on the unfortunate occupants and may use deserted burrows as a convenient domicile while subsisting on their neighbors."[51]

Reminiscences and all kinds of stories written later exist, and tell all kinds of things, but I have found no other pre-1860 pioneers' contemporary statements about this subject beyond those quoted. Of these only one — Reid's — erroneously speaks of harmony between the three concerned species, and the rest, once read, disprove his error and already establish with actual evidence what the best science has more recently learned. So why, in the name of fairness, do we still get statements disparaging our explorers indiscriminately, such as the following one? "Early settlers and pioneer explorers wrote of an apparent friendship existing between the prairie dog, burrowing owl and rattlesnake, all of which were often found occupying the same burrow. The friendship theory was later shattered when closer observation proved that a rattlesnake entered a prairie dog burrow not as a comrade but in search of young prairie dogs to eat...."[52]

It is my hope that all of the explorers' judgments on any given subject will be read and taken into account before they are all devalued because of the error of any one. That is the reason that I take up so much space with sometimes almost repetitious quotations from them. The explorers' big picture of a large Texas can hardly be in one man's paragraph.

The prairie dogs had other enemies — among them badgers, ferrets and coyotes, as well as the cats and the raptorial birds. But from the millions of them that there were, all their natural predators together did not actually threaten their existence. It took a new and unnatural enemy to do them in. This cunning new prairie dog exterminator was man — not Indians or just any man — only the new European Texans. As Robin Doughty says in his study of the decline of wildlife in Texas, "Ranchers and government agents in west Texas and throughout most of the Southwest set about poisoning dog towns so that the rodents were eradicated quickly and comprehensively."[53] But that sad episode took place well after the time of our explorers, so we are spared the ugly details here.

We can ponder instead what might have been if our forebears had not carried out the virtual elimination of these little prairie animals. And our explorers give us a hint of one novel advantage there might have been in having prairie dogs on our modern prairies.

We will never know who the first pioneer to taste prairie dog was, but he didn't have to be either a complete fool or such a great hero, because we know that many Indians in the region where these animals flourished ate them. Still, many an explorer must have had qualms about his first bites of their meat. We can sense this in James G. Bell's journal note when he writes, "By the by, on the fourth I eat a piece of prairie dog. They are better than the Jackass rabbit, the name might not suit some, but I don't mind such little things."[54]

Apparently, explorers in West Texas were soon depending upon prairie dogs for easy meals when larger game was elusive. Frederick Marryat makes it sound that way, plus adding another supposed value of these animals, when, finding himself east of present Lubbock in Dickens or King County in 1843, he wrote: "We halted an hour or two on reaching this beautiful table land [the Llano Estacado], to rest ourselves and give our horses an opportunity to graze. Little villages of prairie dogs were scattered here and there, and we killed half-a-dozen of them for our evening meal. The fat of these animals, I have forgotten to say, is asserted to be an infallible remedy for the rheumatism."[55] George Kendall and other early travelers told of similar reliance on this food source. It should give us pause to think about this lowly but valuable part of the wild game bounty which was spread like a multi-course feast all over the wilderness, allowing the survival of explorers wherever they chose to wander. Since we have practically wiped the platters clean, what would be our chances as explorers living off the land today?

Let's let our imaginations go about prairie dogs as a food staple. There were something between 400 and 800 million of them in wilderness Texas. This is equivalent in both vegetation required for feed as well as possible meat production to between 10 and 20 million cattle, which is near enough to the total cattle population of modern Texas to invite comparison. If we had not eliminated those prairie dogs and substituted cattle, couldn't we have gone a long ways toward feeding the whole population of a more recent Texas on systematically harvested prairie dog drumsticks instead of on steaks? And if we had allowed Texas' whole wild game assortment to survive and harvested it carefully, couldn't we have been dining all along on buffalo instead of beefalo, on elk and antelope as well as deer venison, on wild turkey instead of caged chickens, and couldn't our big hunters be real, heroic providers instead of sort of silly slaughterers of foreign game props set out on our ranches? Couldn't we have much of the explorers' Texas with us still?

Why did we eliminate the prairie dogs, anyway? Someone may maintain that all their holes in the prairies were hazards. Merriam claimed this in 1901, writing, "running horses often trip and break their legs and riders are sometimes injured and even killed," from tripping over prairie dog holes.[56] But this was said at the peak of the prairie dog-eradication mania, and so is suspect. We turn back to our explorers, who had as yet no case against the little animals to stimulate their imaginations, and we note a significant thing. Of all our explorers who were riding hell-for-leather either after or from buffaloes, all sorts of other game, prairie fires, and all over the wilderness just for the fun of it, as well as all of our army expeditions which deployed at breakneck speed after Indians, big game and each other, none of the early pioneers at all have recorded one instance of a horse and rider going down because of a prairie dog hole. And whole *cavelads* of mustangs outran them all without either hesitating or stumbling at prairie dog towns. There should have been a better excuse for exterminating them than that.

Doughty explained it as follows: "The herbivores were not permitted, however, to remain in such colossal numbers for long . . . because they competed with incoming cattle and sheep for the grass."[57] So we eliminated what has sometimes been described as a megalopolis occupying more than one-third of Texas. Its number of residents was certainly twice the total number of humans in the U.S. today. The prairie dogs provide one more evidence that the explorers' Texas was more rich in life than ours.

TEXAS UNDERGROUND RODENTS

We come now to a group of little animals which were apparently numerous in Texas as discovered, but which apparently had little importance in the pioneers' lives, and so were seldom and only very casually mentioned in their writings. In fact, most of what our explorers wrote about them was so informal that we cannot always tell just which animal they were referring to. But we note that, as usual, our forebears did observe these shy animals.

These truly covert animals are represented in Texas by the ground squirrels and the pocket gophers. Modern students recognize several species or subspecies of ground squirrels, such as the thirteen-lined, the Mexican or nine-lined and the spotted ground squirrels. Most early Texans did not bother to count their lines or spots, but Baird, in 1857, did distinguish two of them. One he called the "Line-tailed Squirrel," which must have been the thirteen-lined one because that form usually has lines of color prolonged onto its tail. Then he had another which had been brought to him from only along the Mexican border, so he called it the "Mexican Ground Squirrel."[58]

Gophers were very seldom mentioned by Texas pioneers. We are also hindered in placing them in the explorers' picture because we cannot be sure whether the pioneer writers really meant specifically the pocket gopher when they used the term. For instance, there is an interesting report written by C. D. Gibbes. When in present Midland or Ector County in 1849, he wrote, "[May] 10th . . . camped for noon in high open prairie without water, start at 2 o'clock and travelled over a rolling mound prairie cut up with gopher holes. . . ."[59]

It would be nice to be able to say that Gibbes was reporting an area infested with pocket gophers, but there are problems with assuming that. Perhaps the most serious one is that pocket gophers do not produce holes at all. Every one of these animals is very careful to push a quantity of loose dirt out of its burrow and to leave the opening plugged with this material, thus producing a characteristic small mound completely capping and hiding its hole underneath. One therefore never sees gopher holes unless he is so fortunate as to be present at the rare, usually night-time intervals when the animals venture out onto the surface of the ground. The term "mound prairie," which Gibbes uses, might indicate these little mounds, but this term in association with the term "holes" in quantities sufficient enough to "cut up" the surface of the area makes one think rather of prairie dogs with their large mounds and open holes. Add to this the fact that various authors assure us that the ground squirrels have often been known as "gophers," or "striped gophers," and even these animals might have been meant — although the fact that ground squirrels do not make mounds militates against it.

If that isn't confusion enough, then decide what animal Benjamin Lundy meant when he wrote of them in present eastern Webb or western Duval County in 1834, as follows: "After traveling several miles to-day, we ascended a high ridge, about three hundred feet above the plain that we had left. This ridge is the highest land between the Rio Bravo del Norte, and the Rio de las Nueces. From its summit, one may see, in a clear day, to a distance of near one hundred and twenty miles. . . . On the summit of this ridge, the ground rats are both numerous and industrious, as in the sandy lands of Texas. They dig up large quantities of the reddest sand and earth that I have ever seen."[60]

Perhaps these creatures should be left as the explorers indicated them to have been then: too seldom seen and too unimportant to be described, but, from their mounds and holes and an occasional glimpse, present just under the surface of original Texas.

THE TEXAS TREE SQUIRRELS

Squirrels appear often enough in early Texas writings to make it clear that they were abundant in the natural animal communities of at least East Texas. And there were several kinds of them. Our explorers recognized that, but they did not always do the job of naming and describing them which we think they should have. This is because they far too often relied solely upon color with which to distinguish them, and one of the first lessons a taxonomist should have learned is that color alone can no more be used to separate animals or plants into discreet taxa than it can be used to separate Mendel's red, white and pink peas into species. So we sometimes have to use internal analysis of our explorers' writings to recapture what species of squirrels they are telling us were originally present in Texas.

Modern specialists list four species of primarily above-ground squirrels now found in Texas, as follows: *Sciurus carolinensis*, the gray squirrel; *Sciurus niger*, the fox squirrel; *Glaucomys volans*, the flying squirrel; and *Citellus variegatus*, the rock squirrel. It is a striking accomplishment and a strong argument for the accuracy of the so often depreciated early accounts of Texas that in a book published in Germany in 1844, Friedrich W. von Wrede already reported that there were four squirrels in Texas, calling them, "the flying, gray, black, and the so-called fox squirrel."[61]

How could the four species of Texas squirrels be more nicely named? It's even better than the Latin, which has the fox squirrel called *niger*, meaning black — better, that is, if you equate von Wrede's black squirrel with the rock squirrel. Of course, some will hesitate at this. While I cannot press this interpretation as certain, it seems to me that there are three reasons why it is not only possible, but probable. First, von Wrede would seem to rule out indicating by his black one the black phases of the gray and the fox squirrels by listing those species separately. Second, the black phases of both the gray and fox squirrels, somewhat common farther east, are rare in Texas. And third, the rock squirrel is the only consistently blackish squirrel in Texas.

Edward Smith, in an account published in 1849, also listed three of the same four exact squirrels, calling them, "the large fox-tail squirrel, the grey and the black squirrel."[62] Various other explorers mention these species in the same words, placing them all solidly in the wilderness of early Texas.

Only one squirrel which is hard to place within the four above species is mentioned by Texas explorers. It is a surprise to find several of them claiming to be seeing red squirrels here. Viktor Bracht, for instance, wrote in 1848, "I have learned to know three kinds of squirrels: namely, the small brown flying squirrel, the large fox squirrel . . . and the less common red squirrel."[63]

It might seem at first thought that Bracht is merely substituting the term "red" for the usual name of the gray squirrel, which he has otherwise missed mentioning here, but that would have been a really glaring error on his part, because the gray squirrel is the least red of them all. David Schmidly describes its color thus: "The gray squirrel is named for its color, which is usually gray on the back and sides, with whitish underparts. It is readily distinguished from the fox squirrel *(S. niger)* by its smaller size, by its basically grayish overall coloration, and by the fact that its underparts are almost always grayish or white, never reddish or orangish, as in the fox squirrel."[64] Some other pioneers also describe red squirrels in early Texas.[65] Nor can we presume that this red squirrel is the usually reddish fox squirrel, because Bracht actually sets the two in opposition when he names them both in the same sentence.

The question therefore arises, whether welcomed or not: Did the actual red squirrel of so much of the rest of the U.S., in any of its races, once exist in Texas? Such explorers' statements as we have just seen may be taken to mean that it once did. It would, of course, require a specimen in hand to establish this. Lacking that, there is nothing but conjecture; however, this must be considered before automatically judging our pioneers as wrong.

In the first place, the red squirrel is said to have once occupied "most of the wooded parts of North America north of Mexico."[66] With Texas having been much more wooded originally than it has been since, doesn't this already imply that this animal may have been here at one time? Then we do have the Mount Graham red squirrels in the Coronado National Forest of southeast Arizona at about the same southern latitude as our western Texas mountains. That little animal, labeled at this writing as an endangered subspecies and the focus of an intense battle over its preservation, is considered a relict population stranded since the end of the ice ages on Mount Graham because it is dependent for survival upon the island of pine forest isolated there in the midst of surrounding desert.

The red squirrels are sometimes called "pine squirrels" because they are never far from the large-seeded pines upon which they seem to depend. They do not live down among the small-seeded, long-leafed, southeastern pines such as we have in East Texas. So how could they have ever been in Texas? Simply because we once had our own forests of lusciously large-seeded pinyon pines. This is attested to by the relict stands of them still found in the western Hill Country. So if red squirrels survived until now in the Arizona pinyons, isn't it possible that some race of them also survived into historic times in the southwest-central Texas pinyon?

But if that were so, why aren't they out there in Texas now, as they are in Arizona, my more skeptical friend replies. I tell him that he could answer that if he weren't so young. There are no stands of pinyons anywhere approaching the Arizona stands or large enough to support species dependent on them left in Texas today. But that is a very recent situation. I, myself, am old enough to vouch for that.

Thirty years ago I visited a Texas ranch where the decaying stumps and logs of mature Texas pinyons still cluttered several square miles of the pastures like jackstraws on a table. This was the remains of an ancient forest clear-cut some years before my visit in order to promote grass. I was there looking for a cactus which apparently had been collected in that forest, whose dried stem has lain unidentified for almost 100 years now in the U.S. National Herbarium, and which I believe was not only a species but a genus totally unknown to science. I had found two men who were able to describe that cactus from earlier sightings of the living plants growing among the trees when that forest was still intact. But by the time I got there, everything which had depended upon that removed pine forest was already gone. That cactus had been doomed to oblivion — along with whatever other creatures depended upon those pines.

The point here is that there might as logically have been red, pine squirrels in this Texas island of pines as in that island of them on Mount Graham, and that they might have existed well past the times of our explorers. But our island is essentially gone. All of the mature pinyons I have seen more recently in Texas are isolated individuals or in very small groves. The only actual stands I know of are second growth started since the great orgy of clearing which tried to turn all of that region into grassland. And gone with the pines would be any squirrels dependent on them. Since there is no carcass of one of them in any museum, we can never know with certainty whether they were there, but is a crumbling specimen in some museum so much more credible than the word of our forebears? I'm not claiming to prove that there were red squirrels in Texas, but shouldn't we consider the possibility before we brand our explorers as either inept observers or prevaricators when they say they saw them? They may be telling us something perfectly logical — that some western races of squirrels which still depend upon mountain conifers from Canada to Mexico frolicked in the western Texas pinyon forests even into the exploratory era.

Although various subspecies of the squirrel species have been named and debated over, none of them were described from within Texas during the exploratory period except one. In 1855, Baird described as a separate species, *S. limitis*, the Texas fox squirrel, taken on the Devil's and Nueces rivers.[67] But by 1857, he wrote that he was "far from feeling sure now that it is anything but a local variety of the common western fox squirrel."[68] In 1899, E. W. Nelson merged *limitis* as a subspecies under *S. ludovicianus*,[69] which Custis had described from Louisiana specimens in 1806, but which J. A. Allen had already reduced to *S. niger ludovicianus* in 1877.[70] More recent writers, except for the very discriminating, have overlooked Baird's subdivision entirely.

The more important thing about Baird's report is that the collections he cites on the upper Nueces and the Devil's rivers constitute the westernmost locations in Texas where any explorer reports finding fox squirrels. This therefore establishes the western limit of that species' original range and places it as another eastern animal ranging to approximately the 100th parallel.

When it comes to the range of the gray squirrel, all of the early reports but one fit nicely within the Texas range usually given for this species today. This range includes approximately the eastern one-fifth of the state. Only Baird records grays taken as far west and south as San Antonio. But on the strength of Berlandier's collections, he also puts this species down in Nueva Leon, Mexico. This latter location is especially challenging, since no other explorer mentions *any* squirrel in Texas south of San Antonio. As far as the reporters on early Texas are concerned, all of the chaparral of South Texas — and more remarkably, the dense *galeria* forests of the Rio Grande Valley — were empty of any squirrels.

Would the squirrels have by-passed this couple-of-hundred-miles-wide swath of territory which included some of the most dense forest cover in the U.S. only to settle again into the Mexican forests? Can any reason for such a gap in squirrel range to occur be seen? The reputation of our explorers as reporters is at stake here. And happily a perfectly ample reason why the squirrels might have and apparently did skip deep South Texas is right at hand in any careful study of the oaks of Texas. Oaks did not grow much farther south of San Antonio than the Carrizo Sands and approximately the Nueces River. They were mostly, if not totally, absent from the Rio Grande forest. This means that deep South Texas was bare of the oak mast upon which the species of squirrels in Texas, except for the red, depend. So one would expect deep South Texas to be devoid of squirrels. Our explorers are thus vindicated by logic as well as by experience.

Little else about squirrels is deemed important enough by the explorers for them to note it down, except statements that they found these animals welcome food items. Bracht, in the passage already quoted, goes on to say that the "large fox squirrel . . . makes excellent roast." And Edward Smith, also already noted, adds that, "Squirrels are very numerous, and are accounted a great luxury, and to my untutored taste the flesh is very rich," with "the fox-squirrel, the grey and the black . . . equally prized." These were an important part of the rich bounty wilderness Texas provided for the incoming pioneers. It is at least interesting that not one of them, in his notes, gives thanks to any deity, earth mother or even natural process for stocking this wilderness with such juicy morsels.

The little flying squirrel was barely commemorated by the explorers. This is not surprising. The animals are too small to be worth taking for food, and so retiring and completely nocturnal that even most people living today where they are found have never seen one. Besides listing them as present in Texas, the only statements made by explorers about them are such off-hand notes as Dr. Roemer's that they are "peculiar" and that they "can easily be tamed."[71] Otherwise these were moving shadows seen less clearly as well as much less commonly in the wilderness nights of early Texas than even the bats.

EARLY TEXAS "INFERIOR ANIMALS"

In his 1836 *History of Texas,* David Edward stated, "The inferior animals of the country, are neither very numerous nor troublesome. . . . As for rats, bats, and mice, they are common annoyances, not worth mentioning."[72] Among all the hundreds of pioneer's accounts of Texas animals there survive only three other references to any rat or mouse.

At first thought it seems very strange that our Texas pioneers almost totally ignored the whole rat and mouse clan. After all, this is a group huge in numbers of both species and individuals. Some modern studies list as many as thirty-eight different rats and mice in Texas, and the populations of some of these in recent times have approached plague proportions. We are apt to imagine the primitive dugouts and cabins of the settlers as crawling with vermin, including rats and mice in everything from the corn husk mats to the sod or thatch roofs. Can we explain our explorers' almost total failure to paint these pests into their picture of the early Texas fauna, or will we have to admit that they underrepresented these animals?

We do well to begin the investigation by following Edward's statement where it leads us. He said that these animals were "neither very numerous nor troublesome" in those days, and thus "not worth mentioning." Is there any reason for us to take this statement seriously?

First, is there any reason why rats and mice should have been less numerous in wilderness Texas than in our claimed-up state? Wouldn't they have been more numerous then, as we have seen that all sorts of other animals were? Logic would seem to retort that such a conclusion is obvious. Restock the whole state with the myriad predators — wolves, coyotes, cats large and small, eagles and hawks, owls, snakes, etc. — which were here then, take away all our guns and traps and let these expert natural hunters scour the country as they once did, then count the surviving rat and mouse prey. The predators would hardly have eliminated any of the many species, but there should come to be a different predator-prey balance. With the predators still present in early Texas the rodent prey should have been much less numerous, just as Edward states and the pioneers' ignoring them argues. Wildlife scientists back far enough to have witnessed anything of the former situation well understand the change in the predator-prey balance which has more recently occurred. For instance, they make statements like the following: "On account of the present scarcity of hawks, owls, and large serpents in portions of the Brazos Valley, Texas, native rats and mice have so increased in numbers that their depredations have assumed almost the proportions of a plague."[73]

So rats and mice, constantly stalked and controlled by now vanished predators, were logically much less in evidence in presettlement days than they have been since. The neglect of our explorer-reporters, except for a few like the very thorough post surgeon of Fort Phantom Hill who placed the field mouse in his list of animals of the fort's environs,[74] to mention them at all would seem to accurately indicate their relative scarcity in the primeval community.

But what of Edward's other claim: that they were also less troublesome then? This would follow naturally from these animals having been less numerous and could be a partial explanation for it. But there is a much more important explanation for those rats and mice which were in early Texas having been less of a problem to people than are the rats and mice of more recent times. It is that the modern rats and mice of Texas include especially bothersome invader species which were not in earliest Texas. Somewhere along the line the black or roof rat, the brown or Norway rat, and the house mouse scurried ashore from some Texas-docked ships. These three foreign species are collectively called the "commensal" rodents because they follow humans, live in human-built structures, and do not venture far from human habitations into any natural environment. Congregating in human environs they wreak havoc on food and fiber and spread filth and disease. Imagine Texas totally without these disgusting imported creatures, with only the native field, woods and desert rodents, and you have a totally different, more wholesome picture of Texas as it was, where these animals were not major troublemakers.

It is well documented that the foreign rodents remain closely linked to humans in Texas as elsewhere. A study was once conducted to "record the observations on rural rats in Texas for comparison with studies in other areas."[75] Lavaca County, Texas, was studied. Norway rats were found only in Yoakum, the largest town in the county. Roof rats were "present throughout the county in towns and on the farms." But both of these were closely limited to the environs of man.

Another study compared the rodents found on Galveston to those on Mustang Island. It determined that the house mouse sometimes ranged at least a mile from the nearest house, but that the commensal rats were not found even that far from human structures. At the time of this 1938 study, it was concluded that, "The exotic rat and mouse, introduced presumably by ships visiting the port, have thoroughly established themselves on the [Galveston] island," but that they had not at that time populated Mustang Island, and the difference was credited to the long history of shipping to Galveston Island which had not then yet been duplicated to Mustang Island.[76]

It being almost certain that these troublesome and disgusting rodents entered Texas through Galveston, it is most significant that the only other mention of rats and mice besides that of Edward's with which we began is the statement of Charles Hooton published in 1847. This immigrant of that time wrote: "I myself rented a cottage.... about half-a-mile from the 'city,' [Galveston] and upon the border of a large bayou about half-way across the island, between the Bay and the Gulf.... It consisted of two large rooms, open to the ridge inside, and constructed with the doors and windows opposite each other, north and south, for the benefit of the air. Daylight shone here and there through the cracks and ill-fitting joints of the plank walls; and on the beams and rafters which supported the shingled roof, various colonies of a gigantic sort of wasp had established their homesteads, in the shape of large masses of mud, filled with holes of a geometrical figure, like those of a honeycomb. Mice also had built their nests on the cross-timbers, ten or twelve feet from the ground; and a small republic of fierce and warlike rats had additionally declared their independence of the tenant below, and hoisted the liberal flag of rats-tail on the roof and upper beams of the building."[77]

What words could more succinctly describe the house mouse and the roof rat than these? What other way could you more certainly confirm the presence of these invading pests already debarked at nearby Galveston? Hooton's roof rats could not have been more true to their name.

With this before us, how much more strongly could you indicate the absence as yet at that time of these revolting creatures other places in Texas than by observing the failure of all the other settlers, from Mrs. Holley at nearby Brazoria all the way to those at San Antonio, down along the Rio Grande and up along the Red River, to complain about or even to mention the presence of such hated houseguests?

Texas must have been a more benign, more pleasant place to settle into before these invading pests spread over it. Native field and woods rodents didn't move into human abodes and, as Edward said, weren't of enough importance to warrant being much mentioned in the tales of the frontier. You must imagine the tepees, dugouts and cabins of early Texans clean of rats and mice and the pioneers' belongings safe at least from these pests. Their picture of early Texas is in this respect beautiful, with just the first rats and mice creeping into the Galveston corner of it as harbingers of dismal things to come.

So different from the rest of the rats and mice as to seem from another continent, but hiding in the far southwest corner of early Texas, was a most remarkable member or this group, and the explorers didn't miss it. His description of it is so complete that we will let James G. Bell, writing from Hudspeth County near the Rio Grande below San Elisario in 1854, sketch this fascinating little creature into the explorers' picture of Texas. Bell wrote:

"Went to the river to water my mule. Killed an animal that somewhat resembled a medium sized rat. It had very long and fine fur, tail twice as long as the body, mouth and teeth like a squirrel, only nearer the throat a pocket on each side the mouth lined with fur, — this I suppose is to carry the young in, and what is most remarkable is the hind legs are about 3 times the length of the fore ones, giving it the appearance of a Kangaroo; in fact by some in camp it is called the Kangaroo Rat; — I skinned it on account of its oddity and beautiful fur. The little fellow was verry fat and would no doubt been verry good to eat."[78]

13

They Rushed Around the Texas Brush

Rabbits are peculiar animals. Their remarkable adaptations to a hostile world pique imaginations young and old and are so unique that scientists have had to set up a separate order for them. Defenseless and expendable, it seems they would long ago have been forfeited, but they're still in the picture, practically worldwide.

Texas always had its share of rabbits. Fray Francisco Casanas de Jesus Maria witnessed this as early as in 1691, writing then concerning eastern Texas: "This country contains various kinds of animals that are good to eat, such as wild hogs. . . . Rabbits are also to be had in great numbers."[1] A century and a half later Jose Enrique de la Pena, recounting the particulars of Santa Anna's relentless march across Texas, wrote about a plethora of these animals just within the southwestern edge of this territory. His words are: "On the 25th [of February 1836] between twelve and one in the afternoon we left the Rio Bravo [Rio Grande] and traveled about eight or ten miles to camp at San Ambrosio, a place without water but with such an abundance of rabbits that the soldiers could catch them by hand as easily as chickens from a hen. . . . On the 26th we camped at Pena Creek, which was no more than a big puddle of water, and we traveled about twelve or fourteen miles. Those of us traveling with the vanguard saw more than two hundred jack hares on the road within two hours. It gave us much pleasure to see them jumping in all directions."[2] Clearly we must include, in almost any scenes of early Texas which we choose to imagine, rabbits crouching under the brush, running away across the prairies or gambolling on the plains. They didn't just start to "rush around the bush" with the cowboy song. The explorers make that certain.

But what, exactly, were those animals of early Texas? It is noticeable that in his passage just quoted, de la Pena spoke separately of "rabbits" and "jack hares." Immediately we must deal with a fundamental split in this group's ranks — a division which, while actually simple, the quirks of language have allowed to become confusing.

The Spanish explorers were usually meticulous observers, and their language promoted that by providing them very specific terms with which to express their careful distinctions. Such is the case here. The Spanish have a word, *conejo,* which means the "rabbit" in the narrow sense, including our so-called cottontails of the genus *Sylvilagus.* It further has the word *liebre,* which is usually translated, "hare," specifying members of the genus *Lepus* among which are the jack rabbits. It was the *conejos,* cottontails, which were so abundant that the soldiers sometimes could catch them, and the *liebre,* jack rabbits, which they enjoyed watching leap around ahead of them on the road to San Antonio.

This distinction is usually kept clear in the Spanish accounts, the Spanish explorers mostly taking the trouble to name these two types of animals separately. Don Juan Antonio de la Pena, writing in 1722, and describing what is now Zavala County northeast of Eagle Pass, used both of these words. The translation is: "Along the banks of the [Caramanchel] Creek there are many turkeys, and along the way thither quail, rabbits and hares can be found in large numbers."[3] In the description of the fauna of the Pereda grant, near the Rio Grande in present Zapata County, written up in 1807, there are listed separately *conejo* and *liebre.*[4]

Early English usage was as precise. The equivalent of *conejo* in the English of the European past was the word "rabbit." Both of these words originally meant, very specifically, European burrowing Lagomorphs of a genus which does not exist in America.[5] Both of these words were therefore applied by those pioneers who used words carefully, to the only American members of this order which burrow at all or even make nests — members of the genus *Sylvilagus*, our cottontails. The equivalent of *liebre*, on the other hand, was the English word "hare," which has always meant, both in Europe and America, members of the genus *Lepus* — larger, very different animals such as the jack, snowshoe and Arctic hares which do not hollow out burrows or even make nests for their precocious young. Words paralleling these two exist in both French and German.

Some pioneer writers, whatever languages they wrote in, used these two words carefully, and so we know precisely what animals they were reporting. For instance, Viktor Bracht, in 1848, wrote about Texas in general: "Among the smaller game found near the homes of the settlers are many rabbits and farther west is the large, long-eared Mexican hare."[6] We can be thankful for such writers' attention to detail.

But we Americans got careless with words, and soon we had confused the names for these animals. An example: In 1853, Brad C. Fowler, in writing about the Rhine Party's trek west, said, "We met with many, very many, curiosities, as not one in company had ever passed the road before, and few even having been to, or above the Cross Timbers, in which and since that time we met with the mule eared Rabbit that seems almost to out strip the wind in point of speed."[7]

Now just what animal is Fowler reporting here? Clearly, the western Lagomorph with the most conspicuous ears and most noted for speed is the jack hare. But he calls it a rabbit, which should mean a shorter-eared, dodging instead of long-distance running cottontail. What is going on here?

For some reason, among Americans the term "hare" lost favor and almost disappeared. As this happened the name "rabbit" began to be applied to any and all Lagomorphs indiscriminately. The jack hare carelessly became the jack rabbit, and soon, for many, it was just another rabbit. This is unfortunate, since it makes it impossible to tell which animal is meant in many accounts. For instance, when out in what is now Pecos County in 1854, James G. Bell wrote, "Have one Deer and some dozen Rabbits in the way of fresh meat."[8] There is no way to tell whether he had bagged jack hares or cottontails or both, and the report is therefore of lesser value than it might have been.

Since from very early in Texas history the term "rabbit" was often enlarged in meaning to include the hares, all explorers' reports of "rabbits" with the term unqualified by any description have to be discounted as inexact. Only reports including with this word descriptions of unmistakable rabbit or hare characters can be concluded to indicate respectively cottontails or hares. While Bell's rabbits, being uncharacterized, could be any of the group, and so are of comparatively little use to us, Fowler's rabbits, noted as being western, and having extreme ears as well as extreme speed, are clearly enough hares to help increase our knowledge.

Now that we know how to tell whether they were writing about rabbits or hares, what do our explorers who separate them tell us about each of these in their times?

THE JACK RABBITS: TEXAS HARES

These have always been most conspicuous in Texas scenes, and have always amazed visitors to the state. Early postcards, back to almost 100 years ago, often used faked pictures of impossibly large jack rabbits to demonstrate to the moderate East the astonishing, sometimes frightening, sometimes comical extremisms everywhere present in Texas natives' adaptations to their extreme environments. It is not surprising that even earlier the explorers of this land-on-the-edge noted well these far-out specializations for survival in special situations. Fowler's words, already quoted, communicate in a minimum space the essence of the jack rabbits' best adaptations for survival — their remarkable ears and their great running speed.

Fowler incidentally aids us in understanding the several common names used for this animal. They include jack rabbit, jackass rabbit, mule rabbit and Fowler's mule-eared rabbit. I believe these names came to be in almost the reverse of this order. These hares were quite conceivably dubbed mule-eared because their ears are not only overlarge like a mule's, but shaped and even held in positions which seem to mimic the mule's curious one up, one down, one forward, one backward, lop-eared manner.

John C. Reid shows the shortening of this name which must have already taken place very early by writing in 1857, about the territory which

Texas Hare by Audubon

was to become Val Verde County: "This was the favorite range of all kinds of Texas game: deer, antelope, wolf, prairie dogs, and mule rabbit, in the greatest abundance. . . . The last named (mule rabbit) has much the form of the rabbit of the States; ears as large as those of a young mule (hence the name). . . ."9

Since the same sort of ears are found on the donkey, perhaps just as early there was coined the term "jackass rabbit." Finally, in their proverbial hurry, Americans shortened this to jack rabbit, which was often further abbreviated to just jacks.

It should be obvious from what has been extracted from the historical record and restated here that there were lots of jack rabbits in early Texas. But where were they? Were they everywhere, or were there parts of the state without them?

Mapping the locations of the explorers' reports of these animals shows that they were definitely western creatures. They were described in almost evenly scattered locations over the whole western part of Texas, but not in East Texas. However, their range did not stop at or near the 100th parallel, as did those of various other western living forms. They were as commonly found considerably east of that dividing line as west of it. They apparently ran east as freely as anywhere right up to some more formidable barrier stretching all across Texas, which stopped them cold.

The locations of Texas explorers' easternmost reports of jack rabbits trace a great arc with the upper end anchored all the way east in Bowie, the northeastern corner county of the state. But from that corner the jack hares retreated west through the northern border counties all the way to Grayson County. From there the limit of the jacks' early range curved southwest through Collin County into Tarrant County, then through Johnson County on down through Travis County past the site of Austin to Bexar County near San Antonio. From this, its westernmost point, the limit curved sharply southeast to end in Calhoun County near the site of Indianola.

Can there be any significance to the location of this range limit and any clues to what factors produced it? The quickest way to answer that is to compare this line representing the explorers' evidence about the eastern edge of the jack hare's range in undisturbed Texas with the lines representing the borders of the major natural vegetational regions of Texas as drawn on typical maps by Texas biogeographers. It will quickly be seen that the edge of the jack's range coincides all the way from Collin County to Bexar County with the eastern Cross Timbers and the western edge of the Blackland Prairies. From San Antonio it just as dramatically traces the northeastern boundary of the Rio Grande Plains until, on some maps, that meets the Gulf in Calhoun County or else, on other maps, where the Coastal Prairies are extended on south, our rabbits crossed those to the Gulf. All of this must be more than a remarkable coincidence. There must have been factors appearing or disappearing where the respective vegetative regions changed which favored the jacks on one hand or deterred them on the other. Perhaps it will clarify our overall picture of Texas as it was to look for these.

It is easy to see why the hares didn't live in Texas' easternmost natural bioregion. The very idea of these speedsters cruising through the pineywoods area is preposterous. Of course there were some prairies there, but those were only islands in the essentially contiguous forest, and these animals wouldn't have made it into those more open plots or tolerated their narrow bounds.

It is more possible to imagine jack hares in the second natural region west into Texas, the one variously called the Secondary Forest and Woodlands, the Post Oak Savannah or Belt. As these names imply, many consider that in this region the trees were only scattered, their growth not very dense. In my previous work on the subject, I have gathered evidence which seems to show that this area as found was still essentially contiguously forested.[10] It appears that the jack hares were confirming that by their absence from it.

But then we come to the third natural region into Texas from the east, the famous Blackland Prairies. This is a long but relatively narrow strip extending from the edge of the Red River Valley down to Bexar County. It always was prairie, so many assume because of their conception of prairies, that this was from first exploration a practically treeless expanse of unobstructed grassland. If it were like that, it should have been perfect for jack rabbits, and we should have explorers' accounts of them all through this region. But we don't, and that is the crux of the matter. For its whole length, the western — not the eastern — edge of the Blackland Prairies was, by the explorers' records, an effective barrier not crossed by these animals to get into the region.

I believe this is explained by two factors. First, I think there were originally many more woody plants in the Blackland Prairies than is today imagined. As I have shown in my earlier publications just cited, this was true, by definition as well as by eyewitness accounts, of all prairies.[11] There could be and usually were tracts of trees dense enough to be real forests and large enough to be significant, included in prairies. But while these might have been disadvantages to jack hares, they couldn't have been contiguous enough in this region to have kept those animals from enjoying the grassland portions of these prairies, as they did the often equally wooded prairies of the Edwards Plateau and mesquite woodlands farther west. So there must have been a second and even more important factor present in the Blackland Prairies which made it untenable for these animals.

I believe this second limiting factor was the type and amount of grass and forb vegetation growing in the Blackland Prairies, together with the residue biomass accumulations typically present on the ground in that region. The Blackland Prairies make up the western and probably the largest part of what have been called the Tall Grass Prairies. In the grassland component of these prairies the accounts agree that the vegetative growth topped out each year at between six and nine feet tall. There are accounts of buffaloes and horses having been hidden from sight by this tall growth.[12] Then, after heading out so high each year, this huge amount of vegetation started sinking down to finally form thick mats of slowly decaying biomass over the soil surface. There are descriptions of the larger animals' pathways which sometimes had to be followed by horses and men to get through this obstructing mass.

This huge glut of biomass was usually present in the undisturbed Tall Grass Prairies because the grazing of wild animals upon them was too uncontrolled and sporadic to keep it down, and the idea of either often-recurring natural prairie fires in the Texas wilderness or of the Indians setting these before the white men taught them how to do so is a modern myth unsupported by early Texas records.

Realizing how preposterous the above picture of these prairies must appear to the present orthodoxy, I must be allowed to bring in one credible eyewitness to that so difficult to imagine situation. My witness is none other than the well-known George Catlin, who is credited with leaving us so much valuable knowledge concerning Indians and their societies. He also left us observations about the Tall Grass Prairies which he experienced in their original condition. While he was a little north of Texas, his prairies must have been similar to those here, and his observations about them as accurate as the ones we accept about his Indians.

In the 1830s, Catlin wrote: "But there is yet another character of burning prairies, that requires another Letter, and a different pen to describe — the war, or hell of fire! where the grass is seven or eight feet high, as is often the case for many miles together, on the Missouri bottoms; and the flames are driven forward by the hurricanes, which often sweep over the vast prairies of this denuded country. There are many of those meadows on the Missouri, the Platte, and the Arkansas, of many miles in breadth, which are perfectly level, with a waving grass, so high, that we are obliged to stand erect in our stirrups, in order to look over its waving tops, as we are riding through it. The fire in these, before such a wind, travels at an immense and frightful rate, and often destroys on their fleetest horses, parties of Indians, who are so unlucky as to be overtaken by it; not that it travels as fast as a horse at full speed, but that the high grass is filled with wild pea-vines and other impediments, which render it necessary for the rider to guide his horse in the zig-zag paths of the deers and buffaloes, retarding his progress, until he is overtaken by the dense column of smoke that is swept before the fire...."[13]

Now it is as impossible to imagine jack hares living in the gloom under such tall growth or barging through such tangled mats as it is to imagine them in the more eastern forests. I believe this explains why they avoided not only the thickly forested East Texas but the lush, variegated and cluttered Tall Grass Prairies in their original state. And it explains how jack rabbits have more lately ignored their old bounds to become common in the Blackland Prairies and scattered in all the rest of East Texas except the Big Thicket. This has been precisely because of the known modern clearing of so much of the dense forest and the absence of obstructing biomass in the overgrazed, burned over, plowed under tracts called prairies today. Dr. David J. Schmidly, professor of wildlife and fisheries sciences at Texas A&M University, has recently traced this process for us, writing: "Their [jack rabbits'] occurrence in the pine-oak forested regions has been a recent event that in most places occurred only in the past forty to fifty years as a result of intensified timber-cutting and land-clearing programs in this area. When pine timber is clear-cut, jack rabbits move onto the cleared lands, especially if there has been some burning of slash to further open up the habitat. Much of this cleared land has subsequently been converted to pastureland for dairy cattle. These pastureland openings, although usually of small acreage . . . are contiguous and extend westward in a dendritic pattern. They undoubtedly serve as avenues for the dispersal of jack rabbits in the central and southern parts of eastern Texas. . . . Jack rabbits remain only as long as the ground is open. Without proper management the burns become scrubby with oak sprouts and miscellaneous shrubs after three or four years, and the jack rabbits disappear."[14]

This inverse relationship between the presence of jack hares and woody or tall, lush, eastern grassland plants and the positive correlation between these animals and landscapes covered with naturally shorter, western plants or else kept clear by chopping, farming or burning should be useful. It would seem to make these hares useable indicator species showing the presence or absence of not only contiguous forests but tall grass versus shorter grass prairies, and between cluttered, scrubby, unchopped, only sporadically grazed, seldom if ever burned natural prairies versus cleared, cleaned, scoured and burned fields generally considered such prairies today.

The use of these correlations is particularly instructive at each end of the arc marking the animal's eastern range in Texas. At the extreme northeast these animals were comfortable in the virgin Red River Valley all the way down to the eastern edge of Texas. They apparently lived in that valley from there all the way west, but they couldn't come out of that valley south into any more of East Texas until, around 150 miles west, in what is now Grayson County, they managed to find agreeable environments down into Texas.

We already understand why they couldn't come down into the bulk of East Texas. Once you topped the divide and were out of the Red River Valley, it was contiguous forest or else Tall Grass Prairie unfit for any galloping jack rabbit. But why could the jacks run on east so far in that narrow strip which was the Red River Valley? Precisely because, while there were narrow strips and clumps of dense riverbottom forest in it, much of that valley was made up of prairie stretches. What kind of prairies were they? The use of them by the hares argues that they were not cluttered Blackland Prairies, but more open, shorter growth, western style prairies, just as explorers, incidentally, describe them.

And this gives us a means with which to critique existing maps of vegetative regions. Some of these continue the Blackland Prairie province and the East Texas forest regions right on up through the Red River Valley to the river. Others terminate the Blackland Prairies at the edge of the valley, but then color that valley as a continuation of the Post Oak Belt all the way west to link up with the Cross Timbers. The jack rabbits tell us that the East Texas prairies and forests should definitely terminate at the edge of that valley, and that that valley strip was not an extension of any contiguous forest in any direction but instead had to have been a projection of western prairies made up of mixed medium growth western grasslands and forests plots — or else these animals could not have been living in that valley at all.

Exactly where the hares halted their eastward range south of the Red River is equally educational. They ranged in wilderness days right through the Western Cross Timbers. This fits nicely with two known facts about that strip. First, it was always composed of scattered and disjunct plots of tree cover interspersed with grassland.[15] Second, it was not heavy, dense forest at all, but trees scattered in growing grass, as were found in so many true prairies. Captain Marcy was writing his description of the Western Cross Timbers a little after our cutoff date — in 1866 — but he was detailing what he had found it like during his explorations when he wrote, "At six different points where I have passed through it, I have found it characterized by the same peculiarities; the trees, consisting principally of post-oak and black-jack, standing at such intervals that wagons can without difficulty pass between them in any direction."[16]

The fact that these hares, dependent upon the western openness of at least mid-grass growth and unable to tolerate Tall Grass environments, ranged right across the Fort Worth Prairie to stop only at or in the narrow strip of timber called the Eastern Cross Timbers bordering the Tall Grass Prairies beyond, tips the balance in a long-argued disagreement over fundamental relationships. It establishes the point that the Fort Worth Prairie's natural climax was not eastern tall grasses, but western mid grasses. This puts the whole of this prairie solidly in Bruner's northwestern True Prairie Association[17] and removes it from the Tall Grass Coastal Prairie Association where so many have submerged it.[18] But most Texans have known all along that the East ends and the West begins somewhere between Dallas and Fort Worth!

After having been blocked from going east all the way down to San Antonio by the Tall Grass Prairie tangles, there the jack hares met up with the so-called Rio Grande Plains. That huge region, early dubbed by some the Mustang Desert, had in early days lots of grass and huge amounts of chaparral, but apparently enough openness that the jacks ran right into it and were at home. Explorers reported them all over deep South Texas right out to the Gulf beaches from Indianola down to Brownsville, and the greatest concentration of early jack hare reports from anywhere in Texas come from the northwestern part of the Rio Grande Plains along the roads between San Antonio and the Maverick and Webb County crossings from Mexico. Nor did the Rio Grande stop them. They were known in early days as the Mexican hares for good reason.

The fact that these animals were comfortable clear out to the southern Texas beaches but apparently never approached the upper coast has bearing upon conceptions of the bioregion usually called the Coastal Prairies. Most maps show this area a comparatively narrow strip all along the deep South Texas coast and some do not show it as extending below Lavaca Bay at all. But most maps show the Coastal Prairies as a wider strip — up to at least two counties and sometimes seventy-five miles wide — from Lavaca Bay northeast to Louisiana. According to the explorers, jack rabbits crossed this strip with impunity only up to as far as Indianola, which was on Lavaca Bay, so it is a question whether this southern end of it was sufficiently different from the rest of the Rio Grande Plains to warrant its separate status. The maps which do not continue the Coastal Prairies below about Cameron County may be the most accurate.

It is most striking that no early Texas account placed one jack hare in the wider strip called Coastal Prairies on up the coast from Lavaca Bay. We can see how they were blocked from entering this area from the north and west by the East Texas forests and the Blackland Prairies, but why didn't they do an end-run on up from Indianola into the wide-open plains west of Houston, for instance?

It is my contention that there was a long-forgotten reason. If they crossed Lavaca Bay and attempted to proceed up the coast, these rabbits would have been faced, in unchopped Texas, with one of the most formidable forest barriers in the state, one of the four contiguous forests originally in Texas. That forest occupied virtually all of present Matagorda and Wharton plus much of Brazoria and Fort Bend counties. That forest is so long gone and forgotten that it is no doubt necessary to interject brief accounts of it here.

W. B. Dewees wrote in 1838, "San Barnard, Cedar lake, and Cane Brake creek lie west of the Brazos. These are all minor bodies of water, but they flow through the most extensive body of excellent land in Texas. This is a district about forty miles in width and fifty or sixty miles in length, covered almost entirely with cane brake and forests."[19]

A visitor to the area wrote anonymously in 1831, "Mr. John Austin, the first settler of Brazoria, went there in 1828. The place for the village had been since cleared of the forest trees which then overspread the country, and at the time of my visit they had been cut away to about the distance of half a mile. Beyond that line, every thing was still wild and in the state of nature. The surface is almost entirely level: and such is the want of every species of landmark, that I was informed that the inhabitants could not venture any considerable distance into the woods in a cloudy or misty day for fear lest they should lose their way. The most expert woodsman, it was thought, would find himself at fault for the want of such means as the forest usually affords for determining the points of the compass. What renders the danger still greater, is the frequency of cane brakes, or tracts of land overgrown with the long reeds of which we make fishing poles in the States. These canes there grow in some places among the forest trees, so thick as to render a passage through them inconvenient. . . ."[20]

It is one of the most glaring examples of our wilful modern blindness to our natural heritage not only that this majestic forest covering at least 2,000 square miles by Dewees' estimate is not only literally gone without even a square mile of canebrake saved and protected today, but that it doesn't even appear on our vegetational maps. On these supposedly accurate maps this awesome and unique forest is merely pasted over with the label "Coastal Prairies," which prairies, we are assured these days, were naturally treeless, open and unobstructed grasslands. But our explorers bring us back down to the reality which was virgin Texas, and in it the jack hares were effectively barred from any southeast Texas prairies or plains by formidable forest barriers on any landward side. And our explorer reporters' picture is consistent in its parts.

We have seen that wherever they encountered them, most Texas pioneers called these animals something like jack hares or rabbits. This would seem adequate for their days, but when they were dealing with an entity which was by 1942 divided by one specialist into twelve separate species with seventeen different subspecies among them,[21] it is not surprising that some of the explorers tried to sort out variations they saw in these animals.

The first to do that was Peter Custis. He called the jacks he found in the Red River Valley *Lepus Timidus*. In annotating this, Dan L. Flores says, ". . . it must be assumed that this was the black-tailed jackrabbit (*Lepus californicus melanotis* Mearns)."[22]

John James Audubon and Bachman had some trouble trying to deal with varieties of jack hares. In 1851, they listed under an already proposed name, *Lepus callotis*, a jack which they describe by quoting John Woodhouse Audubon's earlier journals where he tells of examining one taken just west of San Antonio. They say that while occurring at Santa Fe, this form is not found on the lower Red River or anywhere ". . . near the Gulf of Mexico indeed, until we get as far south as about latitude 30, from which parallel to the southward it becomes more abundant, and may be said to be the common Hare of Mexico."[23] This latitude runs near enough to San Antonio and the Matagorda forest to not only confirm other early records of the original limit of these jacks' southeast Texas range, but to make it evident that the South Texas jacks now occupying about the same range and known as *L. C. merriami* are the original Mexican hares.

In their third volume, published in 1854, J. J. Audubon and Bachman put forth yet another form of jack which they called *Lepus texianus*, the "Texas Hare," or "Vilgo Jackass Rabbit." They say this is the largest of the jack rabbits and that it "appears to inhabit the southern parts of New Mexico, the western part of Texas, and the elevated lands . . . of Mexico."[24]

In 1857, Baird dealt in detail with the jack hares he knew of in Texas.[25] He had in his system:

Lepus callotis Wagler, the Jackass Rabbit or Texas Hare, taken in various places in Texas west and north of San Antonio.
Lepus sylvaticus Bachman, the Gray Rabbit, taken at Indianola.
Lepus artemisia Bachman, the Sage Rabbit, taken at Matamoros, San Antonio to El Paso and on the Llano Estacado.

Lepus bachmani Waterhouse, Bachman's Hare, taken at Brownsville.

Baird said, "I have never met with any specimens having the peculiar characters of *L. texianus* of Audubon & Bachman. . . ."

Fortunately we do not have to trace the vicissitudes through which all these names have gone since our explorers' times or bother with the newer ones since coined. Our forefathers knew a jack hare when they saw one. We can be sure of that.

So of what importance were these animals to our pioneers? Of course, as speed-demon novelties they provided welcome diversion along the wilderness roads, but anything else? Jack rabbits were surprisingly important to at least some of the pioneers as — of all things — items of food! Several of them admit this.

In the continuation of his statement about the "mule rabbit" already quoted, John C. Reid went on to remark, "They run with unusual swiftness; their flesh is excellent."[26]

J. J. Audubon and Bachman make statements which require us to treat Reid's with better than contempt and which explain how eating jack hares must have been learned. Speaking of a form of the jack which they say ranged from Texas to California — seeming, therefore, to encompass most of the *Lepus* tribe — they maintain, "The Mexicans are very fond of the flesh of this animal, and as it is widely distributed a great many are shot and snared by them. It is very good eating, and formed an important item in the provisions of John W. Audubon's party whilst passing through Mexico, they at times killing so many that the men became tired of them."[27]

I grew up on western prairies where rabbits, both jacks and cottontails, were always present, and I have eaten of many a fine wild cottontail, but I have never tasted a jack rabbit. It was always easier to shoot a jack rabbit, which typically started up, loped off and then sat down not too far away to mock both myself and my dog, than to get a cottontail with that quick shot before he ducked into some brush or else to go to the trouble to trap him. We often shot jacks for the fun of it, but always left them for the coyotes, while we worked at hunting and trapping cottontails to eat. During the depression of the 1930s, I had schoolmates who even brought sparrows for their lunches, but no one I knew ever ate jacks. Why was this? Everyone must have assumed, as I know I did, that muscles which could propel anything the way the jack rabbit's did would be entirely too tough to chew. I still think they are. So from whom did the explorers learn to eat them, and how did they manage to do it?

Audubon and Bachman imply that the early explorers of the southern latitudes learned from the Mexicans that the jacks were edible, and I think that they also learned from them how to manage it even if jack rabbit is practically unchewable. I believe I can show how this may have taken place by tracing a parallel scenario which I have watched develop in my own very much more recent time.

We find *fajitas* popular today not only in Texas, but all the way to Alaska. *Fajitas* originated in Mexico. Anyone who has had the experience of eating *fajitas* in the interior of northern Mexico before they became popularized and Americanized in the U.S. knows what they originally were and why they were invented. It was in days when there were few high-bred, pampered and tenderized cows in Mexico. Steaks had to come from the semi-wild cattle rounded up from the chaparral. Steaks from these Mexican cattle, even the best steaks you could get in any remote village where you might get hungry, were truly unchewable. They made these steaks no more than one-fourth-inch thick so you could at least cut them up, but you still couldn't chew them. For that reason I used to see greenhorns on field trips into northern Mexico throw both a whole cafe and themselves into confusion upon ordering steaks. The establishment wasn't used to serving steaks and my *nord-Americano* couldn't eat the tough things when they did. What to do?

Someone, probably soon after the Spanish cow got toughened up on merciless Mexican ranges, solved such impasses by inventing the *fajita*. If it helped a little to cut the steak thin but it still couldn't be chewed, then cut the thing entirely into little strips which didn't have to be chewed at all if you had a strong stomach, and the brilliant one had the solution — the *fajita!* In the old days this was what you ate in northern Mexico if you had to have beef. It was strong fare, but it was a way to live on an otherwise useless resource — the skinny, mean, tough Mexican cow. And somehow it got introduced to Texas, and if it was edible with tough Mexican beef it was downright great with top quality American steak meat in strips which are bigger because you can chew them. And *voila*, I recently saw on a menu a "shrimp fajita." We have really absorbed Mexican culture!

Similarly, I believe, the explorers learned from the Mexicans how to eat the tough jack rabbit, and I am more serious than facetious when I say I imagine they were eating jack rabbit *fajitas*. But I am glad I was never that hungry! I can sympathize with J. W. Audubon, whose men "became tired of them." I'll bet they did. And I claim on my side of the to-eat-or-not-to-eat jack rabbit controversy, James G. Bell, who wrote in 1854, "By and by, on the fourth I eat a piece of prairie dog. They are better than the Jackass rabbit."[28] But the jack hares have managed to survive into our day, and perhaps they should be remembered if things really get tough again.

THE COTTONTAILS: TEXAS *SYLVILAGUS*

Because of the inconsistency in its uses, with it meaning on the one hand any member of the family *Leporidae* whatsoever and on the other just cottontails of the genus *Sylvilagus*, we cannot rely upon the term "rabbit" for anything more than the general range of the tribe unless descriptive details are added which make clear in which sense the word is used. Fortunately such information is supplied with many of the explorers' rabbit records. They give us assurance that the eastern cottontail, *S. floridanus*, was common throughout the eastern half of primeval Texas.

The westernmost pre-1860 cottontail records are from present Tom Green, Irion and Upton counties, near and just west of San Angelo.[29] It is certain that these could not have been jack hares because in each of these reports these animals were specifically said to have taken refuge in prairie dog burrows. Over thirty years ago I spent much time, during a two-year stay in the Oklahoma Panhandle, observing events in some large prairie dog towns then in the area. I witnessed jack hares being chased through these towns, and even when their lives were at stake, they never entered dog burrows. As a youth in western Kansas some of my first spending money was earned by trapping rabbits alive, and I soon learned that jack hares would never enter any kind of enclosures — not even box traps lying open on the surface of the ground. Those speedsters who depend upon the quick get-away do not nest, and simply will not enter any enclosed space where they cannot see from their crouching positions the totality of at least their immediate surroundings and leap out in any direction.

Bartlett is the explorer who mentioned these rabbits in the prairie dog towns, but he did not name them. It was Baird who, a few years later, christened them *Sylvilagus auduboni*.[30] Others have mentioned the close relationship between this rabbit and prairie dogs. W. B. Davis, for instance, has written, "I have found it . . . especially in prairie dog towns in short grass areas. In the plains regions it is so commonly associated with prairie dog towns that it is known locally as 'prairie-dog rabbit.'"[31]

These, then, since they are the explorers' westernmost cottontails, bring up both interesting and vexing questions. For instance, why were these rabbits commonly found using the burrows of the eastern prairie dog towns yet never reported by any expedition as even seen in the very huge dog towns abundantly described west of the Pecos River? What does it mean that there isn't a single report of cottontails west of Upton County by any of the numerous pre-1860 expeditions and caravans — some starving — whose hunters scoured West Texas for any game and some of whom tell of eating prairie dogs, jack hares and even snakes? They had shot and eaten cottontails voraciously in East Texas. Sterling Brown Hendricks of the 1842 Somervell Expedition, for instance, after a march from Mexico almost to San Antonio wrote, ". . . we at last arrived at an old, uninhabited rancho on the Laredo road thirty miles from San Antonio. Here we found a drove of beeves that had been generously brought on to meet us from the Medina by two of Colonel Cook's men. . . . We had for many days before this been feeding on hawks and rabbits, and almost everything else that we could find."[32]

We could simply credit the pioneers' picture as another example of the explorers' accuracy — showing these as eastern animals conforming rather well to the 100th parallel east-west dividing line — except for one thing. These rabbits apparently didn't stay put. The more recent picture is radically different from the early one.

We have W. F. Blair showing the extent of the cottontails' more recent range in West Texas in his series on the mammals of the different Texas biotic provinces. In 1949, he had found *S. auduboni*, together with another form called *S. robustus* (the Davis Mountains Cottontail), in the Big Bend.[33] By 1952, Blair wrote that *S. auduboni* ranged over approximately the whole western half of Texas, and he therefore called it "the desert cottontail."[34] By 1966, W. B. Davis mapped this cottontail's range as all of Texas west of a line from the Gulf Coast a little above the mouth of the Rio Grande to the Red River in the vicinity of Wichita Falls.[35]

This is a huge reversal: from our pre-1860 explorers finding the cottontails as wholly eastern forms not present in at least the western one-third of Texas, to the best surveys 100 years later finding them literally everywhere in the state. It is hard to know what to make of such a discrepancy.

Consider how provoking the questions arising here are. Of course, the explorers' not reporting these rabbits in the trans-Pecos doesn't prove that they weren't there in their times. We don't maintain that. But is it likely that the explorers, including the earliest Spanish who traveled various routes up from the Mexican presidios through West Texas as well as the military expeditions and California-bound travellers who went through the Limpia and other Big Bend passes or around the prow of the Guadalupes, describing such inconspicuous things as kangaroo rats along the way, just totally missed or ignored rabbits which were hopping around them? On the other hand, if the rabbits were not there in the untamed wilderness, why did they sometime after 1860 pick up and move west when they couldn't before? Why should the "prairie dog rabbit," after living in only the easternmost prairie dog towns and apparently being unable to colonize the huge trans-Pecos dog towns, move west over those same towns and beyond toward the end of the nineteenth century, just when the prairie dogs were being reduced drastically? Why, if those went west, didn't the common eastern cottontail go too, instead of staying contentedly in eastern Texas?

Now ask the next one carefully, but ask it. Isn't it just possible that the eastern, common cottontail is one entity never going west of the Pecos but making good use of the prairie dog holes east of that river, while *S. auduboni* and *S. robustus* are western forms which weren't originally in Texas at all, but which came into the trans-Pecos more recently as we grazed down the tall grass and encouraged the brush, finally spreading with this process as far east as Davis found them in 1966?

We are in no position to answer these questions here, but maybe we should thank our pioneers for prompting us to think about them and perhaps nudging someone to answer them.

There is in today's Texas another rabbit which introduces new confusion we must try to deal with. This one doesn't fit into the hare versus rabbit categories at all well, and worse than that, it is mysteriously absent from the explorers' accounts of early Texas. But it's here now, so we must deal with it as best we can with the few clues to its history there are.

This animal is the so-called "swamp rabbit." It has long been known in southeastern states as the "cane-cutter," perhaps from having been observed feeding on the tender sprouts of various canes in the lowlands where it lives. The species is usually classified today as *Sylvilagus aquaticus*, thus defined as an aquatic cottontail. There have been some subspecies of it coming and going as the authorities change, but we do not need to be concerned with those here.

Our first problem is to make some sense out of proposed relationships of this rabbit to the other Texas rabbits and hares. But that isn't easy, because the swamp rabbit has been classified by some specialist or other in each of the groups of *Lagomorpha* in this part of the world. So a little history is necessary.

The swamp rabbit was first described by Bachman in 1837, when he discovered it as far east as Alabama. He named it *Lepus aquaticus* and described its peculiar habits which prompted him to give it the species name which is so accurate that it is one of the few which have never been questioned.[36] This rabbit really is aquatic. It inhabits lowlands along streams and swamps, nests often among reeds and thickets almost literally in the water, jumps into water of its own volition not only to swim and cavort, but sometimes to use the water as an escape from pursuit, in which case it can stay entirely submerged except for its eyes and nose for some time.

Bachman apparently considered this a hare, since he put it in the genus *Lepus*, and others followed him to at least as late as Allen, in 1894.[37] And this does not seem illogical, since the animal grows up to one-third larger than a typical cottontail,[38] and is much more rangy, with proportionally longer legs. I have always thought, upon seeing one, that it looked like a jack hare with short ears.

But there are also reasons for considering the animal a large cottontail. Perhaps the chief one of these is that the swamp rabbit makes a nest, as do the cottontails, to shelter its blind and helpless young, while the young of the hares are so precocious, bright-eyed and ready to travel right after birth that no nest is made by the parent. So the swamp rabbit has become recognized as a rabbit in every sense of that word.

But even after placing it among them, some have had trouble relating the swamp rabbit to the ordinary cottontails. It just seems too different from either the eastern cottontail or those coming into West Texas to really be one of either group. In looking around for something else to tie this animal to, they have come across the so-called "wood rabbits." These form a group in the same genus living from South America up into Mexico, but which does not have representatives in the United States — unless this is one. It has therefore been proposed that the swamp rabbit may be a relict species left behind and isolated from wood rabbits which may once have ranged out of Mexico north and east all the way to Illinois and the Carolinas.[39]

This proposal is interesting, but it does not answer two Texas questions. First, why does the swamp rabbit range down out of East Texas to about the Nueces River and stop there, leaving the whole of deep South Texas including the seemingly most inviting environments of the lower coastal marshes and the *resacas* of the Rio Grande *galeria* forests uninhabited by either its supposed wood rabbit relatives of Mexico or by itself? And more to the point here, why does no explorer, pioneer, settler or soldier who wrote describing anything in early Texas so much as mention the swamp rabbit? For immigrants in a strange land to fail to report a rabbit which went swimming and could even hide under water seems about as passing strange as it would be to fail to report a cat if it did the same thing. I have no answer to the question of whether this means that the swamp rabbit came into East Texas after the explorers or that they failed to notice and report such a strange animal which was there all the time. It seems everything about this particular rabbit must remain an open question at least for now.

The big picture seems to be that we have rabbits postulated to have come into Texas from several directions. The common cottontail is the eastern cottontail, whose scientific name is *S. floridanus*. Then there are the West Texas cottontails and the hares, which may have come in from farther west. And most tentatively Texans of all are the swamp rabbits, which while living now from East Texas almost to the Atlantic, may be survivors from south of the border.

One thing is clear in all this. As surely as explorers and settlers were attracted from most directions into a magnetic Texas, so too were the rabbits. Unraveling the details of when and from where the various ones came may be a task never completed, but it's no doubt they got here. Witness what Auguste Fretelliere wrote in 1844, about San Antonio's west side: "The one street which is now called Commerce Street then bore the name of *el Potrero*. . . . Three quarters of *el Potrero* was a field of nopals where we went to shoot rabbits which were very plentiful."[40]

14

Merely Noted in Passing

There are some animals which are barely mentioned in the wealth of surviving explorers' accounts of the creatures they found in Texas. These are merely mentioned in passing, but even though they merge into the shadowy background of the Texas pictured by the pioneers, we must consider them here and try to understand their places in both the wild community and the pioneers' lives.

BATS MOVING IN

Texas has been called the bat capital of the U.S. — and with good reason. Specialists have listed at least twenty-nine species of bats found in Texas — more than in any other state. And the number of individual bats here is truly legion. Some idea of their importance, as well as of their numbers, can be gotten from the estimate that just the population of the Mexican free-tailed bat living in Texas can eat about 140,000 *tons* of insects annually.[1] Think of this negatively and it may sink in: Do away with just the bats of that one species in Texas and you would apparently have 140,000 tons more insects in Texas to plague you each year! In the light of this, doesn't it behoove us to conquer our illogical aversion to these harmless animals, to be good to them and to preserve the caves and other places where they live?

None other than a medical man, Dr. Charles R. A. Campbell, understood this many years ago, and did something about it. In order to increase the sweeping of mosquitoes from San Antonio's throbbing summer atmosphere by more bats, he designed and had built a number of structures which he called "bat roosts," placing them in a ring around the city. These were small wooden buildings in the shapes of truncated pyramids. Each was up on stilts and consisted of an enclosed space containing appropriate supports for bats to cling to, with slotted openings in its walls through which they could fly in and out. One of these still stands as a preserved historic structure in its original situation on the edge of the small town of Comfort, Texas.

It is said that these bat-houses were successful, but it was hard to really assess the effect of the addition of the bats which lived in the provided housing upon a city already swept by untold millions of bats deploying every summer evening from the great caves which actually underlaid some of the city and whose entrances dotted the countryside northwest of town. However, since it was an attempt to provide for bats — those creatures judged most ugly and disgusting by the majority of people — way before birdhouses were erected for our more beautiful, most loved creatures, doesn't the project tell us something about the prevailing attitude of Texans toward their animal populations? Don't we see here, even in Dr. Campbell, the eminent scientist who understood the interactions of disease, parasites and predators so well, an example of a questionable attitude toward wilderness — this being a tendency to notice and even to attempt to encourage only the wild creatures perceived to in some way contribute to those all-important humans who were moving in, while failing to value any animal for its own sake, ignoring and even exploiting it?

The pioneers, in general, seemed to pioneer this attitude. In regard to bats, consider the picture: Any realistic vision of presettlement Texas has to have bats by the millions dipping and darting through the dusk of its prairies, plains and forests. We know they were here. The great caves of the state, as discovered, contained mountains of their wastes — bat guano enough that they used it to make saltpeter to turn into gunpowder for several wars, and also hauled it off by wagon, truck and railroad car to fertilize untold acres of crops. Bats have been a very important part of all the Texas wilderness communities from the shadowy past. Yet it is a strange thing to turn to the explorers' picture of bats in Texas. In all of their writings I have been able to find only three pioneers who even mention bats at all. This may be one of the most remarkable failures of their reporting to square with what we know had to have been here when they were. What can explain it?

It may be significant that it was Dr. Alexander B. Hasson, post surgeon of Fort Phantom Hill, who alone noticed and named bats in any report of the animals in any Texas region.[2] Dr. Hasson was not only the most meticulous reporter of the wildlife around his post of any military personage, but he may have been especially conscious of bats from being concerned about mosquitoes and the health of his charges, as Dr. Campbell was fifty or so years later. He too may have been thinking of bats as contributors to the well-being of humans, rather than for interest in them.

Beyond this one mention, bats in the pioneers' writings are not pictured in the open, but only when they got inside buildings, intruding where they shouldn't be.

In 1849, while in or near where the city of Austin is now, W. Steinert wrote, "Since yesterday afternoon we have been resting at the home of our host, Mr. Ziller. It is too bad, though, that bats disturbed our sleep last night."[3] What is this? How would bats disturb anyone's sleep?

Picture early cabins. Few, if any, had their windows closed with anything, even in coldest weather, except perhaps with skins as thin as they could make them, and surely their very small openings were left unobstructed during hot weather to encourage any breeze there might be. Also, there must often have been unblocked cracks in places like under eaves, where logs and unevenly hewed out rafters had to meet. Pioneers' cabins must have been very inviting, very easily entered structures to bats. So Steinert's story about bats invading Mr. Ziller's home is not prima facie questionable. It may have described a common sort of problem.

But what about the bats disturbing the sleep of this cabin's occupants? First imaginations would picture the little intruders wheeling about in the room or sleeping loft. But, while this might be disconcerting to the fastidious, it surely would pose no threat to anyone, and sleepers would hardly be conscious of it, since the animal's flight is remarkably noiseless to human ears. So is Steinert kidding us or showing an exaggerated aversion to bats, even for that day? I might have thought so, except for my own experience with bats.

Once bats moved into the attic of my old German rock house in the Texas Hill Country. We might not have known they were there except that suddenly there was, throughout the house, an unceasing clamour almost like hundreds of mice or birds twittering and squeaking constantly. Even the tweeting of chimney swifts nesting in a chimney — which we also experienced in that house — never equaled this. Clearly, many somethings were in our attic. When I climbed up there, my flashlight showed about a square yard of dark, throbbing, chattering bats hanging from my roof. They were the source of the tumult, and their gabble went on all day long without a break. It was going on when we awoke in the morning and it was still there no matter how late we went to sleep. Although most of the little mammals went out to hunt at dusk, apparently there was always a remnant at home, keeping up the racket. So I can imagine the disturbance to sleep caused by bats not in an attic but in the single room of a primitive cabin open to the rafters, where the creatures would not only wheel in and out over those trying to slumber, but chatter too near them to be ignored. I don't think Steinert was exaggerating.

The third and last bat account from early Texas I have found was written by Herman Ehrenberg in 1836. This traveler gave very detailed descriptions of San Antonio at that time. Among other things he told of exploring was the old San Jose mission. The mission era was already past in 1836, and when he was there the mission buildings must already have become a grand collection of ruins. Ehrenberg writes, "As we passed through the cloisters adjoining the church a few bats and a small owl, frightened by the noise of our footsteps, brushed by us and flew wildly around the spacious, cool, shadowy depths of the church nave and transept."[4]

That's it from Texas explorers about bats. So it looks like early Texans could hardly care less about those animals. They show no evidence of being afraid of them — as so many moderns so illogically are — but this may be explainable. The modern fear of bats probably has been engendered by the more recent constant propagandizing about bats carrying rabies. Since, as we noticed in dealing with skunks in early Texas, rabies appears to be a more recently introduced scourge not in the early scene at all, the pioneers were probably not conditioned against bats like we are. In fact, it would be hard to explain it if they were. So only one of the early scribes even thought to list bats among the worth-mentioning creatures of the wilderness, one more mentioned bats because they kept him awake, and the third mentioned them, as any good writer would, because they are among the best image-makers for a large, abandoned building. In short, there is no sign of appreciation of the bat for its own sake in our pioneers. I think this points up a lack in their approach to wildlife in general — but if so, it is certainly not a feature unique to their era. Is it too late to atone for this today?

THE PORPOISE PROBLEM

There must have been porpoises — or dolphins, if you prefer — in the bays and passes of the Texas coast from ancient times. I have found no one who doubts that. But how common they were and what part they played in the early history of that coast is hard to learn from either explorers or scientists.

Henri Joutel, one of the first explorers to see Texas, establishes the fact that porpoises were on our coast when our earliest scouts first arrived. Chronicling the 1685 La Salle expedition along the Texas coast, Joutel wrote that after going ashore, presumably in the area of present Calhoun County, "They [the native Indians] brought us some . . . pieces of Porpois, which they cut with a Sort of Knife, made of Stone, setting one Foot upon it, and holding with one Hand, whilst they cut with the other."[5]

This makes the case not only that porpoises were present, but that when those earliest explorers came ashore they found the coastal Indians routinely catching and using those animals. Speculation has rooted here and proliferated like the swampgrass. By 1891, Albert S. Gatschet had deduced and published that not only had the Karankawa Indians dined on porpoises but those animals were originally very numerous in Texas bays.[6] Then our ever-present, reminiscing old-timers began adding stories about impressive herds of porpoises in the good old days. By the time some of us arrived it was practically gospel in most of the tales of Texas that porpoises were once almost as numerous in the state's coastal waters as deer on her lands. Even serious scholars bought these stories. Witness Gordon Gunter, who wrote in 1942, "Gatschet, who described the conditions of Texas bays when the coast was inhabited by the Karankawa Indians, prior to 1840, says the bays teemed with porpoises. To-day old fishermen on the coast say that schools of 75 to 100 were to be seen 40 years ago. I have never observed dolphins in Texas bays in schools greater than five or ten animals and usually they are in threes, pairs, or alone. It seems that the bottlenose dolphin is less numerous to-day on the Texas Coast than in former years."[7]

But wait a minute. We are trying to reconstruct the early Texas scene from what those who were actually present at the time tell us, and our imaginations should not run ahead of their reports. So I read again through all the descriptions of the Texas coastal waters and the animals which were in them which more than 100 different explorers and pioneers who experienced them between Joutel's time and 1860 have left us. And what do I actually find? Would you believe that all those various explorers who went to such great pains to write down details about redfish, drum, gars and eels, about sea turtles and alligators, about oysters and crabs — about all sorts of things which they found in Texas' coastal waters — didn't once mention having the beautiful and exciting experience of seeing porpoises leaping? Only one of them even uses the name, "porpoise," and his account of what he calls a porpoise is included in the discussion of the manatee, because I feel that his life-threatening encounter was actually with one of those animals instead of with a porpoise.

This is not positive testimony by the pioneers that there were *not* porpoises in our bays, but if their word means anything, this must mean that none of them, over a period of 250 years, witnessed herds of these spectacular beauties gamboling before them. How could those continually surfacing animals have been as common as some would maintain and still been so ignored? Fortunately, Joutel's report establishes that porpoises were present in the beginning of the era of our concern. Beyond that our explorers' silence about them would seem to require us to question exuberant claims about large quantities of them present on the Texas coast at any time in our history, while granting that they were probably here in less significant and hardly noticeable numbers.

If we can look beyond the mere question of the numbers of animals patrolling the early Texas coast, may we not learn here that one of our explorers' greatest contributions may be to sometimes temper our overly exuberant reconstructions of the past? And that may be a worthwhile lesson.

TEXAS' ACTUAL SEA MONSTERS

There is still a curious sea mammal called the manatee. Now-a-days, because there are only a very few of them left in the U.S., and these apparently limited to southern Florida, that state claims the animal and it is usually called the Florida manatee. But that is not the way it always was. It used to be called the American or West Indian manatee — this because it had been found in the West Indies and from near Wilmington, North Carolina, down the Atlantic Coast and through Florida, as well as in tropical America. It is easy to see that this leaves a large gap in the manatee's range, consisting of the Gulf Coast and all its estuaries from Alabama through Texas. The question of whether or not that gap really existed in the past has made the matter of manatees being in Texas waters or not a central issue.

The manatees may with some justification be called "sea monsters." They may become over fifteen feet long and weighing up toward a ton. They have bodies the shape of fat torpedoes and are fitted with flippers and a tail. With little, pig eyes and a wide mouth in a broad, flabby face, they are far from beautiful and give no hint of either the desire or the ability for speed or agility. They do not leap or arch above the water to blow, but ease noiselessly to the surface for breaths sometimes up to at least twelve minutes apart. Typically, they laze around in shallow waters of bays and estuaries, feeding on underwater vegetation as they slowly and methodically work the bottoms. Those in captivity have been described as consuming as much as 100 pounds of vegetable matter a day. They might be called the "hogs" of the estuaries.

The records of manatees in the Texas coastal waters are not many, but they are definite and nicely distributed not only timewise, from 1853 to 1986, but geographically — from a tributary of Sabine Bay almost on the Louisiana border, from Bolivar Peninsula, Copano Bay, Laguna Madre, and from the mouth of the Rio Grande at the Mexican border. There have been eleven of these animals reported from Texas during the past one and a third century, and we know they were here because in all cases their carcasses were examined or the live animals captured. None of them got away. Individuals captured alive in Laguna Madre from 1911 to 1913 were actually put on live exhibition in New Orleans, Chicago and New York. In those years there was either a peak in the number of manatees in Texas or else it was only then that fishermen had means with which to snare them. Details of the records are found in two papers, one by Gunter,[8] and the other by Fernandez and Jones.[9]

It may have been noticed that the earliest of the mentioned records comes from within the time-frame of our concern here. It consisted of a manatee skull which was sent by Jean Berlandier to the U.S. National Museum in 1853. The location given for its collection was simply "Brazos, Texas." It has been assumed by most that this location was in the vicinity of Brazos Island, which lies between the mouths of the Rio Grande. But there is another possibility, because a town named Brazoria is near and one called Brazosport is at the mouth of the Brazos River, far up the Texas coast. There is no conclusive evidence to show which location Berlandier's manatee came from, but it is not crucial to know, since either location is within the known range established by other records.

Berlandier's is the only obvious record of a manatee in Texas waters from prior to 1860. It is clear that these animals were not any more common here then than since that time. Our explorers give us no additional information about whether manatees were only rare visitors to our waters or very marginal residents barely clinging to life in them. However, there is one additional description in the pioneers' early writings which it seems may record an early instance of human meeting manatee in Texas with almost tragic results. The participant calls the animal he met up with a porpoise, but I reproduce here most of his account of the episode so that you can, keeping in mind the nervous, quick-moving, never-resting, fish-catching, noisily surfacing and blowing porpoise versus the placid, slow-moving, vegetarian, noiselessly breathing manatee lazing around under water, decide for yourself which animal he tangled with.

It was in 1835 that S. W. Cushing found himself marooned for some months in Galveston. He apparently had quite a time there, and made no bones about that, even calling his account of his adventures, "Wild Oats Sowing." He reports the following happening as occurring during that time.

"Angling for red-fish was likewise a favorite amusement, and nearly cost me my life at one time, the circumstances of which I will here relate, first giving the reader an idea of the *modus operandi* usually observed: First, a line is procured . . . to which is attached a single hook. . . . A noose at the end of this line is then slipped over the hand, and a fresh mullet of suitable size being impaled on the barbed instrument, the operator usually wades into the water . . . until . . . the water reached to the middle of the thigh, when the line was cast as far in advance as the skill of the sportsman could throw it; and it was seldom the case that more than five minutes elapsed before a victim was hooked, when all the fisherman had to do was to turn and make his way to the shore, dragging his prize after him. . . . Arming myself with line, bait, etc., I proceeded to the outer and most eastern point of the [Galveston] island. . . . Having reached the spot, I found, to my great disappointment, that the place was unfit for fishing, as at the distance of forty feet from the shore there was very deep water. However, determined to try my luck, I waded in to the depth of my knees, and threw out my line. I had not long to wait. Something of a dead, heavy weight seemed to have taken hold of the hook, and thinking all right, from its partial yielding to my pull, which enabled me to reach the water-mark of the shore, I began to anticipate a prize; but at this point the object stopped suddenly and commenced to draw slowly off again. Wondering what it could be, I continued to give it line, of which I had considerable slack in my hand, occasionally gently trying to check its farther escape from me, which I found could not be done. I had but one coil left upon my wrist, when I recollected that I was already nearly to my waist in the water, and that I could not swim, and the line was fast to my wrist by a slipnoose which was drawn tight already. I got my knife in my hand in an instant, and it was none too soon. The strain drew the line tighter and tighter. I was up to my armpits, and it would not do to go farther. I cut the line, and the next instant an enormous porpoise rose to the surface at about the length of my line from me, and turning flukes, he disappeared, carrying my fishing apparatus with him. I was so astonished that I could not make out, as his ugly length passed in review before me, whether he had my hook in his mouth, or whether, as was probably the case, it had caught in some part of his shining black carcass. These fish, the shape of whose nose is like that of a hog, are known to resemble that animal in their great propensity for rooting, in which they principally gather their subsistence from the worms which abound to the sand and mud at the bottom of the sea. The individual who had so recently endeavored to introduce me to the mysteries of the Gulf, was probably engaged in the agreeable occupation of procuring his breakfast, when he either swallowed my bait, or got it hooked into his covering of fat or blubber (another peculiarity in which they resemble the porker,) and this turned the tables upon me."[10]

Of course it is impossible to know whether the animal Cushing hooked was a porpoise or a manatee, but if you tally up the characteristics of it which his account actually states or implies, I believe there are more of them typical of the manatee. If he had hooked one of those dashing porpoises I doubt he would have had time to get out his knife and cut himself free before the lightning-fast creature took off with him, and if his line held I don't think he would have survived to tell about it. It is more plausible that he hooked a manatee peacefully grazing underwater, that only a manatee would have waited around for him to tighten up his line, and that only this placid animal would have reacted and moved off so slowly after his hook had penetrated its flesh. So I think this may be the only account of a manatee from the exploratory period to supplement Berlandier's specimen. Whether this is so or not, the manatee is left a rare animal barely in the picture of early Texas.

But things don't look even that good for it now. With speedboats, which are killing these slow-moving animals in Florida, lacing all the waters of our Texas bays and estuaries and nets regularly criss-crossing them, what chance would these sluggish grazers have today?

15

Absent Without Leave

The explorers' picture of primeval Texas has been drawn. Their own accounts have been fitted together like pieces of a jigsaw puzzle to bring the scene into being. The result is a grand and tumultuous mosaic with some animals strutting and stampeding center stage, others stalking and pouncing in the thickets, and some barely seen hiding in the dim corner places or even underground. More recent information and analysis have been used in an attempt to bring the picture into the best possible focus.

But no sooner is the scene before us than we are approached by several animals straight out of present-day Texas with the question, why aren't we in the explorers' picture? And this does present a problem, because there are several animals which we might think should have been included which are totally missing. Can their absence be explained? All we can do is to try, and it must be emphasized that our efforts here are only conjecture. But whether we succeed or not, maybe we can learn by the errors.

THE MUSKRAT DIDN'T RAMBLE THAT MUCH

One of the most remarkable absences from all early accounts of Texas is that of the muskrat. Its absence may not be entirely explainable at this late date, but to examine some possibilities may bring this animal into its rightful place in our understanding of Texas as it was.

The problem is that the muskrat became, in comparatively recent times, one of the most economically important fur-producers in Texas.[1] After the beavers, mink and otters were essentially wiped out, muskrats played a large part in keeping the East Texas fur industry alive. In 1936, for instance, muskrats produced 54 percent of the fur-produced income for Jefferson, Chambers and Orange counties.[2] With this in mind, it seems strange that the records of the active pre-1860 fur trade in East Texas do not even list muskrats at all, and neither do any pioneers. What might explain this?

The first proposed explanation is that, with all the superlative fur-producers from beavers, mink and otters to deer and buffaloes to take, the trappers and hunters, Indian and immigrants alike, may have ignored the smaller and lowly muskrats entirely. And there is a point here. With mink in view, who — male or female, trapper or wearer — can even see muskrat? So this possibility would explain the absence of muskrats from our picture by saying that our exploring reporters merely ignored the ratty things because of better, more beautiful animals all around them.

But there are doubts about this explanation. We may imagine the professional hunters and trappers for whom all these animals were nothing but sources of income ignoring muskrats while they were bringing in the richer fur-bearers, but they did not always have those top quality species — even before 1860 — with which to make their fortunes. Witness to this is left us by William Kennedy, for instance, who had already written in 1839, "In the list of amphibious animals are the otter and beaver, which formerly abounded to the district of Nacogdoches, but have been greatly thinned by the hunters and trappers."[3] Concerning East Texas in general, an unnamed writer stated so early as 1846, "Beaver and otter were frequent in the past, but now they have become rare because of the hunters...."[4]

So it seems that those then dependent upon the fur trade would have become very conscious of any animals whose pelts they could buy and sell, including muskrats. Strengthening this is the fact that they were doing a brisk business in raccoons and skunks in those times, so why not muskrats, if in fact those animals were common in East Texas at the time?

The whole above conjecture may be unnecessary because almost none of our writing explorers were actually hunters, trappers or fur-traders. Those outdoorsmen probably had neither the verbal ability, the inclination or the time to write about the animals they preyed upon. Our pioneering reporters had to be at least to some extent educated, comfortable with the pen, and conscious of either a personal mission or an official commission to produce accounts of what they had time and ability to observe. These reporting persons, if not an elite, had to be individuals with special abilities and sensibilities, and we have seen that they left reports of almost every animal we know must have been in early Texas. So how do we explain their failure to ever mention having met up with a muskrat in Texas?

For instance, when Thomas Jefferson arranged his 1806 Red River Expedition, he "went to considerable length to appoint the first trained naturalist to accompany an American exploring expedition." The choice was Peter Custis, who "had been educated in a diversified natural history program," and who "clearly possessed impressive taxonomical skills as well as a command of contemporary Latin binomials."[5] This scholar's commission included reporting on the flora and fauna of the Red River Valley, and he reported beavers, otters, opossums, skunks, etc. — even down to gophers, moles and species of mice previously unknown.[6]

The question therefore looms large. Why didn't Custis report any muskrat? It would be easy to say: Because there weren't any muskrats, and consider the matter closed. But that won't do. We know well that the failure to be reported does not automatically mean any creature did not exist. Archaeology, geology and biogeography already have too many erroneous histories built on that sort of negative evidence.

Another explanation left us is that while muskrats must have been present in early Texas, three factors probably worked together to hide them from our explorers, namely, muskrats must have ranged over only a small part of Texas, they must not have been very numerous at that time even where they existed, and they are very reclusive, inconspicuous creatures easily overlooked even when present. If these three things were all working together, it would not be so surprising that our explorers missed these animals. So what about these three factors?

Concerning the first — I had always just assumed that muskrats lived wherever in Texas there were appropriate wetlands with lush swamp growth. I suspect many who blame the explorers for missing them assume this also. But I was surprised to learn that, far from claiming Texas as their own, muskrats have only ventured very tentatively into our state and managed to colonize only relatively narrow areas along or near some Texas borders.

A recent, authoritative work describes the muskrat as a northern animal only managing to approach the Gulf Coast in spots, Louisiana being the main one of those. In Texas, it shows the animals only occupying narrow strips along the state's eastern and northern boundaries and along the Pecos River.[7] It is questionable whether the animals own even the upper part of that East Texas border strip, because another scholar says: "Muskrats are confined in East Texas to the coastal prairie from the Louisiana-Texas border west at least to Harris County. In this area they are found in marshes which range from fresh to saline. At one time muskrats from Oklahoma were stocked in Trinity County but the population eventually disappeared."[8]

The muskrats must have come down into the three Texas areas so long ago and from such different regions that scientists consider there to be three separate subspecies in Texas. These are: the Pecos River muskrat, which has come down out of New Mexico along the Pecos and has also been reported a time or two as far down the Rio Grande as at El Paso; the Great Plains muskrat, which comes down out of Oklahoma into the Panhandle and maybe into some of the Red River Valley, although David J. Schmidly recently stated that its occurrence in eastern Texas "must be considered tentative"[9]; and the common muskrat, which spills out of Louisiana and is limited to the immediate southeastern corner of Texas. The last of these is the only one of the three occurring in numbers enough in Texas to have ever been a commercial fur-producer.

So look where we are. The doubts about the muskrat ever having been in northeastern Texas lets Custis and all the others who didn't report it along the Red River off the hook. And don't both the limited ranges and numbers of the two western subspecies go far toward explaining the explorers of West Texas having missed them? If they had reported them often out there, that would have been misleading. This leaves only the common Louisiana muskrat in the southeastern corner of Texas as perhaps numerous enough that explorers should have noticed and reported them. And those have sometimes been very numerous. There have been times when trappers could take fifteen to twenty animals there per acre without endangering the overall population.[10] If they were that common in early times, it is hard to excuse the pioneers for not telling us of it.

But were they so common before the pioneers worked their influence on that southeast Texas watery wilderness? One explanation I have heard for the absence of muskrats from the explorers' picture of Texas is that perhaps only after the hunting out of its many predators by the settlers were the muskrats freed to multiply into the impressive populations seen in southeast Texas when they were in their heyday. Maybe in the untamed wetlands muskrats were uncommon and so especially reclusive because of their many enemies that the explorers missed them. After all, the muskrat is a prey species. It is said that the greatest natural predators upon it are the mink, water snakes, turtles and alligators, followed by a regiment made up of hawks, owls, raccoons, foxes, etc. We know that settlers always warred against such predators, and we have seen that among the first predators on muskrats eliminated was the mink. All of these predators were no doubt reduced by the pioneers, freeing up this belabored prey to multiply and appear almost casually until modern development began co-opting and fouling their habitats.

The explorers' failure to report muskrats may be taken to point toward this purely speculative scenario or some other possible explanation. On the other hand, it may just point to a deficiency in those pioneers themselves and their accounts. Each must decide between those alternatives for himself or herself. But who can deny that they have prompted us to learn more about the muskrat and about Texas as it was?

IS THE PORCUPINE A NATIVE TEXAN?

Comes the porcupine. And when "porky" comes around, there's little question of knowing it. These creatures are famous for lumbering along, day or night, as though completely oblivious to everybody else, or for climbing a particular tree and staying in it, often clearly visible, all day — or days on end. Out in the West Texas spaces and where there aren't that many trees, this creature, up to three feet long and weighing up to twenty-five pounds, is hard to miss. They're seen now on our West Texas highways, either ambling through the bar-ditches or, all too often, lying killed by the traffic they ignore like they do most everyone else.

So the big question becomes: why, if porcupines were in antebellum Texas, didn't any of the wagon trains, military expeditions, their many hunters and scouts, or any of the other explorers, surveyors and pioneers ever report seeing even one of these animals? Wouldn't you think that if they were present some of those sharp-eyed frontiersmen would have included them along with their lists of other animals in their official reports or written home about these very strange animals covered with barbed darts instead or fur?

Fortunately we don't have to look for any explanation for our explorers' having missed porcupines. The case is already practically made that this animal may not have been in Texas in their days at all. Oh yes, the porcupine is clearly here now, but just trace the known history of this animal in Texas.

The earliest record of porcupines here seems to be those reported from the Davis Mountains of the Big Bend in 1940.[11] From that date on, the animals have been seen at various places in the trans-Pecos. Soon after 1940, the animals began to be reported in the Panhandle and in the western high plains. Its debut farther south and east has been much delayed, but it has definitely invaded in those directions. It was collected in Wichita County in 1984,[12] Clay County in 1988,[13] and in Coke County in 1986 and 1987 by Simpson and Maxwell, who state: "Porcupines taken in this [Coke County] study are the first on record for the western half of the Edwards Plateau other than from Terrell County (Davis, 1974)."[14] Today the animals are supposed to be ranging almost throughout the Hill Country.

So what should be said about the history of the porcupine in Texas? Milstead and Tinkle ventured an opinion on that in 1959, writing, "These mammals have not been abundant until recent years. This paper reports several records from northwest Texas from where the porcupine has been previously unrecorded.... The apparent increase of porcupines in both range and number in Texas is interesting and may be of considerable biological importance."[15]

Well, if it might be important, let's consider it. This known history of invasion and increase is apparently accurate as far as it goes, but it is open-ended. It makes it look as if there were no porcupines in Texas — at least in historical times — before about 1940. Could this have been?

It is always dangerous to argue from a negative, but we do it much more often than we admit. All scientists' range maps assume that where there are no verifiable records of a presence, none of the animals or plants under consideration are present — and the boundaries are drawn after reasoning from this negative. Thus up-to-date maps show the porcupine's present range to include about half of Texas, but also imply that they are not present in the eastern half of the state. And the fact that no zoologist could report a porcupine in Texas before 1940, and therefore none of Texas could be included in any verified range map of the animal before that date, at least allows a presumption that they were not here earlier. Is there any other evidence which might support or cast doubt on this implication?

Forward step our explorers. They did not report meeting up with one porcupine during two previous centuries in which some of their expeditions traversed northwest Texas and many of them went through the very mountains of southwest Texas where these animals first appeared in the present century. So to the fact that no zoologist found porcupines here before 1940, we have to add that the dozens of other people who traversed West Texas before 1860, and wrote about animals they found there, didn't find them either. The agreement is complete. Science has only confirmed the explorers' picture of an early Texas without "porky."

Regardless of how early they started to enter Texas, the obvious question today is: Why have these animals fanned out over about half of this state within the space of only about fifty years, when they had not before? What new situation has arisen here in which the porcupines could be at home? What new factor or factors have come to be present which make the region newly tolerable to them?

It is true that these animals are to a large extent dependent for their food upon the bark and twigs of trees. However, the idea that they have been moving into Texas because of a supposed increase of tree cover over the state does not seem to follow. This is because the porcupines first came into the northwest part of Texas and are still seen in the parts of Texas where there are the fewest trees. And even in these areas it is noted that they are often seen out in the open, far away from trees. Beyond that, there is comment about how often these creatures are seen on and near highways, and about how many are killed because of their preoccupation with prospecting for something in ditches and on the actual pavements. Is anything known which might account for these facts?

A biologist friend of mine says that he would never jeopardize his credibility by saying it publicly, but that he believes the porcupines have come into Texas specifically as a result of our practice of de-icing our highways with salt. I cannot either prove or disprove this idea, but I will risk my credibility by pointing out some evidence which would seem to point toward that possibility.

In his major study of the North American porcupine, Uldis Roze has a whole section upon what he calls the porcupine's "salt drive."[16] He relates the fact that all herbivores face a problem maintaining the necessary potassium-sodium ratios in their bodies because of the low sodium content of their plant food. He speculates that this may be an especially critical problem for porcupines for two reasons: first, because the bark and twigs which they eat are especially low in sodium, and second, because they do not appear to have an internal sodium reservoir such as moose, deer, goats and other browsers have in their rumen fluid. He shows that this necessity for salt availability is a factor limiting where these animals may live and a clue to much of their behavior.

Roze studied porcupines in New England, where they are common. Yet he tells how surprised he was, one night, to observe five porcupines on a mere three and a half miles of highway right-of-way. Puzzled by their attraction to this particular stretch of highway, he stopped near one which was busy with something in the bar-ditch, and observed that it was gnawing upon a small piece of deadwood. This seemed to be the behavior of all of the porcupines on that stretch of highway that night, and he saw the search for such material in the same place repeated — often with fatal results due to traffic.

This prompted him to question why these animals would so rashly come out to gnaw sticks in such an open and hazardous place when the forests just next to it were strewn with similar deadwood. His investigation showed that this stretch of highway, being hilly, was routinely salted to melt snow and ice. He performed tests which showed that, although the last salting had been weeks before his observations and rains had washed most of the salt out of the soil, porous plant material along the roadside still held some salt. He concluded that this was what attracted the porcupines. He even reports that he later observed one of these animals licking a wet spot on the pavement itself for traces of salt.

Roze thus established that, in their long-occupied home territory where they could survive with naturally occurring salt, porcupines were still strongly attracted to any salt-treated stretches of highway. Is it not logical, then, to think that these animals may have been enabled to immigrate into Texas, an area where they could not survive before for lack of adequate salt, since we began spreading salt upon our roads and highways? Their movements seem to be just such as should result from the furnishing of some such limiting factor as salt could be for them.

But a quick thinker will immediately reply: Why should our spreading salt on roadways facilitate things for these animals in West Texas where there are salt flats, salt deposits and even rivers running salty?

Roze has a possible answer for that. He set up experiments in which he attracted many porcupines by setting out pieces of wood soaked in salt solutions. By using various salts he found not only that the presence of sodium was the attractant, but that any presence of other elements such as potassium along with the sodium always reduced the attraction, and that when these were present in any high proportion along with the sodium it caused them to avoid the deposits entirely. It seems porcupines could no more make salt licks of West Texas deposits of mixed salts than other animals do of those toxic outcrops and pools. In contrast, our spreading of nice clean sodium salts in ribbons across Texas may have provided the porcupines literal highways into the state.

In the light of all this, do I sacrifice my credibility by merely suggesting that it may be we have spread a welcome mat for "porky" by weaving networks of salt over almost all of Texas? If it is true that the moving in of the porcupines may have "considerable biological importance," as we have seen expressed, may it not be a service to bring this possible reason for it to the attention of those who might then, with study and experiment, determine what effects this peculiar salt-sowing behavior of ours actually has upon not only this animal but upon a host of other Texas organisms?

Be that as it may, we now have the porcupine, which was not in the picture of early Texas, and we may as well adopt him. He's spectacular enough to make a great Texan!

HAS THE COATI REALLY COME IN?

While Texas was being invaded by the porcupine from the north and by humans from all directions, yet another and perhaps even more peculiar creature was apparently trying to enter from the south into this state which seems to attract most everyone. This was the coati.

This animal is a relative of the raccoon and the ringtail, and is intermediate in size between those two, but it is not as quick or as graceful as either. It is a great climber, so it has a very long tail, but this is not beautiful like those of its relatives. Instead, its tail is covered with only short hairs colored in only faded bands. It depends upon this tail for balance, so it holds it up and out stiffly. This, together with extra long rear legs, make the coati look ungainly on the ground, and along with the animal's tendency to stand hunched and peering fixedly at any stranger, gives it a rather stupid look. This, however, doesn't reflect its true nature at all.

Coatis seem to be practically omnivorous. They apparently hunt for both animal and vegetable food high in trees, around rocky crevices and by rooting in ground litter. They are active during daylight hours, and tend to range in troops, so it should be more easily known when they are present than the secretive, nocturnal raccoons or ringtails.

Coatis are semitropical animals. They have been fairly numerous in Mexico, so it would not be surprising to find them also in at least southern parts of Texas. Yet none of the persons who trooped back and forth over South Texas in Spanish expeditions to the north, American expeditions to the south, marches to and from American-Mexican wars, activities in Spanish and later international trade, surveying or ranching over more than 200 years — and wrote about it — ever mentioned a coati. One would almost have to conclude that these animals weren't in Texas at all during all that time. Yet, more recently they are supposed to have been here.

The earliest record of a coati in Texas was of one taken somewhere near Brownsville in 1877.[17] On the basis of this it was long imagined that the animal ranged all along the southern border of Texas. However, actual records of it were not soon forthcoming or very convincing. There was not a second one recorded captured in Texas until 1938. This one was taken alive near Eagle Pass, but it was not possible to prove that it was not an escaped pet, since these animals were often sold alive in Piedras Negras, just across the Rio Grande. The third one consisted of only a skin confiscated as an illegal fur from a trapper in the Texas Big Bend in 1939. It was never possible to determine whether this one was actually taken in Texas or in nearby Mexico. In 1940, F. Wallace Taber summed up the situation to that time with these words: "Two of the three records thus far discovered appear not to have been natural invasions." He goes on to say that, "In southern parts of Arizona and New Mexico a definite northern invasion is taking place," but that he hasn't seen that in Texas.[18] However, as early as 1943, W. B. Davis reported a coati killed on the Rio Frio about forty miles north of Uvalde, Texas. On the strength of this, Davis stated that the animal was extending its range north in Texas.[19] But since, as lately as in 1981, Hall lists only one more record in Texas, one from Aransas County in 1961,[20] we must surely conclude that any invasion of the coati into Texas is only very sporadical and has resulted in no obviously established population here.

How do we best relate the absence of the coati from the explorers' Texas during those first two and a half centuries of Texas history to what we know from the above? The animal's absence from their accounts certainly lets us know that we have not been seeing any surviving individuals from some relict population of these animals. It makes it clear we must turn things around the other way — that any coati actually in the wild here must be a recent immigrant, and that if coatis do become established here it will only then be a true invasion. In the meantime, isn't it clear that our explorers have not misled us, even with their silence on this animal?

SEALS: OUR IMMIGRANT REFUGEES

Is it surprising to learn that seals as a group are among the most widely occurring tribes of animals in existence? They have been found on coasts, far up rivers and even in upland lakes practically worldwide. Their greatest proliferation has been in the colder zones, but they are not only polar creatures. They seem to have been permanently absent only from the central tropic zone. Until recently, seals have been found in various local habitats along the North American coasts down into lower California on the Pacific and to Honduras on the Atlantic.[21]

Never common, but occasionally found in the warmest outposts tolerable to seals on the Atlantic Coast of America, was the West Indian monk or hair seal *(Monachus tropicalis)*. Hall gives this animal's original range as "Florida and Bahama Islands, thence southwestward in the Gulf of Mexico to Honduras."[22] Others describe its known range as including the Gulf of Mexico and Caribbean Sea as far south as Honduras, eastward to Jamaica, Cuba and Hispaniola and northward through the Bahamas to Florida, with its most successful colonies having been on islands off the coast of Yucatan.

If this seal was in the Gulf, did it come west to Texas? And if not, why not? Certainly our coasts would not have been too hot for an animal adapted to the Caribbean, and it is hard to see Texas as too cold for any seal.

Our explorers give us a negative answer to the first question. There is no account of any seal in their writings — not even a hint that over their 250-year era anyone ever saw a seal in or even near Texas. And for decades after that the scientists who combed the region found no trace of this animal here. It seems as probable as any reasoning from negatives can be that the seal did not live on the Texas coast in early historical times.

But then the picture changed. There was a sudden set of seal sightings on the Texas coast, beginning in 1926, but lasting only a few years. Gordon Gunter, of the Marine Laboratory of the University of Miami, has written up details of those sightings.[23] The seals were only reported in and near the Brazos Santiago Pass at Port Isabel and Bolivar Pass into Galveston Bay. At both of these places they were seen over a period of time, often sitting on the rocks of jetties and therefore were called locally "land porpoises." Gunter sums up his paper by writing, "From these facts it seems justifiable to conclude that the West Indian seal ... has been seen at widely scattered points on the Texas coast as recently as 1932."

Assuming, as the lack of early records seems to indicate, that neither explorers nor scientists ever saw a seal on the Texas coast in two and a half centuries, but then suddenly the animals were seen and then so soon disappeared again, we have three questions to deal with. Why weren't seals present on the wild, undeveloped Texas coast? Why did they suddenly come to only two such widely separated locations and nowhere else we know of? Why did they disappear so soon again?

The answer to the first of these questions must be that either something which prohibited the seals' living here must have been present on our coast in its original, wild state, or else something which they needed in order to be successful here must have been missing in the beginning. The answer to the second question would then be that sometime before 1926, that factor prohibiting them by being present must have been eliminated, or else whatever inhibited them by being absent though needed must have been added for the first time. Can we discover anything which was either removed or added that might have been that limiting factor?

This determinant could hardly have been temperature, since the species has prospered in more torrid regions than the Texas coast, while the southern tip of Texas is as far south as southern Florida, where the species has lived. Nor have we seen any general climatic or physical change before 1926 which might have made our coast suddenly favorable to these seals. But was there any local, specific change which might have benefited them?

Immediately it is noticeable that the two locations where the seals were sighted were both at the entrance to major bays and estuaries — though hundreds of miles apart. No one reported seeing seals elsewhere along Texas beaches or even around minor passes. They were only at the two major passes where the most shipping went in and out of major harbors. What might, at so late a date, have made those passes attractive for the first time to these animals?

There are some clues. Gunter quotes Mexican fishermen who reported seals on down the Mexican Gulf Coast as being only "where rocks run out into the water." In the Texas accounts it was specifically stated that the animals were seen when they moved out onto the rocks of jetties at the passes mentioned. This was why they were called "land porpoises."

And this is not only understandable, but may provide an answer to the first two of our questions. A seal, with only a pair of flippers and a streamlined body, has a special problem moving over some surfaces. Out of the water, on a flat surface, it has to pull itself along with its flippers while pushing itself with serpentine undulations of its body. This works well on hard surfaces where the body can find solid unevenness for traction, but such movements are mostly counterproductive in sand. This, plus the difficulty they have swimming up onto sandy beaches through the shallows which typically extend out for some distance from such beaches, means that seals usually avoid sandy shores. Just try to picture seals on a sandy beach, and it becomes obvious how incongruous this image is. They are found on ice and packed snow or else on rocky shores where they can barrel up in deep water and use their momentum to flop out onto some shelf-like solid surface.

Now, where were the rocky shores of early Texas? Wasn't our whole shoreline hundreds of miles of sandy beaches slanting with tantalizing gradualness from under shallow wavelets? Try to imagine a seal wallowing in the inches-deep water, struggling to get either up onto a Texas beach or back down off of it. Trying to find accounts of any natural rocky shores along Texas and failing, I no longer wonder why the seals passed up this coast.

But then, why did they suddenly appear here? Isn't it obvious? Where in Texas did they come ashore? Once those structures were produced, the seals swam up in the deep waters of our ship channels and gracefully leapt out onto the massive rocks of our jetties. These structures were almost as ready made for them as any rocky coasts. I propose that they stopped at the two places in Texas having jetties, even though those were hundreds of miles apart. They came only after and because we built our jetties, which gave them accommodations in Texas for the first time.

Perhaps we have answered the first two of our three questions. If so, we are left with the last one. Once we had rocky jetties, why didn't the seals stay here? We see no reversal of climate or physical situation which would work against them. The jetties remain. But the seals lasted only a few years. It seems we have to once again look for some local cause working on individuals, and this search is especially sobering because Gunter says that the last written report of a West Indian seal anywhere was one which was killed at Key West in 1922. Hall states that, "Lack of recent sightings [of this seal] suggests that this species is extinct."

Do you realize that this would mean that those individuals seen between 1926 and 1932 in Texas — there was only a single individual seen at Brazos Santiago Pass over a period of time and "several" at Bolivar jetties — may have been the last individuals of the species in existence, looking for a refuge where they could survive? Think of it: Texas might have had these refugees to enrich our fauna uniquely and, through offsprings, permanently! They came, we could have welcomed and encouraged them, and they might have added a new dimension to our culture and our history, as so many human refugees have, without our having to build a zoo or a Sea World! But they did not survive, so the suspicion must follow. Isn't it clear that only a few shots from some *macho* Texans with guns or a few lucky hauls by Texas fishermen with the big nets could have put the end to this beautiful species not only here — but entirely exterminated the species?

Perhaps it is fitting to conclude our survey with this admittedly tragic story of the seal Texas had for so short a time and has already forgotten. We have tried to see as clearly as possible the explorers' Texas that once was, before it fades entirely away with the death of too many of its animals and the crumbling of the pages on which our forefathers told about them. In the process we have seen something of the changes we have imposed upon their Texas, with some animals wiped out by our developments and others adapting or even profiting. But for all too many, like the seals, the apparent gifts we devise hide traps. Are we changing Texas so that not only its original denizens but its immigrants — and that includes most of us — can no longer recognize or gain homes in it?

Notes

References to explorers' statements are indicated by the surname of the author followed by the number of the source in the included bibliography. This is followed by the page number of the reference in that source. References to other sources are given in full.

INTRODUCTION
    1. Edward, 82, pp. 74, 177-178.
    2. Edna Kahlbau, *Amarillo Sunday News & Globe*, August 14, 1938; Del Weniger, *The Explorers' Texas: The Lands & Waters*, Austin: Eakin Press, 1984, p. 186.
    3. Froebel, 112, p. 330.
    4. Frank Gilbert Roe, *The North American Buffalo, A Critical Study of the Species in its Wild State*, Toronto & Buffalo: Univ. of Toronto Press, 2nd ed., 1970.
    5. Wayne Franklin, *Discoverers, Explorers, Settlers, The Diligent Writers of Early America*, Chicago: University of Chicago Press, 1979, p. 123.
    6. Peter Matthiessen, *Wildlife in America*, New York: The Viking Press, 1959, p. 133.
    7. Frank Gilbert Roe, *The North American Buffalo, A Critical Study of the Species in its Wild State*, p. 679.
    8. *Ibid.*, p. 671.

Chapter 1: THE BUFFALO IN EARLY TEXAS
    1. Tom McHugh, *The Time of the Buffalo*, New York: Alfred A. Knopf, 1972, p. 4.
    2. Zaldivar, 351, p. 229.
    3. Antonio Espejo, "Account of the Journey to the Provinces and Settlements of New Mexico, 1853," in Bolton, *Spanish Explorations in the Southwest*, New York: Charles Scribner's & Sons, 1916, p. 189.
    4. Wavel, 333, p. 91.
    5. Holley, 156, p. 99.
    6. Baird, 11, p. 682.
    7. Richard Irving Dodge, *The Hunting Grounds of the Great West*, London: Chatto & Windus, 1877, p. 119.
    8. Zaldivar, 351, pp. 227-228.
    9. Berlandier, 24, Vol. 2, pp. 356-357.
    10. Erik K. Reed, "Bison Beyond the Pecos," *The Texas Journal of Science*, Vol. 7, #2 (June 1955), p. 130.
    11. Teran, 319, p. 17.
    12. Manzanet, 211, pp. 65, 191, 530.
    13. Mendoza, 226, pp. 336-337.
    14. Manzanet, 211, pp. 54-56.
    15. Mezieres, 227, Vol. 2, p. 228.
    16. Lafora, 188, p. 152.
    17. Rivera, 279, pp. 491-492.
    18. Roemer, 281, p. 198.
    19. Berlandier, 23, p. 34. Note: Ohlendorf's translation is "three immense herds of bison." 24, Vol. 2, p. 358.
    20. Berlandier, 23, p. 37. See also: 24, Vol. 2, p. 358.
    21. Harrell, 145, pp. 113-114.
    22. Shain, 291, p. 259.
    23. Pena, 262, p. 97.
    24. De Cordova, 66, p. 258.
    25. Roemer, 281, p. 141.
    26. Whipple, 338, Vol. 4, p. 4.
    27. Solis, 305, p. 28.
    28. Talon, 315, p. 8.
    29. Maria, 222, p. 211.
    30. Freeman, 107, p. 190.
    31. Ker, 181, pp. 85-86.
    32. Espinosa, 87, p. 157.
    33. Solis, 304, p. 540.
    34. Borroto, 352.
    35. Yoakum, 349, pp. 22-23.
    36. Joutel, 176, p. 97.
    37. De Leon, 69, p. 420.
    38. Teran, 319, p. 23.
    39. Holley, 155, p. 76.
    40. Bonnell, 28, p. 30.
    41. Colt, 53, p. 33.
    42. Fisher, 99, p. 33.
    43. Manzanet, 211, p. 51.
    44. De Leon, 68, p. 394.
    45. De Leon, 69, p. 406.
    46. Ben Cuellar Ximenes, *Gallant Outcasts*, San Antonio: The Naylor Co., 1963, p. 125.
    47. Baird, 11, p. 684.
    48. J. A. Allen, "History of the American Bison," *Ninth Annual Report of the U.S. Geological and Geographical Survey*, 1875, pp. 519, 545.
    49. Bethel Coopwood, "Route of Cabeza de Vaca," *The Quarterly of the Texas State Historical Association*, Vol. 3, #4 (April 1900), pp. 233-234.
    50. Erik K. Reed, "Bison Beyond the Pecos," *The Texas Journal of Science*, Vol. 7, #2 (June 1955), p. 134.
    51. Lindheimer, 200, Letter: Mirador, Jan. 17, 1835.
    52. Berlandier, 23, pp. 21-23.
    53. D. B. Hiatt, *Ever the Wildebeest*, Kerrville: The author, 1978, p. 186.
    54. Mendoza, 226, p. 329.
    55. Pope, 270.
    56. Luxan, 204, p. 57.
    57. See: Tom McHugh, *The Time of the Buffalo*. New York: Alfred A. Knopf, 1972, p. 17; Larry Barsness, *Heads, Hides and Horns*, Ft. Worth: Texas Christian Univ. Press, 1985, p. 21.
    58. Wayne Gard, *The Great Buffalo Hunt*, Lincoln: Univ. of Nebraska Press, 1959, p. 7.
    59. Mari Sandoz, *The Buffalo Hunters*, New York: Hastings House, 1954, p. 35; Frank Gilbert Roe, *The North*

American Buffalo, Univ. of Toronto Press, 2nd ed., 1970, pp. 334-520.

60. See: Tom McHugh, *The Time of the Buffalo*, pp. 15-16; Frank Gilbert Roe, *The North American Buffalo*, 2nd. ed., pp. 353-354.
61. J. L. Hill, *The Passing of the Indian and Buffalo*, Long Beach, CA: Geo. W. Moyle Co., n.d., p. 32.
62. Unknown member of the Black River California Company, in letter, "Santa Fe, May 23, 1849," in *Southern Trails to California in 1849*, ed. Ralph P. Bieber, Philadelphia: Porcupine Press, 1974, pp. 301-302.
63. Mendoza, 226, pp. 338-339.
64. Mezieres, 227, Vol. 2, p. 228.
65. Amangual, 5, p. 478.
66. Dewees, 76, p. 26.
67. Moore, 238, p. 114.
68. Whipple, 337, Vol. 4, p. 3.
69. Falconer, 96, p. 214.
70. Yoakum, 349, p. 38.
71. Teran, 319, p. 17.
72. Lafora, 188, p. 152.
73. Moore, 238, p. 35.
74. Freeman, 107, p. 208.
75. St. John, 287, p. 179.
76. See: Bonnell, 28, p. 70-71; Lafora, 188, p. 148; Wavel, 333, p. 91; Berlandier, 23, pp. 21-25.
77. Bracht, 31, p. 42.
78. Don H. Biggers, "The Buffalo Butchery in Texas," *Frontier Times*, Vol. 3, #5 (Feb. 1926), p. 6.
79. J. I. Hill, *The Passing of the Buffalo*, p. 35.
80. Mari Sandoz, *The Buffalo Hunters*.
81. See: Tom McHugh, *The Time of the Buffalo*, pp. 173-178.
82. Larry Barsness, *Heads, Hides and Horns, The Compleat Buffalo Book*, pp. 19-20.
83. For a concise description of this constricting process see: C. C. Rister, "The Significance of the Destruction of the Buffalo in the Southwest," *Southwestern Historical Quarterly*, Vol. 33, #1 (July 1929), pp. 34-35.
84. "The Talon Interrogations," in *La Salle, The Mississippi and the Gulf*, ed. R. S. Weddle, College Station: Texas A&M Univ. Press, 1987, p. 228.
85. Onate, 249, p. 255.
86. Don H. Biggers, "The Buffalo Butchery in Texas," p. 6.
87. Richard Irving Dodge, *The Hunting Grounds of the Great West*, pp. 120, 123-234.
88. Roemer, 281, p. 207.
89. Dewees, 76, pp. 120-121.
90. J. P. Simpson, 294, pp. 26-27.
91. Larry Barsness, *Heads, Hides and Horns*, p. 183-184.
92. Frank Gilbert Roe, *The North American Buffalo*, p. 142.
93. Onate, 249, pp. 254-255.
94. Pena, 263, p. 30.
95. Amangual, 5, p. 478.
96. Edwin James, 168, p. 133.
97. Unknown member of the Black River California Company in letter, "Santa Fe, May 23, 1849," in *Southern Trails to California in 1849*, pp. 301-302.
98. Pena, 263, p. 24.
99. Richard Irving Dodge, *The Hunting Grounds of the Great West*, pp. 125-126.
100. Alexander Ross, *The Fur Hunters of the Far West*, London: Smith, Elder & Co., 1855, New edition, Norman: Univ. of Oklahoma Press, 1956.
101. Nuttall, 246, p. 210.
102. Talon, in *La Salle, the Mississippi, and the Gulf*, p. 228.
103. Joutel, 176, p. 112.
104. Wavel, 333, p. 93.
105. Gregg, 137, pp. 56-57.
106. Amangual, 5, pp. 494-495.
107. Thadis W. Box, "Range Deterioration in West Texas," *Southwestern Historical Quarterly*, Vol. 71, #1 (July 1967), p. 40.
108. James, 168, Vol. 16, p. 125.
109. Espinosa, 88, p. 7.
110. Mares, 230, pp. 299-300.
111. Roemer, 281, pp. 198-200.
112. Del Weniger, *The Explorers' Texas: The Lands & Waters*, Austin, Texas: Eakin Press, 1984, p. 11.
113. R. M. Ballantyne, *The Dog Crusoe And His Master, A Tale of the Western Prairies*, n.d., pp. 74-78.

Chapter 2: THE DEER STORY IN EARLY TEXAS

1. Bell, 19, p. 223.
2. Solis, 304, p. 540.
3. Wrede, 346, p. 76.
4. Smith, 299, p. 71.
5. *Ibid.*, p. 66.
6. Reid, 277, pp. 57-58.
7. Roemer, 281, p. 141.
8. Anon., 321, p. 75.
9. Bracht, 31, p. 159.
10. Pena, 263, p. 14.
11. Pages, 254, p. 611.
12. Pancoast, 255, p. 89.
13. Peck, 261, p. 5.
14. Shain, 291, p. 259.
15. Bracht, 31, p. 187.
16. Ikin, 165, pp. 40-41.
17. Moore, 238, p. 35.
18. Audubon & Bachman, 8, Vol. 2, p. 226.
19. Anon., 321, p. 75.
20. Parker, 257, p. 176.
21. Holley, 156, p. 99.
22. See: *National Wildlife*, Vol. 16, #6 (Oct./Nov. 1978), p. 9.
23. See: *Texas Parks & Wildlife*, Nov. 1973.
24. Dan Klepper, "Buzzards Get Fat in the Hills of Texas," *The Sunday Express-News*, Oct. 10, 1982, and "Spotty is the Word for This Season," *Express-News*, Oct. 23, 1988.
25. Audubon & Bachman, 8, Vol. 2, p. 226.
26. Baird, 11, p. 649.
27. Bell, 19, p. 231.
28. V. Bailey, "Mammals of New Mexico," U.S.D.A., *American Fauna Bulletin*, #53 (1931).
29. Dan Klepper, *The Sunday Express-News*, Oct. 10, 1982.
30. Wrede, 346, p. 101.
31. Anon., 84, p. 30.
32. Bracht, 31, pp. 41-42.
33. Audubon & Bachman, 8, Vol. 2, p. 226.
34. Baird, 11, p. 659.
35. Michler, 232, p. 17.
36. Miles, 233, p. 16.
37. Bell, 19, p. 229.

38. Byrne, 41, p. 57.
39. LeGrand, 198, p. 183.
40. O'Crouley, 247, p. 25.
41. Article: "Texas," from *The Texas Republican*, Aug. 28 or Sept. 11, 1819 (date uncertain because paper does not survive). Reprinted in *The Clarion*, and the *Tennessee State Gazette*, Oct. 5, 1819. Reprinted in *Papers Concerning Robertson's Colony in Texas*, ed. Malcolm D. McLean, Ft. Worth: Texas Christian Univ. Press, 1974, p. 254.

Chapter 3: ANTELOPES: The Texas Speedsters
1. See Dan L. Flores, *Jefferson & Southwestern Exploration*, Norman: Univ. of Oklahoma Press, 1984, p. 276, note #278, for confirmation of this location.
2. Joutel, 176, p. 164.
3. Pena, 263, p. 13.
4. Hicks, 152, p. 77.
5. Kendall, 179, p. 94.
6. Almonte, 4, p. 202.
7. Flores, *Jefferson & Southwestern Exploration*, p. 275.
8. Leach ?, 192, p. 122.
9. Johnston, 173, p. 130.
10. Bartlett, 16, p. 100.
11. Moore, 237, p. 264.
12. Marryat, 223, Vol. 2, p. 63.
13. R. M. Ballantyne, *The Dog Crusoe And His Master: A Tale of the Western Prairies*, London: Ward, Lock & Co. n.d., p. 135.
14. Froebel, 112, pp. 413-414.
15. William B. Davis, *The Mammals of Texas*, Texas Parks & Wildlife Dept., Bulletin #41, revised, 1966, p. 232.
16. Myer, 244, p. 71.
17. Echols, 81.
18. Reid, 277, p. 24.
19. Froebel, 112, p. 457.
20. Marcy, 214, p. 53; Michler, 230, p. 37.
21. Gray, 129, p. 44.
22. Kendall, 179, p. 148.
23. "H," 143, p. 189; Johnston, 171, pp. 484-485.
24. Weaver, 334, p. 188.
25. Lawrie, 191, p. 251.
26. Hasson, 147, p. 75.
27. Johnston, 173, p. 135.
28. Bartlett, 16, Vol. 1, p. 87; Ormsby, 250, p. 69.
29. Bartlett, 16, Vol. 1, pp. 83-84.
30. Echols, 81.
31. Myer, 244, pp. 43-44.
32. Cox, 55, p. 45.
33. Mendoza, 226, p. 338.
34. Roemer, 281, p. 204.
35. Harrell, 145, p. 128.
36. Ullrich, 327, p. 190.
37. Bracht, 31, p. 42.
38. Bollaert, 27, p. 9.
39. Johnston, 173, pp. 129-130.
40. Barry, 15, pp. 146, 151.
41. Hicks, 152, pp. 77-78.
42. Gauldin, 121, pp. 163-165.
43. Redfield, 276, p. 121.
44. Suthron [Page], 253, p. 116.
45. J. C. Duval, *Early Times in Texas*, Austin: Steck-Vaughn Co., 1967, p. 69.
46. Pena, 263, p. 13.
47. Olmsted, 248, p. 192.
48. Peck, 261, p. 14.
49. Gaines, 115, p. 39.
50. Bartlett, 16, Vol. 2, pp. 525-526.
51. *Ibid.*, p. 521.
52. Pereda Title, 322, p. 86.
53. Baird, 11, pp. 666-670.
54. Vernon Bailey, "Biological Survey of Texas," *North American Fauna*, U.S.D.A. Biol. Survey, #25, 1905, p. 67.
55. Robin W. Doughty, *Wildlife and Man in Texas*, College Station: Texas A&M Univ. Press, 1983, p. 53.
56. E. W. Nelson, *Wild Animals of North America*, Washington, D.C.: The National Geographic Society, 1930, p. 219.
57. Roger A. Caras, *North American Mammals*, New York: Galahad Books, 1967, p. 457.
58. Doughty, *Wildlife and Man in Texas*, p. 197.
59. Stanley Paul Young, *The Wolf in North American History*, Caldwell, ID: The Caxton Printers, 1946, pp. 100-101.

Chapter 4: TEXAS ELK
1. *Oxford English Dictionary*, entry Moose.
2. Baird, 11, p. 632.
3. Onate, 249, p. 255.
4. Edna Kahlbau, *Amarillo Sunday News & Globe*, August 14, 1938.
5. See: Vernon Bailey, "Our Noblest Deer," *Nature Magazine*, Vol. 30, #3 (Sept. 1937).
6. Sibley, 293, Vol. 2, p. 75.
7. See: H. R. Schoolcraft, *View of the Lead Mines of Missouri*, New York: Charles Wiley, 1819, p. 253; ———, "Journal of a Tour Into The Interior of Missouri and Arkansas," In Sir Richard Phillips, *New Voyages and Travels*, London, 1821, Vol. 5, p. 56; J. F. Ellis, *The Influence of Environment on the Settlement of Missouri*, St. Louis: Webster, 1929, p. 76.
8. Bean, 18, pp. 405-406.
9. Ikin, 165, p. 41.
10. Marcy, 214, pp. 21-22.
11. C. De M. (Charles De Morse), 72.
12. Kendall, 179, p. 102.
13. Kennedy, 180, p. 173.
14. Bonnell, 28, pp. 110-111.
15. Audubon & Bachman, 8, Vol. 2, pp. 93-94.
16. John Dean Caton, *The Antelope and Deer of America*, New York: Forest and Stream Pub. Co., 2nd Ed., 1877, p. 78.
17. See Dan L. Flores, *Jefferson & Southwestern Expedition*, Norman, OK: Univ. of Oklahoma Press, 1984, p. 276, note 278.
18. Richard Irving Dodge, *The Hunting Grounds of the Great West*, London: Chatto & Windus, 1877, p. 155.
19. Parker Gillmore, *Prairie and Forest: A Description of the Game of North America*, London: Chapman & Hall, 1874, p. 77.

Chapter 5: THE TEXAS BIGHORN MOUNTAIN SHEEP
1. Quoted in J. A. Allen, "Historical and Nomenclatorial Notes on North American Sheep," *Bulletin of the American Museum of Natural History*, Vol. 31, 1912, pp. 3, 4.
2. C. M. Barber, "Notes on Little Known New Mexican Mammals and Species Apparently Not Recorded from the Territory," *Proceedings of the Biological Society of Washington*, Vol. 15, 1902, p. 191.

3. V. Bailey, "A New Subspecies of Mountain Sheep from Western Texas and Southeastern New Mexico," *Proceedings of the Biological Society of Washington*, Vol. 25, 1912, pp. 109-110.

4. See Ben Tinker, *Mexican Wilderness and Wildlife*, Austin: Univ. of Texas Press, 1978, pp. 30-31.

5. See William B. Davis, *The Mammals of Texas*, Texas Parks and Wildlife Dept., Bulletin # 41, Revised, 1966, p. 242.

6. Sibley, 293, Vol. 2, p. 75.

7. Marcy, 217, p. 186.

8. Ikin, 165, p. 41.

9. Fowler, 103, p. 145.

10. Froebel, 112, p. 458.

11. Helmut K. Buechner, "The Bighorn Sheep in the U.S., Its Past, Present and Future," *Wildlife Monographs*, 4 (May 1960), p. 13.

12. W. B. Davis & W. P. Taylor, "The Bighorn Sheep of Texas," *Journal of Mammology*, Vol. 20, #4 (1939), pp. 445-455.

13. Allen, "Historical and Nomenclatorial Notes . . . ," p. 4.

14. Barber, "Notes on Little Known . . . Mammals and Species . . . ," p. 191.

15. Davis & Taylor, "The Bighorn Sheep of Texas," p. 450.

16. G. B. Grinnell, "Mountain Sheep," *Journal of Mammology*, Vol. 9, #1, 1928, pp. 2, 3, f.

17. Tinker, *Mexican Wilderness & Wildlife*, p. 31.

Chapter 6: THE BEARS OF THE TEXAS HILLS

1. Marin de Porras, 271, p. 27.

2. Olmsted, 248, p. 130.

3. Domenech, 77, p. 34.

4. Olmsted, 248, pp. 130-131.

5. Wrede, 346, p. 112.

6. Smith, 299, p. 65.

7. Clopper, 50, pp. 77-78.

8. Berlandier, 23, pp. 16, 36.

9. Nuttall, 246, p. 210.

10. Parker, 257, p. 192.

11. Audubon & Bachman, 8, Vol. 3, p. 189.

12. Fowler, 103, p. 145.

13. Bracht, 31, p. 43.

14. Marcy, 217, p. 186.

15. Berlandier, 24, pp. 134-135.

16. John O. Whitaker, Jr., *Audubon Society Field Guide to North American Mammals*, New York: Knopf, 1980.

17. Bailey, *North American Fauna*, p. 187.

18. William B. Davis, "Identity of the Central Texas Bear," *Journal of Mammology*, Vol. 26, #4 (1945), p. 434.

19. Bailey, *North American Fauna*, p. 186.

20. See: Dan L. Flores, *Jefferson & Southwestern Exploration*, p. 230, note #89.

21. Marryat, 223, Vol. 2, pp. 89-90.

22. James, 168, Vol. 16, pp. 100-101.

23. Abert, 2, p. 76.

24. Marcy, 214, p. 61.

25. Sanchez, 288, p. 256.

26. Espinosa, 87, p. 157.

27. Lafora, 188, pp. 171-172.

28. Evia, 94, p. 416.

29. Talon, 315, p. 4.

30. Austin, 10, p. 307.

31. Holley, 155, p. 162.

32. Anon., 331, p. 61.

33. Cushing, 60, p. 209.

34. Morgan, 240, p. 67.

35. D. J. Schmidly, *Texas Mammals East of the Balcones Fault Zone*, College Station: Texas A&M Press, 1983, p. 307.

Chapter 7: WOLVES AT THE DOOR

1. Cushing, 60, pp. 208-209.

2. Guenther, 142, letter 11 (Feb. 1, 1851).

3. Tennery, 318, p. 24.

4. Reid, 277, p. 100.

5. John T. Hughes, 163, p. 390.

6. James, 168, Vol. 16, p. 103.

7. Custis, 62, p. 274.

8. Solis, 305, p. 18.

9. Roemer, 281, p. 80.

10. Bollaert, 27, p. 7.

11. McClintock, 208, p. 28.

12. Moore, 237, p. 264.

13. Sibley, 293, Vol. 2, p. 75.

14. Reid, 277, p. 124.

15. Tennery, 318, pp. 32-33.

16. Sr. M. Patrick & Sr. M. Joseph, 175, p. 350.

17. Bracht, 31, p. 45.

18. A. A. Parker, 257, p. 191.

19. James Ohio Pattie, *The Personal Narrative of James O. Pattie . . .* , ed. Timothy Flint, Cincinnati: E. R. Flint Publisher, 1833, pp. 28-29.

20. Berlandier, 23, pp. 16-18.

21. R. M. Ballantyne, *The Dog Crusoe And His Master, A Tale of The Western Prairies*, London: Lock & Co., undated, pp. 138-140, 247-248.

22. David H. Coyner, *The Lost Trappers; A Collection of Interesting Scenes and Events in the Rocky Mountains; Together With a Short Description of California; Also, Some Accounts of the Fur Trade*, Cincinnati: H. M. Rulison, Queen City Pub. House & Philadelphia: Quaker City Pub. House, 1855, pp. 58-60.

23. Audubon & Bachman, 8, Vol. 2, pp. 156, 157, 161.

24. Hasson, 147, p. 75.

25. Richard Irving Dodge, *The Hunting Grounds of the Great West*, London: Chatto & Windus, 1877, p. 209.

26. J. C. Duval, *Early Times in Texas*, 1967.

27. O. C. Fisher, *It Occurred in Kimble*, Anson Jones Press, 1937, pp. 33-34.

28. V. Bailey, "Biological Survey of Texas," *North American Fauna*, 25, 1905, pp. 171-172.

29. Colt, 53, p. 33; Fisher, 99, p. 33.

30. Holley, 156, p. 95.

31. Roemer, 281, p. 113.

32. Audubon & Bachman, 8, Vol. 2, p. 131.

33. V. Bailey, "Biological Survey of Texas," pp. 173-174.

34. Roemer, 281, p. 233.

35. *Ibid.*, p. 80.

36. Gregg, 133, p. 247.

37. Audubon & Bachman, 8, Vol. 2, p. 151.

38. Baird, 11, p. 113.

39. Audubon & Bachman, 8, Vol. 2, pp. 240, 241, 243.

40. Baird, 11, p. 113.

41. Dan L. Flores, *Jefferson & Southwestern Exploration*, Norman: Univ. of Oklahoma Press, 1984, p. 274, note.

42. Parker Gillmore, *Prairie and Forest: A Description of the Game of North America*, London: Chapman & Hall, 1874, pp. 161-164.

43. See the Pereda Title, August 10, 1810, Spanish Archives of the General Land Office, Vol. 67, p. 11, quoted and translated in Virginia H. Taylor, *The Spanish Archives of the General Land Office of Texas*, Austin: The Lone Star Press, 1955, p. 86.
44. Ehrenberg, 83, p. 42.
45. *Ibid.*, p. 30.
46. Audubon & Bachman, 8, Vol. 2, p. 151.
47. Pages, 254, p. 603.
48. Richard Irving Dodge, *The Hunting Grounds . . .*, p. 209.
49. See William B. Davis, *The Mammals of Texas*, Texas Parks & Wildlife Dept., Bulletin #41, revised, 1966, p. 108; David J. Schmidly, *Texas Mammals East of the Balcones Fault Zone*, pp. 235-236; William B. Davis & David J. Schmidly, *The Mammals of Texas*, Austin: Texas Parks & Wildlife Dept., 1994, p. 214.
50. See S. P. Young & H.H.T. Jackson, *The Clever Coyote*, Harrisburg, Pennsylvania: The Stackpole Co., and Washington, D.C.: The Wildlife Management Institute, 1951, p. 14. See: J. L. Paradiso, "Recent Records of Coyotes . . . from the Southeastern U.S.," *Southwestern Naturalist*, Vol. 2, 1967, pp. 500-501; J. L. Paradiso, "Canids Recently Collected in East Texas, with Comments on the Taxonomy of the Red Wolf," *The American Midland Naturalist*, Vol. 80, #2 (Oct. 1968), p. 529.
51. Sweet & Knox, "Coyote," *Sketches From Texas Siftings*, N.Y.: Texas Siftings Pub. Co., 1882, pp. 94-98.
52. Steinert, 309, Vol. 81, p. 47.
53. A. A. Parker, 257, p. 192.
54. Ikin, 165, p. 50.
55. Kendall, 178, p. 55.
56. Audubon & Bachman, 8, Vol. 2, p. 160.
57. J. L. Paradiso, "Candis Recently Collected in East Texas . . . ," pp. 529-530, 533. Also see: David J. Schmidly, *Texas Mammals East of the Balcones Fault Zone*, College Station, Texas: Texas A&M Univ. Press, 1983, pp. 241-243.
58. See: James, 168, Vol. 16, p. 135.
59. Edward Smith, 299, p. 65.
60. Steinert, 309, Vol. 80, p. 75.
61. Tips, 326, Letter, New Braunfels, Jan. 8, 1850.
62. Anon., 321, p. 75.
63. Coyner, 56, pp. 74-75.
64. Talon, 315, p. 14.
65. John C. Reid, 277, pp. 57-58.
66. David J. Schmidly, *Texas Mammals East of the Balcones Fault Zone*, College Station, Texas: Texas A&M Univ. Press, 1983, p. 235.
67. William B. Davis, *The Mammals of Texas*, Texas Parks & Wildlife Dept., Bulletin #41, revised, 1966, p. 113.
68. David J. Schmidly, *Texas Mammals East of the Balcones Fault Zone*, pp. 241, 243.

Chapter 8: TEXAS CATS
1. Bracht, 31, p. 183.
2. Francis Moore, Jr., 238, p. 33.
3. E. W. Nelson & E. A. Goldman, "Revision of the Jaguars," *Journal of Mammology*, Vol. 14, #3, 1933, pp. 221-240.
4. Anon., 84, p. 30.
5. Ullrich, 327, p. 190.
6. Audubon & Bachman, 8, Vol. 3, p. 9.
7. See: Dan L. Flores, *Jefferson & Southwestern Exploration*, Norman: Univ. of Okla. Press, 1984, p. 271, note #269.
8. Talon, 315, p. 4.
9. Domenech, 77, pp. 142-143.
10. Field, 98, p. 48.
11. Lindheimer, 200, letter.
12. Bracht, 31, pp. 43-44.
13. Baird, 11, pp. 83, 86.
14. Audubon & Bachman, 8, Vol. 3, p. 4.
15. Almonte, 4, p. 202.
16. The Pereda title, August 10, 1810, Spanish Archives of the General Land Office, Vol. 67, p. 11, quoted & translated in Virginia H. Taylor, *The Spanish Archives of the General Land Office of Texas*, Austin: The Lone Star Press, 1955, p. 86.
17. Bracht, 31, pp. 183-184.
18. Audubon & Bachman, 8 Vol. 3, p. 9.
19. *Ibid.*, p. 4.
20. Ben Tinker, *Mexican Wilderness & Wildlife*, Austin: Univ. of Texas Press, 1978, p. 89.
21. Audubon & Bachman, 8, Vol. 3, p. 6.
22. *Ibid.*, p. 9.
23. O. C. Fisher, *It Occurred in Kimble*, Anson Jones Press, 1937, pp. 34-35.
24. Audubon & Bachman, 8, Vol. 3, p. 9.
25. Baird, 11, p. 86.
26. V. Bailey, "Biological Survey of Texas," *North American Fauna*, Vol. 25, 1905, pp. 163-164.
27. A. F. Halloran, "The Goldthwaite Jaguar," *Texas Game and Fish*, Vol. 4, #7, 1946, p. 25.
28. See Nelson & Goldman, "Revision of the Jaguars."
29. Anon., 84, pp. 30-31.
30. Bracht, 31, pp. 43-44.
31. Eliza Johnston, 171, pp. 489-490.
32. Audubon & Bachman, 8, Vol. 3, pp. 3-4, 10.
33. Field, 98, p. 48.
34. Nelson & Goldman, "Revision of the Jaguars."
35. Ben Tinker, *Mexican Wilderness & Wildlife*, p. 89.
36. Henry, 149.
37. O. C. Fisher, *It Occurred in Kimble*.
38. W. P. Taylor, "Recent Records of the Jaguar in Texas," *Journal of Mammology*, Vol. 28, #1, 1947, p. 66.
39. Ben Tinker, *Mexican Wilderness & Wildlife*, pp. 87-88, 89.
40. Gordon Chaplin, "El Tigre Hombre," *Audubon Mag.*, July 1985.
41. *The Encyclopedia of Mammals*, ed. Macdonald.
42. Olmsted, 248, p. 111.
43. Editor of letter by J.M.C., 170, p. 3.
44. C. De M. (Charles De Morse), 70.
45. Marcy, 214, p. 55.
46. Bracht, 31, p. 187.
47. Ikin, 165, p. 42.
48. Audubon & Bachman, 8, Vol. 2, p. 306.
49. Roemer, 281, pp. 260-261.
50. Bracht, 31, p. 44.
51. Richard Irving Dodge, *The Hunting Grounds of the Great West*, pp. 217-219.
52. Webber, 335, pp. 406-408.
53. J.M.C., 170, p. 3.
54. Kennedy, 180, p. 125.
55. O. C. Fisher, *It Happened in Kimble*, pp. 34-35.
56. Froebel, 112, pp. 412-415.
57. Wrede, 346, p. 101.
58. Shain, 291, p. 262.

59. Domenech, 77, pp. 29-30, 65-66, 142-143, 160.
60. Anon., 166, p. 340.
61. Marcy, 214, pp. 54-55.
62. Steinert, 309, Vol. 80, p. 178.
63. C. De M. (Charles De Morse), 70.
64. Edward Smith, 299, p. 70.
65. W. B. Conger, "The Real Cougar," *Nature Magazine*, Oct. 1938, p. 491.
66. W. H. Hudson, *The Naturalist in La Plata*, New York: Appleton & Co., 3rd ed. 1895, pp. 36-58.
67. Audubon & Bachman, 8, Vol. 2, p. 309.
68. Stanley P. Young in *The Puma: Mysterious American Cat*, by Young and Goldman, Washington, D.C.: The American Wildlife Institute, 1946, p. 99.
69. *Ibid.*, pp. 51-52.
70. A. A. Parker, 257, p. 192.
71. Olmsted, 248, p. 111.
72. Anon., "Thereby Hangs a Tail," in *Tales of Frontier Texas, 1830–1860*, Dallas: Southern Methodist Univ. Press, 1966, pp. 220-221. (Reprinted from *Spirit* XXII, #44 (Dec. 18, 1852) p. 520), this said to be reprinted from the New Orleans *Picayune*.
73. Maverick, 225, p. 336.
74. Ker, 181, p. 118.
75. F. W. True, "The Puma, or American Lion: *Felis concolor* of Linnaeus," *Annual Reports*, U.S. National Museum, 1889, p. 603.
76. W. H. Hudson, *The Naturalist in La Plata*, p. 38.
77. Francis Moore, Jr., 238, p. 33.
78. Roemer, 281, pp. 141-142.
79. Francis Smith, 300, p. 280.
80. Bracht, 31, p. 44.
81. Almonte, 4, p. 202.
82. Dresel, 78, p. 82.
83. V. Bailey, "Biol. Survey of Texas," p. 166.
84. Baird, 11, p. 87.
85. W. B. Davis, "Unusual Record of the Ocelot in Texas," *Journal of Mammology*, Vol. 32, 1951, pp. 363-364.
86. Audubon & Bachman, 8, Vol. 2, p. 260.
87. Wrede, 346, p. 101.
88. Anon., 84, p. 31.
89. Berlandier, 23, p. 46.
90. Audubon & Bachman, 8, Vol. 2, p. 295.
91. Ullrich, 327, p. 190.
92. William B. Davis, *The Mammals of Texas*, p. 120.
93. Baird, 11, p. 88.
94. Hollister, "The Spotted Tiger Cat in Texas," *Proceedings of the Biological Society of Washington*, Vol. 27, 1914, p. 219.

Chapter 9:   TEXAS LITTLE FOXES
1. Baird, 11, p. 130.
2. See: Richard Clapham, *The Book of the Fox*, New York: The Derrydale Press, 1931, pp. 11-12.
3. See: Robin W. Doughty, *Wildlife & Man in Texas*, College Station: Texas A&M Press, 1983, p. 93.
4. See: Hasson, 147, p. 75; Bracht, 31, p. 45; Ullrich, 327, p. 190.
5. Wrede, 346, p. 115.
6. Holley, 156, p. 99.
7. Anon., 84, pp. 30-31.

Chapter 10:   TEXAS HOGS: Native and Naturalized
1. Ganilh, 119, Vol. 2, p. 70.
2. Roemer, 281, p. 250.
3. Holley, 155, p. 162.
4. Ullrich, 327, p. 190.
5. Sibley, 293, Vol. 2, p. 75.
6. Dewees, 76, p. 25.
7. Fretelliere, 111, p. 94.
8. Pickett, 266, p. 54.
9. John C. Reid, 277, pp. 97-98.
10. Holley, 156, p. 95.
11. Bracht, 31, pp. 43, 159.
12. Roemer, 281, p. 142.
13. Porras, 271, p. 27.
14. O. C. Fisher, *It Occurred in Kimble*, Anson Jones Press, 1937, p. 31.
15. Audubon & Bachman, 8, Vol. 1, p. 239.
16. Baird, 11, p. 627.
17. William B. Davis, *The Mammals of Texas*, Austin: Texas Parks and Wildlife Dept., Bulletin 41, Revised 1966, p. 229.
18. Nuttall, 246, p. 216.
19. Webster, 336, p. 4.
20. Ganilh, 119, Vol. 2, p. 70.
21. Fretelliere, 111, p. 94.
22. Gregg, 133, p. 247.
23. De Cordova, 66, p. 258.
24. Francis Moore, Jr., 238, p. 33.
25. John C. Reid, 277, p. 97.
26. French, 110, p. 52.
27. Mezieres, 228, p. 340.
28. Rupert Norvel Richardson, *The Frontier of Northwest Texas 1846 to 1876*, Glendale, Calif.: The Arthur H. Clark Co., 1963, p. 131.
29. Lynn A. Simpson & Terry C. Maxwell, "The Mammal Fauna of Coke County, Texas," *The Texas Journal of Science*, Vol. 41, #2, 1989, p. 188.
30. Holley, 155, p. 162.
31. Kendall, 179, p. 87.
32. William B. Davis, *The Mammals of Texas*, p. 230.
33. *Ibid.*
34. Holley, 156, p. 95.
35. Bracht, 31, p. 43.
36. Ikin, 165, p. 42.
37. Audubon & Bachman, 8, Vol. 1, p. 238.
38. Ann Raney Coleman, *Victorian Lady on the Texas Frontier, The Journal of Ann Raney Coleman*, ed. C. Richard King, Norman, OK: Univ. of Okla. Press, 1971, pp. 64-65.
39. W. H. Flower & R. Lydekker, *An Introduction to the Study of Mammals Living and Extinct*, London: Adam & Charles Black, 1891, pp. 290-291.
40. Webber, 335, pp. 385-387.
41. Audubon and Bachman, 8, Vol. 1, p. 238.
42. Bracht, 31, p. 43.
43. Roemer, 281, p. 251.
44. Miles, 233, p. 14.
45. John C. Reid, 277, p. 98.
46. A. A. Parker, 257, p. 192.
47. Jose Enrique de la Pena, 262, p. 101.
48. Brooks, 35, pp. 55-56.
49. Holley, 156, p. 96.
50. Steinert, 309, Vol. 80, p. 285.
51. Domenech, 77, p. 66.
52. Hooton, 158, p. 47.
53. See: Del Weniger, "Wilderness, Farm, and Ranch," *San Antonio in the Eighteenth Century*, San Antonio: San Antonio Bicentennial Heritage Committee, 1976, pp. 111-113.

54. Olmsted, 248, pp. 33, 37.
55. Talon, "Voyage to the Mississippi Through the Gulf of Mexico," translated Ann Linda Bell, in *La Salle, the Mississippi, and the Gulf*, ed. Robert S. Weddle, College Station: Texas A&M Univ. Press, 1987, p. 233.
56. Maria, 222, p. 211.

Chapter 11: MORE THAN CRITTERS
1. Friedrich W. von Wrede, 346, p. 101.
2. See for reports on: Chambers County, Anon., 331, p. 61; Sabine, San Augustine & Nacogdoches counties, Wrede, 346, p. 120; Starr & Hidalgo counties, Tennery, 318, pp. 39-40; Comal County, Ullrich, 327, p. 190; Jones County, Hasson, 147, p. 75; El Paso County, Baird, 11, p. 214.
3. Bracht, 31, p. 44.
4. Roemer, 281, p. 142.
5. Audubon & Bachman, 8, Vol. 2, p. 78.
6. Steinert, 309, Vol. 80, p. 285.
7. Dresel, 78, p. 85.
8. David J. Schmidly, *Texas Mammals East of the Balcones Fault Zone*, College Station: Texas A&M Univ. Press, 1983, p. 258.
9. Baird, 11, pp. 212-214.
10. Roemer, 281, p. 259.
11. Audubon & Bachman, 8, Vol. 2, pp. 316 & 218.
12. See David J. Schmidly, *Texas Mammals East of the Balcones Fault Zone*, pp. 252-253.
13. *Ibid.*, p. 254; W. P. Taylor, "Food Habits and Notes on Life History of the Ringtailed Cat in Texas," *Journal of Mammology*, Vol. 35, #1, 1954, p. 61.
14. Fowler, 103, p. 142.
15. William B. Davis, *The Mammals of Texas*, Austin: Texas Parks and Wildlife Dept., Bulletin 41, revised 1966, p. 102.
16. Baird, 11, p. 205.
17. Lindheimer, 200.
18. See: W. B. Davis, "Additional Records of Badgers Killed on Highways," *Journal of Mammalogy*, Vol. 26, #1, 1945, p. 89; V. S. Schantz, "Three New Races of Badgers (Taxidea) from the Southwestern United States," *Journal of Mammalogy*, Vol. 30, #3, 1949, pp. 301-305.
19. David Schmidly, *Texas Mammals East of the Balcones Fault Zone*, p. 266.
20. Eugene C. Barker, "A Glimpse of the Texas Fur Trade in 1832," *The Southwestern Historical Quarterly*, Vol. 19, #3 (January 1916), p. 280.
21. Ronald M. Nowak & John L. Paradiso, *Walker's Mammals of the World*, Baltimore & London: The Johns Hopkins Univ. Press, 4th ed., 1983, Vol. 2, p. 1009.
22. Quoted in *The Oxford English Dictionary*, entry Polecat.
23. *Ibid.*
24. *Ibid.*
25. Berlandier, 23, p. 18.
26. Abert, 2, p. 54.
27. Audubon & Bachman, 8, Vol. 1, p. 320.
28. *Ibid.*, Vol. 2, pp. 19-20.
29. See: Dragoo, Fagre, Schmidly & Peenry, "First Specimen of a Hog-nosed Skunk . . . from Bexar County, Texas," *The Texas Journal of Science*, Vol. 41, #3, 1989, pp. 331-333.
30. See David J. Schmidly, *Texas Mammals East of the Balcones Fault Zone*, pp. 279-283.
31. See J. A. Allen, "On the Mammals of Aransas County, Texas," *Bulletin of American Museum of Nat. History*, Vol. 6, 1894, pp. 165-198.
32. Audubon & Bachman, 8, Vol. 3, p. 13.
33. Baird, 11, pp. 197-199.
34. Bracht, 31, p. 44.
35. David Macdonald, *The Encyclopedia of Mammals*, New York: Facts on File Publications, 1984, p. 122.
36. Mari Sandoz, *The Buffalo Hunters*, New York: The Hastings House Publishers, 1954, p. 131.
37. *Ibid.*, p. 133.
38. J. D. Mitchell, " 'Mexican Polecat,' 'Hydrophobia Cat,' *Spilogale Indianola* of Southern Texas," *Journal of Mammology*, Vol. 4, 1923, pp. 49-51.
39. V. Bailey, "Joseph D. Mitchell," *Journal of Mammology*, Vol. 4, 1923, p. 48.
40. W. K. Cuyler, "Observations on the Habits of the Striped Skunk," *Journal of Mammology*, Vol. 5, 1924, p. 183.
41. William B. Davis, *The Mammals of Texas*, p. 94.
42. Berlandier, 23, p. 18.
43. Clopper, 50, p. 77.
44. Abert, 2, p. 54.
45. W. H. Hudson, *The Naturalist in La Plata*, New York: D. Appleton & Co., 1895, p. 120.
46. Audubon & Bachman, 8, Vol. 2, p. 4.
47. *Ibid.*, p. 10.
48. Bracht, 31, p. 44.
49. Burnet, 38, pp. 88-89.
50. Nowak & Paradiso, *Walker's Mammals of the World*.
51. Jean Berlandier, *The Indians of Texas in 1830*, Washington, D.C.: Smithsonian Institute Press, 1969, pp. 47, 108, 120.
52. Friedrich W. von Wrede, 346, p. 76.
53. Kennedy, 180, p. 125.
54. Custis, 62, p. 274.
55. Solis, 305, pp. 25-26.
56. Anon., 84, p. 30.
57. Audubon & Bachman, 8, Vol. 2, pp. 8-10.
58. David J. Schmidly, *Texas Mammals East of the Balcones Fault Zone*, p. 29.
59. Bracht, 31, p. 44.
60. J. A. Allen, "A Preliminary Study of the North American Opossums of the genus Didelphis," *Bulletin of the American Museum of Natural History*, Vol. 14, 1901, pp. 149-188.
61. W. B. Davis, "Notes on Mexican Mammals," *Journal of Mammology*, Vol. 25, 1944, p. 375.
62. W. B. Davis, *The Mammals of Texas*, p. 29.
63. Joutel, 176, p. 124.
64. Baird, 11, p. 234.
65. Francis Moore, Jr., 238, p. 35.
66. Bracht, 31, p. 44.
67. Ullrich, 327, p. 190.
68. Friedrich W. von Wrede, 346, p. 76 and Friedrich Wilhelm von Wrede, Jr., 347, p. 115.
69. Friedrich W. von Wrede, 346, p. 120.
70. See: Carl G. Hartman, *Possums*, Austin: University of Texas Press, 1952.
71. See: *Oxford English Dictionary*, entry Opossum.
72. Audubon & Bachman, 8, Vol. 3, p. 224.
73. Webster, 336, p. 4.
74. Baird, 11, pp. 623-624.
75. Bracht, 31, p. 45.
76. Tennery, 318, p. 24.
77. Audubon & Bachman, 8, Vol. 3, p. 225.

78. John K. Strecker, "The Extention of the Range of the Nine-banded Armadillo," *Journal of Mammology*, Vol. 7, 1926, p. 207.
79. See: F. W. Taber, "Extention of the Range of the Armadillo," *Journal of Mammology*, Vol. 20, 1939, pp. 490-491.
80. See: Fitch, Goodrum, & Newman, "The Armadillo in the Southeastern U.S.," *Journal of Mammology*, Vol. 33, 1952, pp. 21-37.
81. See: W. K. Clark, "Ecological Life History of the Armadillo in the Eastern Edwards Plateau Region," *American Midland Naturalist*, Vol. 46, 1951, pp. 337-358.
82. David J. Schmidly, *Texas Mammals East of the Balcones Fault Zone*, p. 103.
83. See: Gordon Chapin, "El Tigre Hombre," *Audubon Magazine*, July 1985.
84. See: E. R. Kalmbach, "The Armadillo: Its Relation to Agriculture and Game," Austin: Texas Game, Fish and Oyster Commission, 1943.

Chapter 12: THE RODENTS AS THEY WERE IN TEXAS

1. See: *Oxford English Dictionary*, entry Varmint.
2. Marcy, 214, pp. 36-37.
3. Froebel, 112, pp. 151-152.
4. Ruxton, 285, p. 170.
5. Solis, 305, pp. 25-26.
6. Calleja, 43, p. 473.
7. Porras, 271, p. 26.
8. Custis, 62, p. 274.
9. Eugene C. Barker, "A Glimpse of the Texas Fur Trade in 1832," *Southwestern Historical Quarterly*, Vol. 19, #3, (Jan. 1916), p. 280.
10. Kennedy, 180, p. 125.
11. Anon., 84, p. 30.
12. Burnet, 38, p. 89.
13. Bracht, 31, p. 44.
14. Maverick, 225, p. 335.
15. French, 110, p. 52.
16. Froebel, 112, pp. 454-455.
17. Marcy, 214, p. 50.
18. W. R. Long, "Prairie Dog," *Texas Parks & Wildlife*, Vol. 29, #5, (May 1971), p. 21.
19. C. H. Merriam, "The Prairie Dogs of the Great Plains," U.S. Dept. Agriculture *Yearbook*, 1901, p. 258.
20. Baird, 11, pp. 331-334.
21. Bryan, 37, p. 22; Bartlett, 16, Vol. 1, p. 128.
22. Bartlett, 16, Vol. 1, pp. 109-110.
23. Falconer, 96, p. 211.
24. Kendall, 179, p. 189.
25. James G. Bell, 19, p. 217.
26. Anthony Glass, "Copy of a Journal of a Voyage from Naekitosh into the interior of Louisiana on the Waters of Red River, Trinity, Brassus, Colorado and the Sabine performed between the first of July 1808 and May 1809," Silliman Family Collection, Historical Manuscript Collection, Yale University Library, unpublished.
27. Dan L. Flores, *Jefferson & Southwestern Exploration*, Norman, Okla.: Univ. of Okla. Press, 1984, p. 272, note #271.
28. Audubon & Bachman, 8, Vol. 2, p. 326.
29. Ehrenberg, 83, pp. 123-124, 130-131.
30. C. B. Koford, "Prairie dogs, whitefaces and blue grama," *Wildlife Monographs*, #3, 1958, p. 62.
31. Whipple, 338, p. 29.
32. Roemer, 281, pp. 252-253.
33. John C. Reid, 277, p. 100.
34. James G. Bell, 19, p. 218.
35. Marcy, 217, p. 184.
36. James G. Bell, 19, pp. 227-228.
37. Bartlett, 16, Vol. 1, p. 69.
38. French, 110, p. 48.
39. Robin W. Doughty, *Wildlife and Man in Texas*, College Station: Texas A&M Univ. Press, 1983, p. 107.
40. C. B. Koford, "Prairie dogs, whitefaces and blue grama," p. 6.
41. *Ibid.*, pp. 8-9.
42. *Ibid.*, p. 37.
43. L. C. Whitehead, "Notes on Prairie dogs," *Journal of Mammology*, Vol. 8, #1, 1927, p. 58.
44. Bartlett, 16, Vol. 1, p. 70.
45. Leach ?, 192, p. 139.
46. John C. Reid, 277, pp. 100-101.
47. William Preston Johnston, 173, p. 144.
48. James, 168, Vol. 16, p. 99.
49. James G. Bell, 19, p. 225.
50. Marcy, 217, p. 185.
51. E. W. Nelson, *Wild Animals of North America*, Washington, D.C.: The National Geographic Society, 1930, p. 124.
52. W. R. Long, "Prairie Dog," p. 21.
53. Robin W. Doughty, *Wildlife and Man in Texas*, p. 107.
54. James G. Bell, 19, p. 226.
55. Marryat, 223, Vol. 2, p. 79.
56. C. H. Merriam, "The Prairie Dogs of the Great Plains," p. 265.
57. Robin W. Doughty, *Wildlife and Man in Texas*, p. 107.
58. Baird, 11, pp. 310-311, 319-320.
59. Gibbes, 123, p. 160.
60. Lundy, 203, pp. 97-98.
61. Friedrich W. von Wrede, 346, p. 101.
62. Edward Smith, 299, p. 31.
63. Bracht, 31, p. 45.
64. David J. Schmidly, *Texas Mammals East of the Balcones Fault Zone*, College Station: Texas A&M Univ. Press, 1983, p. 123.
65. See: Domenech, 77, p. 24.
66. See: E. W. Nelson, *Wild Animals of North America*, p. 134.
67. Baird, *Proc. Acad. Nat. Sci. of Philadelphia*, Vol. 7, 1855, p. 331.
68. Baird, *Mammals of North America*, p. 256.
69. E. W. Nelson, "Revision of the Squirrels of Mexico and Central America," *Proceedings of the Washington Acad. of Science*, Vol. 1, 1899, pp. 97-98.
70. J. A. Allen, *Monograph of North American Rodentia*, 1877, p. 724.
71. Roemer, 281, p. 142.
72. Edward, 82, p. 75.
73. John K. Strecker, "Notes on the Texas Cotton and Attwater Wood Rats in Texas," *Journal of Mammology*, Vol. 10, #3, 1929, p. 216.
74. Hasson, 147, p. 75.
75. David E. Davis, "Notes on Commensal Rats in Lavaca County, Texas," *Journal of Mammology*, Vol. 28, #3, 1947, pp. 241-244.
76. R. H. Baker & D. W. Lay, "Notes on the Mammals of

Galveston and Mustang Islands, Texas," *Journal of Mammology,* Vol. 19, #4, 1938, p. 505.
   77. Hooton, 158, pp. 43-44.
   78. James G. Bell, 19, p. 234.

Chapter 13:   THEY RUSHED AROUND THE TEXAS BRUSH
   1. Maria, 222, p. 211.
   2. Pena, 262, pp. 32-33.
   3. Pena, 263, p. 12.
   4. The Pereda Title, August 10, 1810, quoted and translated in Virginia H. Taylor, *The Spanish Archives of the General Land Office of Texas,* Austin: The Lone Star Press, 1955, p. 86.
   5. *The Oxford Dictionary,* entry: Rabbit.
   6. Bracht, 31, p. 44.
   7. Fowler, 103, p. 142.
   8. Bell, 19, p. 222.
   9. Reid, 277, p. 100.
   10. Del Weniger, *The Explorers' Texas, The Lands and Waters,* Austin: Eakin Press, 1984, pp. 30-53.
   11. *Ibid.,* pp. 3-7.
   12. *Ibid.,* pp. 7-11.
   13. Catlin, 47, Vol. 2, pp. 19-20.
   14. David J. Schmidly, *Texas Mammals East of the Balcones Fault Zone,* College Station: Texas A&M Univ. Press, 1983, pp. 112-113.
   15. See E. J. Dyksterhuis, "The Vegetation of the Western Cross Timbers," *Ecological Monographs,* Vol. 18, July 1948, Map, p. 329.
   16. R. B. Marcy, *Thirty Years of Army Life on the Border,* New York: Harper & Bros., 1866.
   17. See W. E. Bruner, "The Vegetation of Oklahoma," *Ecological Monographs,* Vol. 1, 1931, pp. 99-188.
   18. See H. L. Shantz & R. Zon, "The Physical Basis of Agriculture: Natural Vegetation," *Atlas of American Agriculture,* U.S. Dept. of Agriculture, Bureau of Agricultural Economics, 1924, Pt. 1, sect. E.; F. E. Clements & B. C. Tharp, "Coastal Prairie (*Stipa-Andropogon* Association)," in *Carnegie Institute of Washington Yearbook,* Vol. 25, 1926, pp. 358-359; J. E. Weaver & F. E. Clements, *Plant Ecology,* New York: McGraw-Hill, 2nd. ed., 1938; F. E. Elements & V. E. Shelford, *Bio-ecology,* New York: John Wiley & Sons, 1939.
   19. Dewees, 76, p. 219.
   20. Anon., 331, pp. 16-17.
   21. See H. Harold Shamel, "The Subgeneric Position of the *Lepus Californicus* Group of Hares," *Proceedings of the Biological Society of Washington,* Vol. 55, May 12, 1942, pp. 25-26.
   22. Custis, 62, p. 272 & note #271.
   23. Audubon & Bachman, 8, Vol. 2, pp. 97-99.
   24. *Ibid.,* 8, Vol. 3.
   25. Baird, 11, pp. 590-608.
   26. Reid, 277, p. 101.
   27. Audubon & Bachman, 8, Vol. 3.
   28. Bell, 19, p. 226.
   29. Bartlett, 16, Vol. 1, pp. 75, 76, 87.
   30. Baird, 11.
   31. William B. Davis, *The Mammals of Texas,* Austin: Texas Parks & Wildlife Dept., Bulletin #41, Revised 1966, p. 224.
   32. Hendricks, 148, p. 139.
   33. See W. F. Blair & C. E. Miller, Jr., "The Mammals of the Sierra Vieja Region, southwestern Texas...," *Texas Journal of Science,* Vol. 1, #1, 1949, pp. 67-92.
   34. W. F. Blair, "Mammals of the Tamaulipan Biotic Province in Texas," *Texas Journal of Science,* Vol. 4, #2, 1952, pp. 230-250.
   35. William B. Davis, *The Mammals of Texas,* p. 225.
   36. John Bachman, *Journal of the Academy of Natural Sciences of Philadelphia,* Vol. 7, 1837, p. 319.
   37. J. A. Allen, "On the Mammals of Aransas County, Texas, with Descriptions of New Forms of *Lepus* and *Oryzomys, Bulletin of the American Museum of Natural History,* Vol. 6, 1894, pp. 165-198.
   38. See: William B. Davis, *The Mammals of Texas,* p. 225.
   39. See: E. W. Nelson, *Wild Animals of North America,* Washington, D.C. The National Geographic Society, 1930, p. 200.
   40. August Fretelliere, 111, p. 92.

Chapter 14:   MERELY NOTED IN PASSING
   1. Rebecca Sherman, "Wild in the City," *Dallas Life Magazine,* January 28, 1990.
   2. Hasson, 147, p. 75.
   3. Steinert, 309, Vol. 80, p. 287.
   4. Ehrenberg, 83, p. 111.
   5. Joutel, 176, p. 82.
   6. See: Albert S. Gatschet, "The Karankawa Indians, the Coast People of Texas," *Archeological & Ethnographical Papers,* Vol. 1, 1891, pp. 69-167.
   7. Gordon Gunter, "Contributions to the Natural History of the Bottle-nose Dolphin... on the Texas Coast..." *Journal of Mammology,* Vol. 23, 1942, p. 268.
   8. Gordon Gunter, "Occurrence of the Manatee in the U.S., with Records from Texas," *Journal of Mammology,* Vol. 22, 1941, pp. 60-64.
   9. Stephanie Fernandez & Sherman C. Jones, "Manatee Stranding On the Coast of Texas," *The Texas Journal of Science,* Vol. 42, #1, Feb. 1990, p. 193.
   10. Cushing, 60, pp. 223-225.

Chapter 15:   ABSENT WITHOUT LEAVE
   1. William B. Davis, *The Mammals of Texas,* Austin: Texas Parks & Wildlife Dept., Bulletin #41, Revised 1966.
   2. D. W. Lay, "Fur Resources of Eastern Texas," *Texas Game, Fish and Oyster Bulletin,* No. 15, 1939, pp. 1-7.
   3. William Kennedy, 180, p. 125.
   4. Anon., 84, p. 30.
   5. Dan L. Flores, *Jefferson & Southwestern Exploration,* Norman, Okla.: Univ. of Oklahoma Press, 1984, pp. 56-57, 60.
   6. Flores, *Jefferson...,* pp. 230-231, 273-274.
   7. See: *Wild Mammals of North America,* ed. Joseph A. Chapman & George A. Feldhamer, Baltimore: The Johns Hopkins Univ. Press, 1982.
   8. Howard McCarley, "The Mammals of Eastern Texas," *Texas Journal of Science,* Vol. 11, #4, 1959, p. 413.
   9. David J. Schmidly, *Texas Mammals East of the Balcones Fault Zone,* College Station, Texas: Texas A&M Press, 1983, p. 209.
   10. Davis, *The Mammals of Texas,* p. 211.
   11. W. F. Blair, *Miscellaneous Publication of the Zoological Museum, Univ. of Michigan,* No. 46, 1940.
   12. W. W. Dalquest & N. V. Horner, *Mammals of Northcentral Texas,* Wichita Falls, Texas: Midwestern State Univ. Press, 1984.
   13. Stangl, Kasper & Schafer, "Noteworthy Range Exten-

sions and Marginal Distribution Records for Five Species of Texas Mammals," *The Texas Journal of Science*, Vol. 41, #4, 1989, p. 436.

14. Lynn A. Simpson & Terry C. Maxwell, "The Mammal Fauna of Coke County, Texas," *The Texas Journal of Science*, Vol. 41, #2, May 1989, p. 185.

15. W. W. Milstead & D. W. Tinkle, "Notes on the Porcupine *(Erethizon Dorsatum)* in Texas," *Southwestern Naturalist*, Vol. 3, 1959, pp. 236-237.

16. Uldis Roze, *The North American Porcupine*, Washington, D.C.: The Smithsonian Institution Press, 1989.

17. E. Coues, "Mammals New to the U.S. Fauna," *American Naturalist*, Vol. 11, pp. 492-493.

18. F. Wallace Taber, "Range of the Coati in the U.S.," *Journal of Mammology*, Vol. 21, #1, 1940, pp. 11-12.

19. W. B. Davis, "A Fourth Record of the Coati in Texas," *Journal of Mammology*, Vol. 24, 1943, pp. 501-502.

20. E. R. Hall, *The Mammals of North America*, N.Y.: John Wiley & Sons, 1981, Vol. 2, p. 976.

21. E. W. Nelson, *Wild Animals of North America*, Washington, D.C.: The National Geographic Society, 1930, pp. 105-197.

22. E. R. Hall, *The Mammals of North America*, Vol. 2, p. 1072.

23. Gordon Gunter, "Sight Records of the West Indian Seal, *Monachus tropicalis* (Gray), From the Texas Coast," *Journal of Mammology*, Vol. 28, #3, 1947, pp. 289-290.

Bibliography

1. Abert, James W. "Note, Extracts from the Report of Lieutenant James W. Abert, Corps of Topographical Engineers, commencing August 29th, about fifty-six miles northwest from the junction of Tucumcari creek with the Canadian," appended to *Report on the Topographical Features and Character of the Country*, Section 3, pp. 17-20, in *Reports of Explorations and Surveys to Ascertain the Most Practicable and Economical Route for a Railroad from the Mississippi River to the Pacific Ocean* (Senate Ex. Doc. #78, 33rd Congress, 2nd Session). Vol. 3. Washington: Beverley Tucker Printer, 1856.
2. ———. *Gúadal P A, The Journal of Lieutenant J. W. Abert, From, Bent's Fort to St. Louis in 1845*, ed. H. Bailey Carroll. Canyon, TX: The Panhandle Plains Historical Society, 1941.
3. Aguayo, Marquis of San Miguel de. Quoted in *Pichardo's Treatise on the Limits of Louisiana and Texas*, by Father José Antonio Pichardo, tr. Charles Wilson Hackett. Austin: Univ. of Texas Press, 1931.
4. Almonte, Juan N. "Statistical Report on Texas," tr. C. E. Castaneda, *The Southwestern Historical Quarterly*, Vol. 28, #3 (Jan. 1925), pp. 177-222.
5. Amangual, Francisco. "Diary of Francisco Amangual from San Antonio to Santa Fe, March 30–May 19, 1808," in *Pedro Vial and the Roads to Sante Fe*, by Noel M. Loomis & Abraham P. Nasatir. Norman: Univ. of Oklahoma Press, 1967, pp. 462-508.
6. "Animals and Things in Texas," *Spirit of the Times*, Vol. 23, #15 (May 28, 1853), p. 172, reprinted in *Tales of Frontier Texas 1830–1860*, ed. John Q. Anderson. Dallas: Southern Methodist Univ. Press, 1966, pp. 42-45.
7. Arricivita, Fray Domingo. Quoted in *Pichardo's Treaties on the Limits of Louisiana and Texas*, by Father José Antonio Pichardo, tr. Charles Wilson Hackett. Austin: Univ. of Texas Press, 1931.
8. Audubon, John James & Bachman, John. *The Quadrepeds of North America*. 3 Vols. New York: V. G. Audubon, Vol. 1 & 2, 1851, Vol. 3, 1854.
9. Audubon, John W. *Audubon's Western Journal: 1849–1850 . . .*, Cleveland: The Arthur H. Clark Co., 1906.
10. Austin, Stephen F. "Journal of Stephen F. Austin on His First Trip to Texas, 1821," *Southwestern Historical Quarterly*, Vol. 7, #4 (April 1904) pp. 286-308.
11. Baird, Spencer F. "Explorations and Surveys for a Railroad Route from the Mississippi River to the Pacific Ocean, Mammals," *Reports of Explorations and Surveys to Ascertain the Most Practicable and Economical Route for a Railroad from the Mississippi River to the Pacific Ocean*, Vol. 8, 33rd Congress, 2d Session, Senate Ex. Doc. #78. Washington, D.C.: Beverley Tucker, Printer, 1857.
12. ———. "Explorations and Surveys for a Railroad Route from the Mississippi River to the Pacific Ocean, Birds," as above, Vol. 9, 1858.
13. Barnard, J. H. "Dr. J. H. Barnard's Journal From December 1835, including the Fannin Massacre, March 27, 1836," in *Remember Goliad*, by Clarence Wharton, Appendix 1, Glorieta, NM: The Rio Grande Press, 1968.
14. Barroto, Enríquez. "Diary," Biblioteca Palacio Real, 2667-ff., 1-50 V., 1687, photocopy at San Antonio, the Old Spanish Missions Research Library. "The Enriquez Barroto Diary," tr. Robert S. Weddle, in *LaSalle, The Mississippi, and the Gulf*, ed. Robert S. Weddle. College Station: Texas A&M University Press, 1987, pp. 149-205.
15. Barry, James Buckner. "The Diary of James Buckner Barry," ed. James K. Greer, *Southwestern Hist. Quart.*, Vol. 36, #2 (Oct. 1932), pp. 144-162.
16. Bartlett, John Russell. *Personal Narrative of Explorations and Incidents in Texas . . . Connected with the U.S. and Mexican Boundary Commission during the Years 1850, '51, '52, and '53*, 2 Vols. New York: D. Appleton & Co., 1854.
17. Beale, Edward Fitzgerald. *Uncle Sam's Camels, The Journal of May Humphreys Stacey Supplemented by the Report of Edward Fitzgerald Beale (1857–1858)*, ed. Lewis Burt Lesley. Cambridge: Harvard Univ. Press, 1929.
18. Bean, Ellis P. "Memoir of Colonel Ellis P. Bean," in *History of Texas From Its First Settlement in 1685 to Its Annexation to the United States in 1846*, by H. Yoakum, comprising Appendix 2, Vol. 1, pp. 403–452. New York: Redfield, 1855.
19. Bell, James G. "A Log of the Texas-California Cattle Trail, 1854," ed. J. Evetts Haley, *Southwestern Hist. Quart.*, Vol. 35, #3 (Jan. 1932), pp. 208–237.
20. Bell, Thomas W. "Thomas W. Bell Letters," ed. Llerena Friend, *Southwestern Hist. Quart.*, Vol. 63, #1 (July 1959), pp. 99–109, #2 (Oct. 1959), pp. 299–310, #3 (Jan. 1960), pp. 457–468, #4 (April 1960), pp. 589–599.
21. Bellisle, Simars de. "Relation," in "De Bellisle on the Texas Coast," ed. & tr. Henri Folmer, *Southwestern Hist. Quart.*, Vol. 44, #2 (Oct. 1940), pp. 204–231.
22. Benedict, J. W. "Diary of a Campaign Against the Comanches," *Southwestern Hist. Quart.*, Vol. 32, #4 (April 1929), pp. 300–310.
23. Berlandier, Jean Louis. "Hunting in Texas in 1828," ed. & tr. Richard G. Santos, unpublished.
24. ———. *Journey to Mexico During the Years 1826 to 1834*, tr. Ohlendorf, Bigelow & Standifer. 2 Vols. Austin: The Texas State Historical Association, 1980.
25. Black, Reading W. *The Life and Diary of Reading W. Black, A History of Early Uvalde*, ed. Ike Moore. Uvalde, TX: Privately printed for the El Progreso Club, 1934.

26. Bollaert, William. "Notes on the Coast Region of the Texas Territory: Taken During a Visit in 1842," in *Notes on a Journey Through Texas & New Mexico in 1841–42*, by Thomas Falconer. London: 1844, pp. 226–240.
27. ———. *Observations on the Geography of Texas*, in *William Bollaert's Texas*, ed. W. Eugene Hollon & Ruth Lapham Butler, Chicago: The Newberry Library & Norman: Univ. of Oklahoma Press, 1956.
28. Bonnell, George W. *Topographical Description of Texas*. 1840, facsimile reprint. Waco: The Texian Press, 1964.
29. Bosque, Fernando del. "Diary," tr. Herbert Eugene Bolton, in *Spanish Exploration in the Southwest, 1542–1706*. New York: Chas. Scribner's Sons, 1916, pp. 291–309.
30. Bowie, Rezin P. quoted in *History of Texas From Its First Settlement in 1685 to Its Annexation to the United States in 1846*, by H. Yoakum. New York: Redfield, 1855, Vol. 1, pp. 282–290.
31. Bracht, Viktor. *Texas in 1848*. 1849, tr. Charles Frank Schmidt. San Antonio: Naylor Printing Co., 1931.
32. Braman, Don E. E. *Information About Texas*. Philadelphia: J. B. Lippincott, 1857.
33. Brebel, Juan. Quoted in *Pichardo's Treatise on the Limits of Louisiana and Texas*, by Father José Antonio Pichardo, tr. Charles Wilson Hackett. Austin: Univ. of Texas Press, 1931.
34. Brite, Thomas R. "Atascosa County," *The Texas Almanac For 1861*. Galveston: Richardson & Co., 1860, pp. 192–193.
35. Brooks, D. B. Letter of Jan. 18, 1836, in *The Papers of The Texas Revolution, 1835–36*, ed. John H. Jenkins. Austin: Presidial Press, 1973, Vol. 4, pp. 55–57.
36. Brotherton, W. W. Quoted in *A History of Constantine Lodge, No. 13*, by R. M. Luck, Bonham, TX: Pub. by Constantine Lodge No. 13, Ancient, Free and Accepted Masons, 1917.
37. Bryan, Francis T. "Report," of Dec. 1, 1849, U.S. Senate Ex. Doc. #64, 31st Congress, 1st Session, Washington, D.C.: Government Printing Office, 1850, pp. 14–24.
38. Burnet, David G. Letter of Sept. 29th, 1847, to H. R. Schoolcraft, in *Texas Indian Papers, 1846–1859*, ed. Dorman H. Winfrey, #78, pp. 84–99.
39. Burrowes, Jack (John Taylor). Letters in "New Jersey Pioneers in Texas," by Charles M. Snyder, *Southwestern Hist. Quart.*, Vol. 64, #3 (Jan. 1961), pp. 348–368.
40. Bustillos, Don Juan Antonio. Quoted in *Pichardo's Treatise On the Limits of Louisiana and Texas*, by Father José Antonio Pichardo, tr. Charles Wilson Hackett. Austin: Univ. of Texas Press, 1931.
41. Byrne, J. H. "Diary of the Expedition," *Reports of Explorations and Surveys to Ascertain the Most Practicable and Economical Route for a Railroad from the Mississippi River to the Pacific Ocean*. Vol. 2. Appendix A. Washington, D.C.: Beverley Tucker Printer, 1855.
42. Calahorra y Sanz, Fray Joseph de. "The Journal of Friar Calahorra y Sanz of the Nacogdoches Mission describing his Journey to a Town of the Tawakoni and Yscani Indians in 1760," in "The Tawakoni-Yscani Village, 1760: A Study in Archeological Site Identification," by Leroy Johnson, Jr. and Edward B. Jelks. *The Texas Journal of Science*, Vol. 10, #4 (Dec. 1958), pp. 405–422.
43. Calleja, Félix. "Nuevo Santander in 1795: A Provincial Inspection by Félix Calleja," tr. & ed. David M. Vigness, *Southwestern Hist. Quart.*, Vol. 75, #4 (April 1972) pp. 461–506.
44. Carleton, William. Letter of Jan. 11, 1856. *Texas Letters*, ed. Frederick C. Chabot. San Antonio: Yanaguana Society, 1940, pp. 170–172.
45. Caro, Fray Joseph Francisco. Quoted by Miriam Partlow in *Liberty, Liberty County and the Atascosito District*. Austin: Pemberton Press, Jenkins Publishing Co., p. 39, and attributed to Curtis D. Tunnell and J. Richard Ambler, *Archeological Excavations at Presidio San Agustin de Ahumado*. Austin: State Building Commission Archeological Program, Report #6 (March 1967).
46. Carrasco, José María. "Itinerary of the First Column of the Army of the Mexican Republic to Texas ...," in "Brigadier General Adrian Woll's Report of His Expedition into Texas in 1842," ed. & tr. Joseph Milton Nance, *Southwestern Hist. Quart.*, Vol. 58, #4 (April 1955), pp. 523–552.
47. Catlin, George. *North American Indians ... Written During Eight Years' Travel Amongst the Wildest Tribes of Indians in North America, 1832–1839*. 2 vols. Philadelphia: Leary, Stuart & Co., 1913.
48. Cazorla, Don Luis. Quoted in *Pichardo's Treatise on the Limits of Louisiana and Texas*, by Father José Antonio Pichardo, tr. Charles Wilson Hackett. Austin: Univ. of Texas Press, 1931.
49. Céliz, Fray Francisco. *Diary of the Alarcon Expedition into Texas, 1718–1719*, tr. Fritz Leo Hoffmann. Los Angeles: The Quivira Society, 1935.
50. Clopper, Joseph Chambers. "J. C. Clopper's Journal and Book Memoranda for 1828," *Texas Hist. Assoc. Quart.*, Vol. 13, #1 (July 1909), pp. 44–80.
51. Cole, J. P. Letter, Cole to Lamar, Sept. 3, 1835, in *The Papers of the Texas Revolution, 1835–36*, ed. John H. Jenkins. Austin: Presidial Press, 1973, Vol. 1, pp. 408–414.
52. Collins, E. "Lamar County," *The Texas Almanac for 1861*. Galveston: Richardson & Co., 1860, pp. 191–192.
53. Colt, S. S. *Emigrant Guide to Republic of Texas ... 1840*, reprint ed. New York: Columbia Educational Prints, 1970.
54. Cooper, Colonel Samuel. "Copy of Report of Colonel Samuel Cooper, Assistant Adjutant General of the United States, of Inspection Trip from Fort Graham to the Indian Villages on the Upper Brazos Made in June, 1851," ed. E. B. Ritchie, *Southwestern Hist. Quart.*, Vol. 42, #4 (April 1939), pp. 327–333.
55. Cox, C. C. "From Texas to California in 1849: Diary of C. C. Cox," ed. Mabelle Eppard Martin, *Southwestern Hist. Quart.*, Vol. 29, #1, pp. 36–50, #2, pp. 128–146, #3, pp. 201–223 (1925–26).
56. Coyner, David H. *The Lost Trappers ...* Cincinnati: H. M. Rulison, Queen City Pub. House & Philadelphia: Quaker City Pub. House, 1855.
57. Crawford, Joseph T. Letter, Crawford to O'Gorman, 13 May 1837, in "Correspondence From the British Archives Concerning Texas, 1837–1846," ed. Ephraim Douglass Adams, *Texas Hist. Assoc. Quart.*, Vol. 15, #3 (Jan. 1912), pp. 205–209.
58. Cuervo, Tienda de. "Tienda de Cuervo's Inspection of Laredo, 1757," tr. Herbert Eugene Bolton. *Texas Hist. Assoc. Quart.*, Vol. 6, #3 (Jan. 1903), pp. 187–203.
59. Curless, William. "Passage of McCulloch's Emigrant Train Across the Staked Plains," *Dallas Herald*, August 7, 1858, reprinted in "Wagon Trains and Cattle Herds on the Trail

in the 1850s," *West Texas Hist. Assoc. Year Book,* Vol. 30 (Oct. 1954), pp. 150–154.
60. Cushing, S. W. *Wild Oats Sowing; Or The Autobiography of An Adventurer.* New York: Daniel Fanshaw, 1857.
61. Custis, Peter. "Custis' Manuscript Report to Dearborn, Natchitoches, June 1, 1806," ed. Dan L. Flores, in *Jefferson & Southwestern Exploration,* by Dan L. Flores. Norman, OK: Univ. of Oklahoma Press, 1984.
62. ———. "The Custis Accounts of the Red River . . . in the Year 1806," ed. Dan L. Flores, in *Jefferson & Southwestern Exploration,* by Dan L. Flores. Norman, OK: Univ. of Oklahoma Press, 1984, pp. 99–279.
63. Dance, Henry B. Letter, Dance to Editor, April 25[?], 1836, in *The Papers of the Texas Revolution, 1835–36,* ed. John H. Jenkins. Austin: Presidial Press, 1973, Vol. 6, pp. 55–63.
64. Davis, T. H. "Llano County," *Texas Almanac for 1861.* Galveston: Richardson & Co., 1860, pp. 172–173.
65. De Córdova, J. Letter of June 29, 1849 to Edward Smith and John Barrow, in "Account of a Journey Through North-Eastern Texas Undertaken in 1849 . . .," *East Texas Hist. Journal,* Vol. 8, #1 (March 1970), pp. 29–91.
66. ———. *Texas: Her Resources and Her Public Men.* Philadelphia: J. B. Lippincott & Co., 1858.
67. De León, Alonso. Diary entry dated 27th day of July 1686, quoted by Juan Chapa in "Of the History of Nuevo León that Starts from the Year 1650, and Onward," *Caverns of Oblivion,* tr. & ed. Carl L. Duaine. Corpus Christi: Pub. by the Author, 1971, pp. 189–195.
68. ———. "Itinerary of the Expedition made by General Alonso De León for the Discovery of the Bahai del Espiritu Santo and the French Settlement, 1689," tr. Miss Elizabeth Howard West, in *Original Narratives of Early American History — Spanish Exploration in the Southwest,* by Herbert Eugene Bolton. New York: Chas. Scribner's Sons, 1930, pp. 388–404.
69. ———. "Itinerary of the De León Expedition of 1690," tr. Herbert Eugene Bolton, in *Original Narratives of Early American History — Spanish Exploration in the Southwest,* by Herbert Eugene Bolton. New York: Chas. Scribner's Sons, 1930, pp. 405–423.
70. [De Morse, Charles], C. De M. Letter from McKinney, *The Clarksville Standard,* April 23, 1853.
71. ———. *The Clarksville Standard,* May 14, 1853.
72. ———. *The Clarksville Standard,* May 28, 1853.
73. ———. *The Clarksville Standard,* June 4, 1853.
74. "Description of Counties," *The Texas Almanac for 1861.* Galveston: Richardson & Co., 1860, pp. 171–193.
75. "A Description of the Fort Belknap Country," by "A gentleman who resides there," *Texas State Gazette,* Nov. 29, 1856, reprinted, *West Texas Hist. Assoc. Year Book,* Vol. 1 (Oct. 1925), pp. 82–83.
76. Dewees, W. B. *Letters from an Early Settler of Texas,* ed. [Cara Cardelle ?]. 1852, facsimile ed. Waco: Texian Press, 1968.
77. Domenech, Abbe Emmanuel Henri [Dieudonne]. *Missionary Adventures in Texas and Mexico: A Personal Narrative of Six Years' Sojourn in Those Regions.* London: Longman, Brown, Green, Longmans, and Roberts, 1858.
78. Dresel, Gustav. *Gustav Dresel's Houston Journal . . . 1837–1841,* tr. and ed. Max Freund. Austin: Univ. of Texas Press, 1954.
79. Drummond, Thomas. Letter of Sept. 26, 1834, to Sir William Jackson Hooker, in *Naturalists of the Frontier,* by Samuel Wood Geiser. Dallas: Southern Methodist Univ. Press, 1937, p. 85.
80. Eastman, Seth. "Journal of a March from the River Leona, Texas, to San Antonio (90 miles), Thence to Laredo on the Rio Grand (170 miles) in August, 1849," in *A Seth Eastman Sketchbook, 1848–1849.* Austin: Univ. of Texas Press, 1961, Introd., pp. xxi–xxv.
81. Echols, William H. "Report," U.S. Senate Ex. Doc., #1, 36th Congress, 2nd Session. Washington, D.C.: Gov. Printing Office, 1861, pp. 37-50.
82. Edward, David B. *The History of Texas; or the Emigrant's, Farmer's, and Politician's Guide to the Character, Climate, Soil and Productions of That Country: Geographically Arranged From Personal Observation and Experience.* Cincinnati: J. A. James & Co., 1836.
83. Ehrenberg, Herman. *With Milam and Fannin,* ed. Henry Smith, tr. Charlotte Churchill. Dallas: Tardy Pub. Co., 1935.
84. *The Emigrant to Texas.* 1846, tr. & ed. Otto W. Tetzlaff. Burnet, TX: Eakin Press, 1979.
85. Ernst, F. Letter of 1832, quoted in *The Cat Spring Story.* San Antonio: The Cat Spring Agricultural Society, 1956, p. 148.
86. Erskine, Michael H. "A Cattle Drive from Texas to California: The Diary of M. H. Erskine, 1854," ed. Walter S. Sanderlin, *Southwestern Hist. Quart.,* Vol. 67, #3, (Jan. 1964), pp. 397-412.
87. Espinosa, Fray Isidro Felis de. "Fray Isidro Felis de Espinosa on the Asanai and Their Allies," tr. Mattie Austin Hatcher, in "Descriptions of the Tejas or Asinai Indians, 1691-1722," Part 4, *Southwestern Hist. Quart.,* Vol. 31, #2 (Oct. 1972), pp. 150-180.
88. ———. "The Espinosa-Olivares-Aguirre Expedition of 1709: Espinosa's Diary," tr. Rev. Gabriel Tous, *Preliminary Studies of the Texas Catholic Hist. Society,* Vol. 1, #3 (March 1930).
89. ———. Quoted in *Pichardo's Treatise on the Limits of Louisiana and Texas,* by Father José Antonio Pichardo, tr. Charles Wilson Hackett, Austin: Univ. of Texas Press, 1931.
90. ———. "Ramón Expedition: Espinosa's Diary of 1716," tr. Rev. Gabriel Tous, *Preliminary Studies of the Texas Catholic Hist. Society,* Vol. 1, #4 (April 1930).
91. Eubank, Mary James. "A Journal of Our Trip to Texas, Oct. 6, 1853," *Texana,* Vol. 10, #1 (1972), pp. 31-44.
92. Everett, Richard. "Things in and About San Antonio," *Frank Leslie's Illustrated Newspaper,* Vol. 7, #163 (Jan. 15, 1859).
93. Everett, S. H. Letter, Everett to Gaines, July 1, 1836, in the *Papers of the Texas Revolution, 1835-36,* ed. John H. Jenkins. Austin: Presidial Press, 1973, Vol. 7, pp. 329-330.
94. Evia, Don José de. Quoted in *Pichardo's Treatise on the Limits of Louisiana and Texas,* by Father José Antonio Pichardo, tr. Charles Wilson Hackett. Austin: Univ. of Texas Press, 1931.
95. Falconer, Thomas. *Letters & Notes on the Texas Santa Fe Expedition, 1841-1842.* New York: Dauber & Pine Bookshops, 1930.
96. ———. *Notes on a Journey Through Texas & New Mexico in 1841-42.1* London: 1844.
97. Fernández, Santiago. "Diary of Santiago Fernandez from Santa Fe to the Taovayas and Return to Santa Fe, June 24-July 21, 1788, and July 24-December [August ?] 17, 1788,"

in *Pedro Vial and the Roads to Santa Fe,* by Noel M. Loomis & Abraham P. Nasatir. Norman: Univ. of Oklahoma Press, 1967, pp. 318-326.
98. Field, Joseph E. *Three Years in Texas.* 1836, reprint ed. Austin: The Steck Co., 1935.
99. Fisher, Orceneth. *Sketches of Texas in 1840.* 1841, facsimile reprint. Waco: The Texian Press, 1964.
100. Folsom, George. *México in 1842 . . . To Which is Added an Account of Texas and Yucatán; and of the Santa Fe Expedition.* New York: Charles J. Folsom; Wiley & Putnam: Robinson, Pratt & Co., 1842.
101. Ford, John S. "Report of Dr. John S. Ford, upon the practicability of a Route from Austin to El Paso del Norte," *Texas Democrat,* June 23, 1849, reprinted in "Letters and Documents Opening Routes to El Paso, 1849," by C. L. Greenwood, *Southwestern Hist. Quart.,* Vol. 48, #2 (Oct. 1944), pp. 262-268.
102. Fortune, James. "Letter from James Fortune, Esq.," in *Guide to Texas Immigrants,* 1835, reprint ed. Waco: Texian Press, 1974.
103. Fowler, Brad C. "The Rhine Party, 1853," *The Standard,* Clarksville, TX, Oct. 1, 1853, reprinted in "Wagon Trains and Cattle Herds on the Trail in the 1850s," *West Texas Historical Assoc. Year Book,* Vol. 30 (Oct. 1954), pp. 141-148.
104. Fragoso, Francisco Xavier. "Diary of Francisco Xavier Fragoso, Santa Fe to Natchitoches, June 20 to Aug. 20, 177-[1788]," in *Pedro Vial and the Roads to Santa Fe,* by Noel M. Loomis & Abraham P. Nasatir. Norman: Univ. of Oklahoma Press, 1967, pp. 327-348.
105. ———. Quoted in *Pichardo's Treatise on the Limits of Louisiana and Texas,* by Father José Antonio Pichardo, tr. Charles Wilson Hackett. Austin: Univ. of Texas Press, 1931.
106. Franklin, W. B. "Memoir B.," appended to U.S. Senate Ex. Doc. #32, 31st Congress, 1st Session. Washington, D.C.: Gov. Printing Office, 1850, pp. 49-51.
107. Freeman, Thomas. "Freeman's Journal as Redacted in the King Manuscript copy," ed. Dan L. Flores, in *Jefferson & Southwestern Exploration,* by Dan L. Flores. Norman, OK: Univ. of Oklahoma Press, 1984.
108. ———. "Freeman's Original Entries as Preserved by Edwin James . . .," ed. Dan L. Flores, in *Jefferson & Southwestern Exploration,* by Dan L. Flores. Norman, OK: Univ. of Oklahoma Press, 1984.
109. Freeman, W. G. "Report of Inspection of 8th Military Department Made by Bvt. Lt. Col. W. G. Freeman, Asst. Adjt. Gen. Pursuant to Instructions from Head Quarters of Army dated April 22, 1853," ed. M. L. Crimmins, *Southwestern Hist. Quart.,* Vol. 51, #1 (July 1947), pp. 56-58, #2 (Oct. 1947), pp. 167-174, #3 (Jan. 1948), pp. 252-258, #4 (April 1948), pp. 350-357 & Vol. 53, #4 (April 1950), pp. 443-473.
110. French, S. G. "Report," dated May 30, 1849, U.S. Senate Ex. Doc. #64, 31st Congress, First Session. Washington, D.C.: Gov. Printing Office, 1850.
111. Fretelliere, Auguste. "Adventures of a Castrovillian," in *Castro-ville and Henry Castro Empresario,* by Julia Nott Waugh. San Antonio: Standard Printing Co., 1934, pp. 80-96.
112. Froebel, Julius. *Seven Years' Travel in Central America, Northern México, and the Far West of the United States.* London: Richard Bentley, 1859.
113. "From Texas to the Gold Mines," *Southern Trails to California in 1849,* ed. Ralph P. Bieber. Philadelphia: Porcupine Press, *The Southwest Historical Series,* Vol. 5, pp. 259-280.
114. Gaillardet, Frederic. In *Sketches of Early Texas and Louisiana,* tr. James L. Shepherd III. Austin: Univ. of Texas Press, 1966.
115. Gaines, John Pollard. "Diary of Major John Pollard Gaines," ed. Dorman H. Winfrey, *Texana,* Vol. 1, #1 (Winter 1963), pp. 20-41.
116. Gallagher, Peter. "Journal of the Santa Fe Expedition," in Appendix to "The Texan Santa Fe Trail," by H. Bailey Carroll, *Panhandle-Plains Historical Review,* Vol. 24, 1951.
117. Gallaher, James. *The Western Sketch-Book.* Boston: Crocker & Brewster, 3rd. ed., 1852.
118. Gammage, W. L. "Topography, settlement, climate, population, botany, and diseases of Cherokee County, Texas," *New Orleans Medical & Surgical Journal,* 12 (1855-6), pp. 626-645, 723-743.
119. Ganilh, Anthony. *Ambrosio de Letinez,* or *The First Texian Novel* (first published as *Mexico versus Texas, A descriptive Novel, most of the Characters of which consist of Living Persons,* "By a Texian," 1838). 2nd ed., Vol. 1 & 2, "By A. T. Myrthe," copyright by Anthony Ganilh, 1842. Facsimile ed. Austin: The Steck Co., 1967.
120. Garay, Francisco. Quoted in "Captain Jesus Cuellar, Texas Cavalry, Otherwise 'Comanche,'" by Harbert Davenport, *Southwestern Hist. Quart.,* Vol. 30, #1 (July 1926), pp. 56-62.
121. Gauldin, Martin Austin. "From Missouri to Texas in 1845: Martin Austin Gauldin's Journal," ed. Jackie McElhaney, *Southwestern Hist. Quart.,* Vol. 83, #2 (Oct. 1979), pp. 151-165.
122. "Gid," "Native or Indigenous Texas Grasses," *The Texas Almanac for 1861.* Galveston: Richardson & Co., 1860, pp. 139-143.
123. Gibbes, C. D. "C. D. Gibbes' Journal of the Thomas Gilbert Party, 1849," *West Texas Historical Assoc. Year Book,* Vol. 19 (Oct. 1943), pp. 153-166.
124. Gibson, George R. Quoted in *Doniphan's Expedition and the Conquest of New Mexico and California,* by William Elsey Connelley. Kansas City, MO: Bryant & Douglas Book & Stationery Col, 1907, footnote, p. 373.
125. Glasco, I. M. "Upshur County," *The Texas Almanac for 1861.* Galveston: Richardson & Co., 1860, pp. 181-185.
126. Goodman, Christopher Columbus. "Christopher Columbus Goodman, Soldier, Indian Fighter, Farmer, 1818-1861," ed. Frances Jane Leathers, *Southwestern Hist. Quart.,* Vol. 69, #3 (Jan. 1966), pp. 353-376.
127. Goras, Don Juan Leal, and others. "Petition to the Governor," tr. Helen Mar Hunnicutt, *Bexar Archives,* Vol. 11 (April 9, 1738, to August 26, 1739), Austin: Univ. of Texas, 1947.
128. "Grasshoppers and Indian Raids," by "A gentleman at Fort Belknap," *Texas State Gazette,* March 24, 1857, reprinted, *West Texas Historical Assoc. Year Book,* Vol. 1 (Oct. 1925), pp. 80-81.
129. Gray, Andrew Belcher. "Fort Chadbourne to the Mustang Springs," in *Texas: Her Resources and Her Public Men.* Philadelphia: J. B. Lippincott & Co., 1858, pp. 40-49.
130. ———. *Southern Pacific Railroad Survey of a Route for the Southern Pacific R.R. on the 32nd Parallel, A. B. Gray for the Texas Western R.R. Company,* 1856, quoted in "Survey-

ing in Texas," by Virginia Houston, *Southwestern Hist. Quart.*, Vol. 65, #2 (Oct. 1961), pp. 227-228.
131. Gray, William F. *From Virginia to Texas, 1835, Diary of Col. Wm. F. Gray.* Houston: Gray, Dillaye & Co., 1909.
132. Green, Thomas Jefferson. *Journal of the Texian Expedition Against Mier . . . 1845,* fascimile ed. Austin: Steck Co., 1935.
133. Gregg, Josiah. "Diary, September 1846," ed. Maurice Garland Fulton, *Diary & Letters of Josiah Gregg, Southwestern Enterprises, 1840-1847.* Norman: Univ. of Oklahoma Press, 1941, pp. 231-247.
134. ———. "Diary, June, 1847," ed. Maurice Garland Fulton, *Diary & Letters of Josiah Gregg, Excursions in México & California, 1847-1850.* Norman: Univ. of Oklahoma Press, 1944, pp. 145-157.
135. ———. "Diary, December, 1847," ed. Maurice Garland Fulton, *Diary and Letters of Josiah Gregg, Excursions in México & California, 1847-1850.* Norman: Univ. of Oklahoma Press, 1944, pp. 185-202.
136. ———. "Into México with Wool's Column, September to December, 1846," ed. Maurice Garland Fulton, *Diary & Letters of Josiah Gregg, Southwestern Enterprises, 1840-1847.* Norman: Univ. of Oklahoma Press, 1941, pp. 251-299.
137. ———. "Last Return from Santa Fe, February to April, 1840," ed. Maurice Garland Fulton, *Diary & Letters of Josiah Gregg, Southwestern Enterprises, 1840-1847.* Norman: Univ. of Oklahoma Press, 1941, pp. 43-69.
138. ———. "Memorandum," appended to U.S. Senate Ex. Doc. #32, 31st Congress, 1st Session. Washington, D.C.: Gov. Printing Office, 1850, pp. 51-57.
139. ———. "Report of March to San Antonio," ed. Maurice Garland Fulton, *Diary & Letters of Josiah Gregg, Southwestern Enterprises, 1840-1847.* Norman: Univ. of Oklahoma Press, 1941, pp. 204-217.
140. ———. "Trip into Texas, June 1841 to June 1842," ed. Maurice Garland Fulton, *Diary & Letters of Josiah Gregg, Southwestern Enterprises, 1840-1847.* Norman: Univ. of Oklahoma Press, 1941, pp. 73-120.
141. Grierson, B. H. "Document G," in "Report of General E. O. C. Ord," House Ex. Doc. #1, Pt. 2, 46th Congress, 3rd Session. Washington, D.C.: Gov. Printing Office, 1880, p. 163.
142. Guenther, Carl Hilmar. *Literal Translation of Diary and Letters of Carl Hilman Guenter,* tr. Regina Beckmann Hurst. San Antonio: The Clegg Co., 1952.
143. "H," "Clay County," *The Texas Almanac for 1861.* Galveston: Richardson & Co., 1860, pp. 188-190.
144. Hardaway, Samuel G. Letter, Hardaway to Collins, June 6, 1836, in *The Papers of The Texas Revolution, 1835-36,* ed. John H. Jenkins. Austin: Presidial Press, 1973, Vol. 7, pp. 39-45.
145. Harrell, Jacob. Quoted in "The City of Austin From 1839 to 1865," by Alex. W. Terrell, *Texas State Hist. Assoc. Quart.,* Vol. 14, #2 (Oct. 1910), p. 114.
146. Harris, Lewis B. Letter to a brother, in appendix to "From Texas to California in 1849: Diary of C. C. Cox," ed. Mabelle Eppard Martin, *Southwestern Hist. Quart.,* Vol. 29, #3 (Jan. 1926), pp. 215-220.
147. Hasson, Alex B. "Report of the Post Surgeon at Fort Phantom Hill, for 1852," *Texas State Gazette,* March 24, 1857, reprinted, *West Texas Hist. Assoc. Year Book,* Vol. 1 (Oct. 1925), pp. 73-77.
148. Hendricks, Sterling Brown. "The Somervell Expedition to the Rio Grande, 1842," ed. E. W. Winkler, *Southwestern Hist. Quart.,* Vol. 23, #2 (Oct. 1919), pp. 112-140.
149. Henry, William Seaton (Pen name: "Guy de L***"). "Panther Tales," *Spirit of the Times,* Vol. 17, #40 (Nov. 27, 1847), reprinted in *Tales of Frontier Texas 1830-1860,* ed. John Q. Anderson. Dallas: Southern Methodist Univ. Press, 1966, pp. 216-217.
150. Herff, Ferdinand von. *The Regulated Emigration of the German Proletariat With Special Reference to Texas.* Frankfurt a/M: Franz Varrentrapp Pub. Co., 1850, tr. Arthur L. Finck, M.A. thesis, Univ. of Texas at Austin, 1949.
151. Herndon, John Junter. "Diary of a Young Man in Houston, 1838," ed. Andrew Forest Muir, *Southwestern Hist. Quart.,* Vol. 53, #3 (Jan. 1950), pp. 276-307.
152. Hicks, Elijah. "The Journal of Elijah Hicks," ed. Grant Foreman, *Chronicles of Oklahoma,* Vol. 13 (March 1935), pp. 68-99.
153. Hill, Isaac L. "Additional Recollections of Isaac L. Hill," "Reminiscences of Early Texans, A Collection from the Austin Papers," #12, *Texas Historical Assoc. Quart.,* Vol. 7, #1 (1903), pp. 53-55.
154. Holland, James K. "Diary of a Texan Volunteer in the Mexican War," *Southwestern Hist. Quart.,* Vol. 30, #1 (July 1926), pp. 1-33.
155. Holley, Mary Austin. In *Letters of an Early American Traveller,* by Mattie Austin Hatcher. Dallas: Southwest Press, 1933.
156. ———. *Texas.* 1836, Fascimile ed. Austin: The Steck Co., 1935.
157. Horton, A. C. "Report," to His Excellency, Mirabeau B. Lamar, President, April 13th, 1839, in *Documents of Texas History,* ed. E. Wallace & D. M. Vigness. Austin: Steck Co., 1960, 1963, pp. 130-132.
158. Hooton, Charles. *St. Louis' Isle, or Texiana.* London: Simmonds & Ward, 1847.
159. "Houston, Texas," *Gleason's Pictorial Drawing-Room Companion,* May 22, 1852.
160. Houstoun, Matilda Charlotte. *Hesperos: Or, Travels in the West.* London: John W. Parker, 1850.
161. ———. *Texas and the Gulf of México.* London: John Murray, 1844.
162. Hughes, George W. "Memoir Description of the March of a Division of the U.S. Army, Under the Command of Brig. Gen. John E. Wool, from San Antonio de Bexar, in Texas, to Saltillo, in México," U.S. Senate Ex. Doc. #32, 31st Congress, 1st Session. Washington, D.C.: Gov. Printing Office, 1850, pp. 1-34.
163. Hughes, John T. *"Doniphan's Expedition . . . 1847,* reprint ed. in *Doniphan's Expedition and the Conquest of New Mexico and California,* by William Elsey Connelley. Kansas City, MO: Bryant & Douglas Book & Stationery Co., 1907.
164. Hunt, Richard S. & Randel, Jesse F. *A New Guide to Texas . . . 1845,* fascimile reprint. Austin & New York: Jenkins Pub. Co., The Pemberton Press, 1970.
165. Ikin, Arthur. *Texas . . .* London: Gilbert and Piper, 1841.
166. "Impressions of Texas in 1860," ed. Joseph Schmitz, S.M., *Southwestern Hist. Quart.,* Vol. 42, #4 (April 1939), pp. 334-350.
167. Irving, Washington. "A Tour of the Prairies," *The Works of Washington Irving.* New York: Peter Fenelon Collier, 1897, Vol. 7, pp. 368-527.
168. James, Edwin. *Account of an Expedition from Pittsburgh to*

the Rocky Mountains Performed in the Years 1819, 1820, comprising Vols. 14-17 of *Early Western Travels, 1748-1846*, ed. Reuben G. Thwaites. Cleveland: The Arthur H. Clark Co., 1905.

169. Jenkins, Albert T. "Milam County," *The Texas Almanac for 1861*. Galveston: Richardson & Co., 1860, p. 185.

170. J. M. C. "Chasing a Mexican Lion," *The Dallas Herald*, April 23, 1853.

171. Johnston, Eliza. "The Diary of Eliza (Mrs. Albert Sidney) Johnston," ed. Charles P. Roland & Richard C. Robbins, *Southwestern Hist. Quart.*, Vol. 60, #4 (April 1957), pp. 463-500.

172. Johnston, J. E. "Report," of April 16, 1850, U.S. Senate Ex. Doc. #64, 31st Congress, 1st Session. Washington, D.C.: Gov. Printing Office, 1850, pp. 39-40.

173. Johnston, William Preston. "With Albert Sidney Johnston in West Texas: Austin to Fort Chadbourne, March 1855," ed. Marilyn McAdams Sibley. *West Texas Hist. Assoc. Year Book*, Vol. 40 (Oct. 1964), pp. 121-145.

174. Jones, W. E. Letter of Sept. 22, 1855, to E. M. Pease, *Texas Indian Papers, 1846-1859*, ed. Dorman H. Winfrey, #148, pp. 243-246.

175. Joseph, Sisters Mary Patrick & Mary Augustine. *Letters From the Ursuline, 1852-1853*, ed. Catherine McDowell. San Antonio: Trinity Univ. Press, 1977.

176. Joutel, Henri. *Joutel's Journal of La Salle's Last Voyage*, ed. Henry Reed Stiles, "reprinted from the first English translation of 1714, of the original French edition of 1713." Albany: Joseph McDonough, 1906.

177. Kapp, Ida Kappell. "A Letter Home by Ida Kappell Kapp, Jan. 13 & Jan. 25, 1850," in *The Golden Free Land*, ed. Crystal Sasse Ragsdale, tr. Oscar Haas. Austin: Landmark Press, 1976.

178. Kendall, George Wilkins. *Letters from a Texas Sheep Ranch*, ed. Harry James Brown. Urbana, IL: Univ. of Illinois Press, 1959.

179. ———. *Narrative of the Texan Santa Fe Expedition*. 2 vols. London: Wiley & Putnam, 1845.

180. Kennedy, William. *Texas: The Rise, Progress, and Prospects of the Republic of Texas*. 2nd. ed. 1841, reprint ed. Fort Worth: The Molyneaux Craftsmen, Inc., 1925.

181. Kerr, Henry. *Travels Through the Western Interior of the United States, from the Year 1808 up to the Year 1816*. Elizabethtown, NJ: Printed for the author, 1816.

182. Kettner, Franz, letter of April 2, 1856, to Parents, in "Letters of a German Pioneer in Texas," ed. & tr. Terry G. & Marlis Anderson Jordan. *Southwestern Hist. Quart.*, Vol. 69, #4 (April 1966), pp. 462-472.

183. ———. Letter of August 12, 1853, to Parents, in "Letters of a German Pioneer in Texas," ed. & tr. Terry G. & Marlis Anderson Jordan. *Southwestern Hist. Quart.*, Vol. 69, #4 (April 1966), pp. 462-472.

184. Kirby-Smith, E. *To Mexico with Scott*, ed. E. J. Blackwood. Cambridge: Harvard Univ. Press, 1917.

185. Kuykendall, Barzillai. "Recollections of Barzillai Kuykendall," in "Reminiscences of Early Texans: A Collection from the Austin Papers," Part 2 #4, *Texas Hist. Assoc. Quart.*, Vol. 6, #4 (April 1903), pp. 311-320.

186. Kuykendall, Capt. Gibson. "Recollections of Capt. Gibson Kuykendall," in "Reminiscences of Early Texans: A Collection from the Austin Papers," #6, *Texas Hist. Assoc. Quart.*, Vol. 7, #1 (July 1903), pp. 29-40.

187. Kuykendall, J. H. "Miscellaneous Remarks by J.H.K.," in "Reminiscences of Early Texans: A Collection from the Austin Papers," #11, *Texas Hist. Assoc. Quart.*, Vol. 7, #1 (July 1903), pp. 51-53.

188. Láfora, Nicolás de. "The Frontiers of New Spain, Nicolás de Láfora's Description, 1766-1768," ed. & tr. Lawrence Kinnaird. *Quivera Society Publications*, Vol. 13. Berkeley: The Quivera Society, 1958.

189. Lamar, Mirabeau B. "Mirabeau B. Lamar's Texas Journal," ed. Nancy Boothe Parker, *Southwestern Hist. Quart.*, Vol. 84, #2 (Oct. 1980), pp. 197-220 and #3 (Jan. 1981), pp. 309-330.

190. Latham, Francis S. *Travels in the Republic of Texas, 1842*, ed. Gerald S. Pierce. Austin: Encino Press, 1971.

191. Lawrie, Arthur. Journal in "Lawrie's Trip to Northeast Texas," ed. V. E. Gibbens, *Southwest Hist. Quart.*, Vol. 48, #2 (Oct. 1944), pp. 238-253.

192. [Leach, James B. ?]. "Journey of the Leach Wagon Train Across Texas, 1857," ed. J. W. Williams, *West Texas Hist. Assoc. Year Book*, Vol. 24 (Oct. 1953), pp. 115-177.

193. Lee, Nelson. *Three Years Among the Comanches*. 1859, reprint ed. Norman: Univ. of Oklahoma Press, 1957.

194. Lee, Robert E. Letter of April 12, 1856, in "Robert E. Lee in Texas: Letters and Diary," by Col. M. L. Crimmins, *West Texas Hist. Assoc. Year Book*, Vol. 8 (June 1932), p. 5.

195. ———. Letter of August 4, 1856, in "Robert E. Lee in Texas: Letters and Diary," by Col. M. L. Crimmins, *West Texas Hist. Assoc. Year Book*, Vol. 8 (June 1932), pp. 6, 7.

196. ———. "Memorandum book," 28th of July, 1856, entry, "Robert E. Lee in Texas: Letters and Diary," by Col. M. L. Crimmins, *West Texas Hist. Assoc. Year Book*, Vol. 8 (June 1932), p. 6.

197. ———. In "Colonel Robert E. Lee's Report on Indian Combats in Texas," by Col. M. L. Crimmins, *Southwestern Hist. Quart.*, Vol. 39, #1 (July 1935), pp. 21-32.

198. LeGrand, A. "Field Notes and Journal of Survey," in *Texas: The Rise, Progress, and Prospects of the Republic of Texas*, by William Kennedy. Fort Worth: The Molyneaux Craftsmen, Inc., 1925, pp. 176-191.

199. Lincecum, Gideon. "Journal of Lincecum's Travels in Texas, 1835," ed. A. L. Bradford & T. N. Campbell, *Southwestern Hist. Quart.*, Vol. 53, #2 (Oct. 1949), pp. 180-201.

200. Lindheimer, Ferdinand Jakob. Unpublished letters.

201. Linn, John J. Letter to Judge David Irvin, in "A Letter From John J. Linn," ed. Robert W. Shook, *Southwestern Hist. Quart.*, Vol. 72, #2 (Oct. 1968), pp. 240-241.

202. Ludlow, James Chambers (Pen name: J. C. L.). "Texas in 1822: A Few Observations," ed. Marilyn McAdams Sibley, *East Texas Historical Journal*, Vol. 5, #2 (Oct. 1967), pp. 112-115.

203. Lundy, Benjamin. *The Life, Travels and Opinions of Benjamin Lundy*. New York: Negro Universities Press, 1969.

204. Luxan, Diego Perez de. "Expedition into New Mexico Made by Antonio de Espejo, 1582-1583, as Revealed in the Journal of Diego Perez de Luxan, a Member of the Party," tr. George Peter Hammond & Agapito Rey, *Quivera Society Publications*, Vol. 1. Los Angeles: The Quivera Society, 1929.

205. McCall, George A. "Description of a supposed new species of *Columba*, inhabiting Mexico, with some account of the habits of the *Geococcyx viaticus*, Wagler," *Proceedings of the Academy of Natural Science of Philadelphia*, Vol. 3 (July 1847), pp. 233-235.

206. ———. "Some Remarks on the Habits, etc. of Birds met with in Western Texas between San Antonio and the Rio Grande, and in New Mexico; with descriptions of several species believed to have been hitherto undescribed," *Proceedings of the Academy of Natural Science of Philadelphia*, Vol. 5 (June 1854), pp. 213-224.
207. McCalla, W. L. *Adventures in Texas Chiefly in the Spring & Summer of 1840.* Philadelphia: Printed for the Author, 1841.
208. McClintock, William A. "Journal of a Trip Through Texas and Northern Mexico in 1846-1847," *Southwestern Hist. Quart.*, Vol. 34, #1 (July 1930), pp. 20-37, #2 (Oct. 1930), pp. 141-158, #3 (Jan. 1931), pp. 231-256.
209. M'Cutchen, M. M. "Coryell County," *The Texas Almanac for 1861.* Galveston: Richardson & Co., 1860, pp. 186-187.
210. McMullen, John. "J. McMullen to Lamar," *Lamar Papers*, #523, ed. Charles Adams Gulick, Jr. Austin: Texas State Library, 1921, Vol. 1, pp. 530-531.
211. Manzanet, Fray Damian. "Diary Kept by the Missionaries," tr. Mattie Austin Hatcher, comprising part 3 of "The Expedition of Don Domingo Teran de Los Rios into Texas (1691-1692)," ed. Rev. Paul J. Foik, *Preliminary Studies of the Texas Catholic Historical Society*, Vol. 2, #1 (Jan. 1932), pp. 48-67.
212. ———. Quoted in *Pichardo's Treatise on the Limits of Louisiana and Texas*, by Father José Antonio Pichardo, tr. Charles Wilson Hackett. Austin: Univ. of Texas Press, 1931.
213. Marcy, R. B. "Captain R. B. Marcy's Reconnoissance of the Headwaters of the Red River," *West Texas Historical Assoc. Year Book*, Vol. 3 (June 1927), pp. 78-117.
214. ———. "Exploration of the Red River of Louisiana, In the Year 1852," *U.S. Senate Ex. Docs.*, 33rd Congress, 1st Session. Washington, DC: Beverley Tucker, Senate Printer, 1854.
215. ———. "Field Notes Concerning Indian Reservations," *Texas Indian Papers*, #128, ed. Dorman H. Winfrey. Austin: Texas State Library, 1960, pp. 193-209.
216. ———. "Marcy's Exploration to Locate the Texas Indian Reservations in 1854," eds. J. W. Williams and Ernest Lee, *West Texas Historical Assoc. Year Book*, Vol. 23 (Oct. 1947), pp. 107-132.
217. ———. "Report of Capt. R. B. Marcy," *U.S. Senate Ex. Doc.* #64, 31st Congress, First Session. Washington, DC: Gov. Printing Office, 1850, pp. 169-221.
218. ———. "Report of Captain R. B. Marcy, of the Fifth Infantry, United States Army, on his Exploration of Indian Territory and Northwest Texas," ed. R. C. Crane, *West Texas Historical Assoc. Year Book*, Vol. 14 (Oct. 1938), pp. 116-136.
219. ——— & Neighbors, R. S. "Report of R. B. Marcy & R. S. Neighbors to P. H. Bell," in *Texas Indian Papers*, #125, ed. Dorman H. Winfrey. Austin: Texas State Library, 1960, pp. 186-190.
220. Mares, José. "Itinerary and Diary of José Mares, Bexar to Santa Fe, January 18 to April 27, 1788," in *Pedro Vial and the Roads to Santa Fe*, by Noel M. Loomis & Abraham P. Nasatir. Norman: Univ. of Oklahoma Press, 1967, pp. 306-315.
221. ———. "Journal of José Mares, Santa Fe to Bexar, July 31 to October 8, 1787," in *Pedro Vial and the Roads to Santa Fe*, by Noel M. Loomis & Abraham P. Nasatir. Norman: Univ. of Oklahoma Press, 1967, pp. 289-306.
222. María, Fray Francisco Casanas de Jesús. "Fray Francisco Casanas de Jesús María to the Viceroy of México, August 15, 1691," tr. Mattie Austin Hatcher, comprising part one of "Descriptions of the Tejas or Asanai Indians, 1691-1722," *Southwestern Hist. Quart.*, Vol. 30, #3 (Jan. 1927), pp. 206-218.
223. Marryat, Frederick. *The Travels and Romantic Adventures of Monsieur Violet.* 3 vols. London: Longman, Brown, Green, & Longmans, 1843, reprint ed. bound in one volume, Upper Saddle River, NJ: Gregg Press, 1970.
224. Martínez, Francisco. Quoted in *Pichardo's Treatise on the Limits of Louisiana and Texas*, by Father José Antonio Pichardo, tr. Charles Wilson Hackett. Austin: Univ. of Texas Press, 1931.
225. Maverick, Samuel Augustus. "Journal [of the] Chihuahua Expedition," in *Samuel Maverick, Texan: 1803-1870*, ed. Rena Maverick Green. Privately printed by Rena Maverick Green, 1952, pp., 333-342.
226. Mendoza, Juan Dominguez de. "Itinerary of Juan Domínguez de Mendoza, 1684," in *Original Narratives of Early American History — Spanish Exploration in the Southwest*, by Herbert Eugene Bolton. New York: Chas. Scribner's Sons, 1930, pp. 320-340.
227. Mezieres, Don Athanase de. In *Athanase de Mezieres & the Louisiana-Texas Frontier, 1768-1780 . . .*, by Herbert Eugene Bolton. Cleveland: The Arthur H. Clark Co., 1914.
228. ———. Quoted in *Pichardo's Treatise on the Limits of Louisiana and Texas*, by Father José Antonio Pichardo, tr. Charles Wilson Hackett. Austin: Univ. of Texas Press, 1931.
229. Mezquia, Pedro Pérez de. "The Mezquia Diary of the Alarcón Expedition into Texas, 1718," ed. & tr. Fritz L. Hoffmann, *Southwestern Hist. Quart.*, Vol. 41, #4 (April 1938), pp. 312-323.
230. Michler, N., Jr. "Report," of January 28, 1850, U.S. Senate Ex. Doc. #64, 31st Congress, 1st. Session. Washington, DC: Gov. Printing Office, 1850, pp. 29-39.
231. ———. "Report of a Reconnaissance of the Country Between Corpus Christi and the Military Post on the Leona . . .," dated July 31, 1849, U.S. Senate Ex. Doc. #64, 31st Congress, 1st Session. Washington, D.C.: Gov. Printing Office, 1850, pp. 7-13.
232. ———. Letter to Boundary Commissioner William H. Emory, *Texas Humanist*, March/April, 1984, pp. 16-17.
233. Miles, William. *Journal of the Sufferings and Hardships of Capt. Parker H. French's Overland Expedition to California in 1850, 1851.* Fairfield, WA: Ye Galleon Press, 1970.
234. Miranda, Bernardo de. "Miranda's Inspection of Los Almagres: His Journal Report, and Petition," ed. and tr. Roderick B. Patten, *Southwestern Hist. Quart.*, Vol. 74, #2 (Oct. 1970), pp. 223-251.
235. ———. Quoted in *Pichardo's Treatise on the Limits of Louisiana and Texas*, by Father José Antonio Pichardo, tr. Charles Wilson Hackett. Austin: Univ. of Texas Press, 1931.
236. Montgomery, Cora. *Eagle Pass; or, Life on the Border.* New York: George P. Putnam & Co., 1852.
237. [Moore, A. W. ?]. "A Reconnoissance in Texas in 1846," *Southwestern Hist. Quart.*, Vol. 30, #4 (April 1927), pp. 252-271.
238. Moore, Francis, Jr. *Map and Description of Texas . . . 1840*, reprint ed., Waco: Texian Press, 1965.

239. Morfi, Fray Juan Augustin. "Excerpt from *Viaje de Indios y Diario del Nuevo Mexico*, tr. Robert E. McDonald, *Our Heritage*, San Antonio Geneaological & Historical Society, Vol. 1, #4 (July 1960), pp. 121-127.
240. Morgan, James. *Fragile Empires: The Texas Correspondence of Samuel Swarthout and James Morgan, 1836-1856*, ed. Feris A. Bass, Jr. & B. R. Brunson. Austin: Shoal Creek Publishers, Inc., 1978.
241. ———. "Letter written by Don Juan de Onate from New Mexico, 1599," as previous entry, pp. 212-222.
242. Murchison, John. Letter of June 23, 1849, to Rev. Chauncey Richardson, in appendix to "From Texas to California in 1849: Diary of C. C. Cox," ed. Mabelle Eppard Martin, *Southwestern Hist. Quart.*, Vol. 29, #3 (Jan. 1926) pp. 212-214.
243. Murray, Amelia M. *Letters From the United States, Cuba and Canada*. New York: G. P. Putnam & Co., 1856.
244. Myer, Albert James. " 'I Am Already Quite a Texan': Albert J. Myer's Letters from Texas, 1854-56," ed. David A. Clary, *Southwestern Hist. Quart.*, Vol. 82, #1 (July 1978), pp. 25-76.
245. Neighbors, Robert S. "The Na-u-Ni, or Comanches of Texas; Their Traits and Beliefs, and their Division and Intertribal Relations," in *Texas Indian Papers, 1846-1859*, #234, ed. Dorman H. Winfrey. Austin: Texas State Library, 1960, pp. 347-357.
246. Nuttall, Thomas. *A Journal of Travels Into the Arkansas Territory, During the Year 1819*..., Phil: Thos. W. Palmer, 1821. Reprinted, *Early Western Travels, 1748-1846*, ed. Reuben Gold Thwaites, Vol. 13. Cleveland: The Arthur H. Clark Co., 1905.
247. O'Crouley, Pedro Alonso. *A Description of the Kingdom of New Spain*, ed. & tr. Sean Galvin, n.p.: John Howell Books, 1972.
248. Olmsted, Frederick Law. *Journey Through Texas, A Saddle-trip on the Southwestern Frontier*. 1857, reprinted. Austin: Von Boeckmann-Jones Press, 1962.
249. Onate, Don Juan de. "True Account of the Expedition of Onate Toward the East, 1601," tr. Herbert Eugene Bolton, in *Original Narratives of Early American History — Spanish Explorations in the Southwest*, by Herbert Eugene Bolton. New York: Chas. Scribner's Sons, 1930, pp. 250-265.
250. Ormsby, W. L. Quoted in "The First Trip West on the Butterfield Stage," by Hybernia Grace, *West Texas Historical Assoc. Year Book*, Vol. 8 (June 1932), pp. 62-74.
251. Pacheco, Rafael. "Instructions Sent Out to the Frontier Posts of Texas," tr. Sandra Myers, in "*La Nigua* — the Chigger in the Spanish Southwest," by Sandra Myers, *Texana*, Vol. 3, #4 (Winter 1965), pp. 365-366.
252. Padilla, Augustín Dávila. *Historia de la Fundación y Discurso de la Provincia, de Santiago de México* . . . Brussels: Ivan de Meerbeque, 1625, facsimile & English tr. by Wm. Mahon ? in *Padre Island, Treasure Kingdom of the World*, by Wm. Mahon. Waco: Texian Press, 1967.
253. [Page, Frederic B.]. *Prairiedom: Rambles and Scrambles in Texas or New Estremadura*. New York: 1845.
254. Pages, Pierre Marie Francois de. "Across Texas in 1767: The Travels of Captain Pages," ed. Marilyn McAdams Sibley, *Southwestern Hist. Quart.*, Vol. 70, #4 (April 1967), pp. 563-622.
255. Pancoast, Josiah. Letter of Feb. 14, 1846, from Fort Bend County, Texas, in *Texas Letters*, ed. Frederick C. Chabot. San Antonio: Yanaguana Society, 1940, pp. 84-90.
256. "Panther Hunting," *Spirit of the Times*, 24, 50 (Jan. 27, 1855), p. 594, reprinted in *Tales of Frontier Texas 1830-1860*, ed. John Q. Anderson. Dallas: Southern Methodist Univ. Press, 1966, pp. 218-219.
257. Parker, A. A. *Trip to the West and Texas*. 1836, reprint ed. Austin & New York: Pemberton Press, 1968.
258. Parker, James W. *Narrative of the Perilous Adventures . . . of Rev. James W. Parker, during a Frontier Residence in Texas* . . . Louisville, KY: Printed at the *Morning Courier* Office, 1844.
259. Patillo, G. A. "Orange County," *The Texas Almanac for 1861*. Galveston: Richardson & Co., 1860.
260. Patterson, N. M. C. "Uvalde County," *The Texas Almanac for 1861*. Galveston: Richardson & Co., 1860.
261. Peck, John James. Letters gathered & published as *The Sign of the Eagle*, by Richard F. Pourade. San Diego, CA: The Union-Tribune Publ. Co., a division of the Copley Press, Inc., 1970.
262. Peña, José Enrique de la. *With Santa Anna in Texas*, ed. & tr. Carmen Perry. College Station, TX: Texas A&M Univ. Press, 1975.
263. Peña, Juan Antonio de la. "Peña's Diary of the Aguayo Expedition," tr. Rev. Peter P. Forrestal, *Preliminary Studies of the Texas Catholic Hist. Soc.*, Vol. 2, #7 (Jan. 1935).
264. ———. Quoted in *Pichardo's Treatise on the Limits of Louisiana and Texas*, by Father José Antonio Pichardo, tr. Charles Wilson Hackett. Austin: Univ. of Texas Press, 1931.
265. Peyton, John Rowzee. *A Virginian in New Mexico*, Series of Western Americana #13. Santa Fe, NM: The Press of The Territorian, 1967.
266. Pickett, A. J. Letter of Dec. 10, 1856, from Old Cony [Cany ?], Texas, in *Texas Letters*, ed. Frederick C. Chabot. San Antonio: Yanaguana Society, 1940, p. 52.
267. Pike, Zebulon M. *The Southwestern Expedition of Zebulon M. Pike*, ed. Milo Milton Quaife. 1810, facsimile ed. Freeport, NY: Books for Libraries Press, 1925.
268. "A Pleasant Country for a Nervous Man," *Spirit of the Times*, 30, 23 (July 21, 1855), p. 273, reprinted in *Tales of Frontier Texas 1830-1860*, ed. John Q. Anderson. Dallas: Southern Methodist Univ. Press, 1966, pp. 46-47.
269. Plummer, Rachel. *Narrative of the Capture and Subsequent Sufferings of Mrs. Rachel Plummer* . . . Louisville, KY: Printed at the *Morning Courier* Office, 1844.
270. Pope, John. "Report of Exploration of a Route for the Pacific Railroad, Near the Thirty-Second Parallel of North Latitude, from the Red River to the Rio Grande," in *Reports of Explorations and Surveys to Ascertain the Most Practicable and Economical Route for a Railroad from the Mississippi River to the Pacific Ocean*, Vol. 2, 1955.
271. Porras, Marin de. Letter of June 20, 1805, tr. Nettie Lee Benson, in "Bishop Marin de Porras and Texas," by Nettie Lee Benson, *Southwestern Hist. Quart.*, Vol. 51, #1 (July 1947) pp. 16-40.
272. Postl, Karl Anton (pen name: Charles Sealsfield). "On the Prairie of Jacinto," *Spirit of the Times*, 13, 41 (Dec. 9, 1843), pp. 483-485. Reprinted in *Tales of Frontier Texas 1830-1860*, ed. John Q. Anderson. Dallas: Southern Methodist Univ. Press, 1966, pp. 11-37.
273. Ramón, Don Domingo. "Captain Don Domingo Ramón's Diary of His Expedition into Texas in 1716," tr. Rev. Paul

J. Foik, *Preliminary Studies of the Texas Catholic Historical Society*, Vol. 2, #5 (April 1933).

274. ———. Quoted in *Pichardo's Treatise on the Limits of Louisiana and Texas*, by Father José Antonio Pichardo, tr. Charles Wilson Hackett. Austin: Univ. of Texas Press, 1931.

275. Rankin, Melinda. *Texas in 1850*. Boston: Damrell & Moore, 1850.

276. Redfield, Syman. Letter of Oct. 11, 1846, from Camp La Bacca, Texas, in *Texas Letters*, ed. Frederick C. Chabot. San Antonio: Yanaguana Society, 1940, pp. 120-122.

277. Reid, John C. *Reid's Tramp, Or a Journal of the Incidents of Ten Months' Travel Through Texas, New Mexico, Arizona, Sonora, and California*. 1858, reprint ed. Austin: Steck Co., 1935.

278. Reid, Samuel C., Jr. *The Scouting Expedition of McCulloch's Texas Rangers*, [1847], facsimile ed. Austin: The Steck Co., 1935.

279. Rivera, Pedro de. Quoted in *Pichardo's Treatise on the Limits of Louisiana and Texas*, by Father José Antonio Pichardo, tr. Charles Wilson Hackett. Austin: Univ. of Texas Press, 1931.

280. "Robertson County," by "A Citizen," *The Texas Almanac for 1861*. Galveston: Richardson & Co., 1860.

281. Roemer, Ferdinand. *Texas with Particular Reference to German Immigration and the Physical Appearance of the Country*. 1849, tr. Oswald Mueller. San Antonio: Standard Printing Co., 1935.

282. Rosenberg, Amanda Fallier von. Letter, "Farm Nassau, March 29, 1850, Mr. dear Hannchen," tr. Walter Wupperman, in *The Golden Free Land* by Crystal Sasse Ragsdale. Austin: Landmark Press, 1976, pp. 118-128.

283. ———. Letter, "Galveston, Dec. 10, 1849, My dear Hannchen," tr. Walter Wupperman, in *The Golden Free Land* by Crystal Sasse Ragsdale, Austin: Landmark Press, 1976, p. 118.

284. Rubi, Marquis de. "A Copy of the Report Sent to his Excellency the Viceroy, Marquis de Croix regarding the Advantages of the Maintaining or Removing the Presidio of San Saba, August 1767," in *Documents of Texas History*, ed. & tr. Ernest Wallace & David M. Vigness. Austin: The Steck Co., 1963, pp. 19-22.

285. Ruxton, George F. *Adventures in México and the Rocky Mountains*. 1847, reprint ed. Glorieta, NM: Río Grande Press, Inc., 1973.

286. Sáenz, Matías. *El Memorial de Fr. Matías Sáenz*, Original in Archivo General de las Indias with the Audiencia de Guadalajara, legajo 209, Biblioteca del Estado de Guadalajara, transcript & tr. Richard C. Garay, Document 10.

287. St. John, Berry B. "A Buffalo Hunt in the Texas Prairie," *The Sportsman*, series 2, Vol. 10 (Jan. to June, 1844) reprinted, *Texana*, Vol. 12, #2, 1974, pp. 179-187.

288. Sánchez, José María. "A Trip to Texas in 1828," tr. Carlos E. Castañeda, *Southwestern Hist. Quart.*, Vol. 29, #4 (April 1926), pp. 249-288.

289. Santa Ana, Fray Benito Fernández de. *Letters and Memorials of the Father Presidente Fray Benito Fernández de Santa Ana, 1736-1754*, transcript & tr. Fr. Benedict Leutenegger, O.F.M. San Antonio: Old Spanish Missions Hist. Research Library, Documentary Series 6, 1981.

290. Sexton, Franklin B. "Travels and Tribulations of a Young East Texas Lawyer, 1849-50," ed. Mary S. Estill, *East Texas Hist. Assoc. Journal*, Vol. 3, #1 (March 1965), pp. 50-58.

291. Shain, Charles B. Letter, Hardaway to Collins, June 6, 1836, in *The Papers of The Texas Revolution, 1835-36*, ed. John H. Jenkins. Austin: Presidial Press, 1973, Vol. 7, pp. 258-265.

292. Sheridan, Francis C. *Galveston Island or, A Few Months off the Coast of Texas, The Journal of Francis C. Sheridan, 1839-1840*, ed. Willis W. Pratt. Austin: Univ. of Texas Press, 1954.

293. Sibley, John. Quoted in *Pichardo's Treatise on the Limits of Louisiana and Texas*, by Father José Antonio Pichardo, tr. Charles Wilson Hackett. Austin: Univ. of Texas Press, 1931.

294. Simpson, J. P. Quoted in *A History of Constantine Lodge, #13*, by R. M. Lusk. Bonham, TX: Pub. by Constantine Lodge #13, Ancient, Free and Accepted Masons, 1917.

295. ———. "Report from the Secretary of War," U.S. Senate Ex. Doc. #12, 31st Congress, 1st Session, 1850.

296. Sitgreaves, Capt. L. "Memoir A," appended to U.S. Senate Ex. Doc. #32, 31st Congress, 1st Session. Washington, DC: Gov. Printing Office, 1850, pp. 48-49.

297. Smith, Ashbel. "An Account of the Yellow Fever which appeared in the City of Galveston, Republic of Texas, in the Autumn of 1839, with Cases and Dissections." 1839, reprint ed. Austin: Univ. of Texas Press, 1951.

298. Smith, Edward. *Account of a Journey Through North-East Texas Undertaken in 1849...* London, 1849.

299. ———. "Account of a Journey through North-Eastern Texas Undertaken in 1849, Embodied in a Report to Which are Appended Letters and Verbal Communications from Eminent Individuals . . . ," Third Part, *East Texas Hist. Assoc. Journal*, Vol. 8, #1 (March 1970) pp. 29-91.

300. Smith, Francis. Letter of March 11, 1832, to A. G. and R. Mills, in "A Glimpse of the Texas Fur Trade in 1832," by Eugene C. Barker, *Southwestern Hist. Quart.*, Vol. 19, #3 (Jan. 1916) pp. 279-282.

301. Smith, Lieut. W. F. "Report of Reconnaissance of a Route for a Road from San Antonio to El Paso," dated May 25, 1849, U.S. Senate Ex., Doc. #64, 31st Congress, 1st Session. Washington, DC: Gov. Printing office, 1850, pp. 7-13.

302. Smith, Spencer. Diary quoted in *the Lyman Wight Colony in Texas*, by J. Marvin Hunter. Bandera: Frontier Times Museum, n.d., pp. 22-25.

303. Smyth, George W. "The Autobiography of George W. Smyth," *Southwestern Hist., Quart.*, Vol. 36, #3 (Jan. 1933), pp. 200-214.

304. Solís, Fray Gasper José. Quoted in *Pichardo's Treatise on the Limits of Louisiana and Texas*, by Father José Antonio Pichardo, tr. Charles Wilson Hackett. Austin: Univ. of Texas Press, 1931.

305. ———. "The Solís Diary of 1767," tr. Rev. Peter P. Forrestal, *Preliminary Studies of the Texas Catholic Hist. Society*, Vol. 1, #6 (March 1931).

306. Solms-Braunfels, Prince Carl of. "Prince Solm's 6th and 10th Reports to the Directors of the Adelsverein, 27 March 1845 on Comal Creek," in *A New Land Beckoned*, by Chester W. & Ethel H. Geue, tr. Chester W. Geue. Waco: Texian Press, 1972, pp. 66-67.

307. ———. *Texas, 1844-1845*. 1846, reprint ed. Houston: Anson Jones Press, 1936.

308. Stapp, William Preston. *The Prisoners of Perote: A First-hand Account of the Mier Expedition*. Austin: Univ. of Texas Press, 1977.

309. Steinert, W. "W. Steinert's View of Texas in 1849," ed. & tr. Gilbert J. Jordan, *Southwestern Hist. Quart.*, Vol. 80, #1 (July 1976), pp. 57-78, #2 (Oct. 1976), pp. 177-200, #3 (Jan. 1977), pp. 283-301, #4 (April 1977), pp. 399-416, Vol. 81, #1 (July 1977), pp. 45-72.
310. Sterne, Adolphus. "Diary of Adolphus Sterne." Part 3, ed. Harriet Smither. *Southwestern Hist. Quart.*, Vol. 30, #4 (April 1927), pp. 305–324.
311. ———. "Diary of Adolphus Sterne." Part 4, ed. Harriet Smither. *Southwestern Hist. Quart.*, Vol. 31, #1 (July 1927), pp. 63–83.
312. ———. "Diary of Adolphus Sterne." Part 6, ed. Harriet Smither. *Southwestern Hist. Quart.*, Vol. 31, #3 (Jan. 1928), pp. 285–291.
313. ———. "Diary of Adolphus Sterne." Part 26, ed. Harriet Smither. *Southwestern Hist. Quart.*, Vol. 36, #3 (Jan. 1933), pp. 215–230.
314. Stiff, Edward. *The Texas Emigrant.* 1840, reprint ed. Waco: Texian Press, 1968.
315. Talon, Pierre, and Jean Baptiste. "Report of Two Canadian Soldiers Who Made the Trip With de la Salle to the Mississippi and Returned." Feb. 14, 1698, photocopy in Missions Library, San Antonio, transcript and tr. Sr., Ann Linda Bell, unpublished.
316. Taplin, Charles L. Letter report to Capt. John Pope on exploration of the Llano Estacado, in *Reports of Explorations and Surveys to Ascertain the Most Practicable and Economical Route for a Railroad from the Mississippi River to the Pacific Ocean.* Vol. 2, 1855, Appendix A.
317. "Tarrant County." *The Dallas Herald,* July 12, 1856.
318. Tennery, Thomas D. *The Mexican War Diary of Thomas D. Tennery,* ed. D. E. Livingston-Little. Norman: Univ. of Oklahoma Press, 1970.
319. Terán, Don Domingo. "Itinerary and Daily Account Kept by General Domingo de Teran, Begun May 16, 1691, Finished April 15, 1692." Tr. Mattie Austin Hatcher. *Preliminary Studies of the Texas Catholic Hist. Society,* Vol. 2, #1 (Jan. 1932), pp. 10–48.
320. "Texas," by Editor of *Texian Advocate,* Feb. 10, 1848. Reprinted in *Texas in 1848,* by Viktor Bracht, 1849. San Antonio: Naylor Printing Co., 1931, pp. 95–99.
321. *Texas in 1837, an Anonymous, Contemporary Narrative,* ed. Andrew Forest Muir. Austin: Univ. of Texas Press, 1958.
322. *Testimonio of Title to José Manuel Pereda,* August 10, 1810. Spanish Archives, General Land Office of Texas, Vol. 67, p. 11, quoted in *The Spanish Archives of the General Land Office of Texas,* by Virginia H. Taylor, tr.(?). Austin: The Lone Star Press, 1955.
323. "Thereby Hangs a Tail." *Spirit of the Times,* 22, 44 (Dec. 18, 1852) p. 520. Reprinted in *Tales of Frontier Texas 1830-1860,* ed. John Q. Anderson. Dallas: Southern Methodist Univ. Press, 1966, pp. 220–221.
324. Thomas, J. W. "Burleson County." *The Texas Almanac for 1861.* Galveston: Richardson & Co., 1860.
325. Tilden, B. P. Jr. *Notes on the Upper Rio Grande.* Philadelphia: Lindsay and Balkiston, 1847.
326. Tips, Frederick Julius Conrad. "Frederick Julius Conrad Tips Correspondence (1849–1859)," transcribed by Mona von Kramer, tr. by Mamie Tips von Kramer, ed. Robert R. Robinson, Jr., being Appendix J, of *Die Bremerverwandischaft in Deutschland und in Texas* by Robert R. Robinson, Jr. Burnet, TX: Nortex Press, 1979, Vol. 2, pp. 1524–1543.
327. Ullrich, George. "Comal County," *The Texas Almanac for 1861.* Galveston: Richardson & Co., 1860.
328. Urrea, Jose. "Answer of Jose Urrea to the Court of Inquiry, Mexico City, Dec. 6, 1836." *Boletin del Archivo General de la Nacion,* Vol. 3, pp. 165–166.
329. Vega, Garcilaso de la. Quoted in *The Florida of the Inca,* ed. & tr. John Grier Varner & Jeannette Johnson Varner. Austin: Univ. of Texas Press, 1951.
330. Viele, Mrs. Teresa. *Following the Drum: A Glimpse of Frontier Life.* 1858, facsimile ed. Austin: Steck-Vaughn Co., 1968.
331. *Visit to Texas in 1831, A.* 3rd. ed., ed. Robert S. Gray, reprint ed. Houston: Cordovan Press, 1975.
332. Wallach, W. D. "Report of W. D. Wallach, Esq., Civil Engineer, on the Examination of the Paso Cavallo," in *Texas: The Rise, Progress, and Prospects of the Republic of Texas,* by William Kennedy, 2nd ed., 1841, reprint ed. Fort Worth: The Molyneaux Craftsmen, Inc., 1925.
333. Wavell, Gen. Arthur Goodall. Quoted in *Guide to Texas Immigrants.* 1835, reprint ed. Waco: Texian Press, 1974.
334. Weaver, William T. G. "Cook County," *The Texas Almanac for 1861.* Galveston: Richardson & Co., 1860.
335. Webber, C. W. *The Hunter-Naturalist. Romance of Sporting; or, Wild Scenes and Wild Hunters.* Philadelphia: J. B. Lippincott & Co., 1856.
336. Webster, J. D. "The Report of Lieutenant Webster of a Survey of the Gulf Coast at the Mouth of the Río Grande," U.S. Senate Ex. Doc. #65, 31st Congress, 1st Session. Washington, DC: Gov. Printing Office, 1850, pp. 2–5.
337. Whipple, A. W. "Report on the Botany of the Expedition," comprising Part 5 of "Report on the Topographical Features and Character of the Country," in *Reports of Explorations and Surveys to Ascertain the Most Practicable and Economical Route for a Railroad from the Mississippi River to the Pacific Ocean,* Vol. 3. Washington, DC: Beverley Tucker Printer, 1856.
338. ———. "Report of Explorations for a Railway Route near the 35th Parallel of North Latitude," comprising Part 2 of "Report on the Topographical Features and Character of the Country," in *Reports of Explorations and Surveys to Ascertain the Most Practicable and Economical Route for a Railroad from the Mississippi River to the Pacific Ocean,* Vol. 3. Washington: Beverley Tucker Printer, 1856.
339. Wickeland, H. "The County of Greer," *The Texas Almanac for 1861.* Galveston: Richardson & Co., 1860, pp. 176–177.
340. Willson, William. "Letter from Wm. Willson, of Boston," in *Guide to Texas Immigrants,* by D. Woodman, Jr. 1835, reprint ed. Waco: Texian Press, 1974.
341. Wizlizenus, Adolphus. "Memoir of a Tour to Northern México, connected with Col. Doniphan's Expedition, in 1846 and 1847," U.S. Senate Misc. Doc. #26, 30th Congress, 1st Session. Washington, DC: Tippin & Streeter, printers, 1848.
342. Wood, Samuel J. "The Grasshoppers of Texas," *The Texas Almanac for 1861.* Galveston: Richardson & Co., 1860.
343. ———. "Travis County," *The Texas Almanac for 1861.* Galveston: Richardson & Co., 1860.
344. Woodman, D., Jr. *Guide to Texas Immigrants.* 1835, reprint ed. Waco: Texian Press, 1974.
345. Woodsaw, W. B. Letter of May 2, 1852, from Bowie County, Texas, in *Texas Letters,* ed. Frederick C. Chabot. San Antonio: Yanaguana Society, 1940, pp. 167–168.

346. Wrede, Friedrich W. von. *Sketches of Life in the United States of North America and Texas*. 1844, reprint ed., ed. Emil Drescher, tr. Chester W. Geue. Waco: Texian Press, 1970.
347. Wrede, Friedrich Wilhelm von, Jr. Letter of Oct. 14, 1841, to Friedrich W. von Wrede, Sr., in *Sketches of Life in the United States of North America and Texas*. 1844, reprint ed., ed. Emil Drescher, tr. Chester W. Geue. Waco: Texian Press, 1970.
348. Wright, Charles. "From the El Paso Train," *Texas Democrat,* August 4, 1849, reprinted in "Letters and Documents Opening Routes to El Paso, 1849," by C. L. Greenwood, *Southwestern Hist. Quart.,* Vol. 48, #2 (Oct. 1944), pp. 262-268.
349. Yoakum, H. *History of Texas From Its First Settlement in 1685 to Its Annexation to the United States in 1846*. New York: Redfield, 1855.
350. Young, J. H. Notes on *Map of the State of Texas From the Latest Authorities*. Philadelphia: Thomas, Cowperthwait & Co., 1853.
351. Zaldivar, de Vicente. "Account of the Discovery of the Buffalo, 1599," in Herbert Eugene Bolton, *Spanish Exploration in the Southwest*. New York: Charles Scribner's Sons, 1916, pp. 223–232.

Unpublished Microfilm

352. Barroto, Enriquez Juan. Diary. Microfilm in Old Spanish Missions Research Library, Our Lady of the Lake University, San Antonio, Texas.

Index

A
Abert, Lt. J. W., 60, 116, 121
Abilene, 129
Adirondack or eastern cougar, 89
Alabama, 157
Alberta, Canada, 113
albino buffaloes, 24
albino deer, 38
Alces alces, 46
Alice, 43
Allen, J. A., 17, 53, 125, 144, 157
alligators, 93, 165
Almonte, Juan, 39, 81
Alpine, 43
Amangual, 19, 27, 29, 48
Amarillo, 20, 134, 138
American buffalo, 17
American deer, 37
American elk, 46, 50
American manatee, 162
Anastasius, Father, 28-29
Angelina River, 14
anteaters, 18
Antelope and Deer of America, The, 50
antelopes: 15, 20, 33, 64, 90, 141; hunting of, 40-41, 44-45; location of, 41-44; naming of, 39-40; numbers of, 41, 44; speed of, 40
Apaches, 14
apes, 18
Aransas County, 169
Arizona, 94, 116, 169
Arkansas, 48, 73, 94, 129
Arkansas River, 20, 120
armadillos, 63, 84, 126, 127-131
Armstrong County, 29, 90, 134, 135
astutus, 111
Atascosa County, 61, 103, 117
Audubon, John James, 6, 35, 36, 50, 57, 67, 68, 69, 70-71, 72, 74, 76, 80, 81, 82, 83, 86, 92, 95, 96, 97, 99, 102, 103, 105, 106, 111, 112, 113, 116, 117, 122, 123, 127, 128, 131, 136, 154, 155
 John Woodhouse, 154, 155, 156
Audubon-Bachman, 37
Audubon Society Field Guide to North American Mammals, 59
Austin, 12, 110, 160
 John, 154
 Stephen F., 35, 62
Austin County, 10, 20, 22
Avery, Willis, 12
Azara, 94

B
Bachman, 35, 36, 50, 57, 67, 69, 70, 72, 74, 92, 103, 105, 111, 112, 116, 117, 122, 123, 127, 128, 136, 154, 155, 157
badgers, 18, 113-115, 141
Bailey, Vernon, 37, 43, 52, 53, 59, 60, 68, 69, 81, 120, 139
Baird, Spencer F., 6, 10, 16, 36, 37, 43, 46, 70, 76, 80, 81, 95, 97, 98, 99, 103, 111, 113, 114, 117, 118, 125, 128, 135, 136, 142, 144, 154, 156
Ballantyne, R. M., 40, 65-66
Bandera County, 12
Banks, 89
Barber, C. M., 52, 53
Barroto, Enriquez, 15
Barry, James Buckner, 42
Barsness, Larry, 22, 26
Bartlett, John Russell, 40, 43, 139, 156
Bassaris Astuta Lichtenstein, 112
Bassariscus, 111
Bastrop County, 12, 22, 30, 35
bats, 145, 159-161
Baylor County, 41
Baylor Mountains, 54
Baylor University, 128
Beach Mountains, 54
Bean, Col. Ellis P., 48
bears: 14, 49, 76, 85, 91, 103, 104; diet of, 56-57, 61, 62; hunting of, 55-56, 57, 61, 62; kinds of, 57-60; location of, 57-62; numbers of, 55, 58; as threats, 55, 56-57, 58
beavers, 123, 132-134, 164, 165
Bell, James G., 33, 36, 38, 135-136, 138, 140, 141, 147, 149, 156
Bell County, 104
Bengal tiger, 79
Berlandier, Jean Louis, 10, 12, 18, 27, 28, 35, 43, 56, 58, 59, 61, 65, 67, 68, 96-97, 110, 116, 121, 123, 128, 144, 162
Bernard River, 83
Bexar, 25
Bexar County, 15, 22, 43, 61, 81, 89, 103, 117, 150, 151
Big Bend, 41, 58, 62, 89, 96, 103, 117, 138, 156, 157, 166, 169
Big Bend National Park, 58
Biggers, Don H., 21, 24
Big Hatchet Mountain, 54
Bighorn mountain sheep, 52-54
Big Thicket, 62, 117, 152
Bison bison athabascae, 24
Bison bison bison, 24
Bison bison L., 9
Bison bonasus, 9
black bears, 56, 57, 58-61
Blackland Prairies, 13, 151-153
black-tail deer, 38
black-tailed jackrabbit, 154
black wolf, 68-69, 70
Blair, W. F., 156
Blanco County, 134
Blue River, 48, 53
boars, 64
bobcats, 79, 96
Bodcau Prairie, 14
Bolivar Pass, 169, 170
Bolivar Peninsula, 162
Bollaert, 42, 64
Bolton, 18
Bonham, 34, 85, 88, 91
Bonnell, George W., 15, 49
Bos Americanus, 10
Bosque County, 12, 19, 49
Bosque River, 39
Bowie County, 150
Box, Thadis W., 29
Bracht, Viktor, 21, 34, 35, 37, 42, 57-58, 58-59, 61, 64, 65, 68, 79, 80, 81, 82, 84, 85, 95, 102, 103, 105, 107, 110, 111, 118, 122, 124, 125, 128, 134, 143, 149
Brazoria, 107, 146, 154, 162
Brazoria County, 15, 22, 62, 154
Brazos County, 11
Brazos Island, 162
Brazosport, 162
Brazos River, 12, 13, 15, 19, 20, 21, 22, 39, 42, 48, 59, 60, 81, 96, 100, 104, 129, 162
Brazos Santiago Pass, 169, 170
Brazos Valley, 60, 104, 145
Brebel, Juan, 48, 53, 64, 101, 103
Brewster County, 41, 135
Briscoe County, 60, 90, 135
British Isles, 113
Brooks, D. B., 107
Brooks County, 43
Brown, George, 26
Brownsville, 97, 153, 155, 168
Bruner, 153
Brushy Creek, 12
Buechner, Helmut, 53
buffalo, 2, 33, 34, 37, 42, 47, 48, 49, 55, 65, 67, 68, 91, 93, 103, 139, 141, 164
Buffalo Bayou, 10
Buffalo Bill, 26
Buffalo Creek, 10
buffalo: effect on the environment, 29-31; ferocity of, 27-29; in herds, 24-25, 30, 32; hunting of,

195

13-14, 18-19, 27, 34, 44; location of, 11-19; movement of, 16-19, 20-24, 30; naming of, 9-11; numbers of, 19, 35, 44; stampedes, 25-27, 32; types of, 24
buffalo grass, 10
buffalo wallows, 30-31
buffalo wolf, 67, 68, 69, 70, 75
Buffon, 82
Burleson County, 22, 35, 95
Burnet, David G., 123, 134
Burns, Rollie, 29
buzzards, 72, 76
Byrd, Col. William, 9-10
Byrne, J. H., 38

C
C. latrans, 71
C. lupus nubilus, 71
C. m. telmalestes, 117
C. mesoleuca mearnsi, 117
C. niger gregoryi, 71
C. niger gregoryi Goldman, 71
C. rufus, 71
cacomistle, 111-113
cacti, 104
Caddo area, 13
Caddo Prairie, 14
Cadillac, Antoine de la Mothe, 5
Caldwell County, 12
Calhoun County, 15, 22, 28, 63, 150, 151, 161
California lion, 86
Callahan County, 42
Calleja, 133
Camargo, 64, 74
Cameron County, 153
Camp Belknap, 63
Campbell, Dr. Charles R. A., 159
Camp Davis, 103
Canada, 21, 22
Canadian River, 10, 20, 22, 47, 48, 60, 116, 121
cane-cutter, 157
Canis albescens, 65, 67
Canis griseus, 68, 69
Canis latrans Say., 70
Canis lupus, 69, 70-71
Canis lupus Linn, 67
Canis lupus lycaon, 71
Canis Mexicanus, 64, 67
Canis occidentalis, 70
Canis occidentalis Richardson, 69
Canoe Creek, 123
cape buffalo, 16
Caramanchel Creek, 148
Carpenter, 30
Carrizo Sands, 61
Castaneda, C. E., 39

Castor canadensis, 133
Castroville, 101, 103
catamounts, 79, 85, 92, 93, 94, 95
Catlin, George, 21, 49, 151-152
Caton, John Dean, 50
cattle, 36
Cayotte, The, 73
Cedar Springs, 87
ceibayo, 59
Cenis Indians, 13
Cervus elaphas canadenis Erxleben, 46
Cervus elaphas merriami Nelson, 46
Cervus leucurus, 36
Cervus Macrotis, 37
Cervus virginianus, 35, 36, 37
Chambers County, 62, 63, 164
Champ de Aisle, 109
cheetahs, 79
Cherokee County, 13, 35
Chihuahua, 58, 89
Chimal, 134
Chocolate Bayou, 15
Cibolo Creek, 13
Cibolo hills, 35
Citellus variegatus, 143
civet cat, 111, 112, 118, 119
Clarendon, 96
Clark, J. H., 128
Clarksville, 91
Clay County, 41, 89, 166
Clayton, J., 115
Clements, 30
Clopper, J. C., 56, 121
Coahuila, 16, 17, 58
Coastal Prairies, 153, 154
coati, 168-169
Coke County, 104, 166
Coleman, Ann Raney, 105, 106
collared peccary, 101-107, 109
Collin County, 117, 150, 151
Colorado, 21, 22, 69
Colorado County, 10, 20, 22, 56
Colorado River, 12, 13, 20, 21, 30, 59, 60, 64, 69, 104, 113, 122
Colt, S. S., 15, 68-69
Columbus, 43, 69
Comal County, 42, 69, 81, 103, 125
Comal Creek, 91
Comal River, 103
Comancheros, 48, 74
Comanches, 13, 20, 21, 123
Comfort, 159
"commensal" rodents, 146
common muskrat, 165
Concho County, 11, 42
Concho River, 21, 135

conejo, 148-149
Conepatus leuconotes, 117
Conepatus mesoleucus, 116
Conger, W. B., 91
Cook, Colonel, 156
Cooke County, 41
Coopwood, Judge Bethel, 17
Copano Bay, 162
Cordova, J. De, 13
Coronado, 2, 26
Coronado National Forest, 143
Corpus Christi, 93, 136
Coryell County, 39, 42
Cottle County, 135
cottontails, 148, 149, 156-158
Cotulla, 43
cougars, 79, 80, 82, 85, 86, 87-90, 94, 95, 131
Cowan, 52
Coyner, David, 66, 76-77
coyotes: 41, 64, 67, 70, 71-75, 78, 113, 137, 141, 145; howling of, 72, 73-74; as threats, 74-76
coyotl, 72
cranes, 63, 128
Crockett, 108
Crockett County, 42, 135
Crosby County, 135
Cross Timbers, 104, 149, 151, 153
Culberson County, 38, 41, 64, 72, 135
Currie's Creek, 55
Cushing, S. W., 62, 63, 162-163
Custis, Peter, 40, 64, 65, 67, 71, 80, 123, 136, 144, 154, 165
Cuyler, W. K., 120, 121-122

D
D. maperito, 117
D. marsupialis, 125
D. mesamericana, 125
Daingerfield, 43
Dallas, 87, 129
Darwin, 94
Dasypus novemcinctus, 129
Dauphine Island, 5
Davis, W. B., 53, 59, 78, 103, 104, 105, 113, 121, 125, 156-157, 169
Davis Mountains, 54, 57, 58, 138, 166
Davis Mountains Cottontail, 156
Deaf Smith County, 38
DeCordova, J., 103
deer: 13, 14, 15, 18, 39, 41, 43, 48, 49, 55, 64, 65, 84, 91, 93, 103, 118, 126, 128, 141, 164; in herds, 34-35, 37; hunting of, 35, 36;

kinds of, 36-38; location of, 33-35, 36-38; numbers of, 33-38, 44; size of, 37
Delaware Creek, 57
Delawares, 91
De Leon, Gen. Alonso, 15, 16
DeMorse, Charles, 49, 88, 91
Denton County, 41
desert cottontail, 156
desert foxes, 100
Dess, Mr., 34
Devil's River, 42, 103, 104, 133, 134, 136, 144
Dewees, W. B., 19, 25, 101, 104, 154
De Witt County, 90
D'Hanis, 90, 108
Dickens County, 141
Dicotyles torquatua L., 103
Didelphis virginiana, 125
Discoverers, Explorers, Settlers, The Diligent Writers of Early America, 5
Dodge, Lt. Col. Richard Irving, 10, 24-25, 28, 50, 67, 70, 72, 86, 88, 89, 93, 120
dolphins, 161-162
Domenech, Abbe, 4, 35, 55, 77, 80, 81, 90, 93, 107-108, 110, 128
Donley County, 96, 134, 135
Doughty, 43, 44
  Robin, 141, 142
Dresel, Gustav, 111
ducks, 20
Duval, J. C., 43, 67
Duval County, 142

E
Eagle Pass, 16, 98, 148, 168
eagles, 63, 128, 145
eastern cottontail, 158
Eastern Cross Timbers, 153
Echols, Lt. W. H., 41, 42
Ector County, 142
Edentata, 130
Edward, David B., 2, 145, 146
Edwards County, 22, 59
Edwards Escarpment, 61
Edwards Plateau, 13, 37, 81, 104, 113, 117, 151, 166
Ehrenberg, Herman, 72, 136, 137, 160
elk: 15, 33, 141; hunting of, 48, 50-51; kinds of, 46; location of, 47-50; naming of, 46; numbers of, 50-51; size of, 46-47, 50; speed of, 47
Ellis County, 40, 42, 64
El Paso, 63, 81, 103, 134
El Paso County, 135
Emory, Major, 135

English, Judge, 34, 91
Espejo, 9
Espinosa, 14, 30, 61, 62
Euphrates Valley, 39
European bison, 17
European deer, 46
Evis, Don Jose de, 61

F
F. c. stanleyana, 89
F. concolor coryi, 89
F. Concolor cougar, 89
fajitas, 155-156
Falconer, Thomas, 20, 135
Falls County, 19, 42, 64
Fannin County, 48
Farnham, Thomas, 19
Fayette County, 10, 20, 30
Felis Aztecus, 89
Felis concolor, 80, 86, 89
Felis coryi, 89
Felis cougar, 89
Felis hippolestes, 89
Felis onca, 79
Felis pardalis, 94
Felis wiedii, 97
Felis yagouaroudi, 97
feral hogs, 107-109
Fernandez, 162
ferrets, 141
Field, Joseph E., 80, 82, 83
Fisher, O. C., 15, 67-68, 68-69, 81, 84, 88, 103
Fisher County, 22
Flores, Dan L., 14, 71, 80, 136, 154
Florida, 69
Florida manatee, 162
Florida panther, 89, 90
Floyd County, 135
flying squirrel, 143, 145
Fontaine, 12
Fort Belknap, 85, 136
Fort Bend County, 34, 35, 154
Fort Davis, 41
Fort Mason, 82
Fort Phantom Hill, 67, 69, 146, 160
Fort St. Louis, 9, 15, 109
Fort Stockton, 18, 19
Fort Worth Prairie, 153
Fouquet, L. C., 26
Fowler, Brad C., 53, 57, 113, 114, 149
foxes, 99-100, 126, 165
fox squirrels, 143, 144, 145
Franklin, Wayne, 5
Franklin Mountains, 3, 92
Fredericksburg, 59, 69, 107, 111
Freeman, Thomas, 14, 21, 136
French, Capt. S. G., 41, 103, 134, 139

Fretelliere, Auguste, 101, 103, 158
Frio County, 39, 43
Froebel, Julius, 40-41, 53, 89, 133, 134
Fulton, Arkansas, 14
fur-producers, 164-165
fur traders, 123-124, 133, 134

G
Gaines, Maj. John Pollard, 43
Galveston, 108, 146, 147, 163
Galveston Bay, 15, 63, 169
Galveston County, 15
Galveston Island, 15
Galveston Pass, 90
Ganilh, Anthony, 101, 103
Garcitas Creek, 15
Garza County, 49
Gatschet, Albert S., 161
Gauldin, Martin Austin, 42
gazelles, 39
Gibbes, C. D., 142
Gillespie County, 12, 20, 68, 128, 134
Gillmore, Parker, 71
Givens, Lieut., 85
Glass, Anthony, 136
Glaucomys volans, 143
goats, 39, 43, 52, 53, 125
Goldman, 83, 84, 89
Goldthwaite, 82
Goliad, 34
Goliad County, 15
Gonzales, 25
Gonzalez, 43
gophers, 142, 165
grasses, 29-30, 43, 151-154
grasshoppers, 139
grassland prairies, 151-154
Gray, A. B., 41
Gray County, 60
gray fox, 99-100
gray rabbit, 154
Grayson County, 150, 152
gray squirrel, 143, 144
gray wolf, 69-70, 71
Great Plains muskrat, 165
Great Slave Lake, 21
Gregg, Josiah, 29, 70, 72, 103
Grierson, Lieut. Charles H., 53
Grinnell, George Bird, 54
grizzly bears, 57-58, 59, 82
Groce, Colonel, 2
Guadalupe County, 22, 72, 76
Guadalupe Mountains, 10, 53, 54, 57, 58, 103, 157
Guadalupe Mountains National Park, 58
Guadalupe River, 12, 15, 16, 43, 90, 122, 124
Guenther, Carl Hilmar, 63
Guerrero, Coahuila, 16

Gulf Coast, 20
Gunter, Gordon, 161, 162, 169, 170

H
Hall, 169
Hardin County, 62, 117
hares: 63, 128, 148-156; as food, 155-156; kinds of, 154-155
Harrell, Jacob, 12
Harris County, 62, 165
Hartman, Carl G., 126, 127
Hasson, Dr. Alexander B., 69, 160
hawks, 145, 165
Hays, Col., 112
Hearne, 19, 101
Hemphill County, 135, 137
Henderson, 123
Hendricks, Sterling Brown, 156
Henrietta, 43
Henry, Capt. William Seaton, 83
heron, 63
Hiatt, D. B., 18
Hicks, Elijah, 4, 39, 42
Hidalgo County, 49
Hill, J. I., 21
Hill County, 12, 42
History of Connecticut, 115
History of Texas, 2
Hite, Mr., 63
hog-nosed skunk, 116, 117
Holland, 4
Holley, Mary Austin, 4, 10, 15, 35, 36, 62, 68, 70, 100, 101, 102, 104-105, 107, 146
hooded skunk, 117
Hooton, Charles, 108, 146
Hopkins County, 76
horses, 64
Houston, 78
Houston, General, 81
Houston County, 13, 35
Hudson, W. H., 91, 92, 93, 122
Hudspeth County, 18, 36, 38, 41, 64, 72, 135, 147
Hughes, John T., 63
Hunt, 12
hydrophobia skunk, 120
hydrophobic cats, 118, 119, 121

I
Ictonys striatus, 116
Ikin, Arthur, 35, 49, 53, 74, 85, 88, 105
Indianola, 90, 150, 153, 154
Indians, nomadic, 14, 18, 21
Indians in East Texas, 14, 18, 34

Indians in South Texas, 18, 19
Indian Territory, 21
Ingram, 12
Irion County, 42, 156
Irish elk, 46, 50
Irving, Washington, 132

J
J.M.C., 87
jackals, 71, 76
jackass rabbit, 150, 154
Jack County, 41
jack rabbits, 148, 149-156
Jackson County, 15, 22
jaguar, 79-84, 95, 131
jaguarundi, 97-98
James, Edwin, 27, 28, 30, 60, 64, 140
javelina, 101-109
Jeff Davis County, 37-38, 41, 64, 72, 135
Jefferson, Thomas, 165
Jefferson County, 164
Jesus Maria, Fray Francisco Casanas de, 14, 109, 148
Johnson County, 150
Johnston, Eliza, 4, 82, 83
  William Preston, 40, 42, 140
Jones, ———, 162
  Buffalo, 26
Jones County, 22, 42, 67
Joseph, Sister Mary, 64
Josselyn, 46
Joutel, Henri, 15, 28-29, 39, 43, 125, 127, 161

K
kangaroo rats, 147, 157
Kansas, 21, 136
Karankawas, 161
Kendall, George, 35, 39, 40, 41, 42, 49, 74, 104, 110, 135, 141
Kendall County, 55, 68, 74
Kenedy County, 49
Kennedy, William, 35, 49, 88, 123, 134, 164
Kentucky, 69
Kerr, Henry, 14, 89, 93
Kerr County, 12, 68
Key West, 170
Kickapoos, 39
Kimble County, 12, 20, 22, 81, 84, 103
King County, 141
Kinny County, 89
Kiowa, 13, 20
kit foxes, 100
Klappenbach, Mr., 91
Kleberg County, 43
Kofort, 139

L
L. C. merriami, 154
L. texianus, 155

La Bahia, 64
Lafora, 12, 20, 61
Lagomorphs, 149
LaGrange, 122
Laguna Madre, 162
Lake Whitney, 49
Lamar, 12
Lamar County, 34, 103, 136
Lampasas County, 40, 42
Landon, C. R., 54
La Porte, 62
Laredo, 17, 43
La Riviere Aix de Boeufs, 9
Larson, 30
La Salle, 9, 13, 15, 20, 28, 50, 108, 161
Las Animas, 12
Las Vegas, 10
Lavaca Bay, 153
Lavaca County, 146
Lavaca River, 15, 43
Lawrie, 41
Leach, James B., 139
Leach wagon train, 40, 139
Lee County, 35
LeGrand, 38
Leona River, 42
Leon Creek, 90
leopards, 79, 81, 82, 83, 88, 95
Leporidae, 156
Lepus, 148, 149, 157
Lepus aquaticus, 157
Lepus artemisia Bachman, 154
Lepus bachmani Waterhouse, 155
Lepus californicus melanotis Mearns, 154
Lepus callotis, 154
Lepus callotis Wagler, 154
Lepus sylvaticus Bachman, 154
Lepus texianus, 154
Lepus Timidus, 154
Les Vaches River, 15
Lewis and Clark, 19, 72
liebre, 148-149
Limpia Canyon, 138, 157
Limpia Mountains, 53
Lincoln region, 10
Lindheimer, Ferdinand, 17, 80, 113
line-tailed squirrel, 142
Linnaeus, 9, 10, 89, 94, 129
lions, 17, 64, 85-94
Lion's Spring, 89
Lipans, 34
Little River, 19, 25, 28, 104
little spotted skunk, 121
little striped skunk, 118
Llano, 134
Llano County, 134
Llano Estacado, 20, 41, 60, 89, 90, 114, 135, 141, 154
Llano River, 19, 118
Llano Valley, 67, 88
loafers, 68, 69

lobo wolves, 67-68, 69, 75, 78
Long, W. R., 135
long-tailed yellow lynx, 97
Louisiana, 50, 62, 64, 69, 72, 93, 94, 129
Louisiana black bear, 59, 62
Louisiana muskrat, 166
Lubbock, 141
Lundy, Benjamin, 142
Lutra canadensis, 122
Luxan, Diego Perez de, 19
lynxes, 79, 96
Lynx maculatus, 96
Lynx rufus, 96

M
McClellan, Capt., 90
McClintock, William, 64, 128
McCown, Capt. J. P., 127, 131
McCulloch County, 42, 136
McCullough, 4
McGillivray, Duncan, 52
McHugh, Tom, 21
McLennan County, 12, 19, 42, 117
Madison County, 35
Mammals of North America, The, 6
manatees, 161-163
Manzanet, Fray Damian, 11, 15, 16
Marcy, Capt. R. B., 4, 41, 49, 53, 58, 60, 85, 90, 132, 133, 134, 135, 136, 138, 140, 153
margay, 97, 98
Marryat, Frederick, 4, 40, 60, 141
Mason County, 117, 134, 136
Matagorda Bay, 61, 128
Matagorda County, 62, 154
Matagorda forest, 154
Matagorda Island, 35
Matamoros, 17, 97, 125, 128, 154
Matthews, Dr., 56, 76
Maverick, Samuel Augustus, 93, 134
Maverick County, 15, 22, 43, 153
Maxwell, 166
Mearns, 53
Medina County, 22, 35, 43, 103
Medina River, 81
Menard County, 12, 42, 86, 112, 137
Mendoza, Juan Dominguez de, 11, 18, 19, 42
Menzel, Father, 4
Mephitis bicolor, 118
Mephitis macroura, 117

Mephitis mephitis, 116
Mephitis mesoleuca, 117
Mephitis mesoleuca Licht, 116
Merriam, 52, 89, 135, 141
Merriam's elk, 46
mesoleuca, 117
mesquite, 12, 15, 104
Meusebach, 55
Mexican badger, 113
Mexican cougar, 88, 89
Mexican free-tailed bat, 159
Mexican ground squirrel, 142
Mexican hares, 153, 154
Mexican hogs, 101, 102, 103, 104, 105
Mexican lions, 80, 85, 86, 87, 88, 93, 94
Mexican raccoon, 111
Mexican tiger, 81
Mexico, 22
Mezieres, Don Athanase de, 12, 19, 104
mice, 126, 145-147, 165
Michler, 38, 41
Midland County, 142
Milam County, 22
Miles, William, 38, 107
Mill Creek, 76
Mills County, 30, 40, 42
Milstead, 166
mink, 122-124, 164, 165
Minneosa Creek, 116
Mirador, Veracruz, 17
Mission del Refugio, 136
Mississippi, 62, 129
Mississippi River, 129
Missouri, 48, 69
Missouri River, 72
Mitchell, Joseph D., 120
Mobeetie, 132
moles, 165
Monachus tropicalis, 169
mongooses, 118
Monterey, 17
Mooar, J. Wright, 24, 25
Moore, ———, 19, 20-21, 80
  A. W., 40, 64
  Francis, Jr., 35, 79, 95, 103
moose, 46, 49, 53
More, Mrs., 82
Morgan, James, 62
Morris County, 39
Morton, T., 46
mosquitoes, 159-160
mountain lions, 80, 83, 85, 86, 88, 89, 92-93
Mount Graham, 143, 144
mule deer, 37-38
mule rabbit, 155
mules, 38
muskrats, 164-166
Musselshell River, 22
mustang, 49
mustang deer, 42

Mustang Desert, 16, 18, 129, 153
mustang horses, 15
Mustang Island, 146
Myer, Albert, 41, 42

N
Nacogdoches, 62, 99, 123, 125, 134, 164
Nacogdoches County, 72, 125
Nacogdoches, Department of, 114
Natchez Creek, 76
Natchitoches, Louisiana, 14
National Geographic Society, 44
Nayarit, 83
Nebraska, 21, 22, 136
Nelson, ———, 83, 84
  E. W., 144
New Braunfels, 13, 34, 35, 69, 91, 103
New Mexican black bear, 59-60, 61
New Mexico, 10, 18, 38, 50, 52, 53, 54, 57, 58, 82, 103, 116, 129, 154, 169
New Washington, 62
Nika, 20
North American Buffalo, The, 3
North Carolina, 69
Norway rats, 126, 146
Nueces County, 43
Nueces River, 59, 81, 133, 144, 158
Nuevo León, 18, 144
Nuttall, 28, 56-57, 103, 104

O
O. canadensis mexicana, 52
O. canadensis texianus, 52
oaks, 145
Oberholser, 43
ocelot, 81, 82, 94-95
Ochiltree County, 22
O'Crouley, Don Pedro Alonso, 38
Odocoileus hemionus, 37
Odocoileus viginianus, 36
Oklahoma, 19, 20, 48, 49, 57, 72, 104, 132, 136, 156
Oldham County, 22, 53, 58, 60, 135
Olmsted, F. L., 4, 35, 43, 55, 56, 85, 93, 108, 110
Onate, Don Juan de, 24, 27, 47-48, 50
opossums, 110, 125-127, 165
Orange County, 164
otters, 122-124, 164, 165
Ovis canadensis, 52
Ovis mexicanus, 52

Index

owls, 139-140, 145, 165

P
P. lotor fuscipes, 111
Page, Frederic B., 43
Pages, Pierre Francois de, 35, 72
painters, 85, 88, 92, 94
Palo Alto, 128
Palo Duro Canyon Park, 60
Pancoast, Josiah, 4, 35
panthers, 80, 85, 86, 87, 88-89, 90, 91, 93, 94, 96, 131
Paradiso, John L., 73, 74
Paris, 104, 136
Parker, A. A., 35, 57, 64, 74, 93, 107
Parmer County, 38
pastores, 48
Patrick, Sister Mary, 64
Pattie, James Ohio, 65
Pawnee, 22
Paxton, Joseph, 14
Peale, Mr., 140
peccaries, 84, 118, 126, 127, 128 (*see* collared peccary)
Peck, Lt. John James, 35, 43
Pecos County, 33, 40, 41, 89, 135, 149
Pecos River, 9, 18, 21, 22, 36, 37, 38, 42, 59, 103, 125, 128, 156, 165
Pecos River muskrat, 165
Pecos Valley, 36, 128
Pedernales, 134
Pedernales River, 59, 61
Pena, ———, 27, 28
  Jose Enrique de la, 13, 107, 148
  Juan Antonio de la, 35, 39, 148
Pena Creek, 148
Pereda grant, 148
Pereda title, 43, 81
Peters, S., 115
Pickett, A. J., 102, 104
Piedras Negras, 168
Pine Springs, 57
pine squirrels, 143
pinyon pines, 143
Platte River, 65
pole cat, 115
Ponchartrain, 5
Pope, Capt. John, 4, 114, 117
porcupine, 166-168
porpoises, 161-162, 163
Porras, Marin de, 55, 103, 133
Port Isabel, 169
Port Lavaca, 15
Possums, 126
Post Oak Belt, 153
Post Oak Savannah, 151
Potter County, 64, 135, 138
prairie dogs: 156, 157; described, 137-138; effect on environment, 138-142; extermination of, 141-142; as food, 141; location of, 135-138; numbers of, 134-136; as prey, 139-141
Prairie Dog Town Fork, 60
prairie wolf, 41, 67, 70, 71, 137
Presidio, 19, 54, 103, 135
Presidio County, 89
Presidio Orcoquizac, 61
Procyon hernandezii, 111
pronghorn antelope, 40, 43
pumas, 80, 83, 85, 86, 87, 88, 91, 92, 94
Punta del Agua, 89

Q
Quadrupeds of North America, The, 35, 67
quail, 39, 148

R
rabbits: 18, 39, 64, 148-158; as food, 155-156; kinds of, 154-155; naming of, 148-149
rabies, 119-121, 161
raccoon-fox, 111
raccoons, 110-111, 126, 127, 165
railroads, 24
Randall County, 29
rats, 145-147
rattlesnakes, 127, 139-140
razorback, 107
Reagan County, 42
red deer, 50
Redfield, Symon, 42
red fox, 99-100
Red River, 14, 20, 23, 40, 42, 48, 49, 53, 59, 60, 64, 71, 80, 81, 87, 93, 96, 101, 103, 104, 106, 112, 123, 134, 136, 146, 153, 154, 165
Red River Valley, 151, 152, 153, 154, 165
red squirrels, 143-144
red wolf, 70-71, 75, 76, 78
Reed, Captain, 53
  Erik K., 17
Reeves County, 135
Reid, John C., 34, 41, 63, 64, 72, 78, 102, 103, 107, 138, 140, 149, 155
Reily, Colonel, 56, 76
reindeer, 46
Resaca de la Palma, 128
Rhine Party, 149
Richardson, Rupert Norval, 104
ringtails, 111-113, 118, 126
Rio Azul, 48, 53
Rio Conchas, 17
Rio de Las Vacas, 20
Rio de la Trinidad, 33
Rio de Medina, 61
Rio de San Marcos, 12
Rio Escaravadra, 20
Rio Frio, 169
Rio Grande, 15, 16, 17, 18, 19, 21, 43, 54, 62, 64, 81, 84, 89, 97, 103, 125, 128, 129, 131, 133, 146, 148, 153, 158, 162
Rio Grande City, 64
Rio Grande Plains, 151, 153
Rio Grande Valley, 18, 81, 97, 128, 129, 130, 131, 144
Rio Negro, 106
Rio Sabinas, 16
Rivera, Brigadier, 12
River of Bullocks, 15
Roberts County, 29
Robertson County, 11, 19, 22, 30, 101, 104
Rock Springs, 43
rock squirrel, 143
Rocky Mountain House, 22
Roe, Frank Gilbert, 3, 4-5, 7, 19, 27
Roemer, Ferdinand, 4, 12, 13, 14, 25, 30, 34, 35, 42, 64, 69, 86, 95, 101, 103, 107, 110, 112, 137, 138, 139, 145
roof rats, 126, 146
Roosevelt, Franklin D., 127
  Theodore, 92
Ross, Alexander, 28
Roze, Uldis, 167-168
Ruxton, 133, 134

S
S. auduboni, 156, 157
S. floridanus, 156, 158
S. limitis, 144
S. ludovicianus, 144
S. niger ludovicianus, 144
S. robustus, 156, 157
Sabine Bay, 162
Sabine County, 72, 125
Sabine Pass, 90
Sabine River, 61, 98, 129
sage rabbit, 154
St. John, 21
St. Joseph's Island, 35
Salt Basin, 10
Salt Creek, 113
Saltillo, 17
Salt Lake, 49
San Ambrosio, 148
San Angelo, 156
San Antonio, 13, 25, 34, 42, 43, 55, 64, 70, 72, 73, 80, 103, 108, 117, 121, 136, 144, 146, 154, 158, 160
San Antonio de Bexar, 18, 87
San Antonio de Padua, 12
San Antonio River, 11
San Augustine County, 72, 125
San Benito, 84
Sanchez, 61
San Diego, 43
Sandoz, Mari, 21, 24, 119
San Elisario, 147
San Jacinto County, 117
San Jacinto River, 81
San Jose Mission, 160
San Juan del Rio, 18
San Luis Pass, 15
San Marcos, 55
San Saba County, 13, 103, 136
San Saba River, 19, 86, 112, 137
Santa Fe Trail, 19, 72
Saskatchewan, 21
Schleicher County, 42
Schmidly, David J., 78, 114, 143, 152, 165
Schultz, James Willard, 26-27
Sciurus carolinensis, 143
Sciurus niger, 143
Scurry County, 19
seals, 169-171
Secondary Forest, 151
selective breeding, 37
Seton, Ernest Thompson, 27, 53
Sevier, Paxton de, 14
Shackelford County, 22
Shain, Charles B., 12, 35, 90
Shawnees, 112
sheep, 3, 36, 48, 74, 84
Sheridan, Gen. Phil, 9
Sherman County, 22
Shoal Creek, 12
Shoreacres, 62
short grass prairie, 30
Sibley, John, 48, 53, 64, 101
Sierra Blanca, 54
Sierra de San Carlos, 17
silver foxes, 99
Simpson, ———, 166
  J. P., 26
Sisterdale, 85, 93
skunks: 18, 115-122, 127, 161, 165; as food, 121; location of, 117-118; naming of, 116, 118-119; numbers of, 116; as pole cats, 115-116; rabies in, 119-121
Smith, Captain, 124
  Edward, 34, 56, 76, 91, 143, 145
  Francis, 95
  Mr., 106
  William P., 105
snakes, 145, 166
Snow, ———, 54

County	County Seat	Location	County	County Seat	Location	County	County Seat	Location
ANDERSON	Palestine	H-17	HASKELL	Haskell	F-11	SAN JACINTO	Coldspring	J-18
ANDREWS	Andrews	G-7	HAYS	San Marcos	K-14	SAN PATRICIO	Sinton	N-15
ANGELINA	Lufkin	I-19	HEMPHILL	Canadian	B-10	SAN SABA	San Saba	I-12
ARANSAS	Rockport	N-16	HENDERSON	Athens	G-17	SCHLEICHER	Eldorado	J-10
ARCHER	Archer City	E-12	HIDALGO	Edinburg	Q-11	SCURRY	Snyder	G-9
ARMSTRONG	Claude	C-9	HILL	Hillsboro	H-15	SHACKELFORD	Albany	G-12
ATASCOSA	Jourdanton	M-13	HOCKLEY	Levelland	E-7	SHELBY	Center	H-20
AUSTIN	Bellville	K-16	HOOD	Granbury	G-14	SHERMAN	Stratford	A-8
BAILEY	Muleshoe	E-6	HOPKINS	Sulphur Springs	F-17	SMITH	Tyler	G-18
BANDERA	Bandera	L-12	HOUSTON	Crockett	I-18	SOMERVELL	Glen Rose	H-14
BASTROP	Bastrop	K-15	HOWARD	Big Spring	H-8	STARR	Rio Grande City	Q-13
BAYLOR	Seymour	E-12	HUDSPETH	Sierra Blanca	H-2	STEPHENS	Breckenridge	Gj-12
BEE	Beeville	N-14	HUNT	Greenville	F-16	STERLING	Sterling City	H-9
BELL	Belton	I-14	HUTCHINSON	Stinnett	B-8	STONEWALL	Aspermont	F-10
BEXAR	San Antonio	L-13	IRION	Mertzon	I-9	SUTTON	Sonora	J-10
BLANCO	Johnson City	K-13				SWISHER	Tulia	D-8
BORDEN	Gail	G-8	JACK	Jacksboro	F-1			
BOSQUE	Meridian	H-14	JACKSON	Edna	M-16	TARRANT	Fort Worth	G-15
BOWIE	Boston	E-19	JASPER	Jasper	I-20	TAYLOR	Abilene	G-11
BRAZORIA	Angleton	L-18	JEFF DAVIS	Fort Davis	J-4	TERRELL	Sanderson	K-7
BRAZOS	Bryan	J-16	JEFFERSON	Beaumont	K-20	TERRY	Brownfield	F-7
BREWSTER	Alpine	K-6	JIM HOGG	Hebbronville	P-13	THROCKMORTON	Throckmorton	F-2
BRISCOE	Silverton	D-9	JIM WELLS	Alice	O-14	TITUS	Mount Pleasant	F-18
BROOKS	Falfurrias	P-14	JOHNSON	Cleburne	G-15	TOM GREEN	Sn Angelo	I-10
BROWN	Brownwood	H-12	JONES	Anson	G-11	TRAVIS	Austin	K-14
BURLESON	Caldwell	J-16	KARNES	Karnes City	M-14	TRINITY	Groveton	I-18
BURNET	Burnet	J-13	KAUFMAN	Kaufman	G-16	TYLER	Woodville	I-19
CALDWELL	Lockhart	K-14	KENDALL	Boerne	K-13	UPSHUR	Gilmer	F-18
CALHOUN	Port Lavaca	M-16	KENEDY	Sarita	P-15	UPTON	Rankin	I-8
CALLAHAN	Baird	G-12	KENT	Jayton	F-9	UVALDE	Uvalde	L-11
CAMERON	Brownsville	Q-15	KERR	Kerrville	K-12	VAL VERDE	Del Rio	K-9
CAMP	Pittsburg	F-18	KIMBLE	Junction	J-11	VAN ZANDT	Canton	G-17
CARSON	Panhandle	B-8	KING	Guthrie	E-10	VICTORIA	Victoria	M-16
CASS	Linden	F-19	KINNEY	Brackettville	L-10	WALKER	Huntsville	J-18
CASTRO	Dimmitt;	D-7	KLEBERG	Kingsville	O-15	WALLER	Hempstead	K-17
CHAMBERS	Anahuac	K-19	KNOX	BENJAMIN	E-11	WARD	Monahans	I-6
CHEROKEE	Rusk	H-18	LAMAR	Paris	E-17	WASHINGTON	Brenham	K-16
CHILDRESS	Childress	D-10	LAMB	Littlefield	E-7	WEBB	Laredo	O-12
CLAY	Henrietta	E-13	LAMPASAS	Lampasas	I-13			
COCHRAN	Morton	E-6	LaSALLE	Cotulla	N-12			
COKE	Robert Lee	H-10	LAVACA	Hallettsville	L-16			
COLEMAN	Coleman	H-11	LEE	Giddings	J-15			
COLLINGSWORTH	Wellington	C-10	LEON	Centerville	I-17			
COLORADO	Columbus	L-16	LIBERTY	Liberty	J-19			
COMAL	New Braunfels	K-13	LIMESTONE	Groesbeck	H-16			
COMANCHE	Comanche	H-13	LIPSCOMB	Lipscomb	A-10			
CONCHO	Paint Rock	I-11	LIVE OAK	George West	N-14			
COOKE	Gainesville	E-15	LLANO	Llano	J-13			
CORYELL	Gatesville	I-14	LOVING	Mentone	H-5			
COTTLE	Paducah	E-10	LUBBOCK	Lubbock	E-8			
CRANE	Crane	I-7	LYNN	Tahoka	F-8			
CROCKETT	Ozona	J-8	McCULLOCH	Brady	I-12			
CROSBY	Crosbyton	F-9	McLENNAN	Waco	H-15			
CULBERSON	Van Horn	I-4	McMULLEN	Tilden	N-13			
DALLAM	Dalhart	A-7	MADISON	Madisonville	I-17			
DALLAS	Dallas	G-15	MARION	Jefferson	F-19			
DAWSON	Lamesa	G-8	MARTIN	Stanton	G-8			
DEAF SMITH	Hereford	C-7	MASON	Mason	J-12			
DELTA	Cooper	F-17	MATAGORDA	Bay City	M-17			
DENTON	Denton	F-15	MAVERICK	Eagle Pass	M-10			
DeWITT	CUERO	L-15	MEDINA	Hondo	L-12			
DICKENS	Dickens	E-9	MENARD	Menard	J-11			
DIMMIT	Carrizo Springs	N-11	MIDLAND	Midland	H-8			
DONLEY	Clarendon	C-9	MILAM	Cameron	J-15			
DUVAL	San Diego	O-13	MILLS	Goldthwaite	I-13			
			MITCHELL	Colorado City	H-9			
EASTLAND	Eastland	G-12	MONTAGUE	Montague	E-14	WHARTON	Wharton	L-17
ECTOR	Odessa	H-7	MONTGOMERY	Conroe	J-18	WHEELER	Wheeler	Cj-10
EDWARDS	Rocksprings	K-10	MOORE	Dumas	B-8	WICHITA	Wichita Falls	E-12
ELLIS	Waxahachie	G-15	MORRIS	Daingerfield	F-18	WILBARGER	Vernon	Dj-12
EL PASO	El Paso	H-1	MOTLEY	Matador	E-9	WILLACY	Raymondville	Q-15
ERATH	Stephenville	H-13	NACOGDOCHES	Nacogdoches	H-19	WILLIAMSON	Georgetown	J-14
FALLS	Marlin	I-15	NAVARRO	Corsicana	H-16	WILSON	Floresville	L-14
FANNIN	Bonham	E-16	NEWTON	Newton	I-20	WINKLER	Kermit	H-6
FAYETTE	La Grange	K-15	NOLAN	Sweetwater	G-10	WISE	Decatur	F-14
FISHER	Roby	G-10	NUECES	Corpus Christi	O-15	WOOD	Quitman	F-18
FLOYD	Floydada	E-9	OCHILTREE	Perryton	A-9	YOAKUM	Plains	F-6
FOARD	Crowell	E-11	OLDHAM	Vega	C-7	YOUNG	Graham	F-12
FORT BEND	Richmond	L-17	ORANGE	Orange	J-20	ZAPATA	Zapata	P-12
FRANKLIN	Mount Vernon	F-18	PALO PINTO	Palo Pinto	G-13	ZAVALA	Crystal City	M-11
FREESTONE	Fairfield	H-16	PANOLA	Carthage	G-19			
FRIO	Pearsall	M-12	PARKER	Weatherford	G-14			
GAINES	Seminole	G-7	PARMER	Farwell	D-6			
GALVESTON	Galveston	L-18	PECOS	Fort Stockton	J-6			
GARZA	Post	F-9	POLK	Livingston	I-19			
GILLESPIE	Fredericksburg	K-12	POTTER	Amarillo	c-8			
GLASSCOCK	Garden City	H-8	PRESIDIO	Marfa	K-4			
GOLIAD	Goliad	M-15	RAINS	Emory	F-17			
GONZALES	Gonzales	L-15	RANDALL	CANYON	G-8			
GRAY	Pampa	C-9	REAGAN	Big Lake	I-8			
GRAYSON	Sherman	E-15	REAL	Leakey	K-11			
GREGG	Longview	G-18	RED RIVER	Clarksville	E-18			
GRIMES	Anderson	J-17	REEVES	Pecos	I-5			
GUADALUPE	Seguin	L-14	REFUGIO	Refugio	N-15			
HALE	Plainview	E-8	ROBERTS	Miami	B-9			
HALL	Memphis	D-9	ROBERTSON	Franklin	I-16			
HAMILTON	Hamilton	H-13	ROCKWALL	Rockwall	F-16			
HANSFORD	Spearman	A-8	RUNNELS	Ballinger	H-11			
HARDEMAN	Quanah	D-11	RUSK	Henderson	G-18			
HARDIN	Kountze	J-19	SABINE	Hemphill	H-20			
HARRIS	Houston	K-18	SAN AUGUSTINE	San Augustine	H-20			
HARRISON	Marshall	G-19						
HARTLEY	Channing	B-7						

1 2 3 4 5 6